BEYOND
"Understanding Canada"

Published by

THE UNIVERSITY OF ALBERTA PRESS
Ring House 2
Edmonton, Alberta, Canada T6G 2E1
www.uap.ualberta.ca

Copyright © 2017 The University of Alberta Press

LIBRARY AND ARCHIVES CANADA CATALOGUING IN PUBLICATION

Beyond "understanding Canada" : transnational perspectives on Canadian literature / Melissa Tanti, Jeremy Haynes, Daniel Coleman, and Lorraine York, editors.

Includes bibliographical references and index.
Issued in print and electronic formats.
ISBN 978-1-77212-269-5 (softcover).—
ISBN 978-1-77212-325-8 (EPUB).—
ISBN 978-1-77212-326-5 (Kindle).—
ISBN 978-1-77212-327-2 (PDF)

1. Canadian literature--History and criticism. 2. National characteristics, Canadian, in literature. 3. Literature and transnationalism. I. Tanti, Melissa, 1975–, editor II. Haynes, Jeremy, 1990–, editor III. Coleman, Daniel, 1961–, editor IV. York, Lorraine M. (Lorraine Mary), 1958–, editor

PS8101.N38B49 2017   C810.9   C2016-908167-2
                                    C2016-908168-0

First edition, first printing, 2017.
First printed and bound in Canada by Houghton Boston Printers, Saskatoon, Saskatchewan.
Copyediting and proofreading by Joanne Muzak.
Indexing by Judy Dunlop.

All rights reserved. No part of this publication may be reproduced, stored in a retrieval system, or transmitted in any form or by any means (electronic, mechanical, photocopying, recording, or otherwise) without prior written consent. Contact the University of Alberta Press for further details.

The University of Alberta Press supports copyright. Copyright fuels creativity, encourages diverse voices, promotes free speech, and creates a vibrant culture. Thank you for buying an authorized edition of this book and for complying with the copyright laws by not reproducing, scanning, or distributing any part of it in any form without permission. You are supporting writers and allowing University of Alberta Press to continue to publish books for every reader.

The University of Alberta Press is committed to protecting our natural environment. As part of our efforts, this book is printed on Enviro Paper: it contains 100% post-consumer recycled fibres and is acid- and chlorine-free.

The University of Alberta Press gratefully acknowledges the support received for its publishing program from the Government of Canada, the Canada Council for the Arts, and the Government of Alberta through the Alberta Media Fund.

This book has been published with the help of a grant from the Canadian Federation for the Humanities and Social Sciences, through the Awards to Scholarly Publications Program, using funds provided by the Social Sciences and Humanities Research Council of Canada.

BEYOND
"*Understanding Canada*"
Transnational Perspectives
on Canadian Literature

MELISSA TANTI, JEREMY HAYNES,
DANIEL COLEMAN, AND LORRAINE YORK,
EDITORS

THE UNIVERSITY OF ALBERTA PRESS

Contents

Acknowledgements	VII
Introduction	XI
Jeremy Haynes, Melissa Tanti, Daniel Coleman, Lorraine York	

I Contexts, Provocations, and Knowledge Territories

1 Beyond ~~Understanding~~ Canada 3
   Belatedness and Canadian Literary Studies
   Smaro Kamboureli

2 The Understanding Canada Program and International Canadian Literary Studies 23
   Christl Verduyn

3 Indigenous Writing in Indigenous Languages 37
   Reconfiguring Canadian Literary Studies and Beyond
   Elizabeth Yeoman

II Roots and Routes

4 Canada in Black Transnational Studies 51
   Austin Clarke, Affective Affiliations, and the Cross-Border Poetics of Caribbean Canadian Writing
   Michael A. Bucknor

5 "Why Don't You Write about Canada?" 79
   Olive Senior's Poetry, Everybody's History, and the "Condition of Resonance"
   Anne Collett

6 Canada and the Black Atlantic 99
   Epistemologies, Frameworks, Texts
   Pilar Cuder-Domínguez

III Mapping Bodies, Place, and Time

7 "Off the Highway" 117
Margins, Centres, Modernisms
Katalin Kürtösi

8 Canadian Photography and the Exhaustion of Landscape 131
Claire Omhovère

9 Posthuman Affect in the Global Empire 151
Queer Speculative Fictions of Canada
Belén Martín-Lucas

IV Border Zones

10 Unexpected Dialogical Space in David Albahari's Immigrant Writing 175
Vesna Lopičić and Milena Kaličanin

11 The Politics of Art and Affect in Michael Helm's *Cities of Refuge* 193
Ana María Fraile-Marcos

V Reading Publics

12 Canada through the Lens of the Communist Censor 211
The Translation of CanLit under an Authoritarian Regime
Lucia Otrísalová

13 Economies of Export 229
Translating Laurence, Atwood, and Munro in Eastern Europe (1960–1989)
Cristina Ivanovici

14 Canadian Literature and Canadian Studies in the Czech Republic 255
Don Sparling

Works Cited 275
Contributors 301
Index 311

Acknowledgements

AS THIS WORK EMBARKS ON ITS OWN transnational circulations—those made in the course of this collaboration, those preexistent, and those beyond the current scope—the editors and contributors to this volume collectively express our thanks to the various bodies that contributed to its production. With sincere thanks to the Department of English and Cultural Studies and the Faculty of Humanities at McMaster for collegiality and financial support; the Canadian Department of Foreign Affairs and International Trade (DFAIT);[1] the McCord Museum; the McMaster President's Seminar Series in Higher Education and the Social Sciences and Humanities Research Council of Canada (SSHRC)'s Connections Grant program in support of the conference that generated this volume; the Awards to Scholarly Publications Program for a grant in aid of publication; McMaster University for support in the form of a Senator McMaster Chair in Canadian Literature and Culture; the Royal Botanical Gardens; Six Nations Polytechnic; SSHRC for funding provided to individual scholars included in this collection; the Spanish Ministry (Research Projects

FFI2010-20989 and Transcanadian Research Networks FFI2015-71921-REDT); the Spanish Ministry of Economy and Competitiveness within the projects "Bodies in Transit: Making Difference in Globalized Cultures" (Reference FFI2013-47789-C2-2-P) and "Globalized Cultural Markets: the Production, Circulation and Reception of Difference" (Reference FFI2010-17282); University of Wollongong for travel funding; and the University of the West Indies for travel grants and research leave.

Gratitude from Michael Bucknor to Leah Rosenberg and J. Dillon Brown for inviting him to consider the role of Canada in Caribbean Literary Development, to Austin Clarke for his generosity, to Daniel and Wendy Coleman for hosting his research visits to McMaster, and to his colleagues, Professors Faith Smith and Curdella Forbes, and his research assistants, Michael Berry and Cornel Bogle for their critical input; from Anne Collett to Olive Senior for her permission to publish her poetry; from Ana María Fraile-Marcos to Gabrielle Dallaporta, research officer in the Department of Canadian Heritage for assistance with statistical calculations and to Cristina Frias, executive director of the International Council for Canadian Studies, for help in accessing information; Katalin Kürtösi wishes to to acknowledge that many ideas presented here were elaborated in more detail in her monograph *Modernism on the 'Margin'—The 'Margin' on Modernism: Manifestations in Canadian Culture* published by Wissner Verlag (2013); from Cristina Ivanovici to Dr. Danielle Fuller (University of Birmingham, UK) and Professor Lorraine York for their excellent and consistent support of my doctoral and postdoctoral projects, as well as for selflessly sharing their wit, time, and collegiality; from Elizabeth Yeoman to Maria Hernáez Lerena for introducing her to Daniel and to these explorations, and to Elizabeth Penashue, for all that she has learned from her. Thanks also to all the people at McMaster involved in supporting the conference and project: from all of us, thank you to Rachel Harvey for ensuring the success of the conference by taking care of administrative and hosting matters; to the graduate student volunteers who helped facilitate transportation and workshop sessions; to Grace Pollock for managing our conference grant application; to Ms. Antoinette Somo for generous assistance and amazing know-how; and to Dr. Peter Walmsley, chair, Department of English and Cultural Studies, for his generous support of all our research endeavours.

Finally, the contributors and editors in this project wish to express thanks to others within the project for the collegiality and conviviality of the experience of working together. This spirit of collective gratitude raises our confidence in the vital futures in store for transnational Canadian literary studies. Many thanks to the University of Alberta Press's Linda Cameron, Peter Midgley, Joanne Muzak, Mary Lou Roy, and Cathie Crooks for yet another wonderful collaboration.

Note

1. Canadian Departments of External or Foreign Affairs have had a variety of names over the years. For the past twenty-five years, it has been known most commonly as "DFAIT" based on the 1993 title, Department of Foreign Affairs and International Trade. It retained the acronym when it was reorganized as Foreign Affairs and International Trade Canada in 2006, but was changed to DFATD (Department of Foreign Affairs, Trade, and Development) in 2013, and then to Global Affairs Canada in June 2015. To retain consistency throughout this book, we retain the acronym longest in use, DFAIT.

Introduction

**JEREMY HAYNES, MELISSA TANTI,
DANIEL COLEMAN, LORRAINE YORK**

THE FACT OF THE MATTER IS that the collegial relationships that generated this volume are indebted to Canadian government funding, and with the termination of that funding, relationships like these live in uncertainty about how to secure and expand our activities as scholars of Canadian literary cultures into the future. From the 1970s until 2012, the Canadian federal government through its Department of External Affairs (or, after 1993, Department of Foreign Affairs and International Trade commonly known as DFAIT) and through various arm's-length agencies such as the Canada Council for the Arts, the Canadian International Development Agency, and the Commonwealth Scholarships programs, provided financial support to promote Canadian culture abroad and to encourage international scholars to make Canada their field of study. Similar to the British Council, the United States Information Service, or the Confucius Institutes, this cluster of Canadian agencies has supported the international study of Canada and Canadian cultural production. Since the mid-1970s, these programs and agencies have financed the translation of Canadian creative and scholarly works into international languages, programs to aid international scholars to carry out research in and about Canada, scholarships for international students to study in Canada, international conferences on Canadian topics both abroad and in Canada, national and regional Canadian studies associations around the world, and the long-standing and now much less secure International Council for Canadian Studies (ICCS).

In accordance with its overall neoliberal policy of defunding public cultural and scholarly programs, which has meant significant cuts to the Tri-Council research agencies and the Canadian Broadcasting Corporation (CBC), Stephen Harper's Conservative government (2006–2015) announced in May 2012, over the objections of many prominent writers, artists, and scholars, that it would eliminate Department of Foreign Affairs funding for the Understanding Canada Program, the current name for the initiative that, under one guise or another, had supported the development of interdisciplinary Canadian studies in fifty countries around the world for almost forty years. The total budget for Understanding Canada (UC) had never been large, reaching $5 million at the time it was cut, and those who protested its removal argued that the return in international interest in Canadian studies had repaid the modest investment several times over (Atwood et al.; Blanchfield, "Foreign Affairs"; "Authors, Academics"; Meisel and Graham). By titling this book *Beyond "Understanding Canada,"* we mean to signal not only the Harper government's elimination of the program of this name, but also the open futures of transnational CanLit scholarship in the aftermath of its defunding. Thinking "beyond" encourages a move away from any project that might try to shore up an "understanding" of national cultural production as a state-sponsored entity, brand, or product and signals instead the possibilities for new relationships and imaginaries that arise when the reiterative process of self-invention that produces any nation-state formation is circulated in the unauthorized and intermediary spaces between official, state-sponsored venues.

In the interim between our submission of this volume to the press and its publication, of course, we have witnessed a palpable rise in the promise of such possibilities, in the form of the unseating of the fiscally conservative Harper government and the election of Justin Trudeau's Liberals on October 19, 2015. And while cultural workers eagerly wait to see whether the "sunny ways" of Canada's new prime minister might yet translate into resurrected support for the arts, we are in the midst of a change, at least for now, in political and discursive positioning on the question of cultural policy. Gone are the Harperesque sneers at subsidy-fed artists basking in rich galas (Petruţ) and in their place is a government and a federal minister of Canadian Heritage who are speaking about reinvestment in the arts. As the newly minted minister, Mélanie Joly told the *Montreal Gazette* that her government sees this policy as part of a larger project to reinvest in infrastructure, and that her job is to "influence my [cabinet] colleagues" when they plan to improve transportation, green energy, housing, and other social infrastructure, to "take into account the importance of the arts and creativity" (Brownstein). Poised at this moment of promise, it is our hope that the essays contained in *Beyond "Understanding Canada"* will speak not only to cultural workers but also to the government and public policy officials who are at this crucial, exciting juncture with us.

It is no overstatement to say that all of the participants in this volume encountered one another—either in person or through each other's scholarship—as a result of this federal support, so, regardless of various views on the wisdom and impact of government sponsorship for Canadian-focused culture and scholarship, the cancellation of UC requires assessment, evaluation, and creative problem-solving as we look to the future and consider how Canadian literary scholarship can flourish in a transnational context. In order to gather scholars from a broad international context to discuss these matters in a focused and intensive way, Lorraine York and Daniel Coleman, long-time colleagues in the Department of English and Cultural Studies at McMaster University in Hamilton, Ontario, invited scholars of their acquaintance from many international regions to attend a three-day workshop-style conference at McMaster to discuss what had been achieved in the era of government sponsorship and how to proceed into the future after it has been cut and its future is uncertain. The relationship between autonomous scholarly inquiry and evolving government priorities is a vexed one, since programs such as UC operated under the aegis of the DFAIT and the priorities of the state tend to shape where and how that funding is spent. Over the forty years in question here, the priorities of successive governments of course have changed. Navigating these shifts in government directives are the bureaucrats, civil servants, and volunteers on academic and cultural committees who have mediated between government policies on the one hand and academic and artistic freedom on the other. It is important to recognize how these workers in the transnational circulation of Canadian culture have buffered the fluctuations in Canadian policy over the years. Nonetheless, transnational circulation depended, if not absolutely, then substantially upon Canadian government funding priorities. UC was no exception. As one of our conference participants noted, funding from this program was never available to scholars in his region, since he came from a country with which the Canadian government had little interest in establishing trade or political alliances. There are twenty-three associations for Canadian studies worldwide that were eligible for UC's small amount of funding. Of these, fourteen are in Europe and North America, four are in Australasia, four are in South America, and one is in Israel. There are none in Africa, the Caribbean, or the Middle East aside from Israel. For this reason, the Canadianists we knew to invite to our conference were "pre-selected" by the history of Canadian federal priorities. Conscious that this would be the case, we had invited scholars from countries that had not had access to UC's programs, and while some were able to attend, the very absence of funding infrastructures for Canadian studies in their own countries, let alone the extra visa and travel requirements for travellers from non-preferred countries, meant that a number of invitees were not able to attend, with the result that some significant world regions were not represented at the gathering. In the end, seventeen international experts on Canadian literature from Australia, the Czech Republic, France, Germany, Hungary, Jamaica, Romania, Serbia, Slovakia, Spain, and the United Kingdom met between September 27 and 29, 2013 to share our research and renew relationships as we explored how to proceed. Jeremy Haynes and Melissa Tanti, members of the editorial team for this volume, were among the group of graduate students and postdoctoral fellows who participated in the workshop as facilitators, interlocutors, and organizers.

From the beginning, our plans were to stimulate widespread discussion of the changing state of affairs in Canadian literary and cultural studies in a *transnational* context, a term we will discuss in some detail below. We aimed to create various public forums for sharing our guests' expertise and experience while they were with us by posting video recordings of five-minute versions of their talks online and by collecting their essays in an edited book. The resulting videos can be viewed at the McMaster Humanities YouTube channel, using the search terms "Understanding Canada Conference 2013." We also invited three prominent Canadian scholars—Smaro Kamboureli (University of Toronto), Christl Verduyn (Mount Allison University), and Elizabeth Yeoman (Memorial University)—to set some context for our discussions by reflecting on their considerable experience with the history and effects of government sponsorship for international Canadian literary studies. Video versions of their recorded talks can also be found at the McMaster Humanities YouTube channel. All of this video material was recorded on September 27, 2013 at the opening day forum to which the wider McMaster and Hamilton–area public was invited. The second and third days of the conference were devoted to workshopping early drafts of the essays collected in this volume. While these arrangements were meant to give the participants opportunities to generate deeply considered and energetically engaged work, they were also meant to strengthen and solidify the relationships among and between us. For, given our broadly dispersed locations, it is going to require creativity and active relationships to ensure a lively future for transnational Canadian literary and cultural studies in the absence of traditional sources of funding.

The narratives performed by transnational perspectives on Canadian literature, then, remain vital for us to parse, listening attentively for what flies beneath the radar of the nation and its manifold others who are located both inside and outside—and in resistance to—its borders. The chapters in this book, taken as a whole, allow us to perceive exactly this multi-positioned glimpse of a national literary culture in the very act of being transnationally consumed, represented, contested, commodified, and much else. The opening part, "Contexts, Provocations, and Knowledge Territories," serves as a series of introductory, ground-setting essays for this book. Together, these introductory essays by Smaro Kamboureli, Christl Verduyn, and Elizabeth Yeoman posit this multiplicity of stance; Smaro Kamboureli fittingly opens the volume by inviting us to consider this volume's primary site of transnational literary exchange—the UC program—as "a web of forces, a multilateral manifestation of how cultural policy and politics interface with scholarship and transnationalism"—an invitation to which these contributors' essays vigorously respond. Christl Verduyn assembles valuable data about the workings of the UC program and, in keeping with Kamboureli's definition of the program as a geopolitical force field, directs attention to the constraints under which international scholars were asked to work. In spirited response to both of these interventions, Elizabeth Yeoman opens up the question of the predominant linguistic binaries of government-funded scholarly work on Canada in English *ou en français*, drawing attention to the invisibility of Indigenous and other languages enforced by this binary. "CanLit," she concludes, "may be multicultural, but it seems it is not multilingual."

The second part of the volume, "Roots and Routes," similarly seeks to break down stultifying boundaries between "Canada" and the "international," "outside" world that discussions of Canadian cultural policy lend themselves to. Taking inspiration from the transnational methodologies that have emerged from Paul Gilroy's notion of the black Atlantic, Michael Bucknor, Anne Collett, and Pilar Cuder-Domínguez explore the implications of Olive Senior's observation (cited in Collett) that "our connections are not one-way flows but are built up of past exchanges." In her essay on Senior, Collett takes a prismatic, transnational look at that old chestnut of an othering question often posed to writers whose works do not, in F.R. Scott's words, "paint the native maple": Why don't you write about Canada? Collett affirms that Senior's writing "acts to insert the Caribbean within the world and to remind Canadians of their relationship to the Caribbean and that world," through the tracing of the entangled circuits of the slave trade and the African diaspora. Michael Bucknor's chapter on Austin Clarke extends this project, specifically exploring the insertion of the Canadian Caribbean "within the world." Taking his cue from archival accounts of the relationships within a circle of West Indian male writers centred around Clarke, Bucknor shows how these diasporic intimacies, in combination with the growing material effects of the CBC's broadcast mandate, reveal the "intricacies of black global networks of political and cultural production from the vantage point of Canada." Picking up on Elizabeth Yeoman's reminder that in reading Canadian culture transnationally we must not overlook "the intra-national dialogues, complex and nuanced conversations among [Canadians] that might enrich the international dialogue and encourage a reconsideration of the maps of the world and of the nation," Pilar Cuder-Domínguez perceives those dialogues at work in the increasingly interactive study of roots and routes in black Canadian criticism that departs from an earlier dichotomy between the roots-centred approach of George Elliott Clarke and Rinaldo Walcott's Gilroyesque paradigm of mobile diasporic routes. As a case study for this "complex and nuanced conversation," she shows how Esi Edugyan's first novel, *The Second Life of Samuel Tyne*, "shifts the terms of the conversation from white–black exchanges to the interaction between several Black

Canadian constituencies, engaging obliquely with a history of colonialism and displacement even while it discloses local, rooted histories, thus playing roots against routes."

As the next two parts of this collection reveal, this model of "oblique engagement" is actively transforming those most binaristic of Canadian cultural truisms: the margin/centre dichotomy and the border. In the part "Mapping Bodies, Place, and Time," Katalin Kürtösi performs a reading of Emily Carr alongside the emerging global theories of Harold Innis, Marshall McLuhan, and Northrop Frye that both relies upon and unhinges the centre–periphery duality. The meeting of centre and periphery becomes, to quote Andreas Huyssen, as Kürtösi does, on the relations between metropolis and colony, a "reciprocal though asymmetrical encounter." Like Cuder-Domínguez perceiving a freshly integrative appreciation of the roles of roots and routes, Kürtösi discerns "a massive mobility" of Carr and other modernist artists "between margins and centres." A parallel movement from stabilizing roots to mobile routes informs Claire Omhovère's reading of the landscape photographs of William McFarlane Notman in the early twentieth century and of Edward Burtynsky and Douglas Coupland in the twenty-first as documenting a "shift from landscape as object to landscape as process, or event." All three photographers explore the dynamic "entanglement of nature and culture," and so "question the role landscape has traditionally played in the Canadian rhetoric of national identifications" as supposedly static and timeless. Changing the conversation from that familiar realist mode of nationalist representation, Belén Martín-Lucas traces how queer speculative fictions by Nalo Hopkinson, Hiromi Goto, Larissa Lai, and Suzette Mayr refuse "the almost compulsory autoethnographic mode" expected of minoritized writers and, instead, embrace a speculative genre whose "project," at heart, is "postcolonial, posthuman, feminist, queer, anti-racist, and anti-imperialist." Michael Hardt and Antonio Negri's concept of the multitude, which informs Martín-Lucas's analysis, resonates with this collection's emphasis on complex intra-national dialogues as seen (or not seen) from an outside vantage point:

"innumerable internal differences," Hardt and Negri call them, "that can never be reduced to a unity or single identity."

The figure of the border has shifted of late from a vehicle for articulating simple binaries to a means of contemplating liminal spaces. Vesna Lopičić and Milena Kaličanin, and Ana María Fraile-Marcos revisit that shifting metaphor in the next part of this volume, "Border Zones." Lopičić and Kaličanin take up a metaphorical border zone in reading the stories of David Albahari: that existing between immigrant and Indigenous subjects in contemporary Canada. In this liminal space, the possibility for alliance is complicated by recent immigrants' preoccupation with gaining equality with nationals at the expense of recognizing their potential solidarity with Indigenous people. Fraile-Marcos's chapter on Michael Helm's *Cities of Refuge* implicitly responds to this ethical question of intra-national border crossings. Fraile-Marcos argues that Helm's novel about refugees and their advocates in Toronto creates a self-estrangement that not only encourages a recognition of the Other, but that moves us to consider ourselves as Other in a world full of violence at the global, local, national, and private levels.

The final part, "Reading Publics," returns us to the question of "Knowledge Territories" that opened the volume, and it invests it with a thoroughgoing awareness of the role of material production. Lucia Otrísalová and Cristina Ivanovici each approach in their chapters the ethics and politics of literary consumption from outside Canada through the lens of translation as a means of ideological production. For Otrísalová, the particular visions of Canada that have been created through translation—in this case, into Slovak—take shape according to the needs of the target audience. Although texts in translation are literary "ambassadors of the culture from which they come," Otrísalová reminds us, "when translated" they "change their values so that they are intelligible to different readers." Ivanovici brings the issue of material production to bear on this question of translation exchange; examining the translation of Canadian writers such as Margaret Laurence, Margaret Atwood, and Alice Munro in Eastern

Europe between 1960 and 1989, Ivanovici directs attention to translation projects that were delayed or left incomplete: a reminder of the material obstacles to the kinds of transnational exchanges that translation aspires to effect. In the final chapter in the volume, Don Sparling reads the burgeoning translation of Canadian texts into Czech "against the broader background of Canadian public diplomacy." He paints a picture of a "precarious discipline," reliant on the goodwill of embassy staff, as well as the grassroots ad hoc initiatives of individual teachers, but one whose precariousness was increased by the Harper government's isolationist retreat from cultural diplomacy. Thus, the book concludes with a set of meditations on the ways in which reading publics have been shaped in Eastern Europe through a combination of domestic social and political policies of the Cold War era and the vagaries of Canadian international cultural diplomacy, as exemplified by the wax and wane of UC.

Interestingly, the criticisms that emerge from the diverse critical regions identified in the volume—from the black Atlantic and Eastern Europe to border and metropolitan locations—overlap and speak to each other in revealing ways. What Anne Collett refers to as "Canada *in* the world," refers to a view that, perhaps, can only be discovered from a collection of transnational perspectives. Beyond the provocations each chapter explicitly offers, there is much left unsaid in the questions that emerge across these works, particularly on issues of gender, legacy, and Indigeneity. It follows that when read together, chapters by Lucia Otrísalová, Cristina Ivanovici, and Don Sparling provide a rich picture of the development of Canadian literary studies in Eastern and Central Europe before, during, and after the lifting of the Iron Curtain in 1989. We come to understand the way certain Canadian texts were authorized and marketed during the communist era and the assumptions that supported their publications. From the seemingly ideologically neutral animal stories of Ernest Thompson Seton to Lucy Maud Montgomery's plucky heroine Anne Shirley, Otrísalová, Ivanovici, and Sparling show that Canadian literature enjoyed a steady presence throughout the regime changes and their fallout from post–Second World War to the present. The reasons and motivations for that persistence, as they surface in these three essays, however, are curious to ponder. We realize in reading these essays in concert with each other that Martha Ostenso's *The Young May Moon* (1929) was the first Canadian book published in Slovakia (1931), the books of Margaret Laurence and Alice Munro were published in high numbers during the communist era, and Margaret Atwood has had thirteen books published in Czech translations since the end of communism. Thus, women writers' books have remained at the forefront of Canadian literary fame in Eastern Europe and within communist regimes.

As Ivanovici explains, Eastern European translations constituted a gateway for readers to access "forbidden (fictional) worlds" and Western cultures under restrictive political systems, despite ideologically marked paratexts such as forewords, afterwords, and book covers that aimed to control readers' responses. It is remarkable, then, that Ostenso's lesser-known book about the choices made by a pregnant single woman torn between two lovers and the undeniably feminist content of Atwood's *The Edible Woman* (1969) passed through strict censors aimed at creating political alignment with dominant ideological systems, though it is telling on this note that the Romanian censors changed the title of Atwood's novel to *An Ordinary Woman*. We might wonder if these politically charged stories benefitted from the historical tendency to treat women's writing as less threatening and thus provided reading communities in Central and Eastern Europe with important gateways to counterdiscourses that would represent more than the "modicum of Canadian influence on other states" that Smaro Kamboureli perceives within transnational dialogues produced by overseas studies of CanLit. Though Otrísalová, Ivanovici, and Sparling show that stories set in one-dimensional and slightly romanticized Canadian settings were consistently popular in all regions, so too were politically visionary texts by women writers. The embedded politics of nonconformist gender roles, ecological themes, speculative fiction, and political criticism could not have been lost on their audiences, and we can infer, then, it must have been at least part of their appeal.

The question of why so many genres of CanLit—and particularly Canadian women's stories—have been translated into foreign languages is never fully answered, though admittedly the question only arises when one reads across these essays. Is it likely, as Sparling suggests, that there is a soft spot for Canada due to the personal links that many Czechs have, for example, with the country as a result of the nation's history of accepting Czech refugees or because, as both he and Otrísalová note, there is a general perception of Canadian landscape as vast and naturally beautiful? Or can this appetite for Canadian texts be set against the broader background of Canadian public diplomacy to suggest a craving by both academic and informal book circulation networks for distinctly Canadian feminist content?

A second set of conversations among these chapters emerges within the context of what Collett calls Canada's "less laudable links," including those to the global south, the African diaspora, and its own settler-invader history. Collett's chapter reminds us of the historical entanglements of Canada and the Caribbean, the legacy of which persists in familiar though unquestioned institutions and markets seeded by the plantation system. In a similar vein, Cuder-Domínguez exposes the neglected histories of "black Canadas," with a particular focus on the ways formal and de facto racism in the Canadian Prairies has shaped prairie blackness. Lopičić and Kaličanin draw our attention to the unrealized potential of possible allegiances between similarly dispossessed immigrant and Indigenous communities—the felt effects of multiple wars of differing kinds in both cultural histories. Thus, together these chapters point to a series of erased or at the very least underrepresented histories that constitute unrecognized traumas woven into the founding fabric of the nation. In her analysis of Michael Helm's work, Fraile-Marcos examines the epistemological and ethical value of both history and storytelling as responses to a preponderance of violence at the global, local, national, and private levels. Similarly, Lopičić and Kaličanin argue that stories are "indispensable for the creation and preservation of one's identity, and their exchange can allow for a successful intercultural communication." Just as Susan Sontag, quoted in Fraile-Marcos's chapter, contends that individuals achieve moral or psychological adulthood by confronting rather than ignoring the gruesome truth of cruelties that humans are capable of inflicting on other humans, so too do these critics seem to be collectively implying that any project of "understanding Canada"—officially funded or not—must involve listening to Canada's own stories of historical injustice and facing the concerns of the marginalized that may contradict the master narrative upheld by popular visions of multiculturalism.

It is intriguing that the Indigenous Canadian voices in Lopičić and Kaličanin's chapter recognize the power of storytelling most explicitly. The transnational accounts of Canadian culture collected in this volume devote little attention to Indigenous perspectives, yet our discussions with the authors of these essays testified to their eagerness to take into account Indigenous knowledge and cultural production while at the same time exposing barriers that have limited access to Indigenous work in certain regions outside of Canada thus far. In fact, in order to account for Indigenous resurgence within and against Canadian studies and reconcile what Sparling concedes to be the customary consumption of "stereotypical Romantic picture of North American native peoples" in the Czech Republic, scholars at Masaryk University initiated the translation of works by Beth Brant, Thomas King, Lee Maracle, Eden Robinson, Ruby Slipperjack, and Jeannette Armstrong in an innovative semester-long translation course. Czech students and teachers worked together to produce *Vinnetou Doesn't Live Here: An Anthology of Contemporary North American Indian Short Stories* (2003)—a groundbreaking publication for Czechs and one that should be of interest to Canadian studies scholars in Canada. It becomes apparent when reading across the essays collected in *Beyond "Understanding Canada"* that writing on and by Indigenous peoples is distributed inconsistently within the field of Canadian studies as it is being constructed in transnational contexts.

The various approaches to CanLit represented in this collection suggest another entry point for understanding CanLit's transnational circulation by the way they highlight the impact of regional location. Thus, in lieu of collecting traditional biographies from our contributors, which tend to focus on scholarly production, we asked the UC conference participants why they started studying CanLit, and what work it allowed them to do. The responses we received to this question highlighted the diverse range of academic experiences that had led our contributors to Canadian literary study. For some, such as Don Sparling and Vesna Lopičić, teaching and researching Canadian studies has meant working in response to a diverse range of institutional agendas and (in)accessible resources. For others, such as Belén Martín-Lucas, Canadian literature represented a path to other theoretical, social, and political lines of inquiry. Elizabeth Yeoman was drawn to the multilingual aspects of CanLit and its cultures, working in Innu-aimun as a natural outflow of "the places I live and the people I meet."

In the search to understand Canada—sometimes in the interests of clarifying global, transnational, and subnational politics—transnational scholarship reveals new ways that Canada might understand itself. For Katalin Kürtösi, for instance, Canada is poised, an engaged periphery, on the edge of the two titanic cultures of Europe and America. For Belén Martín-Lucas, Canada is a distinctly transgressive culture due to its "queer" postcolonial position as simultaneously an ex-colony, a colonizer of its Indigenous nations, and a nation arguably subservient to the United States. This notion of queer Canada is provocative, especially in light of the nation's global reputation as a destination for those escaping persecution on the basis of sexual orientation. However, the tendency to conflate the queer with any kind of transgression risks reductionism. The national positions signalled here are explained well, however, within the notion of "transing" introduced by Susan Stryker, Paisley Currah, and Lisa Jean Moore whose work enables us to apply the term as developed within gender and sexuality studies in a different register. We use the term *transnationalism* to signal the more "porous and permeable" (Stryker et al. 12) spatial territories in which CanLit circulates. This shift recognizes the ways that "transing" stands in contradistinction to notions of crossing (gender or otherwise), which suggests a horizontal movement from one fixed and bounded space to another. Instead, as Stryker et al. explain, "trans" is a modality that needs no particular root word to be politically effective, evident in the variety of trans- conditions: trans-gender; -national; -racial; -generational; -genic; -species. It is differentiated then from "inter"(national) in that transing disrupts dichotomies while international relations function according to understandable or readable boundaries that may either clash or blend. The field known as "international relations," for example, emphasizes the system of bounded, autonomous nation-states between which trade and politics are negotiated, whereas the *trans* in *transnationalism* emphasizes the porosity and cross-pollination that occur throughout a planetary ecology.

There is a tension between transnational critiques and the critical authority of scholars outside Canada in the global discourse of Canadian literary studies. Similar to an interdisciplinary perspective, international scholarship of Canadian literature is forced to continuously reorient its critical gaze between the domestic "inside" and the foreign "outside" (Kamboureli qtd. in Verduyn, "Critical" 231). This dichotomy results in a critical hierarchy that at times holds the domestic perspective above that of scholars outside of Canada. An international critique can cross the conceptual borders of inside and outside, but it cannot shift them, broaden them, or occupy the spaces in between. In this way, an international critique represents a politically neutral "value-added" (Liu qtd. in Verduyn, "Critical" 231) with little room for reciprocal exchange. Transnationalism, on the other hand, acknowledges the shift in Canadian literary discourse away from the thematic performance of "Canadianness" and instead toward the pursuit of self-knowledge within a body politic that includes and exceeds those residing in Canada. Within a Canadian thematic discourse, the international perspective does little to shift a sense of national identity. A literary discourse that pursues self-knowledge, however, benefits "from the knowledge of other lands and other times essential to our understanding [of self]" (Symons qtd. in Verduyn, "Critical" 236). Transnationalism represents an exchange of cultural capital that has the potential to not only move between borders but also resist them, and even exceed them. In this way, transing provides an opportunity to unsettle the profitability of any singular notion of national identity.

Drawing on Kit Dobson's examination of economic and market influences on Canadian transnationalism in *Transnational Canadas* (2009), we, alternatively, consider the cultural-conceptual process of transing that registers circuits that fly under radars prioritized by trade, diplomacy, and formal networks. This collection exudes a transnational awareness in the attention that our contributors have paid to both the diplomatic and economic scaffolds that supported the UC program and the circulation of Canadian literature within global circuits. The popular belief that Canadian literature has become a "world literature" is the result of diplomatic, cultural, and academic programs that have cultivated a specific network of international acquaintances, conferences, translations, and awards committees. Collectively, these programs have shaped Canadian literature as an international discourse.

The scholarly contributions collected in this volume represent a transnational critical discourse that is as tethered to the shifting economic and diplomatic agendas of a succession of Canadian governments and policies, as it is to the evolving climates of the global market. As Reingard M. Nischik describes in the concluding chapter to *Gaining Ground* (1985), financial support for Canadian studies programs went to "priority support countries," particularly those who at the time had existing political and economic ties to Canada (253). The UC program, therefore, was a contemporary iteration of the diplomatically and economically motivated initiatives of the 1970s and 1980s. This political underpinning of the program suggests that the longevity of international Canadian literary scholarship is particularly vulnerable to shifts in foreign policy and global market economies that can influence the mobility, exposure, and collectivity of transnational Canadian literary scholars.

To borrow a set of scales from Christl Verduyn's concluding essay in *Critical Collaborations* (2014) on transdisciplinarity—as opposed to interdisciplinarity, which maintains and often favours epistemological borders—the adjectives "thin" and "thick," when applied to transnationalism (231–32) can help to articulate the unevenness with which international scholarship is supported. The distinction between "trans" and "inter" highlights the different economic and diplomatic relationships of scholars hailing from different nations and regions, and the varying degrees of impact their research has on the field. While scholars who work on CanLit outside of Canada have continued to engage in a transnational discourse, the support structures made available to these scholars are varying in degree, not counting issues of technological and material accessibility even in countries with UC support. The relationship between changes in DFAIT priority areas and the critical discourses of the field reveals another major aspect of this collection's transnational perspective. In our collection and editorial process, the asymmetry with which funding was distributed, as well as the geographic, political, and infrastructural constraints that shaped the UC program, became increasingly clear. For example, it wasn't until we began the editing process that we collectively realized the obvious, yet understated influence of the Cold War on not only the critical perspectives of our contributors but also on the stark contrasts in accessible resources within many countries of the former Soviet Bloc when compared to West Germany, France, Italy, and Britain.

Beyond "Understanding Canada," like the program whose cancellation brought this volume into being, is another reminder of the very real material obstacles to transnational intellectual exchange, but it is also a reminder of its persistence despite those obstacles. The transnational nationalism that our contributors have pondered in these pages is a complexly multidirectional one best summed up in Olive Senior's wise words: "Awareness of history would affirm that our connections are not one-way flows."

I

Contexts, Provocations, and Knowledge Territories

1

Beyond ~~Understanding~~ Canada
Belatedness and Canadian Literary Studies

SMARO KAMBOURELI

"THERE IS SUCH A THING as Canadian Literature," wrote the late German scholar Walter Pache in 1976.[1] He made this announcement, the title of his review of two anthologies of short stories by Canadian authors translated into German,[2] in the feuilleton pages of *Süddeutsche Zeitung*. In her 2009 essay "Telling Canada's 'Story' in German," Luise von Flotow identifies Pache's review as "a landmark text" (19) in the history of "the Canada-Germany connection" (18). Pache's review does not merely support her central thesis that translation has been "the primary vehicle of export for Canadian culture," a "vital factor" that has "mobiliz[ed] literary works, especially those that tell mainstream stories" (17); in her argument, it also stands out as a singular turning point in the development of Canadian literature itself.

A literature signifies only insofar as it finds readers, and its cultural legitimacy is proportionally increased when it is distributed beyond its national borders. Reviews play a seminal role in a literature's mobility because they have the potential to influence as much the national as the global cultural market place, especially when they appear in newspapers that have long enjoyed, as *Süddeutsche Zeitung* has done since its inception, a reputation for "pointed criticism" (Stahl). But while an author may never forget a bad or good review, newspaper reviews rarely, if ever, become more than an ephemeral part of the critical canon. Even though von Flotow does not mention anything specific about Pache's review, she nevertheless acknowledges its publication as a historic moment. In yet another chapter by von Flotow in the same book, this one co-authored with Brita Oeding, Pache's review is again lauded, this time as "groundbreaking" (81). If Pache's review of two, by now outdated, anthologies still warrants mention over thirty years later, it is not because it offers any extraordinary insights about Canadian literature, but rather because it is seen as an inaugural act that has played a performative role for three reasons. First, his declaration proclaims that Canada does have a literature, a gesture that appears to correct an image of Canada lagging behind; second, his review is perceived to be the occasion of the founding of Canadian studies as a new field of inquiry in Germany and other German-speaking countries, thus helping expand the circulation horizon for Canadian literary titles; and, third, he announces the existence of Canadian literature at a time when "this may still have been news— even to Canadians" (von Flotow 20).

The historical significance attributed to Pache's review, then, does not derive so much from his analysis of individual texts but, instead, from the pivotal role his declaration has played as a double apostrophe: a heralding moment for Canadians, deemed to be in 1976 still oblivious to the fact that they had a national literature, but also for German academics who are, implicitly, prompted to pursue a new field of study. At the time of Pache's review the institutionalization of CanLit might have still been in its early stages, but Carl F. Klinck's *Literary History of Canada*, including Northrop Frye's "Conclusion," had already appeared two years before the Centennial and Expo 67, two events Pache cites as evidence that Canada was already a nation-state well into its maturation process. But institutionalization should not be seen here as referencing only the formation of CanLit as a distinct field. Although

Pache's analysis barely ventures beyond literature, I take his review to be embedded within the trans/national policies—and politics—of that period, specifically the bilateral agreement between Canada and Germany that was signed in 1975,[3] but also within concurrent events internal to Germany that are equally relevant.

And this is why I am focusing here on what is admittedly old news. Both the exceptional status von Flotow and Oeding ascribe to Pache's review[4] and the timing of its publication make it paradigmatic of the conditions typifying the export of Canadian literature and its study beyond the Canadian borders. Looking back at the inception of Canadian literary studies in Germany, Reingard Nischik notes that "the academic reception of Canadian literature in Germany developed within the wider framework of a *cautious* opening up toward Commonwealth literatures" ("New Horizons" 251, emphasis added). She uses "cautious" twice on the same page, thus drawing attention to the reluctance of English studies in Germany to include literatures beyond those of the British and the American traditions that have defined the field, but also providing a more nuanced picture of the "arrival" of Canadian literature on the German scene than Pache and von Flotow do. It cannot be a coincidence that the year in which Pache's review appeared was also the same year that the University of Bayreuth, established only in 1975, announced, as Nischik mentions, "the first two German professorships with a specialization in Commonwealth literature" (251). Considered in the context of these disciplinary and institutional shifts, as well as that of the Canada–Germany cultural agreement and the funding attached to it, Pache's review no longer functions as a singular generative act. What has been identified as exceptionalist about it is best seen as exemplary: he is not so much making a call for the study of a new literature as he is responding to the call to promote Canadian culture. It thus belongs to a series of contingencies that set in motion a consistent plan for transnational exchanges, including the fact that in 1971–72, with the support of a Canada Council postdoctoral fellowship, Pache studied Canadian literature at the University of Toronto.

The exemplarity of this review is constituted by the different layers of belatedness inscribed in it. The terms in which Pache's announcement is granted such a canonical standing by his German peers reveal the general belatedness that characterizes literatures in relation to European culture. A sign of Eurocentrism, this kind of belatedness belongs to the genealogy of imperial and colonial politics whereby a literature exists only insofar as it is recognized within a Eurocentric context. What renders Canada as a sign warranting critical attention in this context is that it is part of the West but also, to evoke an old paradigm, a "new" country, one whose special appeal comes from the fact that, given its settler history, it is a newer product of the "old" world. It is this difference that posits CanLit, on the one hand, as a form of escape literature since it offers to German readers relief from "the weighty themes and post–World War II soul searching of much contemporary German literature" and, on the other hand, as "an attractive North American alternative to the United States" (von Flotow 10). This comparative frame not only speaks directly to the ambivalent history of CanLit's origins but also to the conditions that characterize and determine its international position as a national literature, as well as its status in the context of disciplinary frames such as American literature or New Literatures in English. As both Eurocentric and a "new" other, CanLit is thus configured by Pache as a critically virginal field, thus inviting his German peers to venture into what is assumed to be a previously uncharted territory—a critical gesture evoking the colonial trope of *terra nullius*.

These conditions allow Canadian literature to gain validation by virtue of its kinship with already established national literatures, but also draw attention to its affiliation with another growing field at the time, that of Commonwealth studies, an affiliation that, inevitably, also serves as a reminder of its colonial history. As a "relatively new political mapping of literature, and one that has grown out of British imperialist politics" (D.S. Roberts 131), Commonwealth literature both belongs to "a fairly well-developed tradition of writing...[that] is not merely the product of post-independence nationalism" (132) and posits itself as a volatile canon with multiple origins. Significantly, Canadian literature was not a latecomer to Commonwealth literature and, therefore, to a world context. For example, the 1917 edition of *The Cambridge History of English Literature* included references to Canadian authors, and in the mid-1950s a dozen North American academics, including Northrop Frye, Carl F. Klinck, John P. Matthews, and the poet Miriam Waddington, circulated a petition that succeeded in organizing a special session on Commonwealth literatures at the Modern Language Association (MLA) convention.[5] As these examples suggest, although still in a developmental stage, Canadian literature already operated as a study field by the first half of the twentieth century.

Situated in this context of a literature that has already gained at least a modicum of international readership, it is Pache's own discovery in 1976 that is belated. It is belated not only in terms of where things stood in Canada at the time of his review,[6] but also with regard to Canadian literature's standing elsewhere: for example, in 1967 the MLA included a special session on Canadian literature, a year earlier than the sessions it featured on African and Australian literatures; 1969 saw the founding of the Center of Canadian Studies at Johns Hopkins University; 1970 the formation of the Centre for Canadian Studies in France at the Université de Bordeaux; 1971 the formation of the Association for Canadian Studies in the United States (ACSUS); and 1975 the founding of the British Association for Canadian Studies.[7] These different time frames suggest that there cannot be a single originary point that demarcates the arrival of Canadian literature as a field of study on the world stage.

Also relevant to consider here is that three years prior to Pache's review the *Times Literary Supplement* (TLS) dedicated an entire special issue to Canadian literature,[8] its cover page announcing a wholly different approach to and perception of the state of literature in Canada from that of Pache. The title, *Canadian Writing Today*, appears against the background of Michael Snow's 1960s iconic sculpture of *Walking Woman*, thus producing a multi-layered message in 1973 that circumscribes the import of Pache's announcement. Snow was already a world-renowned filmmaker and artist at the time. TLS's choice of *Walking Woman* as a cover image, far from pointing to a culture barely out of the woods, situates it within an international avant-garde scene. Moreover, while in the case of Pache's review we hear about Canadian literature from a German scholar, in the case of the TLS it is a chorus of Canadian voices that speak about it. Equally significant in the latter case is that, although the issue focuses primarily on literature, the title's emphasis on *Writing* declares a broader approach, a concerted desire to engage not only with different literary genres but with cultural production in general. Thus, the issue includes a page of new poetry by Margaret Atwood, Earle Birney, Patrick Lane, Gwendolyn MacEwen, Michael Ondaatje, and Tom Wayman; long articles by Atwood, Betty Bednarski, Tony Kilgallin, Brian Stock, and Ronald Sutherland that discuss cultural nationalism, economics and culture, and language politics in Quebec; and reviews of poetry and academic books. Equally importantly, the advertisements by the University of Toronto Press, McClelland & Stewart, PaperJacks, and Oberon Press, together with a full-page advertisement that invites readers to "COME TO CANADA" by visiting the Commonwealth Book Fair where "CANADIAN BOOKS— around 3000 titles!—can be seen and bought from BooksCanada [London, UK]" (1301), contribute to an aggregate portrait of a vibrant culture and literary scene, never mind its anxiety about the "absence of greatness" (Kilgallin 1300). Given the timing of this special issue, it would be safe to assume that its publication was designed to complement the Commonwealth Book Fair.[9] This fact, along with the diverse contents, reveals not only a well-orchestrated effort to promote Canadian literature but also that there is a Canadian literature to promote. Thus the tenor of *Canadian Writing Today*, though it thematizes CanLit's growing pains, is one of neither overwhelming anxiety—can Canadian literature measure up to established traditions?—nor of the need to broadcast aloud its existence—there is such a thing as Canadian literature. The emphasis in this special issue's title on *Today* clearly suggests a literature with a history, unlike the discovery tone of Pache's title.

My intention here is not to compare a single review to an entire special edition of a magazine. Rather, my juxtaposition of Pache's review to the TLS special issue is meant to convey the extent to which the reception and perception of Canadian literature as a national literature and/or as a distinct literary field is specific to the national and trans/cultural contexts within which it is translocated. The TLS issue and the list of events I mention above demonstrate that Pache's review was written in isolation and not in dialogue with what was going elsewhere vis-à-vis CanLit, that is, in a fashion that is ironically analogous to Canada's tradition of the "two solitudes." This fact, coupled with the review's timing and the cultural capital of *Süddeutsche Zeitung*, points to the instrumentalist character of this review. Pache is being strategic when he positions himself, in effect, as CanLit's German father, evidenced by how his review has been historicized thirty years later: strategic in the sense that such an announcement as "There Is Such a Thing as Canadian Literature" had no direct bearing on launching CanLit as a field, but was instead of immediate interest to German scholars keen to pursue the study of "new" literatures. Read in this light, his proclamation is still marked by a double apostrophe, though one that speaks to different parties: it validates and practices the Canada–Germany cultural agreement, and provides fodder for the call to establish Commonwealth studies in Germany. More specifically, in the larger context of disciplinary shifts within Germany, he pioneers a "new" field, putting himself at the helm of it. Symptomatic of the Cold War period's intensified attempts to further internationalize the academy, Pache's review, especially its tone, can be seen as having played a particularly constructive role within the power dynamics of the humanities in German universities.

So the news Pache announced was news of a different kind. The belatedness of the news his review proclaims echoes the same syndrome of belatedness that has been a recurrent mark in discussions about the formation of Canadian literature and Canadian studies in Canada.[10] Perhaps, then, it would be more accurate to say that it was not the Canadians' obliviousness to the existence of their literature that Pache discovered, as von Flotow suggests, but rather CanLit's own ambivalence about itself as a "new" Western literature—certainly not the same thing. This ambivalence speaks as much to CanLit's lingering anxiety of not measuring up to its European origins as to an anxiety of influence. When we consider CanLit as a field positioned at the crossroads of local and European reception, the question of its emergence—and what this entails—should take into account how it has evolved within Canada but also how it has been deployed outside of it. To wit: "Where is here?" We can then detect the same centrifugal and centripetal trajectories of the formation and recalibration of CanLit as an institution in Canada in the ways in which it has come to be a field of interest in Germany. To appropriate Harold Bloom, writing about American literature's own belatedness, CanLit "is *consciously late*" (534). There is surely a difference between being consciously late and being oblivious to one's lateness, a distinction that has often gone unnoticed in criticism of Canadian literature outside of Canada. And let's remember that to be a latecomer is not necessarily a bad thing; it is after all immigrants, latecomers in relation to settlers, who have reconstituted, to a great extent, our understanding of CanLit. The double fact that the Canadian canon was no sooner established than it was reconfigured as a multicultural literature and that it took years before Canadian scholars began to pay due attention to First Nations authors poses an interesting twist to CanLit's condition of belatedness.

CanLit's desire and need to be recognized by others as a distinct yet equally valuable literary tradition undergirds the various attempts by the Canadian state to support Canadian culture within Canada and to promote it beyond its borders via different means of export. This was made abundantly clear in the 1951 Massey Report, which stated that, "If modern nations were marshaled in the order of the importance which they assign to...[national culture], Canada would be found far from the vanguard; she would even be near the end of the procession" (272). If one of the mandates of the Massey Report was to seek ways to withstand the threat posed at the time by the expansionism of American culture, its chapter entitled "The Projection of Canada

Abroad" shows that one of its primary goals was to recommend ways in which Canada, like other "nations," would "project" itself "on the international screen in various ways" (253). The cinematic metaphor draws attention to the construction process and production conditions (often restrictive) that accompany the packaging of Canadian literature for the purposes of export. Despite the Massey Report's finding that "Ignorance of Canada in other countries [was] very widespread" (253), little systematic action was taken by the Canadian state to amend the situation. Indeed, A.B. Hodgetts's 1968 book, *Quelle culture? Quel heritage? / What Culture? What Heritage?* demonstrated that the relative ignorance from which Canadian culture suffered overseas was also to be encountered within the Canadian borders, specifically in the Canadian secondary school system.

Four years later, the Association of Universities and Colleges of Canada, with the assistance of the Canada Council, commissioned Thomas H.B. Symons to undertake a major inquiry on this matter, this time focusing on postsecondary education. Known as the Symons Report, this three-volume publication was pivotal to the Canadian state's strategic plans to promote Canada via its cultural products. As Serge Jaumain notes, in *The Canadianists: The ICCS / 25 Years in the Service of Canadian Studies,* the Symons Report "represent[s] a watershed in the development of Canadian Studies" (16) inside and outside of Canada. This doesn't mean there weren't already Canadian studies centres overseas prior to the release of this report. Including the ones I mention above, the Symons Report identified fifty such centres. In typical Canadian—that is, belated—fashion, the Association for Canadian Studies was established in 1973 during the Learned Societies' meeting at Queen's University in Kingston, Ontario, two years after its American counterpart. Thus, as Jaumain states emphatically, "the Symons Report constituted the real point at which public policy began to be adapted to reflect the need to promote the study of Canada" (17). Still, according to Nischik, "even in April 1975, before the Symons Report had recommended that a sustained interest in Canada be created abroad...the Department of External Affairs in Ottawa had officially established a Canadian Studies Program" ("New Horizons" 252–53), which provided seed and matching funds to foreign institutions and scholars to pursue such studies.

This cultural policy was a response to "the urgency of developing... contacts and resources as a means of helping Canadians to understand themselves and of enabling citizens of other countries having close ties with Canada...to arrive at a better *understanding of Canada* the nation and of some of its contributions to the world community" (Gibson 66; emphasis added). These goals graph an interesting triangulated movement: cultural products are created and manufactured in Canada through what the cultural industries call "welfare-style grants...[that] serve to keep the publishers in business from year to year but [do] nothing to make Canadian publishers more competitive against foreign firms" (Lorimer 21); these products are then exported to countries via means and investments that are commensurate to those countries' political and economic relevance to Canada; and a study of these products abroad is expected to be undertaken, at least until recently, with the support of yet further Canadian investment that produces, in turn, this sought-after thing called "understanding Canada."

As a policy, Understanding Canada—the more recent name under which Canadian studies overseas has been known—has functioned as a national episteme that calibrates in decisive ways the relationship between Canadian cultural production and foreign relations. It should be said that cultural policy is not exactly synonymous with foreign policy. While it is the Department of Foreign Affairs that has traditionally handled the export of Canadian culture, the cultural agenda in diplomacy has usually operated as a means to achieve better trade and political alliances. It has been a tool employed for the advancement of goals that are at best only peripherally related to culture in general and to literature in particular,[11] though this often depends on the ideological bent of individual federal governments. As John Meisel and John Graham write, "the Understanding Canada program was set up... as part of our cultural projection overseas. Its challenge was to rectify an image of Canada subject to more distortion than other countries of comparable political and economic weight." As a corrective instrument, then, Understanding Canada emerged from the recognition that knowledge economies could play a major role as much in producing knowledge about others as about contributing to economic development at large. I use "others" here in both senses of the word: those who are different from us and those who, because of their particularities, are minoritized and/or seen as a potential threat or rendered invisible or inconsequential. Remaining mindful of all the permutations of otherness in this context is crucial for two reasons: first, because historically the Canadian concerted efforts toward developing a cohesive cultural policy, a policy that was both reactive and proactive, took place in the middle of the Cold War era; and, second, because in the present neoliberal climate otherness has become further complicated due to the biopolitics of disjunctive moral economies as is reflected, for example, in the policies of the Stephen Harper government.

Interestingly, while the United States in the Cold War period was aggressively establishing its state policy by means of "the intelligence-university nexus" (B. Cummings 262)—namely, area studies in American universities designed to "fill the vacuum of knowledge" (B. Cummings 268) about others through "massive information retrieval that constituted the study of non-Western cultures" (Chow, "Theory" 106)—Canada was developing a reverse policy whereby its sponsoring and funding of area studies had itself as a subject. The time lag between the Canadian model of cultural policy and the American model of area studies adds yet another layer to the scenario of belatedness I have been developing. It would be helpful to remember here Homi Bhabha's notion of the time lag; the time lag as a moment of delay is also "a contingent moment" that produces a space where the subaltern subject that has fallen behind vis-à-vis modernity can exercise its agency, and thus initiate a process of reinscription and negotiation that allows it to enter the intersubjective realm, a realm of otherness but also of the social (*Location* 183–85). This process sheds some light on the Canadian maneuvers regarding Canadian cultural capital in relation to the global sphere at large. Thus, while the United States proceeded from a status of hegemonic self-confidence, Canada acted from a locus of self-awareness about its paradoxical position—paradoxical because Canada emerged from the Second World War as a major international player but one that lacked a strong cultural signature. If area studies about others reflects the American state's self-interest in the power and control it may garner from knowledge production, Canadian studies as the equivalent of area studies is similarly mobilized by self-interest, but this kind of interest is to be actualized by seeing oneself in and through the eyes of others. Thus the establishment of Canadian studies programs abroad was about "self-formation," "a process of *Bildung*" (Dowler 339). This is the reason why both the Massey and Symons Reports were equally concerned with what happened both within and outside of Canada.

As a result, in part, of these reports' shared emphasis on and instrumentalization of culture, culture operates as a sign that "marks the moment when the Canadian state performs on its own behalf the transformation from preoccupation with issues of sovereignty toward a form of governmentality" (Dowler 339). In this context, Canadian cultural policy has exerted its regulatory power in two sites simultaneously: within Canada, it has focused on "the production of cultural citizens," and showed a concern "with the maintenance and development of cultural lineage via education, custom, language…and the acknowledgement of difference in and by the mainstream" (Lewis and Miller 1); at the same time, it exports this regulation of cultural economy and its production of "compliant citizen[s], who learn self-governance in the interest of the cultural-capital polity" (Lewis and Miller 2). It goes without saying that this double process of promoting an understanding of Canada has a nationalist and therefore ideological agenda. As Philip Resnick wrote about the cultural industries in the 1970s, "the self-serving connection between the publishing of Canadiana and the espousal of Canadian nationalism need come as no surprise, or put another way, Canadian nationalism could also mean good business" (174). Ryan Edwardson agrees: those who have participated in the process of understanding Canada "stood to collect" "economic benefits...though the greatest gains were in many ways ideological" (139).

So what has this cultural agenda as foreign policy accomplished vis-à-vis the Canadian state's goals? By 2012 Understanding Canada generated an average of $70 million a year for the country's economy (Graham qtd. in Blanchfield, "Canada Axes"), a figure cited as evidence of Understanding Canada's beneficial role. But beyond this focus on the bottom line, which demonstrates that, from the Canadian government's perspective, Understanding Canada has been an investment policy, what kinds of understandings of Canada has this policy advanced? To what extent have European or Asian literary critics become, unwittingly perhaps, the instruments of this national episteme that has traditionally promoted a homogeneous and mainstream view of Canada? How can we gauge the wealth and range of overseas studies about CanLit in relation to Canada's own national imaginary, an imaginary that has shown itself to be less stable and progressive than its earlier claims? Has it generated transnational dialogues that have produced a more complex understanding of Canada through the eyes of others, dialogues that might have at least exercise a modicum of Canadian influence on other states? Might there be a correspondence between, say, studies of Canadian multicultural literature and the fact that Canada has become one of the most desirable destinations for new immigrants? Or can we identify, for example, an explicit link between Stephen Harper's EU free trade deal in the summer of 2013 and Understanding Canada's effectiveness as policy at a larger scale? Answers to these questions might not reveal a direct correlation between politico-economic agreements and the study of Canadian literature overseas, but they should, nevertheless, be pursued if only because these, among other, issues can help us understand better the relationship between literary scholarship and the range of contingencies that shape it.

~§§§~

When the Canadian government announced in 2012 that it was going to "abolish" Understanding Canada,[12] there was a general outcry against this sudden decision—sudden, yes, but it must be said utterly consistent with other policies of the Harper government, including the closing down of seven regional libraries in the Department of Fisheries and Oceans. The decision to end the program was rationalized in the name of fiscal responsibility, which has included, among other things, closing consulates and selling off diplomatic residences. But as John Graham, "former career diplomat who headed the [Foreign Affairs] department's academic relations division in the 1970s," put it, "It's just the most appalling false economy to take it away...Canadian studies works as a hybrid engine. You put in a little gas and foreign universities and governments keep the battery charged...It is a no-brainer" (Blanchfield, "Canada Axes").

Nevertheless, at the same time that I was similarly appalled by the program's termination, I was equally troubled by the noticeably uniform and ultimately simplistic nature of the collective outcry. It is not that I do not acknowledge the value of Canadian studies programs overseas or that I do not appreciate the high caliber of scholarship non-Canadian scholars have produced about Canada. After all, I have benefitted directly, in more ways than one, from many of these programs and from my colleagues' scholarship for close to forty years. It is the sacrosanct status that has been ascribed to Understanding Canada that makes me nervous, especially since its success has been appraised virtually exclusively in numerical terms: how many dollars Canada has gained as a return of its investment policy; how many foreign scholars and students have received grants; how many Canadian content courses have been taught abroad; how many articles or books foreign Canadianists have published; etc. This quantitative approach is too limited to offer us a true appraisal of the program and its overall efficacy. While the $5 million the Canadian government saved by abolishing Understanding Canada may be miniscule compared to Canada's overall budget, the impact of its loss on the programing it supported will be comparatively widespread and compounded.

Still, in light of the ambivalences and complicities characterizing cultural policy as diplomacy, I do not think we should just bemoan the passing of Understanding Canada by simply celebrating its accomplishments. Such obituary tropes do not encourage us to ask, for example, why we need a nation-centred study program at a time when the nation and the state have been radically questioned and reconfigured; or what the relevance of a program established in the early 1970s might be in the second decade of the twenty-first century; or why Canada should continue to subsidize its study in our post–Cold War and rampantly global times. Not to mention the need to take stock of what is perhaps a most awkward aspect of the program, namely, the fact that, while it has been used well—indeed, admirably so—by many scholars, it has also been abused by as many (Canadians and non-Canadians alike). Instead, we should view the termination of Understanding Canada as a timely occasion to take a critical look at its legacy from a variety of perspectives. It may be wildly optimistic to assume that the termination of Understanding Canada might, unwittingly, signal the suspension of its namesake meta-narrative, a meta-narrative that forged an understanding of things Canadian built on governmentality. For what does Understanding Canada imply as a moniker if not the regulated desire to be "understood," a desire marked by vested interests no matter how thinly veiled?

Seeing Understanding Canada's termination as a kind of temporary or conditional release from the ways in which scholarship can be managed—a kind of critical wager—we can revisit this program as a web of forces, a multilateral manifestation of how cultural policy and politics interface with scholarship and transnationalism, with individual scholars and today's corporate university environment. Such work would best be transdisciplinary and collaborative, engaged as much with the past as with the present, and cover a broad terrain of trans/national contexts. Indeed, under the present circumstances, it would be valuable to consider situating the body of knowledge designated as "Canadian" beyond the familiar niches of Canadian studies in order to trouble the territoriality of knowledge that comes under this sign. One of the shifts such a critical gesture implies is not simply studying, say, Carol Shields or Canadian multiculturalism in relation to their country of export but in direct dialogue with the different pedagogical, institutional, and cultural sites within which they are studied overseas. Such a self-reflexive approach would inevitably broaden the exclusive focus on Canada's geopolitical and cultural landscape that was fostered by Understanding Canada to include a dialogue between Canada *and* the locations of its export and reception. Taking into account that much of what constitutes Canadian culture, and specifically Canadian literatures today, is shaped by the elsewhereness of Canadian artists and writers, such a dialogue would also invite a critique of the power/knowledge dynamic that has long marked the export of CanLit under the aegis of federal policies. In other words, it would help bring to light the professional conditions within which such work is undertaken and thus thematize the contingencies, as well as complicities, of these critical and pedagogical acts.

If the Canadian studies that Understanding Canada supported are, as I have proposed, a particularly Canadian configuration of area studies overseas, then we should also consider these programs in the larger post–Cold War context and the crisis of area studies today. Reminding us that it "is impossible to disentangle the project of area studies from its political surround" (3), Ali Mirsepassi, Amrita Basu, and Frederick Weaver argue that this crisis "concerns the very fate of area-based knowledge in a globalizing world" (2), the fact that "many policy-makers, universities, and foundations view area studies as anachronistic" (3). As a result, since the mid-1990s, in the United States major foundations such as the Ford Foundation, the Mellon Foundation, and the Social Science Research Council, which had been instrumental in establishing and supporting area studies, began discontinuing their funding for them while major research universities were "re-orienting graduate students away from area studies training" (5).

The American and Canadian contexts of area studies may not be identical, as I have already suggested, but they do share structural similarities in terms of knowledge production about particular locations. In this regard, although the Harper government never offered a clear rationale for its decision to cancel Understanding Canada, it seems to follow suit. This fact alone should serve as a special instigation to take a closer look at Understanding Canada in relation to Canada's ideological and/or strategic (in the case of the Harper government these two may be readily reduced to one another) position/s on, or aversion to, the kind of knowledge produced by this particular form of study.

Arjun Appadurai states that "traditional thinking about 'areas' has been driven by conceptions of geographical, civilizational, and cultural coherence that rely...on immobile aggregates of traits, with more or less durable historical boundaries" (7) and that, as a result, "the area studies tradition has probably grown too comfortable with its own maps of the world" (17). This may very well be the case, but if the area studies crisis today revolves, as David Ludden writes, around the tension generated by two different modalities of knowing, the universal and the contextual, both of which have their origins in the Enlightenment, these two approaches to pursuing knowledge have, nevertheless, always fed each other (131–36). Mobility is the operative concept here not only because of the accelerated mobility of capital, cultural commodities, knowledge, and people today, but primarily because it tends to be embedded in asymmetrical exchanges. Relying on the complementarity that links these universal and contextual approaches, while remaining mindful of the asymmetries underlying their relationship, can help us forge new understandings of Canada through a range of projects. Such projects should involve acknowledging the shifting of conceptual and disciplinary boundaries that have already occurred both in Canada and elsewhere; developing research styles and networks that are more relevant to our times' disjunctive temporalities and mobility; and problematizing mobility itself. Thus, although crucial funding has been withdrawn, the cancellation of Understanding Canada should not be seen as a terminal but, rather, as a turning point, albeit a critical one: an invitation to launch a range of synergetic projects—be they individual or collaborative—that would raise concerns of interest both to non-Canadian and Canadian scholars alike.

Notes

1. I am indebted to Martin Kuester for sending me a copy of Pache's review, and to Heidi Schaefer for its translation.
2. These anthologies are *Moderne Erzähler der Welt: Kanada. Mit elf Graphiken kanadischer Kunstler*, ed. Walter Riedel, published in West Germany (Tubingen: Erdmann-Verlag 1976), and *Die weite Reise: Kanadische Erzahlungen und Kurzgeschichten*, ed. Ernst Bartsch, published in East Germany (Berlin: Volk und Welt Verlag, 1974).
3. As the Government of Canada's website on "Academic Relations" states, in Germany "the scholarly study of Canada dates back to the 19th century. German geographers, historians, economists and scholars of literature dealt with Canadian topics intermittently in the first half of our [twentieth] century."
4. Barbara Korte's chapter in the same volume, "'Two Solitudes'?: Anglo-Canadian Literature in Translation in the Two Germanies," also references Pache's review in a similar fashion (27–51).
5. See A.L. McLeod's Introduction in his edited collection *The Canon of Commonwealth Literature: Essays in Criticism*.
6. For example, 1972, beyond seeing the publication of Atwood's *Survival: A Thematic Guide to Canadian Literature*, was also the year when the federal government introduced a number of initiatives to support various Canadian cultural sectors, including block grants and translation grants through the Canada Council.
7. It would be relevant to note here that the first book on a living Canadian author was written by Paul Goetsch, *Das Romanwerk Hugh MacLennans: Eine Studie zum literarischen Nationalismus in Kanada* and published in Hamburg in 1961. Goetsch also edited a collection of essays on MacLennan, *Hugh MacLennan*, published in Toronto by McGraw-Hill Ryerson in 1973. He is also a contributor, as is Walter Pache, to *Gaining Ground: European Perspectives on Canadian Literature*, a collection of essays edited by Robert Kroetsch and Reingard Nischik (Edmonton: NeWest Press, 1985).
8. I am indebted to Linda Hutcheon and Nick Mount who drew my attention to this TLS special issue.
9. The date of the special issue, October 27, overlaps with the fair's dates, October 17 to November 7.

10. See, for example, Imre Szeman's essay, "Belated or Isochronic?: Canadian Writing, Time and Globalization."
11. It is worth mentioning here that the Canadian diplomatic service has been directly involved in the administering and monitoring of much of the funding provided through Understanding Canada to foreign scholars, students, and institutions. Traditionally, Canadian embassy and consulate personnel have also exercised their own discretion in allocating funds toward Canadian literature conferences, as well as individual scholars, in their areas.
12. See the DFAIT letter to the ICCS that announces the termination of this program: http://www.iccs-ciec.ca/dfait-scholarships-overview.php.

2

The Understanding Canada Program and International Canadian Literary Studies

CHRISTL VERDUYN

THE RELATIONSHIP BETWEEN INTERNATIONAL Canadian literary studies and the Canadian government-sponsored program Understanding Canada comprises two features that are interestingly in tension with one another. On the one hand, the Understanding Canada program, which was in place from 2008 to 2012, introduced constraints on the study of Canadian literature by excluding this long-standing and major focus of international—as well as national—Canadian studies from the program's five new priority funding themes. On the other hand, international scholars of Canadian literature managed to continue their work during the four-year existence of the program and in spite of its constraints. This chapter undertakes a brief study of this twofold relationship. Beginning with some information about the Understanding Canada program and the International Council for Canadian Studies (ICCS), which administered the program on behalf of its sponsor, the Department of Foreign Affairs and International Trade (DFAIT), I present data on the extent of Canadian literary studies funded under the program. This data indicates that a little over 12 per cent of awards granted during the four years of the Understanding Canada program involved Canadian literary studies, with the balance awarded to projects addressing the program's new priority themes. I then turn to four examples of international Canadian studies research contributions to Canadian literary studies during the 2008–2012 period of the Understanding Canada program. As these examples show, international scholars of Canadian literature produced and published important work despite the exclusion of literary studies as a priority funding area under the program. Notwithstanding the non-priority position of Canadian literary studies during the Understanding Canada period, when the Canadian government abruptly cancelled the program in May 2012 members of both the national and international Canadian literary community were among the most vocal and active in expressing consternation, dismay, and protest. The third and final section of this chapter includes some of the communications sent to Prime Minister Harper and Minister of Foreign Affairs John Baird by prominent Canadian writers such as Margaret Atwood, Neil Bissoondath, Dionne Brand, Wayson Choy, Elizabeth Hay, Thomas King, Alistair MacLeod, Rohinton Mistry, and Rudy Wiebe, and by literary scholars across Canada and around the world. Protests highlighted the modest financial investment of a program that generated not only tremendous return in terms of knowledge about Canada and Canadians but also major economic return. As president of the International Council for Canadian Studies (2011–2013) Patrick James reported, the federal government's annual investment of $5 million in the program generated "$200 million spending on Canadian Studies globally by roughly 7,000 Canadianists working in 290 Canadian Studies programs researching and offering courses on Canada in 50 countries" (Nimijean 14–15).[1] None of the protests undid the former Canadian Conservative government's decision to discontinue Understanding Canada, leaving scholars of Canadian literature, as this chapter concludes, with an ongoing search for support of research and publication about Canada's literary production.

The Department of Foreign Affairs and International Trade introduced Understanding Canada on April 1, 2008. The program replaced DFAIT's existing and long-standing Canadian Studies Program and established five priority areas or themes for international Canadian studies. These included peace and security in Afghanistan; North America partnership (Canada–US relations); managing diversity; environment/energy; and economic development and prosperity. The new program did allow for possible additional themes, provided they were directly related to the new strategic priorities. Like the five priority themes, however, this provision did not point in any obvious way to the kind of research or publications on Canadian literature that had for so long been such a significant part of Canadian studies work, at both the national and international levels.

It is helpful to note here the difference between international and national Canadian studies, which work collaboratively but are funded separately. The international Canadian studies community, formally represented by the ICCS, until 2012 received funding from DFAIT. Founded in 1981, by 2012 the ICCS comprised twenty-eight member and associate member associations from around the world—Europe, Asia, South America—representing some seven thousand scholars from over seventy countries.[2] Canada figured among the ICCS member associations through its national Association for Canadian Studies (ACS) until 2007 when the ACS executive at the time withdrew the association from the ICCS. The ACS, established in 1973 and supported by the Department of Canadian Heritage, represented Canadian studies scholars in Canada until 2010, when, for many Canadian studies academics in Canada, a new organization—the Canadian Studies Network–Réseau d'études canadiennes (CSN–REC)—assumed that role. Supported by fees from its individual and institutional members, the CSN–REC held associate membership with the ICCS until May 2014 when it achieved full member status.

It can be a humbling experience to attend the ICCS's annual meeting or its biennial conference and to recognize how many scholars around the world are dedicated to the study of Canada in its many different dimensions—cultural, political, geographic, demographic, economic, and so on. Amongst these areas of research and publication, Canadian literature and literary studies long held pride of place, a fact worthy of note particularly in light of the change in funding focus under the Understanding Canada program.

In 1987 the ICCS began to serve as the administrative and adjudicative agent for DFAIT's Canadian studies programming, which included a number of different programs for individuals and institutions. These were programs for non-Canadian applicants and as such were not available to Canadians. This held for the Understanding Canada program and for other DFAIT Canadian studies programs designed for individuals and for institutions.[3] Thus, for example, the Faculty Enrichment and Faculty Research programs (FEPS and FRPS) were developed to support travel to Canada of non-Canadian scholars involved in teaching and research on Canada. The Doctoral Student Research Awards (DSRA) were available to non-Canadian PHD students. The ICCS's role was to ensure the eligibility and academic quality of applications to these programs and to carry out their financial administration. It has, therefore, been a major player on the international stage of Canadian studies.

This brief information about the ICCS, DFAIT, and the Understanding Canada program serves as background and context for the further information to which I turn now in considering the contributions and accomplishments of international scholars of Canadian literature under the Understanding Canada program. I will proceed in two ways: first, by presenting data from various programs administered by the ICCS on behalf of DFAIT between 2008 and 2012; and second, by considering four case study examples of international Canadian studies research contributions to Canadian literary studies during the Understanding Canada program. The case studies include the first two volumes of the Polish Association for Canadian Studies journal *TransCanadiana* (*Essays in Red and White*, 2008 and *Canada and Its Utopias*, 2009); two recent collections of essays

TABLE 2.1 Canadian Studies Disciplines by Priority Areas

Priority Areas	2008–09	2009–10	2010–11	2011–12
Democracy, rule of law, human rights	14%	10%	13%	12%
Economic development and competitiveness	14%	14%	12%	6%
Environment/energy	14%	11%	12%	12%
Managing diversity	37%	42%	49%	29%
North America partnership (Canada–US relations)	4%	10%	1%	6%
Peace and security	5%	2%	7%	7%
Others	12%	11%	6%	28%

Source: Information provided by the International Council for Canadian Studies Ottawa office.

edited by international Canadian studies literary scholars, *Unruly Penelopes and the Ghosts: Narratives of English Canada* and *Re-exploring Canadian Space / Redécouvrir l'espace canadien*, both published in 2012; and finally the 2013 publication, *Cultural Challenges of Migration in Canada / Les défis culturels de la migration au Canada*, issuing from the ICCS's May 2012 conference. The data that follows draws on research grant results administered by the ICCS during the four-year period of the Understanding Canada program, and in particular on the key Canadian studies programs funded by DFAIT, including the Faculty Enrichment Program (FEP), the Faculty Research Program (FRP), the Doctoral Student Research Awards (DSRA), and grants in support of conferences (CONF).[4]

In 2008–09, 259 awards were granted under the Understanding Canada program administered by the ICCS, with distribution as follows: 81 FEP grants of which 27 (33%) dealt with topics in literature; 135 FRP grants, of which 7 (5%) targeted topics in literature; 33 DSRA grants, with 5 (15%) focusing on topics in literature; and 10 conference grant awards (CONF), none in support of a topic in literature. Of the total 259 awards granted under the Understanding Canada program in 2008–09, then, 15 per cent were for projects dealing broadly with literature. Overall results were even more modest the following year.

In 2009–10, 253 awards were granted under the Understanding Canada program. They included 74 FEP grants of which 10 (13%) featured topics in literature; 132 FRP grants with 14 (11%) displaying topics in literature; 26 DSRA grants, only 2 of which (8%) had topics in literature; 10 CONF grants, none supporting a literary conference; and finally 3 Canadian Publishing Awards for Japan (CPAJ), none for a topic of literature. Thus, 10 per cent of the total 253 awards granted under the 2009–10 Understanding Canada program dealt with the topic of literature. This percentage increased slightly in 2010–11.

Of the 256 awards granted under the Understanding Canada program in 2010–11, 62 FEP grants included 11 (18%) on literary topics; 123 FRP grants included 10 (8%) with a literary focus; 48 DSRA grants featured 7 (15%) in the domain of literature; 6 CONF grants featured, none with a literature focus; similarly of 2 CPAJS, neither dealt with a topic of literature; and finally of 15 Special Awards for Canadian Studies (SACS),[5] 2 (13%) dealt with literature. In 2010–11, then, 12 per cent in all of the total 256 awards granted under the Understanding Canada program dealt with the topic of literature.

Finally, in 2011–12, 229 awards were granted under the Understanding Canada program administered by the ICCS. Of 62 FEP grants, 14 (23%) dealt with topics in literature; of 108 FRP grants, 9 (8%) dealt with literature; of 34 DSRA grants, 3 (9%) dealt with the topic of literature; of 8 CONF grants, none had a literary focus, and of 15 SACS, 1 (7%) dealt with the topic of literature. In conclusion for 2011–12, 12 per cent of the total 229 awards granted under the Understanding Canada program dealt with the topic of literature.

One might reasonably observe that these figures are not terribly favourable as far as production in the field of Canadian literary studies is concerned; over the four years from 2008 to 2012 an average 12.25 per cent of grants awarded to applications presented a literary focus. Of these successful applications, their titles suggest that they were included primarily under the program priority theme of "managing diversity." Thus, for example, in 2008–09, successful titles included, from Argentina: "Canadian Women Writers: How Canadian Women See Their Indigenous Heritage"; from Brazil: "Canadian Literature: A Historical Multicultural Overview"; from Romania: "Quête identitaire et ouverture sur la diversité dans la littérature québécoise"; from China: "The History of Canadian Literature: Marginality, Heterogeneity and Crisis." Similarly, in 2009–10, samples of successful applications featuring literary content include, from Australia: "Homelessness and Social Justice in Canadian and Australian Children's Literatures"; from Hungary: "Intercultural Identity Shifting; Longing for an Indigenous Identity; Othering in Canadian and American Literature and Culture"; and from India: "Indian Women Writers in Canada: Lessons for India." Similar examples may be found among the titles awarded grants in 2010–11 and 2011–12. As Table 2.1 confirms, the program theme of "managing diversity" garnered the highest percentage of total grants awarded.

In short, despite the fact that literary studies were not identified for priority funding under the Understanding Canada program, some support was nevertheless secured, under the theme of "managing diversity," for example, and work was produced. Moreover, as the case studies that follow illustrate, *quality* work was accomplished—though not necessarily through Understanding Canada, DFAIT, or ICCS program funding. Some scholars, as these examples show further, proceeded with their research and publication without this funding. I begin, however, with an example of work from one of ICCS's member associations, the Polish Association for Canadian Studies and its journal *TransCanadiana*, issues 1 and 2, 2008 and 2009, respectively, funded through the association's annual DFAIT grant.

As mentioned, the amount of Canadian studies research activity and expertise in countries around the world can be a humbling realization for Canadians. Poland is a case in point. The extent of research and work on Canada by Polish scholars is impressive. The publication of the Polish journal of Canadian studies is just one branch of that research and activity. Published in 2008, the first issue of *TransCanadiana* coincided with the tenth anniversary of the Polish Association for Canadian Studies and with the first year of the Understanding Canada program. In that regard, the contents of the journal's first issue reflect earlier years during which, as the volume's introductory essay on the history of Canadian studies in Poland makes clear, Canadian literature remained a dominant discipline (16). This is certainly borne out by the number of Canadian and Québécois authors and critics whose names appear in the table of contents: Margaret Atwood, Carol Shields, Marian Engel, Douglas Glover, Robert Lalonde, Myrna Kostash, Michael Ondaatje, Janice Kulyk Keefer, Émile Ollivier, Dionne Brand, and Smaro Kamboureli. The list is even longer one year later in *TransCanadiana 2*, where essays on transculturalism and on work by authors such as Quebec's Sergio Kokis, Pan Bouyoucas, and Anne Hébert, and on work by English Canada's Joy Kogawa, Ann-Marie MacDonald, and Yann Martel confirm the contributors' knowledge of Canada's multifaceted literature and its place in the study of the country.

Fast forward to the end of the Understanding Canada period, 2012, and to the publication of two separate volumes by international Canadianists, each offering considerable Canadian literary and Canadian literary criticism content. In their introduction to *Re-exploring Canadian Space / Redécouvrir l'espace canadien*, Cornelius Remi and Jeanette den Toonder reflect on how research priorities changed under DFAIT's Understanding Canada program. They propose that rather than a substitute for "traditional research themes, such as arts, literature, linguistics, history, sociology and geography" (xi), the changed focus adds "a new dimension to the study of Canada" (xi). As such, their collection "encompasses the writings by those studying the arts and literature as well as writings by social scientists, and it includes both English and French-speaking scholars" (xviii). Remi and den Toonder assert the richness of such a multitude of perspectives and approaches to exploring Canadian space, declaring that it "is characteristic of the way in which Canadian Studies is practiced nowadays. It is therefore an appropriate volume to celebrate 20 years of Canadian Studies in the Netherlands" (xviii).

The point here is that literary studies continued to feature in work published with support from DFAIT and its Understanding Canada program. Alongside such essays as "The Netherlands and Canada in Afghanistan" or "A Forest for the Future: 'Making Place' in the Great Bear Rainforest," appear literary studies such as "The Troubled Spaces of Lynn Coady's Cape Breton," "Lire dehors: Les oeuvres littéraires dans l'espace public canadien," "Ghost Towns in the Making: Hugh Hood's 'The Village Inside' and Duncan Campbell Scott's *In the Village of Viger*," "Le discours identitaire des Acadiens du sud-ouest de la Nouvelle-Ecosse," or, a final example, "L'espace poétique chez Leonard Cohen et Hélène Dorion." This volume, therefore, contains a solid component of Canadian literary criticism.

A second case study from 2012, Eva Darias-Beautell's edited collection *Unruly Penelopes and the Ghosts: Narratives of English Canada* points to what may be the future path for international Canadianists seeking to share their interest and expertise in Canadian literature. That path is publication with Canadian presses—in this case Wilfrid Laurier University Press—of research resulting from funding outside of DFAIT, Understanding Canada, and the ICCS. Darias-Beautell is one of a productive group of Spanish specialists of Canadian literature who have made Canadian literature and literary criticism the heart of their academic careers. While some Spanish scholars have benefitted from DFAIT-funded ICCS programs such as FEP and FRP grants, the collection *Unruly Penelopes and the Ghosts* is the result of work funded by the Spanish Ministry of Education, with support through Wilfrid Laurier University Press, the Canada Book Fund, and one of the contributors to the volume, Smaro Kamboureli, from the TransCanada Institute at the University of Guelph. The volume offers eight essays on the evolving character of Canadian literature and literary criticism, beginning with editor Eva Darias-Beautell's "Why Penelopes? Why Unruly? Which Ghosts?: Narratives of English Canada," and continuing with British scholar Coral Ann Howells's "Rewriting Tradition: Literature, History, and Changing Narratives in English Canada since the 1970s," Canadian critic Smaro Kamboureli's "(Reading Closely) Calling for the Formation of Asian Canadian Studies," Spanish scholars Ana María Fraile's "When Race Does Not Matter, 'except to everyone else': Mixed Race Subjectivity and the Fantasy of a Post-Racial Canada in Lawrence Hill and Kim Barry Brunhuber," Belén Martín-Lucas's "Of Aliens, Monsters, and Vampires: Speculative Fantasy's Strategies of Dissent (Transnational Feminist Fiction)," Eva Darias-Beautell's "The Production of Vancouver: Termination Views in the City of Glass," Canadian academic Richard Cavell's "Jane Rule and the Memory of Canada," Spanish contributor María Jesús Hernáez Lerena's "Confession as Antidote to Historial Truth in *River Thieves*," and concluding with Canadian academic Michèle Lacombe's "Indigenous Criticism and Indigenous Literature in the 1990s: Critical Intimacy"—a catalogue of topics clearly reflecting major concerns of Canadian literary criticism.

A final example of the contribution to Canadian literary studies by international scholars is the most recent publication proceeding from ICCS's biennial conference—the collection *Cultural Challenges of Migration in Canada / Les défis culturels de la migration au Canada*. This 460-page volume is co-edited by Klaus-Dieter Ertler, former president of ICCS and prior to that of the Association for Canadian Studies in German-speaking Countries, together with Patrick Imbert, Canada Research Chair at the University of Ottawa. Given the termination of the Understanding Canada program, which was announced on May 1, 2012 and signalled the end of funding for international Canadian studies, this collection of essays may be not only the most recent but also the final volume produced through the ICCS. There is no reference to the ICCS conference with which the volume originated, a conference that was planned in keeping with the priority areas of the Understanding Canada program, and that took place in the immediate aftermath of the cancellation of the program. Over half the essays in the collection appear in the third section entitled "Literature and Language

– Littérature et Langage." The first two sections—"Social Science – Science Sociales," and "(Meta)-History – (Méta)-Histoire"—each offer six essays for a combined total of twelve, with the balance of the book—fourteen essays—on Canadian and Québécois literatures, in English, French, and one in Spanish.[6] Thus, literary studies dominate this project on the contemporary social experience of migration, demonstrating their ongoing importance for international Canadian studies scholars despite the stipulated priories of the Understanding Canada program.

In the wake of the cancellation of Understanding Canada, many prominent individuals and organizations voiced public dismay and concern about the loss of the program. Letters and columns in one of Canada's national newspapers, the *Globe and Mail*, articles in national and international newsletters, email and fax communications from Canadian studies associations and centres around the world to Prime Minister Stephen Harper and Foreign Affairs Minister John Baird, as well as to provincial premiers who were not party to the decision-making process that led to the termination of the program, all questioned the elimination of a program with a record of return not only in terms of knowledge but also of finance. On June 19, 2012, twenty of Canada's foremost writers and scholars of Canadian literature signed a collective lament on the loss of Understanding Canada published in the *Globe and Mail*. They included Margaret Atwood, Neil Bissoondath, George Bowering, Dionne Brand, Wayson Choy, Elizabeth Hay, Jack Hodgins, Thomas King, Alistair MacLeod, Rohinton Mistry, Timothy Taylor, Jane Urquhart, Aritha van Herk, Rudy Wiebe, D.M.R. Bentley, Neil Besner, Eva-Maria Kroller, W.H. New, David Staines, and Brian Trehearne. "Visiting scholars," the group pointed out, "return to their home institutions, having agreed—one of the stipulations of their grant—to teach, in the next five years, three courses related to Canada. Many scholars spend as much as seven times the amount of their grants on expenses related to Canada. And many of them are now producing some of the finest studies of Canadian economics, politics, and culture." Gone, the signatories added, are the many activities and research highlighting "Canada's major role in the political life of

North America, in the economic challenges of the present day and in the astonishing culture life that is being seen and read across the globe." Publishing their concerns in the *Globe and Mail* as well (July 12, 2012), John Meisel, former chair of the Canadian Radio-television and Telecommunications Commission and former president of the Royal Society of Canada, together with John Graham, who developed the Canadian studies overseas program as part of Canadian cultural foreign policy in the 1970s, reminded readers of the purpose and value of the Understanding Canada program:

> to rectify an image of Canada subject to more distortion than other countries of comparable political and economic weight. Canada had changed and was changing; what was (and still is) needed was more informed awareness and more balanced understanding. The program was directed at educators and, through them, an enlarging body of students around the world with a focus on the distinctiveness, quality and innovations of Canadian society, science and scholarship...Foreign governments contribute directly or indirectly— India, for example, supports four Canadian Studies Centres. The program provided platforms from which two generations of Canadian authors have been publicized, translated and sold in foreign book stores...The value to Canada's profile and to the enrichment of Canadian universities and scientific establishments through cross-fertilization has been incalculable. All this for an annual government investment of barely $5-million.

Globe and Mail columnist Jeffrey Simpson weighed in on May 4, 2012 with a list of cuts by the Harper government, including the Understanding Canada program. Patrick James, ICCS president from 2011 to 2013 and director of the Centre for International Studies, University of California, Los Angeles, wrote to Prime Minister Harper on June 1, 2012, citing the "negative effects [of the cancellation of the program] on how Canada is perceived internationally" (*Globe and Mail*, 20 June 2012). This view was expressed around the world in reactions from presidents of associations for Canadian studies across the globe, from Argentina (Annette Pfeiffer, email to Patrick James, 3 May 2014) to China (Wang Bing, email to Patrick James, 2 May 2012). On May 4, 2012, Serge Jaumain, vice-rector for international relations and director of the Centre for North American Studies at the Université Libre de Bruxelles, as well as vice-president of the Association internationale d'études canadiennes, gave an interview on Radio-Canada on the "killing" of Understanding Canada. The same day, the Honourable Stéphane Dion raised the matter in Parliament (41st Parliament, 1st session) to receive the following response from Minister of Foreign Affairs John Baird: "We have made decisions in the Department of Foreign Affairs on what we can best spend our valuable taxpayer dollars, and we believe this is the right decision toward that end." Canadian literature professor Paul Martin, head of the Canadian Studies Program at the University of Vermont from 2006 to 2011, contributed an in-depth reflection on the impact, both short-term and long-term, of the cancellation of Understanding Canada to *University Affairs*. With modest funding from Understanding Canada, Martin recounted, he had been able to raise matching funds and to bring in speakers from Canada, "from Canadian politicians and Native leaders to writers such as Michael Ondaatje, Joseph Boyden and Alistair MacLeod. These rich educational experiences brought Canada to life for our students and helped demonstrate to them the relevance of Canada to the United States." Martin was also able to take a group of nearly one hundred students on an annual trip to Ottawa, where they visited Canada's National Gallery and museums, attended a session of Question Period and met with members of Parliament. The long-term impact of the loss of Understanding Canada, Martin concluded, is "an attack on knowledge, and in particular the knowledge that other countries can gain about Canada."

Canadian literary studies and international scholars' contributions to the field are part and parcel of the knowledge loss that Martin and many other commentators lamented following the cancellation of the Understanding Canada program in May 2012. As noted, protests did not change the government's decision to discontinue the program. But as the examples presented in this chapter show, the work of understanding the country—in particular its literature and literary criticism—has continued in the face of the new reality and, it is to be hoped, will continue, through the commitment, efforts, and contributions of international and national Canadian literary scholars alike.

Notes

1. See also Paul Martin, "Canada's Image Abroad: Fade to Black." Other articles related to the cancellation of Understanding Canada presented different figures. *The Long Report* calculates that "a total of over $70 million enter[s] the Canadian economy in any given year as a consequence of Canadian Studies activity undertaken abroad. Simply adding the GST to this amount would make the Understanding Canada: Canadian Studies program essentially self-funding. Adding in all the other taxes that are taken at the provincial and federal levels would more than pay for the program. It is doubtful that any other Canadian Government program can make such a claim" (Long 28).
2. The ICCS website (www.iccs-ciec.ca) may be consulted for updates to these figures.
3. For individuals, these programs include Faculty Enrichment and Faculty Research programs (FEPS and FRPS) designed to support travel to Canada of non-Canadian scholars involved in teaching and research on Canada; Doctoral Student Research Awards (DSRA); Canada-Asia-Pacific Awards, Canada-Latin American-Caribbean Awards; and International Research Linkages Awards. For institutions, these programs include Conference Travel Assistance Program; University Library Support Program; Canadian Publishing Awards for Japan; Canada Conference Grant Program; and Book Display Program.
4. I wish to thank Cristina Frias, executive director of the ICCS, for help in accessing the information on which the percentage calculations were made, and Gabrielle Dallaporta, my former student and now a research officer in the Department of Canadian Heritage, for assistance with the calculations. We were generous in our inclusion of what counted as "literary," basing our interpretation largely on project titles. Therefore, the figures presented in this chapter are to be understood as broad guidelines.
5. SACS: Fifteen Chinese scholars are selected annually for this award through a competition. Recipients come to Canada for five weeks of research in their respective areas of study. After their return to China, SACS scholars are expected to publish scholarly articles or books on issues of importance to Canada or to teach courses on Canada so as to further research in key areas and promote bilateral academic relations between Canada and China.
6. Authors and titles of these essays are available on the publisher's website. See Contents at https://www.peterlang.com/view/product/16372?v=toc.

3

Indigenous Writing in Indigenous Languages
Reconfiguring Canadian Literary Studies and Beyond

ELIZABETH YEOMAN

UNLIKE ALL THE REST OF THE CONTRIBUTORS to this book, I am not a Canadian literary studies specialist, though perhaps I could say that the work I am currently doing, a collaborative project with Elizabeth Penashue, an Innu author who writes in Innu-aimun, falls into that category. Yet, at the same time, it is work that calls into question the whole idea of Canadian studies or area studies and that asks questions similar to those asked by Smaro Kamboureli, but from a different place. I'll say more about that work later but first I want to mention my own experiences in the Understanding Canada program and the earlier DFAIT Canadian Studies Program in Spain and China and the constraints and possibilities of different research funding programs. Following that, I will respond to some of the key points made by Christl Verduyn and Smaro Kamboureli in this volume, in particular the financial impact of the funding cuts and the future of area studies in general and Canadian studies in particular. I was deeply disappointed when the Understanding Canada program was cancelled as my experiences with it and the preceding Canadian Studies

Program had all been overwhelmingly positive. However, I was not the main applicant on any of the grants I was involved in and therefore had not put a lot of thought into the orientation of the program. Until I read Verduyn and Kamboureli's chapters, I was not completely aware of the emphasis on promoting business and international trade, or of the change in policies in 2008.

Prior to the changes to the program in 2008, my Chinese colleague Liming Yu and I visited each other's universities, co-wrote a book called *Theories of Bilingual Education: The Implications of Canadian Immersion Education for Bilingual Instruction in Chinese Universities* and organized an international conference, the proceedings of which were also published. All of this work was funded by DFAIT's Canadian Studies Program. Unlike the project I was involved in later with literary scholars Daniel Coleman, Ana María Fraile-Marcos, and Maria Hernáez at the University of Salamanca in Spain, these activities had more of a linguistic focus than a literary one. We didn't have a prescribed theme because this was before 2008, but we did have to orient our projects to highlight Canadian research in a way that was somewhat artificial. Thus, perhaps oddly, we were more constrained before the reorientation of the program than after. While I was in China, someone from the Canadian Embassy in Beijing told me that it was all about "branding Canada." I was a bit shocked by that at the time since I still thought of scholarly work as having intrinsic value and as being somehow separate from other more crassly commercial concerns. Now I am amazed that I ever believed that. However, perhaps the embassy was also somewhat naive to think that a few scholars (or even a lot of scholars) could really have much impact on "branding Canada" in China.

At one of the guest lectures I gave during my four months at Shanghai Jiao Tong University, I was on the podium with former Manitoba Premier Howard Pawley. Our topic was language policy. Following our presentations, the first question from the floor came from a young graduate student. Her question to Mr. Pawley was, "How can an advanced country like Canada permit the barbaric and primitive seal hunt to continue?" So much for our informed and earnest discussion of language policy in Canada! Mr. Pawley, being a politician, hastily pointed to me and said, "Elizabeth is from Newfoundland so perhaps she can answer your question better than I can!" This in turn reminded me of a letter I had received from someone in France in the 1970s who wrote that all he knew about Canada was "Margaret Trudeau and the baby seals." We get branded in ways that seem to be entirely beyond our control. However, as Verduyn points out in her contribution to this volume, the ultimate purpose of the branding was an economic one and the program had "a record of return not only in terms of knowledge but also of finance." An editorial in *University Affairs* at the time of the cut argued that "this $5-million cut by DFAIT [would] result in a blow to the Canadian economy worth 14 times what DFAIT [would] save" (Martin).

As Verduyn describes, the reoriented program from 2008 onwards, presumably still about branding Canada and bringing an economic return, outlined specific themes "directly related to the mission's strategic priorities in the region" (DFAIT). Verduyn suggests that "the theme of 'managing diversity' offered a particularly productive venue for a literary focus" ("Understanding" 6). In Spain we oriented our DFAIT application towards diversity and the environment, the latter being another priority theme, and were able to find ways of making that fit with what we wanted to do (as opposed to making what we wanted to do fit with the program—though perhaps it worked both ways). We organized a seminar for undergraduates at the University of Salamanca called Representations of Diversity in Canadian Cultural Production (I don't think we ever used the word *managing*, which suggests there was some leeway in how the themes were interpreted). Despite the constraints of the DFAIT criteria, the seminar gave us scope for talking about the literary works we wanted to discuss.

In a third experience with DFAIT funding, this one also in the revised post-2008 program, Liming Yu and I brought students from Shanghai Jiao Tong University to Memorial University of Newfoundland under the same themes of diversity and the environment. I am quite sure that we did not use the words *managing* or *energy* (which was paired with *environment* in the DFAIT criteria at the time). I suppose we were still branding Canada though, in the sense that the students—potential future leaders from one of China's top-ranked universities—came here, got to know us, and had a good time. They went tobogganing and snowshoeing, navigated a ship using a mind-bogglingly realistic simulator, learned a lot about food security and the cod moratorium, drank Tim Hortons hot chocolate, ate moose stew and seal sausage, and stayed with local families. I believe they really did learn quite a lot about diversity and the environment as well.

At the University of Salamanca too, I think that, despite the constraints of the program, approximately one hundred undergraduates were exposed through our seminar to exciting new ideas about diversity and the role of film and literature in cultural and social change. I remember being both disturbed and moved when one of them told Ana that it was the first time she really felt as though she were at a university. This from a student at one of Spain's, and perhaps Europe's, most famous universities! We may have been branding Canada but we were also having a sustained and challenging conversation about culture, politics, ecology, and social responsibility.

The DFAIT-mandated focus on diversity and the environment, along with our interdisciplinary connections (English, education, Aboriginal studies, Canadian studies) brought "a new dimension to the study of Canada" (Remi and den Toonder x) in our collaboration in Salamanca. Quoting Cornelius Remi and Jeanette den Toonder, Verduyn also mentions the advantages of bilingualism and interdisciplinarity through the inclusion of "both English and French-speaking scholars" (Remi and den Toonder xviii) and the richness that can be found in the multitude of perspectives and approaches to exploring Canadian space. The idea of richness to be found despite the constraints of the funding source is intriguing, and I think this insight is accurate, or at least it reflects my own experiences of Understanding Canada. However, I'm troubled by Remi and den Toonder's phrase "both English and French-speaking scholars." Why, nationally or internationally, is it limited to English and French? I would have thought that translation could open the possibility of work in other languages and also that Canadian Indigenous languages would be included as well. Inuktitut and Inuinnaqtun are official languages in Nunavut, and Chipewyan, Cree, Gwich'in, Inuinnaqtun, Inuktitut, Inuvialuktun, North Slavey, Slavey, and Tłįchǫ or Dogrib are also officially recognized in the Northwest Territories. There are people writing in other Indigenous languages as well as these, yet they seem to be invisible here. It is as if writing, and literary production, only really exist if they are in a colonizing language.

Here are two examples of what I mean: one from Inuit cinema and one from my own work with Elizabeth Penashue, the project I referred to earlier. I think these examples may suggest one kind of answer to Kamboureli's challenge to consider new kinds of networks, affiliations, and research styles as well as opening up another aspect of her critique of area studies. I hope this will generate discussion of other possibilities.

Paul Apak Angilirq, of Igloolik Isuma Productions, discussed funding for the film *Atanarjuat (The Fast Runner)* in an interview with anthropologist Nancy Wachowich:

> NW: So let me get this straight, it was written out on paper from tapes of the elders speaking in Inuktitut, then turned into an English story, and then turned into an Inuktitut script, and then turned into an English script?
>
> PA: Yes, that is the system that we had to use in order to get money. Because... Canada Council and other places where we could apply for money, they don't read Inuktitut (qtd. in Nolette).

Elizabeth Penashue and I had a similar experience in the work we are doing. We have been working together for several years, translating Elizabeth's diaries, stories, and essays from Innu-aimun (related to Cree, one of the most widely spoken Indigenous languages in Canada) into English and French and editing both the originals and the translations for publication. We do have Social Sciences and Humanities

Research Council of Canada (SSHRC) funding, but it was a challenge to get it. One problem was that to get SSHRC funding one must write in English or French. Elizabeth writes only in Innu-aimun. Despite the fact that Aboriginal research is a SSHRC priority area, Indigenous knowledge holders cannot apply for funding if they are not affiliated with a university and applications cannot be submitted in any Indigenous language.

This is clearly a constraint, perhaps a much more challenging one, at least for some Indigenous writers, but really for all of us, than any imposed by DFAIT. As Nicole Nolette puts it, however, "both the process and the result of translation are telling manifestations of the power dynamics at play, dynamics that not only lead to language loss but also to a certain gain." The loss of language, and of funding opportunities and recognition, seems clear. Another loss, which Claire Omhovère pointed out at the workshop to develop this book, is that in France, and perhaps other countries, Canadian literature can only be taught in the original language, not in translation. This means that nothing written or produced in an Indigenous language can be taught in Canadian studies unless, of course (marvellous but implausible idea!), there were a whole class of European students able to read an Indigenous language. CanLit may be multicultural, but it seems it is not multilingual. Although Inuktitut, Cree, and other Indigenous languages are widely spoken in the North and, as I have mentioned, a number of them are officially recognized in two territories, speakers of these languages are forced to use cumbersome multi-layered translation processes in dealing with funding institutions. And the more dominant English is, the more likely the Indigenous language will be lost.

The gain Nolette is referring to may be less obvious. What gain might there be in translating back and forth, in endless explaining, in trying to live simultaneously in two worlds? Perhaps doing so can help to synthesize what really matters about the work, to reconceptualize, to encounter each other in conversation about the texts, and to find spaces where, as Paul Angilirq does in the example above, speakers of the dominant language are reminded that it is they who are deficient.

After all, they are the ones who can't read Inuktitut, or Innu-aimun, or Cree, or Dene. In her important book *First Person Plural: Aboriginal Storytelling and the Ethics of Collaborative Authorship* (2011), Sophie McCall discusses Zacharias Kunuk's use of partial translations in *Atanarjuat*. Parts of the dialogue are presented in Inuktitut but not explained in the subtitles. Thus, a non-Inuktitut-speaking audience might realize they are excluded, and can only follow the story on certain levels. The use of partial translation is a way of reminding the dominant group that they are missing something, something they might want to know, might even long to know.

This kind of work demands recognition that Indigenous writers may write in their own languages as well as colonizing ones. As Maria Tymoczko suggests, the translation of such works can contribute to changing "structures of feeling" (23), referring to shared perceptions and values common to an era or cultural group and circulated through aesthetic forms and conventions. In *Culture and Imperialism*, Edward Said applied the concept (originally developed by Raymond Williams in *The Long Revolution* and other works) to postcolonial contexts, showing how such structures and the aesthetic forms that support them could uphold or counter imperialism. Translation in such contexts often involves collaboration, as in the two examples I've just given, and perhaps both translations and collaborations could be considered in the examination of future directions and the creation of new kinds of networks and affiliations proposed by Kamboureli.

Edith Grossman, the translator of writers ranging from Cervantes to the Chilean antipoet Nicanor Parra, suggests that English-speaking regions of the world are not exposed nearly enough to writers in other languages because of a cultural antipathy toward translated works. She argues that we lose not only the opportunity to read those works but the possibility of relationships beyond the English-speaking world (the term *English-speaking world* also highlights the impossibility of "understanding Canada" since we both are and aren't part of the English-speaking world):

> Translation not only plays its important traditional role as the means that allows us access to literature originally written in one of the countless languages we cannot read, but it also represents a concrete literary presence with the crucial capacity to ease and make more meaningful our relationships to those with whom we may not have had a connection before. Translation always helps us to know, to see from a different angle, to attribute new value to what once may have been unfamiliar. As nations and as individuals, we have a critical need for that kind of understanding and insight. The alternative is unthinkable. (x–xi)

Language is an important aspect of the kinds of alliances I'm interested in, and perhaps Kamboureli is thinking of as well, but so is geography. In a wonderful book called *The Highway of the Atom*, which draws on Dene stories as well as other records of the uranium industry in Canada, Peter van Wyck writes,

> [Stories from the North] are inaccessible, if we mean by that geographically remote from the south: a pious and ironic alibi. But, more than this...many from elsewhere have not had ears with which to hear them. It seems clear as well that voices from the North seldom gather sufficient force to rise above the colonial din of southern settler life. (16)

Here is a possible agenda for Canadian studies scholars looking for new kinds of networks and affiliations. How can voices from the North "gather sufficient force"? Perhaps the example I have given of Inuit film productions, some of which are based on earlier writing in Inuktitut, suggests an answer. Another possibility comes from Japan, but with a Canadian connection.

Canadian scholar Valerie Henitiuk's award-winning research on translations of eleventh-century Japanese classics *The Tale of Genji* and *The Pillow Book* shows how they have become part of world literature in English translation and subsequently made their way back to Japan in new forms.[1] Students study the classic versions in high school and traditionally thought of them as difficult and dry, if not completely incomprehensible, but manga comic books and other pop cultural adaptations have led to renewed excitement about the texts. According to Henitiuk, a main reason for this new interest is the fact that, in English translation, they have become part of world literature, thus raising international interest that made its way back to Japan. I offer this as a fragment, the beginning of an idea, but one that suggests that translations and adaptations might play a role in enabling voices from the North to be heard, not only in the Canadian south but globally. Immigrants, as Kamboureli argues, have played a key role in reconstituting our understanding of CanLit, but Indigenous writers are currently doing so. It is beyond the scope of this chapter to discuss the contribution of Indigenous writers writing in English or French in the detail that would be necessary to do it justice, but my particular interest is in writing in Indigenous languages, translations and collaborations, and how they might challenge our understanding of CanLit (and indeed literature itself) and open up new possibilities and insights. For one thing, as McCall has suggested, they call into question the concept of the single author and oppositions such as oral/written and teller/recorder (212). For another, original writing in Indigenous languages has often been discounted because much of it has not been seen as literary writing, yet it could be understood and explored as opening up that category and taking it in new directions. While there are Indigenous writers producing work in Indigenous languages that is clearly literary—for example, Innu poet Joséphine Bacon—there are also numerous examples, present and past, of diary keepers, life writers, film makers, and others working in Indigenous languages, particularly Inuktitut. These include the film makers of Isuma, mentioned above, Labrador Inuk Abraham Ulrikabe who kept a diary while he and his family were exhibited in European zoos in the 1880s; Peter Pitseolak, whose *People from Our Side* consists of his own manuscript and photographs along with a narrative by Dorothy Harley Eber; and autobiographers John Ayaruaq and Nuligak, the former having published his autobiography in syllabics in 1968 and the latter a book edited by Maurice Metayer around the same period and more recently made into an award-winning film, *I, Nuligak: An*

Inuvialuit History of First Contact, produced by White Pine Pictures in 2005. Apart from the films, these examples are not contemporary but the recent production of the film version of *I, Nuligak* and new versions of *People from Our Side* and *The Diary of Abraham Ulrikabe* suggest that they still have much to offer through translation, and through the kinds of retellings Valerie Henitiuk is working with in Japanese contexts. Elizabeth Penashue's writing is a current example of what might be called life writing, though it transcends genres as it ranges from heartbreaking firsthand accounts of the devastating changes in Innu life in the past fifty years to political satire to prayers to poignant lists of people, places, and items that read like found poetry.

Can translation from Indigenous languages to ones that are widely spoken internationally, and adaptation—another form of translation—into popular forms such as films or graphic novels, lead to further international interest in Indigenous writing? And, if so, what might be the effects of these forms of translation?

~ʃʃʃ~

Kamboureli asks whether the Understanding Canada program has generated transnational dialogues that have produced a more complex understanding of Canada—an important question. I am also interested in intra-national dialogues, complex and nuanced conversations among ourselves that might enrich the international dialogue and encourage a reconsideration of the maps of the world and of the nation. As Kamboureli asks, why do we need nation-state-focused study programs at a time when the nation and the state have been radically questioned and reconfigured, when we study borders, peripheries, diasporas and liminality, feminist geographies, Indigenous writing, and the challenges of translation and collaboration? When many, perhaps most, of us are not very interested in a mainstream homogeneous understanding of Canada? As a Canadian who has lived much of her life as an anglophone among francophones, then as a non-Newfoundlander in Newfoundland—a place with a passionate regional identity that is often defined in opposition to the nation—and now doing collaborative work with an Innu writer in Labrador, I have never had any particular sense of Canada as a homogeneous, understandable, or brandable place. And yet it may be that within the nation-state we could have crucial discussions that would reconfigure our understanding of who we are and what we are doing here, as well as whose writing counts, and for what.

Kamboureli suggests that international scholars of Canadian studies use the cancellation of the Understanding Canada program as an opportunity to broaden the imaginary it fostered and critique the very concepts of Canadian studies and area studies. This process might also promote the development of new kinds of "research styles and networks that are more relevant to our times' disjunctive temporalities and mobility"; it could lead to exciting new kinds of work that, like *The Tale of Genji* in Japan, might find their way back home.

Finally, I want to juxtapose Verduyn's concluding points about the financial benefits of the Understanding Canada program and the ability of scholars to continue working despite thematic constraints with Kamboureli's arguments about the limitations of a quantitative approach and the opportunities brought by the cancellation of the program. Both are right, of course. Any funding is a window of opportunity and there are ways of subverting the stated goals and the constraints of any program. It is also true that thematic and disciplinary framings limit and shape the work we do, or can even imagine doing. However, lack of funding also limits what can be done and scholars, especially in countries and regions that have been hard hit by recent as well as ongoing economic trends. As we consider where to go from here and how to begin to conceptualize new kinds of networks, affiliations, and research styles, we also need to think about funding sources and about the kinds of work that can be done in times of limited funding.

Note

1. See the profile of Henitiuk's work at the SSHRC Postdoctoral Prize website: www.sshrc-crsh.gc.ca/results-resultats/prizes-prix/2005/postdoctoral_henitiuk-eng.aspx.

II

Roots and Routes

4

Canada in Black Transnational Studies
Austin Clarke, Affective Affiliations, and the Cross-Border Poetics of Caribbean Canadian Writing

MICHAEL A. BUCKNOR

Dept of History
UWI
2 April, 1964

Dear Austin X,

Good good good to hear from you. Being hearing so much about you recently [sic]. Canadian girl teaching at a secondary school here...Peter Kempadoo....Colly....

First thing, let me congratulate you on your work....Those stories in BIM, esp. the first one in dramatic monologue. Had this performed (author's permission?) when I was in St. Lucia last year. They loved it madly. Looking forward now to your novel...Kempadoo says you're coming out soon... summer?...to do a[n] assignment for CBS...[CBC] or whatever radio network I hear you practically own.

But seriously, all of us who remember you are very happy and excited about your success and I hope you will let me know if and when you are coming to Jamaica so I can do something about it.

Brath[1]

THIS LETTER FROM KAMAU BRATHWAITE to his fellow Barbadian writer Austin Clarke in 1964 celebrates the emerging significance of Austin Clarke as a writer, acknowledges his role at the Canadian Broadcasting Corporation (CBC), and hints at his intimate connection with other writers across the globe. These clues about Clarke, the CBC, Canada, and this band of letter-writing black Atlantic writers represent a story that is yet to be excavated. This story might lead us to understanding Canada's multi-textured relationship to the networks of the black Atlantic. While Afro-Caribbean diasporic figures such as Claude McKay feature in the work of Brent Hayes Edwards, who has given priority to Paris, France, as a metropolitan centre for viewing transnational black coalitions at work, and Michelle Ann Stephens similarly focuses on such figures as Marcus Garvey in Harlem, United States, I have argued that Toronto, Canada, is another black Atlantic site of cultural production with reference to Austin Clarke and the broadcast media provided at the CBC. Yet one distinctive mark of Canada's black Atlantic manifestation via Clarke is the virtual transnational community of affective alliance that provided the solidarity, support, and improvisational collaboration that gave these writers the opportunity for economic sustenance, even as they preserved their humanity and agency in the economies of cultural production. Though the importance of Caribbean literary figures in African diaspora studies has now been generally acknowledged,[2] the place of Austin Clarke—or even of Caribbean Canadian writing and Canada in black transnational studies more generally—has neither been given significant disciplinary recognition nor sufficient attention.[3]

In African diaspora studies, the Afro-Canadian situation has often been overshadowed by the Afro-American and black British contexts.[4] Although literary/cultural critics George Elliott Clarke (*Eyeing the North Star: Directions in African-Canadian Literature*), Rinaldo Walcott (*Black Like Who?: Writing Black Canada*), and David Chariandy ("Black Canadas and the Question of Diasporic Citizenship" and other essays) have made important contributions to African Canadian scholarship, the way in which Caribbean Canadian writing positions Canada as a black transnational space has been a source of critical ambivalence.[5] Indeed, on one hand, these scholars have been sensitive to the ways in which the raced construct of Caribbean Canadian writing can so easily obscure other black Canadian histories and have warned against what Walcott calls "the hyper-visibility" of Caribbean Canadian writing in black studies in Canada (*Black Like* 39).[6] On the other hand, Walcott has also argued that "discourses of black diaspora(s) and the black Atlantic" have largely left Canada out of their consideration of these exchange routes, even in the context of a cross-border black politics between America and Canada (*sic*, 17–33).[7] Like Walcott, Chariandy, in various essays, and Pilar Cuder-Domínguez, in previous work as well as in this collection, have also exposed this lacuna and shown important ways in which black Canadian studies can benefit from Gilroy's black Atlantic paradigm. As Cuder-Domínguez argues, "Canada is yet another location—and a crucial one—to add in order to restore the full picture of a criss-crossing network of black consciousness" ("African Canadian Writing" 57).

Yet, between the hypervisibility of binational discourses that obscure and the transnational mappings that erase, there is very little attention to the black (Canadian) Atlantic via Caribbean Canadian writing. Consequently, though recognizing, like Walcott, the importance of the politics of erasure, I propose shifting the critical lens of analysis beyond an oppositional black politics of recognition to the crisscrossing networks of Austin Clarke's black Atlantic politics of improvisational collaboration, black global economy, and "diasporic [maroon] intimacy."[8] In this regard, Caribbean Canadian writers might help to show how Canada, through its cultural institutions such as the CBC, becomes a central node in the black Atlantic network and expands, as well as complicates, black transnational studies. Moreover, I want to emphasize the need to consider African diasporic networks beyond institutions and to account for the role of literary friendships, the affect of political passion, and the effectiveness of improvisational strategies that mark the collaborative maneuvers of "maroon intimacy" that are evident in Canada's black Atlantic cultural production. Arguably, the four main correspondents of Clarke, among many others, are Samuel Selvon (from Trinidad), Andrew Salkey (from Jamaica), Kamau Brathwaite (from Barbados), and Jan Carew (from British Guyana). Wedded by race, cultural marginalization, a search for an economic means to support their work, and their love for writing, an important literary club is formed and sustained through the "airmail circuits above the waves of the Atlantic" by their affection for and friendship with each other (Ball 109).

While Caribbean Canadian literature is positioned uneasily within black Canadian studies and its writers are generally omitted from black transnational studies, the disciplinary value of Clarke and Caribbean Canadian writing can be seen in various other area studies such as ethnic/Canadian literature, Jewish/Canadian studies, Canadian multicultural studies, and immigrant trauma literature. To a large extent, Caribbean Canadian writing has been mobilized to question nationalist constructs and dominant paradigms in artistic and academic operations. In the academy, Smaro Kamboureli demonstrates the ways in which Caribbean Canadian writing becomes a site of interrogation, innovation, and expansion of the content, fields, and areas of study that dominate academic offerings in Canada ("Canadian Ethnic Anthologies" 11–20). Accordingly, the Canadian Multiculturalism Act is put under the critical microscope for the way it seems to influence the production of "ethnic literature" in such a way as "to neglect the relationship between ethnicity and nationalism, to leave little room, if any, for cross-cultural influences" (Kamboureli 27). This kind of critique is further elaborated by Chariandy, who uses Austin Clarke's work and its reception to show how "multiculturalism is understood not simply as a government policy specific to Canada, but rather as a broader 'politics of recognition'" that set the "discursive and epistemological terms that govern how ethno-racial minorities are recognized or misrecognized" ("'That's What You Want'" 143). Also, in the essay "Experiences of Arrival: Jewishness and Caribbean-Canadian Identity in Austin Clarke's *The Meeting Point*," Clarke's novel is used by Sarah Phillips Casteel to explore inter-ethnic relationships: "Clarke capitalizes on the racial ambiguity of the Jew in order to highlight his Caribbean immigrant characters' unstable relationship to blackness in post-war Toronto" (115). Whitney Edwards sees even wider application of the same novel by Clarke to explore "migration trauma" (319). The ever expanding issues and constituencies that Clarke and, by extension, Caribbean Canadian writing have been made to serve, including Asian Canadian studies,[9] make its omission from African diasporic studies curious, even more so given the value of Gilroy's notion of the network in his conception of the black Atlantic.

Yet the disciplinary significance of black Canadas to black transnational studies has been a concern for Canadian scholars such as Rinaldo Walcott from as early as, if not earlier than, the appearance of his *Black Like Who?* In the first chapter of that book, "'Going to the North': The Limit of Black Diasporic Discourses," he uses a 1905 example of an African American political organization's exclusion of Canadian blacks at their Ontario meeting as a marker of "the historical limit of the current discourse of diaspora...in black studies and black cultural studies" (19). Given the geographic proximity of the United States to Canada, the black border crossings (e.g., the Underground Railroad), and the currency of pan-national black politics at the time, this erasure of black Canadas is glaring, as Walcott shows. Productively, Walcott has used the "unacknowledged" pathways of Canadian black writing, culture, and history to conceptualize detour routes, additional routes that Gilroy's black Atlantic needs to take. He stresses the importance of the politics of (mis)recognition that leads to the disavowal of historical, genealogical, and discursive connections in black Atlantic crossings, because of reconstituted hegemonies that resurrect "ethnic absolutism" in diasporic black studies. While I am very sympathetic to this caution about how diasporic black studies can "re-marginalize" other fields of black studies and can fail to attend to "the cross-cutting constitution of black cultures" (28), I am nevertheless wary of the seduction of the politics of recognition and erasure, since it creates a scenario of political competition among black marginalities that potentially produces new hierarchies of power. While I am not dismissing the importance of Walcott's politics of erasure/recognition and his interrogation of uneven representational power, I also want to take up his challenge for black studies to "seriously consider diasporic exchanges, dialogues and differences" (32). In this embrace of such cross-cutting exchanges, I want to account for, as well as move beyond, the politics of hypervisibility and obscurity—the necessary oppositional politics of internal black ideological conflict—to map the black Atlantic cross-cultural networks in Austin Clarke's politics of improvisational collaboration, black global capital, and "diasporic [maroon] intimacy."

> 203 Almond Street,
> Georgetown,
> Guyana.
> 19th September 1966
>
> Dear A.P.,
> Glad like hell to hear from you, man. Congratulations on having finished the new novel. I will send off in the next two days a half hour radio play THE FIVERMAN, it should fit better than UNIVERSITY into your programme....
>   I booked a passage to Toronto for the 7th of October (PAA) the cost of a return ticket is six-fifty Guyanese dollars, and living expenses you can estimate better than I can.
>   I can pay my passage one way (three twenty-five dollars) but wouldn't mind a subsidy for the rest....I will arrive loaded with articles, stories, plays for radio, stage, TV.
>   At the moment I am loaded down with fame, acclaim etc., but broke, the Govt. hasn't got any money until next year, so the Canadian trip will be a godsend....

This letter from Jan Carew to Clarke clearly establishes Canada as a site of black diasporic capital and recognizes literary friendship as valuable to writers' development; Carew's literary career is facilitated by Clarke's connections at the CBC and other institutions important to literary production and the livelihood of artists.

It has been difficult to see the diasporic intimacies and intricacies of black global networks of political and cultural production from the vantage point of Canada because of the emphasis on an oppositional politics of disruption that is so dominant in black Canadian studies. The imprint of nationalist and postcolonial conceptual pressures on the theoretical work of black Canadian scholars has often emphasized the productive potential of marginality and the desire for representational recognition and power. Consequently, as Chariandy has astutely pointed out in his very useful survey of black Canadian scholarship, critics have often taken up the posture of discursive effrontery and rudeness, engaging in what he calls "readerly mischief" in order to challenge the orthodoxies of racial and nationalist hegemonies ("Locating" 198). In "'Canada in Us Now': Locating the Criticism of Black Canadian Writing," Chariandy identifies the necessary political "incivility" of black scholarly negotiations as part of demanding representational recognition in nationalist discourses. He alludes to the word *rude* in the title of one of Walcott's books[10] as paradigmatic of the desire in black scholarship to position black Canadian culture as "discursively disruptive" and "politically contestatory" ("Locating" 207).[11] Austin Clarke demonstrates this disruptive rudeness in a letter written at 1:35 p.m., April 26, 1978 when he writes these words to Howard Engel, executive producer of the CBC's program *Anthology*: "I thought it was better to read your comments carefully, and then write you, instead of calling you on the telephone, to tell you that really, you are full of shit. It now behoves [sic] you to call sooner than later than you wanted to, to invite me for that drink" (Box 36).

The usually civil Chariandy himself deploys his own interpretive strategy of "readerly mischief" when he speculatively queers Harold Head's phrase "Canada in us now" in the question, "Have Black people been inseminated with Canada during some unspecified encounter (climactic? anticlimactic? traumatic? queer?)" ("Locating" 198). In less civil language, Chariandy speculates inter alia on whether Head is meaning to say by that phrase, "Canada in us now," that blacks have been "fucked by Canada" and/or blackness has "fucked up Canada." What has been valuable to me in this rude speculation on Chariandy's part is the invocation of a kind of unexpected intimacy in the context of the "intensification of power relations" (Foucault qtd. in Gandhi 41). Yet Howard Engel's response to Clarke was to suggest that their close friendship would not allow their rude exchanges and difficult politics to shatter their intimacy: "For years I've heard that you have the ability to write the best letters of abuse in this country, and yet, when I at last get mine, it fails to strike sparks. Could it be that our friendship is too deep for harsh words? Have we seen too much together?" (Letter of May 1, 1978, Box 36). In the generative, paradoxical intimacy that Chariandy reads in Head's statement, both the black body and the Canadian national body are optimistically positioned as sites of exchange that can reduce the discursive distancing of blackness from Canadianness. In addition, I am also suggesting that the traumas of exclusion for various ethnicities including blacks have led to another kind of unexpected intimacy in the "commonwealth of blackness" that Head sees inhabiting Canada (Bucknor and Coleman ix). In this regard, I am suggesting that Gilroy's black Atlantic notion of "diasporic intimacy" that is manifested in the "ties of affiliation and affect which articulated the discontinuous histories of black settlers in the new world" has a Canadian manifestation (Gilroy 16). If we read Head's "Canada in us now," as Chariandy does, as an indication of both the insemination of transnational blackness by Canada and the insemination of the Canadian nation by local and transnational blackness, there is the suggestion of an intimate engagement in two ways. First, there is the idea of the intimate coalition of black Canadas and, second, the intimate exchange between transnational blacks and Canada. It is important, then, to ask these questions: What would Canada as site for cross-cultural exchange offer to black Atlantic studies? What would black transnationalism offer to Canada's cultural and political landscape? And how does the concept of "affect" help us to unpack Gilroy's concept of "diasporic intimacy," which is so important to understanding political negotiations and cultural exchanges in "postcolonial diasporas"?[12]

Several cultural critics have shown the ways in which the ideological pressures of racial and cultural hegemonies in metropolitan cities have made racial minorities marginal in the discursive and material distribution of power so that new transnational diasporic "black" communities are formed. Using London in the 1950s as an example, Barbadian writer George Lamming has acknowledged that "No Barbadian, no Trinidadian, no St. Lucian, no islander from the West Indies sees himself as a West Indian until he encounters another islander in foreign territory" (214). In this way, Lamming suggests that the immigrants' shared otherness[13] leads to the discovery of a common culture that facilitates the creation of a diasporic community: "the category West Indian, formerly understood as a geographical term, now assumes cultural significance" (214). For Lamming, "What holds Selvon and myself together is precisely what could hold Indians and Negroes together in Trinidad. It is their common background of social history which can be called West Indian" (224–25). Though "Indian" and "Negro" evoke different ethnic and racial histories, the political fight for both discursive and material power in which both figures have become embroiled becomes the source of diasporic intimacy—the closeness between disparate islanders from different classes, ethnicities, races, genders, and geographic enclaves. Lamming describes this bond developing between himself and Selvon from as early as their encounter on the ship from the Caribbean to England as an example of "comradeship" and as a kind of maroon intimacy: "Selvon and I, like members of some secret society, were always together" (212). I turn to Ronald Cummings and Jarrett Brown's conception of maroon intimacies as a way of unpacking Gilroy's concept of "diasporic intimacy"; both are kinds of intimacies developing in the context of the uneven distribution of power and in situations of trauma. The hegemonic pressures of metropolitan spaces also sideline Caribbean subjects racially, making all variations of non-white pigmentation to be read as black.

As Bill Schwarz explains, "Those who journeyed from the Caribbean recall that they became West Indian[14] (as opposed, say, to Antiguan or Guyanese or St. Lucian) in London or Birmingham: indeed for many of them this was part and parcel of *becoming black*" (13). This understanding that Schwarz and Lamming have of Caribbean subject formation in England is similar to Head's construction of black Canada in his collection *Canada in Us Now*. While Head traces an originary source of black cultures to Africa, he eventually upholds an *improvisational* construct of blackness that is a response to the economic pressures of a predominantly white metropolis, so that "Head's black commonwealth is marked off by common poverty" (Bucknor and Coleman x–xi). As Daniel Coleman and I argue elsewhere, "a shared circumstance that suggests that class issues can provide common ground for political coalitions" is also part of Head's optimistic configuration of black Canada (xi). Lamming's and Head's conception can be aligned with Leela Gandhi's notion of how intimacy is borne out of a "shared catastrophe" (45) and with Lisa Lowe's idea of how intimacy develops in the context of "volatile contacts of colonized peoples" (203). This improvisational production of diasporic intimacy is one illustration of what Walcott conceives as the detour routes that Gilroy's black Atlantic can take,[15] and that Caribbean Canadian affiliative networks of literary and cultural production is worthy of further study.

It is not surprising that Gilroy sees artistic and political coalitions of racial minorities as a source for diasporic intimacy marked by ties of "affiliation and affect" (Gilroy 16), since art has played a major role in black liberation projects, and minorities shut out from access to public systems and resources are often forced to turn to the informal and the personal.[16] In a four-page letter to Jan Carew, Austin Clarke, even in 1978, continues to use the many resources and connections he has to make ends meet. After receiving a loan that he describes as a "bailout," he tries to place his novel *More* with McClelland & Stewart,[17] he is working on four stories (one of which is bought by the CBC), he is considering taking up another offer by Yale University to return there to teach, he has come up with a scheme to ask the CBC to sponsor a trip to Guyana to do some reporting on the Jonestown Massacre, and he is also planning to organize a conference on West Indian writers by approaching the Canada Council. In this last venture, he identifies a number of connections that he hopes to approach: "We do...have a great number of extraordinary people who can play a part in such a conference, and I am sure, in spite of the spite and cut-backs, that I will get some financial backing. Vince D'Oyley in the West has much experience in these things, and I will call on him. Also, Professor Lloyd Brown of the University of Southern California; and Elliott Parris who is now at Howard in the Afro-American programme" (Letter of 30 Nov. 1978, Box 36). As Chariandy has argued, "historically disenfranchised peoples have developed *inventive tactics* for transforming even the most sinister experiences of dislocation into vibrant and revolutionary forms of political action and cultural life" ("Postcolonial Diasporas" 1, emphasis added). For Gilroy, "the contemporary black arts movement in film, visual arts and theatre, as well as music... have created a new topography of loyalty and identity," leaving behind the "outmoded" nation-state (16).[18] While I don't agree with Gilroy that this "new topography of loyalty and identity" discards nationalist affiliations, I am intrigued by his suggestion that black transnational political activism in art can be a source of affective alliances and political intimacies. Against the dominance in some aspects of black Canadian studies of a politics of separation, I want to tease out Gilroy's politics of intimacy as a way to understand what role Austin Clarke and his letter-writing buddies and, by extension, Caribbean Canadian writing might play in marking iterations of black transnationalism in Canada. One set of discourses that offers some insight into the idea of political intimacy is recent work on "postcolonial intimacy."

Both the article "Black Atlantic, Queer Atlantic: Queer Imaginings of the Middle Passage" by Omise'eke Natasha Tinsley and the introductory essay, "Postcolonial Intimacies: Gatherings, Disruptions, Departures," in the special issue of *Interventions* called *Postcolonial Intimacies* by Antwi et al. begin to tease out a relationship between affect and resistance in the black Atlantic that exposes intimacy as a politically valuable concept. For Antwi et al., the idea of "'post-colonial intimacies' relocates the concept of intimacy to conditions of post-colonial exchanges, with inter- and intra-continental circuits of passionate politics, and to acts and interested networks of globalization, with all its economic, ecological and informational concerns" (2). In this regard, they recognize the decolonizing value of affect and intimate alliances in global networks that would include the black Atlantic. Affect, for them, is one of the channels of establishing the networking community as well as of engaging politically with dominant power. These editors, much like Head read through Chariandy's rude speculation, see the very "ideological frameworks as knowledge systems of intimacy" (Antwi et al. 2). The arguments about postcolonial intimacies draw attention to the inventive strategies of resistance articulated in the personal and affective affiliations that diverse peoples form in the wake of "shared catastrophe" (Gandhi 45). Their attention to the "emotional economy of belonging, labour and migration; ethics and responsibility; and the affective and cultural tensions surrounding public and private demonstrations of care, comfort, familiarity and/or unease" (Antwi et al. 2–3) creates a critical space for Clarke's black Atlantic letter-writing community and for understanding how their bonds of intimacy renegotiate the terms on which global capital is engaged. Clarke's facilitation of Jan Carew's visit in which personal arrangement supersedes or augments institutional arrangements that are tardy and bureaucratic is only one example of such collaborations. Jan Carew writes in a letter of September 19, 1966, "My publishers have an office in Canada (Longman's, Green) I will write off to them and they will write their man, but on the sponsoring side, it would take them ages. So we've got to swing this business without them." In a letter of July 30, 1966, Andrew Salkey, though outlining the possible paths of economic success for black Atlantic writers like himself and Clarke, is equally taken up with commiserating over Edgar Mittleholzer's death. He spends half the letter lamenting the CBC's and Robert Weaver's non-acceptance of his poem in tribute to Mittleholzer: "it was quite near to Edgar's anniversary and I thought that possibly Weaver might like to mark the occasion with a poem written by another West Indian writer....Of course, the poem is personal: a buddy's death by suicide is a bloody personal loss, yes." While seeking to participate in the global labour market of literary production, Clarke and other Caribbean writers do not necessarily succumb to the capitalist imperative of gaining individual profit at the expense of human and community value. Their strategies of inventive collaboration facilitated their participation in economic opportunities that were negotiated through their intimate bonds of friendship that preserved human value in a capitalist culture of dehumanization.

Indeed, these affective alliances of collaboration and resistance are not only conceptualized through the lens of postcolonial intimacy, but also through queer postcolonial intimacy, as demonstrated by Tinsley in her reading of the black Atlantic. In the capitalist configurations of the Atlantic slave trade, blacks were subjected to dehumanizing strategies, maneuvers to evacuate any sense of humanity and agency. Yet, as Tinsley shows, the "shared catastrophe" (Gandhi 45) and "volatile contacts" (Lowe 203) of the Middle Passage and indentureship produced unexpected intimacy that was a source of rebellion and collaboration. Consequently, Tinsley argues that

> this bloody Atlantic was also the site of collaboration and resistance. In the early eighteenth century, ship captains like John Newton and James Barbot repeatedly record with horror how despite such conditions slaves conspired to rebel against captors. At the same time, unnamed rebellions took place not in violent but in *erotic* resistance, in interpersonal relationships enslaved Africans formed with those imprisoned and oozing beside them. (198)

Using the concept of "shipmates"[19] as a sign of intimate encounter, Tinsley suggests that queer intimacy was developed between same-sex shipmates whose sympathy, shared anguish, and bodily alignment allowed for affiliations and erotic agency that facilitated resistance to imperialist logic and began the process of re-humanization. The queer conception in these alliances is deployed by Tinsley not necessarily to restrict the concept to gay erotic connections, but to a larger project of postcolonial intimate resistance.[20] For her "queer" is used

> not in the sense of a "gay" or same-sex loving identity waiting to be excavated from the ocean floor but as a praxis of resistance—*queer* in the sense of marking disruption to the violence of normative order and powerfully so: connecting in ways that commodified flesh was never supposed to, loving your own kind when your kind was supposed to cease to exist, forging interpersonal connections that counteract imperial desires for Africans' living deaths. (Tinsley 199)

Therefore, postcolonial resistance conceptualized through a queer lens allows for conceiving of intimacy as a political tool of disruption of the dominant order of capitalism and its negotiations through racial hierarchies and hegemonies. This disruptive conception is consonant with Chariandy's theorizing of black Canadian scholarship, but this disruptive challenge does not preclude intimate collaboration in the context of a hegemonic oppression. Following Chariandy's queer reading of Head, Caribbean Canadian writing and Clarke's infiltration of the institutions of cultural production help us to see how queer postcolonial intimacies can complicate Canada's black Atlantic as a space of disruptive politics that is not outside of collaboration.

This queer postcolonial intimacy may also carry embedded in it a kind of "maroon technology" (J. Brown 20) that allows it not to be easily detected in public, institutional operations. Following on Tinsley's productive use of the "shipmate" concept, I would like to refer to my earlier take on Lamming's description of his shipmate alliance with Selvon (while sailing on the *Windrush* to London) as a kind of maroon intimacy. Ronald Cummings, for example, makes good work of the story "This Dance," by Jamaican writer Kei Miller, to invoke a maroon tradition of private (even secret) society of alliance and rebellion; it is based on "the Maroon tradition of transgression, resistance and subterfuge" as Cummings claims ("Queer Theory" 328). Jarrett Brown adds the idea of "improvisation" as a key concept in maroonage, what he calls a "poetics of contingency" residing in "maroon ancestry" (20). In this way, maroon intimacies are associated with guerrilla warfare against dominant power structures using strategies of improvisation, transgression, and rebellion. Yet it is also a space for creating a community for support, identity consolidation, and intimacy. The improvisational collaborations, rebellion against the dehumanizing economic logic, as well as exploitation of the economic opportunities of global capital, and diasporic intimacy seen in the private space of letters among Caribbean writers in capital sites of cultural production (Bridgetown, Kingston, Georgetown, London, and Toronto) mark the detours of black Atlantic culture in Canada.

As I have argued elsewhere, much of the work that laid the foundation for this further burgeoning of anglophone Caribbean literature was done by Clarke, who detoured to Canada in 1955 when funding opportunities for studying in London were delayed. In "Beyond Windrush and Other Black Atlantic Routes," I have already shown the importance of linking Clarke's cultural institution building in Canada, as well his transnational coalitions, to the work of the first wave of development by the Windrush generation of Caribbean writers and the British Broadcasting Corporation (BBC). I also pointed out that "Anne Walmsley's history of the Caribbean Artists Movement" (an organization formed by students, artists, writers from the Caribbean living in London) "provides an account of some of the [capital] advantages that London afforded Caribbean writers in the post–World War II period" (208). Significantly, she identifies opportunities for work and publishing, media exposure, support from an artistic community, and political agitation around issues of race as contributing factors to Caribbean literary production at the time (208).[21] All these factors are linked to Caribbean writers' search for an economic environment in which their art could be successful. As James Procter reminds us, writers such as Samuel Selvon in London had to be inventive in selling stories to various magazines, including non-traditional printing spaces, in order to survive. Clarke's own story about Selvon on his visit to London in 1965 confirms the economic struggle of these writers.[22] Clarke knew this struggle personally when he was forced to find a variety of jobs in order to maintain his family. According to his biographer, Stella Algoo-Baksh, in 1957 after leaving the University of Toronto without completing his studies and in short order marrying Betty Reynolds, "Clarke acquired immigrant status in Canada and embarked on a search for employment" (18). In his search for suitable work, "he was in turn an employee in a paint factory, a cleaner in a school on College Street, a janitor at a Baptist Church House, and a stage hand with the Canadian Broadcasting Corporation" (18). Nevertheless, it was only later, after several stints as a journalist in Ontario at the *Daily Press* of Timmins, the *Northern Daily News* in Kirkland Lake, the Toronto *Globe and Mail*, at the magazine *Canadian Nuclear Technology*, and then much later as a freelance journalist at the CBC that Clarke began to exploit the institutional mechanisms of broadcast culture for the promotion of anglophone Caribbean writing in Canada.

Through a collaborative effort, a building of a transnational network, and an investment in human value, Clarke was also able to facilitate and consolidate a second renaissance of anglophone Caribbean writing from a Canadian cultural centre—so much so that, by 1998, a subfield of Canadian literature had been developed and identified as Caribbean Canadian writing. Yet the work of black Atlantic cultural production is not complete without consideration of the work of intimacy as detailed in his letters to fellow writers in which improvisational collaboration helps us to see black Atlantic networks and coalitions that are both Canadian and black transnational at the same time. Just as the *Caribbean Voices* radio program comes to an end at the BBC in 1958, the CBC and its associated *Tamarack Review* appear to be new sites for anglophone Caribbean literary promotion and production.[23] Jamaican literary critic and poet Edward Baugh, who spent 1958–59 as a graduate student at Queen's University in Kingston, Ontario, reports that "the first substantial recognition of West Indian literature in a big, First World country other than Great Britain" was "Canada's prestigious *Tamarack Review*" (special issue, no. 14, winter 1960), which focused on the West Indies (247). According to Baugh, it was an impressive selection of work by writers who were already on their way to becoming the "classics": Martin Carter, John Hearne, George Lamming, Victor Reid, Samuel Selvon, and Derek Walcott. An essay by Reid, "The West Indies: A New Nation," provided the historical background to the literature, while Frank Collymore gave an overview of the literature in his essay "Writing in the West Indies" (247).

By 1961, if not earlier, Clarke was already knocking at the doors of opportunity in the person of Robert Weaver, then program officer, Special Programs at the CBC and co-founder and editor of the *Tamarack Review*, to have his work published and promoted. For several decades, Clarke built relationships with officials such as Weaver, Robert McCormack, Harry J. Boyle, and Howard Engel of the CBC. Through them and others such as Janet Somerville, he was able to have his work read, reviewed, performed, and featured on various literary programs of the broadcasting network. In addition, he was also able to gain assignments as a journalist for the CBC in conducting interviews, sourcing literary material from other Caribbean writers and exploring race-based issues that were so dominant in the 1960s. It is also clear that Weaver was aware of the economic struggles of emerging writers and, much like Henry Swanzy of the BBC,[24] facilitated the financial support of writers. What would make Weaver and others of the CBC be disposed to non-resident anglophone Caribbean writers who did not publish in Canada? Granted, from reports about Weaver's work at the CBC, it is clear that he was interested in helping to promote Canadian literature of which Clarke could be seen as a part.[25] Yet, owing to this collaboration between Clarke and Weaver, George Lamming (Barbados/UK), Ismith Khan (Trinidad/US), Jan Carew (Guyana/UK/Spain), Derek Walcott (St. Lucia/Trinidad), Samuel Selvon (Trinidad/UK, not yet living in Canada), all non-resident Canadians, were also being featured on the CBC. How far can we take the black Atlantic networking connections, and can white establishment collaborators be seen as part of that economic network? In "The Intimacies of Four Continents," Lisa Lowe points out that "Robin D.G. Kelly emphasizes that the significance of black diaspora projects to the field of US history may be precisely their capacity to chart *more* than black identities and political movements, what he calls 'other streams of internationalism not limited to the black world'" (205). This view is echoed in England by Peter J. Kalliney in the *Commonwealth of Letters: British Literary Culture and the Emergence of Postcolonial Aesthetics*, in which he argues for the recognition of cross-racial alliances in publishing and radio networks. I think it is worthwhile to begin thinking through what the political stakes are for widening and whitening the black Atlantic in Canada.

Though Clarke would accuse Weaver and others at the CBC of veiled racism, though he would be considered at times rude in his aggressive demand for air space,[26] and though there would be conflicts about language, length, and complexity of material that would disqualify various pieces of writing submitted by him from being broadcast, there was still a relatively respectful, caring, sensitive relationship evidenced, even in testy letters, that suggested that institutional responses did not ignore the personal. In a letter of November 14, 1961, Weaver responds to Clarke's submission of fiction for consideration in the *Tamarack Review*, indicating that he had more than enough fiction already, but would continue to think about other possibilities for the submission: "I have read the story quickly and want a chance to read it a second time. Unfortunately for you, we really have too much fiction on hand just now for *Tamarack Review*. However, let me think a little further about the story" (Box 36). He goes on to advise Clarke about applying to the Canada Arts Council and invites him to call him for them to meet. Even when Clarke tells Howard Engel that he is "full of shit" and it is clear that Clarke's "effrontery" and rude contestations were necessary to get the attention of and fair treatment from the literary establishment, Engel and Clarke's personal friendship helps to negotiate such tensions. As Engel asks, "Can it be that our friendship is too deep for harsh words?" (Letter from Engel to Clarke, 1 May 1978, Box 36). There are various invitations to talk on the phone and to go for lunch in the correspondence in the 1960s and 1970s and several officials at the CBC clearly enjoyed drinking with Clarke.[27] In 1968, the day after Martin Luther King Jr. is assassinated, April 5, Weaver writes to Clarke wishing him luck in his journey back to Yale University, invites him to lunch and commiserates on the death of King: "I am sorry to have to write today because the Martin Luther King business last night certainly does not make life easy on this planet just now" (Box 36). These expressions of sensitivity across the divide of race are also played out in correspondence about payment to Clarke. For example, Harry Boyle writing to Clarke on January 23, 1967 assures him that "we are processing a contract for One Thousand Dollars ($1,000.00) for the programme 'The World of Graham Coughtry' for Project '68. We are giving you an advance of $300.00 which we will put through as quickly as possible" (Box 36). Such sensitivity seems to suggest that the economic channels of Canadian cultural production, through broadcast culture, did not ignore the human side of things. Alternatively, perhaps it is Clarke's insistence and rude rebellion against unfair economic treatment that force the officials to tread carefully as evidenced in this letter to Clarke by Janet Somerville, producer of the program *Ideas* in the Public Affairs Department:

> I think I told you that we're into our "repeat" season—a long cool summer of re-arranging old packages, during which I have not one cent of budget....
>
> I got officially informed last week by the Talent Relations Office that... all CBC programs, even those without a written contract, can be broadcast once on every CBC transmitter, so that means I can use your gems on "Best of IDEAS" without further payment. Since that's the deal, I will—because they're such good programs—but I don't mind admitting that I feel crummy about not having a budget to pay you extra. You worked hard for your $130.00 per....
>
> I hope you're not going to be furious about the bread-less AM exposure.
> (16 June 1967, Box 36)

That there might be sensitivity expressed by the CBC does not mean that there were not elements of economic exploitation or racism faced by black content producers such as Clarke.

In their discussion of postcolonial intimacies, Antwi et al. list "passionate politics" as a way of framing how political agendas can carry embedded in them strong personal feelings and emotions. Much of the alliance among the Caribbean writers with whom Clarke establishes strong friendships is linked to their sense of outrage at racism in the metropolitan centres in which they found themselves searching for cultural capital. Clarke, in his memoir, describes their emotional reaction to one of their own, V.S. Naipaul, whom they felt became a dissident in his accommodation of racism in statements he made on the BBC in 1965:

> There was fierceness in Handrew's[28] disapprobrium; passion in his disappointment with a "brother" gone wrong, with a friend who had misunderstood the Inglish congratulation, and had mistaken it for acceptance. "Rass!"[29] Handrew said. "'Bro,' what you expect from the rass-man?" There was no need, in either case, from either evaluation, for further enlargement.
> (*A Passage* 42–43)

Yet the emotional reaction of these friends was not uniform. As Clarke reports, "when I called Sam [Selvon] back that night of the *Third Programme*, to talk about Naipaul's contribution, he said simply, 'Well, boy you know Vidia! [V.S. Naipaul] Vidia does-do his thing. That is Vidia" (*A Passage* 42). While the contrasting responses from the Afro-Jamaican (Salkey) and the Indo-Trinidadian (Selvon) might suggest they were not wedded in their common emotional reaction to this issue or that they did not share the same passion, I would argue that their reaction revealed their differing emotional registers. Selvon, though seeming to be milder in his response, is equally sensitive to the race issue, which comes up from time to time in his letters to Clarke, through humour. In his letters, often he playfully refers to him as "Copper" or "copper-plate" and makes a great deal of fun about race. Just before Carifesta 1972 in Guyana (often referred to in the letters as B.G.—British Guyana), for example, Selvon writes to Clarke, obviously excited about the trip, but as is customary, makes some racial remarks: "My/our buddy ISMITH KHAN is going to be there, so it will mean two coolie against one nigger. If you like, I could bring one of them straight-hair wig: it had a lot selling in London, so you wouldn't feel so conspicuous when walking about town with we" (7 Aug. 1972, Box 42). As Lowe has argued about the post emancipation period, "intimacies...formed the political unconscious of modern racial classification," in spite of the deliberate attempts to erect hierarchies of race between former slaves and indentured labourers (204).

In the letters I examined in the Austin Clarke archives at McMaster University from the early 1960s to the 1970s, Clarke and his literary friends provide an important support group for each other as they struggle to survive and remain relevant in the competitive literary scene of the day. Much of the expressions of affect are detailed in the fond names they call each other, the expressions of comfort and encouragement, the sharing of personal stories about their love lives, their homosocial bonding, their articulations of vulnerabilities and distress, and their networking connections for economic benefit. Jan Carew refers to Clarke as "Clarky" and "A.P.," while Clarke refers to Jan Carew as "Jancrow"; Selvon calls him "Copper" and "Copper-plate"; Brathwaite addresses him as "Tom" (reminiscent of his informal Barbadian name) and sometimes, "my brother"; and Salkey uses variations on "my brother": "Brother Austin," "My dearest Brother Man," and "My dear Austin, Brother Man"; all these names are laced with affection and a sense of the close fraternity of writer friends. They also feel free to share their vulnerabilities: Carew in letter of April 25, 1966 (Box 36) shares from London with Clarke his ordeal in Ghana when he was imprisoned: "For trying to organize a general strike on the day of the coup, and taking a number of people who were in danger to safety, I was imprisoned by the army, spent twelve days in Usher Fort," and Clarke writing to Carew on November 30, 1978 (Box 36) reveals his anxiety over the reception of his novel *More* and his dire financial circumstances:

> I am working on four short stories at the same time. One of them will be bought by the CBC and I am about to run down there this afternoon, and see if Howard Engel, that latter-day literary critic will be Jewish enough as to put through the cheque so that I might buy some salt fish and rich [rice] for Christmas. If this does not go through, I will be feasting on salt and water.

Years before, on September 28, 1965 (Box 42), it is Salkey who is writing concerned about Carew's seemingly aimless life:

> Incidentally, Jan has left London for good, you know. He has gone to live in Spain temporarily, maybe B.G. afterwards, or if that does not work (as it certainly didn't when he tried it some years ago), he might try some other West Indian territory. I think he is in a very bad way, no real home to go to, no real aim (apart from his writing which is picking up nicely again, but Jan wants "the political life" too), no real friends to speak of, and alas no wife either. I am very concerned about him. If you want to drop him a line of cheer, write to:...

Almost a month later, Jan is writing back to Clarke indicating how happy he was to hear from him, sharing his various writing projects, inviting him to "rendezvous" in "B.G. for independence, sometime between Feb. and June 66" and asking to be invited to Canada (26 Oct. 1965, Box 36).

There is not enough space to detail the various accounts of intimacy in these letters in this chapter, but the clear homosocial practice of hypermasculine cussing and retailing stories about womanizing is only part of a larger story of caring, thoughtfulness, comfort, support, confessions of vulnerabilities, and building of networks for participation in the global economies of broadcast culture and literary production. The growing recognition of the value of broadcast culture is expressed by Salkey in a 1965 letter to Clarke: "Anyway, if you can get a few minutes on radio and TV that ought to spread the word even quicker and more evenly than by the old printed word" (30 July 1966, Box 42). That Clarke and other Caribbean writers could gain access to Canada's elite institutions of cultural production (the CBC, the *Tamarack Review*, and later the Canada Arts Council) is one way of understanding how transnational black cultures inseminated Canada and Canada provided an alternative metropolitan cultural centre for the black Atlantic cultures to expand black global economies, however modest. The fact of Canada's nationalist engagement around that time and its multicultural mechanisms for publication support were further institutional facilities for the development of Caribbean Canadian writing affording a second renaissance for anglophone Caribbean writing. Though the "passionate politics" about race wedded black Atlantic writers in a fierce fight for discursive space, this fight produced unexpected intimacies as well with white collaborators whose positions of power made discursive and material space for the cultural products of the black Atlantic. Read through the lens of affect, the dehumanizing logic of capitalist cultural institutions is resisted and the very terms of engagement preserve humanity and agency.

Mervyn Morris's "Making West Indian Literature" explicitly indicates the value of institutional processes and implicitly hints at the significance of literary friendships to "nurturing" literary production: "Critics can be important to a literature. But the literature must be produced before it can be sifted for analysis. It may be that, even in the academy, we should pay more attention to nurturing production and trying to understand its processes" (1). In his account of West Indian literary history, he demonstrates the way in which chance encounters, informal connections, and personal interest led to his nurturing role in the development of dub poetry:

> Serendipities led me to "dub poetry"—a disputed term. Late in 1975, when I was on secondment to this centre, I had a telephone call from Leonie Forbes. She asked me to look at some poems she had received from a man in prison, Orlando Wong. I saw talent in the poems, and I told her so. She urged me to visit Orlando. I survived his initial inspection, and became one of his regular visitors at the St Catherine District Prison and, later, at Fort Augusta where the regime seemed less strict. He was already writing reggae rhythms in his poems, and outlining an explanatory aesthetic. He examined poetry by Langston

Hughes and younger black American poets. I introduced him to reggae-related work by Linton Kwesi Johnson, whom I had met in England in 1972–73. (9)

I agree with Morris's clearly articulated point that institutional mechanisms have to be in place for the development of literature. However, I am also keenly aware of the value of literary friendships and affective alliances. Clarke and his letter-writing buddies show that black Atlantic networks of cultural production in Canada were ever widening through and beyond national borders, ethnicities, races, and cultures. In this regard, Clarke, Caribbean Canadian writing, and Canada help to expand and complicate the black Atlantic project and black transnational studies. Even so, one wonders if this moment in broadcast history in Canada has radically changed cultural institutions to the point that black Atlantic cultures are fully accommodated or, even more importantly, other constituents than writers have now been able to enter or adjust global capital. Has Harold Head's optimistic claim been realized three decades later? Is Canada in the black Atlantic now, and has black Atlantic culture been accommodated in Canada?

Notes

1. This letter (from Box 35) and all subsequent letters quoted in this chapter are courtesy of the Austin Clarke Archives from The William Ready Division of Archives and Research Collections, McMaster University Library.
2. See, for example, the recurring significance of Caribbean intellectuals and activists to African diasporic studies in books such as Paul Gilroy's *The Black Atlantic: Modernity and Double Consciousness* (1993), Brent Hayes Edwards's *The Practice of Diaspora: Literature, Translation and the Rise of Black Internationalism* (2003), and Michelle Ann Stephens's *Black Empire: The Masculine Global Imaginary of Caribbean Intellectuals in the United States, 1914–1962* (2005).
3. See, for example, the call for papers for the 42nd Annual Convention, Northeast Modern Language Association (NemLA), April 7–10, 2011 titled, "Canada and the African Diasporic Literary Imaginary," which states that "'African Canada' is often elided from conceptions of the African Diaspora. And yet the history of Canada within the African Diaspora is rich and diverse." See http://call-for-papers.sas.upenn.edu/node/37376.

4. Rinaldo Walcott argues that while "*The Black Atlantic* has inaugurated a discussion of Black British and African American cultural and political identifications and sharing," Gilroy seems reluctant "to seriously consider Black Canada" ("'Who Is She'" 40).
5. One exception is recent work by Phanuel Antwi on Caribbean Canadian dub poetry.
6. See Bucknor and Coleman's Introduction, "Rooting and Routing Caribbean-Canadian Writing," x.
7. See also Diana Brydon, "Re-Routing the Black Atlantic." In this review essay, she concludes, "Although Gilroy's focus fell on rethinking the relations of the Caribbean, the United States, and Africa from the perspective of black Britain, his theorizing of the Black Atlantic invites the expansion of his thesis into other domains" (95).
8. I am using the concept of "diasporic intimacy" that is suggested in Gilroy's work. However, I am also inflecting that by considering concepts of maroonage as explored by Caribbean critics Ronald Cummings and Jarrett Brown.
9. See Bucknor and Coleman's "Rooting and Routing," xi.
10. See *Rude: Contemporary Black Canadian Culture Criticism*.
11. For him, "Barbara Godard appears to share both Padolsky's and Walcott's hope that Black Canadian writing can be discursively disruptive" ("Locating" 207).
12. I am adopting Chariandy's very useful twinning of the concepts of postcolonial and diaspora in his essay "Postcolonial Diasporas."
13. The fact that the predominantly non-white Caribbean subjects are often collectively "othered" in a white dominated space of London is the source of their oppression.
14. The phrase "becoming West Indian" covers both the idea that the Caribbean subject's particularities are erased in a generalized ghettoized identity that all peoples with a certain accent, ethnicity, and cultural expression are interpellated into and, at the same time, signals the way that particularities are suppressed in a strategic identity of coalition and intimacy that allows for survival in a hostile economic and discursive environment.
15. See Walcott's elaboration on the concept of "detour" in his work: "The detour is both an improvisatory and an in-between space which black diasporic cultures occupy" (*Black Like* 18).
16. Aligning marginalized minorities with personal contact does not suggest that big capitalist enterprises do not mobilize personal connections, but they are not restricted to these efforts since they usually have access to institutional structures of power.
17. This novel was only published in 2008.

18. See my PHD thesis "Postcolonial Crosses," in which I argue that in these transnational configurations of cultural exchange, the nation is not totally abandoned. See as well Chariandy's very lucid engagement with Gilroy's work specifically in which he argues that to "pit nation against diaspora" is problematic ("Postcolonial Diasporas").
19. Tinsley quotes Byran Edwards's *The History...of the British West-Indies* (1794) to define "shipmate" thus: "the term *shipmate* is understood among [West Indian slaves] as signifying a relationship of the most endearing nature; perhaps as recalling the time when the sufferers were cut off together from their common country and kindred, and awakening reciprocal sympathy from the remembrance of mutual affliction" (Bryan 20 qtd. in Tinsley 198).
20. While Tinsley is foregrounding the concept of queer as a way of reading history, it is not an attempt to deny or disavow the significance of the lived experience of queer subjectivities.
21. In fact, many writers had come with the hope, she claims, "that in Britain they would obtain training and experience, a responsive audience, and opportunities to live by the practice of their craft" (Walmsley 8). See also my "Beyond Windrush and the Original Black Atlantic Routes."
22. See Clarke's *A Passage Back Home*, 23–24.
23. Katherine McLeod indicates that the Robert Weaver's CBC-run program "*Anthology* participated in and was part of events following the Massey Commission in 1951 to support and encourage the arts in Canada. We can see a burst in Canadian writing in the 1950s and early '60s leading toward the Centennial celebrations. Looking at radio allows us to see that connection" (qtd. in Vowles, "CBC Radio"). By means of this new emphasis on Canadian literary programs, Clarke is able to get more Caribbean literary voices broadcast at the CBC.
24. See, for example, Glyne Griffith's remark that "neglect of the literary talent of a new generation of Caribbean writers was, in Swanzy's mind, not only an aesthetic matter: it was economic too" (196).
25. See, for example, Elaine Kalman Naves's book, *Robert Weaver: Godfather of Canadian Literature*, in which she argues that "as CBC's program organizer for literary content, he [Weaver] became its driving force of cultural programming through shows such as *Anthology*, *CBC Wednesday Night*, and *Critically Speaking*. Over the decades, he worked tirelessly as producer, editor, talent scout, and impresario" (12).
26. See letter to Clarke from Weaver on January 4, 1966 (Box 36) in which he states inter alia, "I did not reply at once to your letter of December 19 because I was afraid that I might be rude in response to your rudeness to me."

27. Lewis Auerbach ends his letter of March 7, 1969 (Box 36) this way: "Come drink with me next time you are in Toronto. I would very much enjoy the honour of getting you stoned."
28. The additional *h* at beginning of Andrew is a way to tease Salkey about the tendency in Jamaican creole speakers to place an unnecessary *h* sound before words beginning with a vowel.
29. Jamaican expletive.

5

"Why Don't You Write about Canada?"

Olive Senior's Poetry, Everybody's History, and the "Condition of Resonance"

ANNE COLLETT

Questions

> ...Come:
> study me. Take my chambered shell apart.
> Brace yourself for whirlwinds
> coiled at my heart.
> (Senior, "Gastropoda," *Shell* 9)

I HAVE BEEN STUDYING OLIVE SENIOR'S POETRY for some years now, and can vouch for the whirlwinds coiled at its heart. She is a poet of great skill, deep compassion, and infectious humour. Her art is a quiet hurricane,[1] whose power is often only apparent after you've been swept away, blown over, hit the ground...shell-shocked. Senior writes almost exclusively "about" the Caribbean; but taken out of the context of her 2007 volume of poetry, *Shell*, the poem "Gastropoda" might appear to have nothing to do with the Caribbean, given it does not reference the Caribbean specifically, and yet it has everything to do with the

Caribbean—a world at whose heart lies a maelstrom of greed, violence, suffering, anger. The shell is an image of a dispersed people, flung far from home to distant and unwelcoming shores by the turbulent currents of human desire. The shell is the vessel of life and the evidence of that life after death. Put it to your ear; listen to the grave story it has to tell:

> The slave ship shell-shock dark
> as night-filled gourd
>
> Cavernous as a grave fault
>
> The viewer's mind
> stretches to fit.
> ...
> Outside: The Sun has his eye on
>
> the truth that spirals out of ( ) hell.
> ("At the Slave Museum," *Shell* 63)

What does this have to do with Canada? Neither "Gastropoda" nor "At the Slave Museum" appears to have anything to do with Canada, given that the poems do not reference Canada specifically, and yet it is my contention that the poems speak to and of Canada—Canada in the world. Perhaps I should ask, what does the Caribbean have to do with Canada? Does it matter? Clearly it matters to the people who regularly ask Senior "why don't you write about Canada?" as though the Caribbean were irrelevant to Canada, and clearly it matters to Senior for whom the Caribbean provides a "condition of resonance": "Home for me," she reflects, "is a place where there is a condition of resonance or sound returned, that is, a place where you speak to a community and it speaks back to you" ("Crossing Borders" 18).

In this chapter I don't want to think about why this question about the absence of "Canada" arises or why and to whom it matters; rather, I want to think about how we might "see" Canada in Senior's work, and what it is she is saying about Canada and the relationship between Canada and the Caribbean. A clue to the latter questions might lie in her observation that "to come here [to Canada] is to suddenly become a member of a visible minority and all that it entails. Visibility here implies over-exposure; you are too readily seen, but you can fade and vanish in the harsh glare of overlooking" ("Crossing Borders" 19). The "problem" and the conflicted feelings with which it is associated are all too familiar to immigrants in Australia; so I also want to insert myself as an Australian into this discussion, and think about what Senior's recognition of entangled histories, the worlding of the Caribbean and of Canada, might encourage me to see about Australia and its similar (if different) colonial history.

I suggest that Canada is a *present absence* in Senior's poetry, a poetry in which her focus on the Caribbean acts not only to assert the value of Caribbean community but to lay claim to, and indeed to remind readers of, the value of that community to Canada. When Senior is asked, why don't you write about Canada?—with the unspoken qualifier that she has resided in Canada since the early 1990s and publishes her work in Canada—Senior might reply with lines from her poem "Canefield Surprised by Emptiness":

> It is not so much the shell shock as questions
> we never asked that leave us cowering still
> among the dead sugar metaphors. (*Shell* 55)

In response I want to ask a question that might enable us to make sense of the other(ing) question, and the "dead sugar metaphors": What does Canada have to do with this condition of "shell shock"? By way of short single answer, I might paraphrase Ngũgĩ wa Thiong'o observation/accusation (via Walter Rodney) that the first world (a.k.a.

Canada) was developed at the expense and thus the underdevelopment, of the so-called third world (a.k.a. the Caribbean). In her essay "Bread out of Stone," Trinidadian Canadian Dionne Brand reminds her "white" Canadian audience:

> Listen, I am a Black woman whose ancestors were brought to a new world lying tightly packed in ships. Fifteen million of them survived the voyage...millions among them died, were killed, committed suicide in the middle passage.
>
> When I come back to Toronto...I will pass a flashing neon sign hanging over the Gardiner Expressway. "Lloyds Bank," it will say. Lloyds, as in Lloyds of London. They got their bullish start insuring slave cargo. (179)

In concert with Brand, but voiced in a different key, Senior's poetry acts to insert the Caribbean within the world and to remind Canadians of their relationship to the Caribbean and that world. She writes "about Canada" by placing it within circuits of the slave trade and a labour market that is utterly entangled in the history of African diaspora (forced and voluntary). Poems in the volume *Shell* remind readers that sugar consumption throughout the British Empire in the eighteenth and nineteenth centuries prior to abolition was reliant on the slave labour of Africans transported to the plantations of the American Tropics;[2] and that the currency of imperial exchange between France and Britain after the Seven Years' War was "a few acres of snow" (Voltaire qtd. in Thorner and Frohn-Nielsen xiii) for Guadeloupe, Martinique, and St. Lucia.[3]

As an Australian reading Senior's volume, I am reminded of the slave labour of captured Pacific Islanders upon which Australia's sugar plantations were reliant for profit[4] and of an incident famous in Australian history, "The Mutiny on the *Bounty*," which was in large part due to the suffering of the crew who saw the scarce resource of fresh water being wasted on the breadfruit plants destined to provide a cheap source of food for slaves on Caribbean plantations. The title of Senior's first collection of poetry, *Talking of Trees*, is an allusion to Bertolt Brecht's question, "What kind of period is it when to talk of trees is almost a crime because it implies silence about so many horrors?" (Senior, *Talking of Trees* 45). Typical of Senior, the volume plays with Brecht's question to suit her own political and poetic ends. Senior's poetry is a "gardening in the tropics" that reveals the horrors of European plantation in the Caribbean as an intimate entanglement of plant and human: "Gardening in the Tropics you never know / what you'll turn up. Quite often, bones" ("Brief Lives," *Gardening* 83). To talk of trees is to *reveal* the darkness at the heart of (en)light(enment). The silent (and silenced) are given voice:

> A Gleaner photographer saw Bustamante bare his chest to the police guns
> Queen Victoria saw everything but is saving it for later
>
> Green was our rage once
> Harder than Almond
>
> Blood fe Blood
> Fire fe fire
> Colour fe colour
>
> Our roots tied up the harbour
>
> Mangroves of resistance.
>
> Cane trash mi life
> Cane break mi spirit
> Cane sweeten mi bizzie
> Banana rotten me clothes
> Stone-bruck mi womanhood
> Cargo strain mi muscle
>
> Police baton bus' mi head
> (Senior, "Talking of Trees," *Talking of Trees* 83)

The answers to complex questions are rarely short or single, but it seems to me that voice is pertinent here—the voices of the poet, the voices of the questioner/listener/readers, and so too is the space into which those voices resound.

Voiced in a Different Key

In order to begin thinking about voice, I need to tell you something more about Senior (she is "black" Canadian) and something about myself (I am "white" Australian), and something of the relationship between us, which has to do with histories of empire, nation, migration, education, and poetry ("Queen Victoria saw everything but is saving it for later"). Being Australian, I am part of the British colonial project, and the subsequent endeavour to "decolonise the mind" (Thiong'o) in order to become postcolonial; but however postcolonial I become I am still a white; my relationship to Senior cannot help but carry the weight, even the taint, of a shared colonial history of winners and losers. Senior herself is the vessel of that unequal sharing because skin colour speaks and determines (no matter how we ourselves wish to determine who and what we are). Nevertheless, I refer to Senior as "black" with some trepidation as I am unsure that she would refer to herself as such or that she would appreciate me doing so. In all that I have read she speaks of herself as Jamaican, and in a 2004 interview for the *Jamaica Gleaner* she claims to be "Heinz 57 varieties because I think I'm a mixture of a whole lot of things but I can't say I'm a quarter this or a half this. Both my parents are of mixed ancestry, British and black and in my father's family there is some Jewish ancestry" (Tanna, "One-on-One, 1"); but for the purposes of this chapter, I will use the term *black* as I wish to situate her work in relation to current debate about the presence and absence of blackness in Canada and in Canadian literature.

I would like, however, to begin with myself, and to admit that I was one of those people who asked why Senior doesn't write about Canada, but I am not a Canadian, and I think this makes a difference as to why the question is being asked and how it might be understood and received by Senior. Senior's response to my question in private discussion indicated that she believes Canadians ask the question from the premise that she *should* write about Canada, as though not to write about the nation that has afforded her the security and support that her native land did or could not is an affront to Canadian generosity, the benefits of Canadian immigration and multicultural policies, or, in a word that I use with reference to the work of Daniel Coleman (and to which I will return), Canadian "civility."[5] I am inclined to go so far as to suggest that the question is coupled with an unvoiced accusation of treason.

I choose this word in order to make connection with Richard Almonte's essay on blackness and Canadian literature, titled "Treason in the Fort," in which he makes the claim that "If the 'fort,' after Frye, is a euphemism for the Canadian community, then 'treason in the fort' [a phrase borrowed from John Richardson's *Wacousta*, 1832] is an apt way of describing the presence of Blackness in fictional Canadian communities. Treason is a betrayal from within" (24). Almonte asserts that blackness in Canadian literature is always already treason, always already dissension and difference that challenge the "true north strong and free" and white. But more, I suggest that by not *overtly* situating her poetry in Canada, this "black" poet is committing treason as much or more than if she situated herself within the black Canadian community, or more specifically, the Jamaican community in Toronto, and ranged herself thereby against or as different from "the rest" of Canada. A direct challenge that accentuates difference can be attacked, removed, or assimilated—it can be dealt with. A strategy of not recognizing Canada is akin to those "mangroves of resistance" that "tie up the harbour," and like all guerrilla offensives, might be taken as offering more offence to those Canadians who ask "Where is Canada?" than a declaration of outright war.

On the other hand, when *I* asked the question of Senior, there was no voice inflection, no unspoken qualifier, no sense of offence (although there may have been some offence taken). When I asked the question of Senior, not being Canadian I had nothing at stake, and yet I now see that a similarity of immigration, multicultural, colonial, and postcolonial structures might suggest that as an Australian there might be something at stake, by association, Australians also being concerned with what it means to be Australian, and often demanding a loyalty to a notion of Australia that remains determinedly multiple and elusive despite nationalist efforts to tie it down to something singular. This possibility aside, I asked the question, somewhat naively perhaps, because I was surprised to discover how much time Senior had spent in Canada and yet how little evidence of this "Canadian life" was to be found in her poetry. Although Jordan Stouck and Stephanie Batcos have identified what Stouck refers to as "an attempt to reconcile a Caribbean past with a North American present" (n.p.), and yes, something of a North American presence can be discerned ("We children fled the blue for northern / light where we buy up all the shoes / in sight" ["My Father's Blue Plantation," *Gardening* 84]), a Canadian presence is even more fugitive:

>...yes maybe
>that isn't the sound of wild
>
>bamboo flutes scaling up and down
>mountain passes which I keep
>hearing from this high window
>
>near St. Clair Avenue Toronto
>Canada which is *not where*
>river-bank of hill is.
>(Senior, "Bamboo," *Gardening* 80, emphasis added)

Although Canada is here, Canada is also "not where," that is, *not* here, indicating that perplexity still dominates at least some aspects of Canadian (migrant) identity, and that answer to the riddle of "where is here" (Frye) is multiple and complex. In this poem, one of the few occasions when Senior references Canada overtly in her poetry, she does so in order to immediately disclaim it—perhaps to disclaim it as the dominant, identity-making, nation-making "here" as theorized by Frye and Atwood: it might be that disassociation is a sign of Senior's determination not to be determined by place (Jamaica or Canada), but to actively choose who she is.

In 2004 Senior spoke of her first experience of living in Canada as a formative one—"part of the process of discovering who I was": "Once you leave home you are in a different, alien environment," she observes. "It really forced me to look at Jamaica…I was becoming more conscious…I came of age at the time of Independence…So my search for personal identity and the search for national identity came together" (Tanna, "One-on-One," F3). In the same interview she makes clear how difficult it is to "choose" when skin, face, hair determine so much: "I have had to deal with race because of who I am and how I look. In that process, I've had to determine who I am…As part of that process, I decided I was a Jamaican. I represent many different races and I'm not rejecting any of them to please anybody." Ten years previously, Senior had remarked that, "I like to go back to Jamaica or somewhere tropical mainly to regenerate myself, to go back to the sources of my being. But I am a pragmatist, I am in Canada by choice, I am not in exile" (Binder 112). Jamaica is heart, Canada is head. Return to the tropics is in part a demonstration of freedom to cross borders and of the choice she makes as a global citizen to insist that "here" is also "there"; but return to Jamaica is also a return to a poetic wellspring, a font that does not spring out of Canadian soil.

There are a number of ways we might attempt to understand the apparent absence (this fugitive, disavowed presence) of Canada in Senior's poetry. We might consider this question in—at least—two ways. The first would be to accept that, with the exception of a very small number of instances, Canada is *not present*, that is, Senior does not talk about Canada in her poetry, and consider why that might be. The second would be to suggest that Canada *is* present in her poetry, and that she does in fact talk "about" Canada in a (clearly) less than obvious way. Attendant on this mode of thinking is to consider what form this *present absence* takes, why it takes this form, and what Senior is saying about Canada by choosing this mode of covert speaking.

Although the first option is interesting to me, it's not what I want to focus on in this chapter, but it would be worth thinking about Senior's work in relation to a kind of poetry that has its roots in a Romantic tradition. This poetry is by nature nostalgic; it is a poetry of loss that derives its power from emotion "recollected in tranquillity" (Wordsworth) and draws its inspiration from "spots in time" (often related to childhood). Although Wordsworth's theory of poetry was closely aligned with a particular place (the English Lake District), and with the notion of "genius" of place, it can be applied to poetry and native place in a larger world picture. So from a Romantic point of view, we might expect that Senior's poetry would grow out of, draw upon, be stimulated by the country of her birth and growth as a poet.

We might also consider Senior's poetry as influenced by an epic tradition, primarily oral in form, and the responsibility of the Afro-Caribbean poet to record and pass on the history of his/her people—the poet as "tribal drummer" (see Kamau Brathwaite). In either case, nostalgia or history, it is the Caribbean, not Canada, of which Senior would write. It is the community to which she belongs, by birth and ethnicity, and it is equally that which has been lost, both in terms of her migration to Canada and the removal and transplantation of African and Indigenous peoples. This way of considering the absence of Canada has its own problems, as in either case she might also have included Canada in a poetry of Caribbean loss and history and to some extent she does—that is, her poetry does in fact speak of and to the Caribbean diasporic community in Canada, but it rarely does so overtly.

This brings me to the second approach, that being a consideration of the ways in which Senior might be understood to write about Canada—Canada as multicultural for example. Given the extent of the Jamaican community in Canada (and particularly in Toronto), in writing about Jamaica, Senior is also writing about Canada (and Toronto); or perhaps more politically, in remembering/reverting to a Jamaican childhood, Senior is writing a childhood of Jamaica and a Jamaican heritage into a Canada that claims to be multicultural but struggles with the reality of multiculturalism: she is making good those claims and insisting on that reality. Or, to take the degree to which Senior's poetry writes a history of the Americas (most overtly, the American Tropics) does Senior thereby insist on Canada as part of that Americas—as a geography and a history that is intimately involved in the African diaspora? Perhaps Canada's allegiance to "the north" is contaminated by relationship with "the south." Although the Underground Railroad is a much lauded link between north and south, there are other less laudable links that might be considered, particularly if we take "the south" to be a metaphor of an American Tropics with which Canada was much entangled, not only through the sale of the cod fish that, dried and salted, fed the slaves on Jamaican plantations (Kurlansky), but also through the first world consumption of sugar, coffee, bananas, and chocolate:

> I've been travelling long
> cross the sea in the sun-hot
> I've been slaving in the cane rows
> for your sugar
> I've been ripening coffee beans
> for your morning break
> I've been dallying on the docks
> loading your bananas
> …
> I've been chopping cocoa pods
> for your chocolate bars

and tourism:

and just when I thought

I could rest

pour my own

—something soothing

like fever-grass and lemon—

...

a new set of people

arrive

...

So I serving them

coffee

tea

cock-soup

rum

Red Stripe beer

sensimilla

I cane-rowing their hair

with my beads

But still they want more

want it strong

want it long

want it black

want it green

want it dread

("Meditation on Yellow," *Gardening* 14–15)

    I discovered Olive Senior through *Gardening in the Tropics*, a volume I promptly put on my Twentieth-Century Women's Writing syllabus, along with Virginia Woolf, Katherine Mansfield, Sylvia Plath, Dorothy Hewett, Alice Walker, and Jamaica Kincaid; Senior being Caribbean and Canadian gave me a little more global and postcolonial reach in the class. Every year I began by performing "Meditation on Yellow," and every year the students were shell-shocked, but also delighted. I use the word *delighted* because it's what I feel makes Senior's work so useful in the classroom, not because it bypasses anger but because it works effectively with anger. Diana Brydon's notion of "cross-talk" is relevant here in that she speaks of "cross-talk" as having the capacity to create an engagement between people and ideas in classroom situations in which anger can close down listening and shut down dialogue (Brydon, "Cross-Talk").[6] I would comment briefly here, however, that anger comes in different forms, takes up different stances, and that, for example, where many of the issues raised by Jamaica Kincaid's work often result in (white) student outrage followed by a stubborn anger that makes it very difficult to encourage the expression of and possible points of connection between a range of views (cross-talk), I have found those issues much more easily drawn out and debated through a poem like "Meditation on Yellow." Anger in each case is voiced differently and invites or gives rise to different response. Kincaid's approach is confrontational, effectively offering a slap in the face to a white reader, where Senior's is cunning—often working to lull the reader into a false sense of security and then delivering a blow to the back of the head. Irony gives an edge to apparent innocence, allied with a bawdiness we might recognize as central to the Jamaican pantomime of the "little theatre":

I like to feel alive
to the possibilities
of yellow

Lightning striking

perhaps as you sip tea
at three in the afternoon
a bit incontinent
despite your vast holdings
(though I was gratified to note

> that despite the difference in our skins
> our piss was exactly the same shade of yellow)
> (Senior, "Meditation on Yellow," *Gardening* 12)

Senior's art draws in the first instance on an Anansi tradition that, although derived from West Africa, has a distinctly Caribbean flavour.[7] We might also understand her approach in light of Homi Bhabha's theory of "sly civility." In *The Location of Culture*, Bhabha quotes from a sermon by Archdeacon Potts, delivered in 1818, in which he observes, "If you urge them with their gross and unworthy misconceptions of the nature and the will of God, or the monstrous follies of their fabulous theology, they will turn it off with a *sly civility* perhaps, or with a popular and careless proverb" (140–41). What the Archdeacon didn't (or refused to) recognize was the combative and careful intelligence that lay behind that apparently casual "turning off" with a proverb. This brings me back to voice and silence, to speaking and listening.

While I agree with Brydon that it is the task of postcolonial pedagogy to prompt cross-talk, and while I also accept that "misguided notions of politeness" can "prevent these debates from emerging" ("Cross-Talk" 68), I think that the kind of "politeness" in which Senior engages offers an enormously productive way of pushing "politeness" towards something more "wry" in the classroom. Significantly, Senior's essay—a piece entitled "'Whirlwinds Coiled at My Heart': Voice and Vision in a Writer's Practice"—was chosen by the editors of *Crosstalk: Canadian and Global Imaginaries in Dialogue* (Brydon and Dvořák) to begin the conversation of the volume. Here Senior acknowledges the "little" (popular/indigenous/oral) and "big" (elite/colonial/scribal) traditions upon which her literary art draws, and remarks that "what I do is mediate between the two worlds" (28). Pertinent to this discussion is her observation that

> Those perceived as voiceless have always had their ways and means. My education in hearing and overhearing inspired an awe that came from my early

exposure to the creative use of words by the real masters of language, the non-scribal for whom words are both tool and weapon...In the minds of the common people, who have only words as weapons, the rich can be stripped of their vanity by a few well-chosen ones...It took me a while to realize that I was the inheritor of a powerful tradition of subversion through voice, through music through gesture. A subversion that can also be subtle, soft, and subterranean. (26–27)

Subtle, soft, subterranean: my understanding of Senior's "politeness" aligns it, somewhat paradoxically, with Rinaldo Walcott's "rudeness"—"rudeness" here being understood as a range of "creative insubordinations" ("By Way of a Brief Introduction" 8–9), along with Bhabha's "sly civility" and Daniel Coleman's notion of a "wry civility." Coleman calls upon Canadians to move from a "*Canadian trance* over a static and reified idea of civility, which has its foundations in White, British gentlemanliness, to a *TransCanadian*, dynamic, self-questioning concept of civility" ("From Canadian Trance" 26–27). Drawing as she does upon the long history of complex and sophisticated linguistic relationship developed between slave and master, colonized and colonizer, Senior's poetry takes an ironic, and yes, often "wry," position that seeks an equally sophisticated, self-questioning, yet civil, response. "Why don't you write about Canada?" is hardly that. The problem with the subterranean of course, and indeed, with irony, is that they can be overlooked—not seen. Recognizing and using nuanced voice, listening to and deploying silence, is a practiced art.[8]

Concluding Observations (If Not Answers)

To bring this chapter to a close, I wish to recall Senior's observation, drawn from a 1988 interview with Charles Rowell: "for what you see on the page is only part of the story. The inexplicable, the part not expressed, the part withheld is the part that you the reader will have to supply from your emotional and imaginative stock, the part that will enable the work to resonate" (483); and a point she made about her craft in the annual Philip Sherlock Lecture (published in the *Journal of West Indian Literature* in 2005):

> What I do as a writer...is mediate the worlds I have inherited, the worlds of the oral and the scribal. While writing is a private act, speaking is a communal one: it implies a teller and a listener, as traditional song consists of call and response. It implicitly invites the community to participate by approval, disapproval, or persuasion, or by contributing different versions of the event. And this is what I invite my readers to do, often by leaving my stories open-ended or presenting poems capable of multiple interpretations. ("The Poem as Gardening" 46)

It is interesting to conjecture why Senior felt the need to attach an "Author's Note" to *Shell* in which she makes the connection between shell and sugar cane painfully clear, explaining that "The sugar cane plant itself is a hard shell imprisoning the gold within. But that shell has to be beaten and crushed to release its sweet juice, the first step in making sugar, a chilling metaphor for the way millions of human beings were beaten and crushed in order to produce it" (95). This paragraph follows one in which she also takes pains to reference Canada: "At one time, sugar made these small West Indian islands the most profitable to their European owners; wars were fought over them. At the close of the Seven Years War (1763), the tiny islands of Guadeloupe and Martinique were returned to the French in exchange for the undeveloped territory of Canada" (95). I always think it sad that authors feel the need to explain their work, but it is usually a response to increasing frustration that what is being said is not heard. In Senior's case it is this and more, for it is also a response to *that* question. There it is—naked—"Canada"—the clothing of metaphor removed, the relationship of the Caribbean and Canada in plain English. "Why don't you write about Canada?" In *Shell*, Senior answers the question: she does write about Canada, and she asks us, why aren't we looking? Why aren't we listening? To quote Coleman, as he reflects on both Brydon and Spivak,

> Reading carefully, paying close attention, not just to another person's voice in a given text but to the way in which that voice is embedded in cultural history, involves what Spivak calls "critical intimacy," a kind of cross-talk between the cultural location of the reader and the voice of the text, which has the potential to dislodge the sanctioned ignorance that repeatedly envelopes us all. ("From Canadian Trance" 41)

While I would agree with Coleman, Brydon, and Spivak, and while I also accept that we are all hampered by the degree to which we can form connections to each other because we see through layers of culture and history as through a glass darkly, maybe seeing "through" could be accomplished if there were a real desire to see. I think the question here is how do we create that desire? It is a question of and about willingness, and receptivity. Just picking up the shell is a start.

> Like other objects beached, beyond
> your ken, inert I lie, bleached and toneless
>
> save for ocean song that only visitors claim
> to hear. What if one day you accidentally
> picked up the right shell—such as I; placed it
>
> to your ear, pressed—by chance—the right
> knob, there would pour out not the croak
> of song soaked up in sea-water and salt
>
> but the real thing, a blast-out, *everybody's*
> *history.*
> ("Shell Blow," *Shell* 33, emphasis added)

In thinking through Senior's position of disavowal—her insistence on allegiance to Jamaica that appears to be strengthened in response to the question about Canada, and the ironic voice she most often employs—I am beginning to wonder if "the lady doth protest too much." It would certainly seem to be the case that in refusing to acknowledge "Canada" as "here" she insists on a Canada that, like the Caribbean, overflows its (arbitrary) borders. The shell (story/poem) contains the silences and the voices of *everybody's history*:

> Mother of origins, guardian
> > of passages;
>
> ...
>
> > summon your children
> > haul the rain down
>
> > white water: blue water
> > the circle comes round
> ("Yemoja: Mother of Waters," *Gardening* 131)

We might understand Senior's work as speaking *both* into the Jamaican community with which she so overtly aligns herself, *and* into a Canadian space that is both "here" and "not-here." It is my contention that Senior's poetry works to create a "condition of resonance" in Canada, and that she has, despite the question that will not be quieted, succeeded. One only has to look to the number of Canadian publications in which her essays appear (often as the opening piece). One such essay titled "Crossing Borders and Negotiating Boundaries" opens a 2012 volume of essays called *Jamaica in the Canadian Experience: A Multiculturalizing Presence*. In this piece, Senior insists on the importance of placing ourselves within "everybody's history," understanding our connections and our connectedness:

> Part of the problem is that the whole experience of border crossings exists in
> an ahistorical framework. The people who come know little of where Canadians

are coming from, and Canadians already here know even less about the new arrivals. And yet if we were to examine each other historically, we would be able to affirm that we are not such strangers after all; in the long ago and not so distant past, people like us met and mingled. Newfoundlanders have been feeding cod to West Indians for centuries, and the West Indies bananas to Canadians...Awareness of history would affirm that our connections are not one-way flows but are built up of past exchanges...To be able to affirm that we have met before...might help to reduce the barriers between "us" and "them," bring "here" closer to "there," get the conversation going. (16)

Author's Note

I would like to thank Daniel Coleman and Lorraine York for inviting me to participate in the symposium that gave rise to the original version of this chapter, and for their generous critique that helped clarify and extend my thinking on this topic. Thanks also for the considered comments of my fellow symposium colleagues.

Notes

1. "Hurricane" (rather than the more obvious "cyclone" in connection with "whirlwinds") has been used here to denote the Caribbean *poetic* significance of hurricane as referred to in Edward Kamau Brathwaite's famous claim that "the hurricane does not roar in pentameters" in History of the Voice, and the four poems in Senior's Gardening in the Tropics on the disruptive/connective significance of hurricane—"Hurricane Story, 1903," "Hurricane Story, 1944," "Hurricane Story, 1951," and "Hurricane Story, 1988."
2. See the American Tropics: Towards a Literary Geography project, which was led by Peter Hulme, at http://www.essex.ac.uk/lifts/american_tropics/index.htm.
3. In Candide, Voltaire wrote, "You realize that these two countries have been fighting over a few acres of snow near Canada, and they are spending on this splendid struggle more than Canada itself is worth" (qtd. in Thorner and Frohn-Nielsen xiii).
4. The islanders' capture was known as "blackbirding" and the peoples referred to as "Kanakas."
5. This is by no means the first instance of the demand that "Canadian" writers write "about Canada," the question and associated debate being raised in relation to a number of high-profile authors and prize winners, including Michael

Ondaatje, Rohinton Mistry, and Esi Edugyan; but it is a question and a debate that just won't die—like the hydra, it keeps growing another and another head.

6. See also Brydon and Dvořák, *Crosstalk: Canadian and Global Imaginaries in Dialogue*.
7. Anansi (also spelt variously, Anancy and Ananse) has become the Caribbean symbol of survival, creativity, and subversion, allied with folk and oral traditions. Senior directly references Anansi in her poem "Colonial Girls School."
8. Of course not everyone agrees that civility of any kind is the best approach (see the dialogue in Gingell and Didur, "Author Meets Critic Forum on Daniel Coleman's *White Civility: The Literary Project of English Canada*"), but as indicated in my comments on response to Kincaid in the classroom, in my experience anger rarely engenders a response that leads to a change of attitude in the party at whom the anger is directed, or to constructive dialogue.

6

Canada and the Black Atlantic
Epistemologies, Frameworks, Texts

PILAR CUDER-DOMÍNGUEZ

Epistemologies: Paul Gilroy and the Impact of the Black Atlantic Concept

PUBLISHED IN 1993, PAUL GILROY's *The Black Atlantic: Modernity and Double Consciousness* critiqued the construction of fake boundaries and misguided notions of racial purity, opening up to scholarly inquiry a broad, complex, fluid field. With the words, "striving to be both European and black requires some specific forms of double consciousness" (1), Gilroy started to unpack the complex relations between black cultures and modern nations across the expanse he called "the black Atlantic." He set out to dispel the myth that "the reflexive cultures and consciousness of the European settlers and those of the Africans they enslaved, the 'Indians' they slaughtered, and the Asians they indentured were...sealed off hermetically from each other" (2). Most strikingly, Gilroy managed to bring together many widely circulated concepts to crystallize around the chronotope of the ship, "a living, micro-cultural, micro-political system in motion" (4) connecting the fixed places of the Atlantic world.

While acknowledging the groundbreaking quality of Gilroy's conceptual model, early reactions were mixed. Simon Gikandi admitted to being energized by the theoretical possibilities of Gilroy's book but also to feeling "a sense of disenchantment with the series of paradigms, cartographies, and histories (or their absences) on which the main argument of the book depended" (1). Some even stronger critiques dwelt on how the book made sweeping claims for a black consciousness that was eventually reduced to Britain and the United States alone.[1] Most of all, critics took issue with the fact that Gilroy's description sidelined Africa, while more generally, the black Atlantic has been taken to task for being decidedly anglophone, thus reasserting at least some of the cultural and linguistic borders that the model allegedly strives to unsettle.[2] Assessing the current state of black transnational studies, Laura Chrisman traces several trajectories. Some forms of transnational scholarship have flourished in African and postcolonial studies, outside of Gilroy's influence, while others, inspired by his idea, have "productively branched out into different methodological or regional directions; and entire new fields, including black roots heritage studies, have developed" (23). Other disciplines have felt its impact less directly. A case in point is American studies, which "has experienced a 'transnational turn' that owes much to Gilroy's critique of US insularity and exceptionalism" (23). Probably inspired by Gilroy's black European reading of African American authors, Brent Hayes Edwards's *The Practice of Diaspora: Literature, Translation, and the Rise of Black Internationalism* undertakes the opposite journey, focusing on African Americans in Europe between the two world wars, although skirting London to touch ground in Paris and engaging more closely with the Négritude movement. John Cullen Gruesser, on the other hand, considers the "formidable similarities" (2) of postcolonial and African American literary studies in *Confluences: Postcolonialism, African American Literary Studies, and the Black Atlantic*. He explicitly claims to be following the path opened by Gilroy, referring to *The*

Black Atlantic as "the most profound attempt to correlate postcolonialism and African American studies" (4).

This chapter aims to consider how Gilroy's paradigm may have affected our understanding of black literature and culture in Canada. I briefly first describe the main threads and trajectories of black Canadian literary scholarship, and next I test what may be the new directions in the cultural representation of black consciousness in Canada by means of a celebrated first novel that fits into Gilroy's paradigm. I am intrigued by Esi Edugyan's *The Second Life of Samuel Tyne* (2004) because of the way that it manages to tap into subjectivities and issues that at first sight would appear to be at odds. This is the kind of work that shifts the terms of the conversation from white–black exchanges to the interaction between several black Canadian constituencies, engaging obliquely with a history of colonialism and displacement even while it discloses local, rooted histories, thus playing roots against routes.[3] In bringing together these three aspects—transnational epistemologies, national frameworks, and the writer's take on them—my aim is to provide a comprehensive account of the field today, placing the overarching questions alongside the individual experience.

Frameworks: The View from Canada

Gilroy's definition of black Britain as "a compound culture from disparate sources" (15) might be applicable to Canada as well. Black Canadians currently constitute the third largest non-Caucasian group in the country, where their presence has been recorded from as early as 1605. Some were brought by their owners, like the rebel slave Angélique in 1730s Montreal.[4] At the end of the eighteenth century, Nova Scotia became the destination of free or slave American Loyalists as well as Maroons deported from Jamaica. A substantial number of runaway slaves from the United States in the 1800s remained in the towns of southern Ontario. Later, black pioneers came north, attracted by the promise of land in the Canadian Prairies, and throughout the twentieth century, successive waves brought black people from several Caribbean locations, many of them encouraged by immigration laws looking for cheap labour to deal with menial tasks. From approximately the 1990s, the origins of black migrants to Canada have shifted to the African continent, particularly Somalia, Ghana, and Ethiopia. Interestingly, practically 50 per cent of all black Canadians live in the Greater Toronto Area, with Montreal coming second, which shows a decided preference for the larger multicultural centres (Mensah 53). Not surprisingly, the presence of black people in rural areas has had little visibility to date. The writer Esi Edugyan, who grew up in rural Alberta, has related that it was her discovery of historical black settlements in a province where there seemed to be very few black people that became the main spur for her novel *The Second Life of Samuel Tyne* (Compton et al.).

Needless to say, tracing the histories and experiences of such an extraordinarily diverse population, or even highlighting their historical struggle for equality, is well beyond the scope of this chapter. Suffice it to say for my purposes here that in the post–Second World War period, civil rights activism instigated scholarly interest in black Canadians as a subject. Robin Winks's *The Blacks in Canada: A History* (1971) was followed by James W. St. G. Walker's *A History of Blacks in Canada* (1980), even though the relative dearth of studies on black Canadians has led to claims that "much of the most interesting historical work then has been generated by scholars not formally trained as historians" (B. Walker 73). As regards black Canadian literary culture, critical interest in this field beyond scattered essays on isolated authors or texts grew in the 1970s and 1980s, and came to fruition with the publication of anthologies that, by making available a sizeable corpus, have contributed to trace the contours of the field and thus to the foundations of what is still a very provisional canon.[5] In the following decades, a number of book-length studies, starting with Rinaldo Walcott's *Black Like Who?* (1997), laid the ground of the field.

All in all, a staggering amount of work has been carried out in the short space of two decades, gathering momentum particularly from the late 1990s, that is, in the post–black Atlantic era. Among the early work that engaged with Gilroy's text, one of the most widely cited is George Elliott Clarke's "Must All Blackness Be American?: Locating Canada in Borden's 'Tightrope Time,' or Nationalizing Gilroy's *The Black Atlantic*" (1996).[6] The title itself voices Clarke's critique of what he considers an impracticable anti-nationalism, while the article opens with the complaint that African Canadian literature is "awash in African-American and Caribbean influences" (56) and goes on to locate its "dynamic dilemma" in the fact that "Euro-Canadian critics often consider it as *Other*, while African-American (and Caribbean) critics read it (unabashedly) as extensions of their own" (57). Clarke's efforts run counter to Gilroy's concept most of all as he is trying to frame the critical terms for valorizing African Canadian literature as a "Canadian" (i.e., national) literature, based on a myth of purity that Gilroy struggles hard to debunk. However, Clarke is trying to assert its value as a "black" literature too, on the same level as African American literature, at least in that respect falling in line with Gilroy's own challenge to the latter's exceptionalism.

The following year saw the publication of Rinaldo Walcott's *Black Like Who?*, a book admittedly inspired by Gilroy's *The Black Atlantic*.[7] Drawing from black British, Caribbean, and African American sources, Walcott takes detours (historical and contemporary, literary and musical) to think through "the circuitous routes of black diasporic cultures, their connectedness and differences" (17). Its first chapter, "Going to the North," both adopts and completes Gilroy's text insofar as it contextualizes the critic's reading of Martin Robinson Delany's *Blake* (19–29)[8] within the black abolitionist circles of southern Ontario, thus bringing black Atlantic exchanges to bear on his depiction of what he terms "black Canadas," that is, "the multiplicities of black peoples in the geographic area called Canada [attending] to the tensions of their differences" (151). Walcott accepts that there are collisions within the different constituents of these black Canadas, and that, in the Canadian nation-state, definitions of blackness have clustered among people of Caribbean descent, so that "the hyper-visibility of Caribbean blackness makes 'indigenous black Canadians' invisible" (39).

These emerging debates around the differing trajectories of "indigenous" versus "diasporic" black subjects were summarized soon afterwards in David Chariandy's path-breaking "'Canada in Us Now': Locating the Criticism of Black Canadian Writing," where this scholar came to acknowledge "the complex articulations of racial identity" (196) in black Canadian literary criticism and went on to identify four different positions: G.E. Clarke's "Africadian Atlantic," Enoch Padolsky's "Canadian crossroads of race and ethnicity," Rinaldo Walcott's "diasporic detours," and Barbara Godard's "feminism(s) and black writing." Of these, Padolsky's (advocating a plural understanding of the workings of race and ethnicity) and Godard's (claiming the specific power of black women's writing to challenge hierarchies of power) are not directly related to my topic.[9] On the contrary, Chariandy perceptively highlights the opposing critical thrusts of Clarke's and Walcott's approaches, as he dwells on how Clarke's laudable project to recuperate a neglected corpus of black Canadian literature clashes with Gilroy's repudiation of national tradition, while Walcott's emphasis on transcultural migrations and exchanges perfectly fits into the black Atlantic model.

These critics' distinctive choices in terminology are most emblematic of their diverging politics. G.E. Clarke consistently uses the term *African Canadian* (or sometimes his own coinage "Africadian" for black Nova Scotians), while Walcott prefers *black Canadian*. Nowadays, as far as I have been able to ascertain, both terms are in common usage, although the occasional critic may continue to insist that the latter term "references identities that are deliberately less self-assured, more unstable, more in flux, and less obedient to the nation" (Davis 47). Similarly, much of the tension between these two positions has defused over the years, as the more nationalist have yielded some ground on their reductive view of blackness and the more diasporic have acknowledged more rooted histories. Last but not least, a younger generation of scholars has started to move the conversation in fresh directions. A case in point is Wayde Compton's *After Canaan* (2010), which creatively weaves together both perspectives. A poet, teacher, anthologist, critic, and activist, Compton's take on blackness is shaped by British Columbia, which boasts numerous interracial families, close proximity to Asians and First Nations subjects, and no recognizable accent despite frequent histories of immigration. This BC black consciousness, emerging "at the outer rim of black centres," he names "Afroperiphery": "Embracing this set of unusual black experiences, rather than trying to return to the imagined essence of a past blackness, is, for me, an assertive Afroperipheralism—in contrast to the redemptive drive of Afrocentrism which iterates everything but a narrow set of perceived traditions as inauthentic and culturally ersatz" (*After Canaan* 14–15). Even though he repudiates essentialism and embraces hybridity and impurity, often by way of his own mixed-racedness or "Halfrican" condition, Compton nonetheless also reclaims the neglected histories of his community, actively engaging in projects concerning the memorialization of Vancouver's lost black neighbourhood, Hogan's Alley. Roots and routes are thus reconciled and put to the service of communal well-being.

In the next section, I aim to look into the creative insights of the younger generation of black Canadian artists by means of an acclaimed first novel—Esi Edugyan's *The Second Life of Samuel Tyne* (2004)—set in just such an Afroperiphery, 1960s and 1970s rural Alberta, where the author herself grew up. As I will explain below, this story masterfully conveys what Walcott terms "the space of pain," enacting a refusal to render displacements or reconciliations as simple and uncomplicated (*Black Like Who?* 49) and postulating the need for reparations as a necessary step towards reconciliation.

Texts: Writing Black Canada(s)

Esi Edugyan's *The Second Life of Samuel Tyne* is set in the fictional northern Albertan town of Aster, loosely based on archival evidence of a sizeable black presence in the area from the early 1900s, when black people came north of the US border in search of "the Last Best West." According to Mensah, approximately three hundred black people settled in Alberta around 1910, many of them originally from Oklahoma. This was the inception of the black northern Albertan community of Pine Creek, later renamed Amber Valley. These pioneers were coldly received, and soon petitions and town council resolutions against the newcomers resulted in new restrictions for black immigration into the province.[10] To these were added the common hardships of farming in a difficult climate and the not quite so common tribulations of having to do so in disadvantaged conditions: "As usual, they were promised good farmlands but, upon arrival, were given poor land and had to create farms from dense bush and swamps with rudimentary implements" (Mensah 51).

When Samuel Tyne and his family arrive in Aster in the late 1960s to claim the house he has inherited from his uncle Jacob, not much remains of its original black history for these Ghanaian Canadians to see, except for two pioneer homes set back from the town itself, and a stone wall neatly marking out the racial borders of the settlement. The wall is now eroded and scarcely two-inches high, but the general belief that it was originally built by the black families attests to their fear of racist attacks. The houses, too, are in a sad state of decay and disrepair. The black population itself dwindled after the Second World War, and only one pioneer family has stayed in town, the Porters, a name with powerful echoes in black Canadian history, as it reminds us of the black porters working on the railway.[11]

Edugyan thus sets up a contrast between the "new" African diaspora (the Tynes) and the "old" black diaspora (the Porters). The latter term refers to the waves of African subjects arriving during the colonization period (resulting from the slave trade), whereas the former names Africans leaving from the end of the nineteenth century, as decolonization starts (Zeleza 36). The cut between both is not quite so neat in this novel, for Saul Porter's wife, Akosia, is Ghanaian as well. Saul is the heir of the black pioneers and the living recipient of their memory, orally transmitting the stories of their displacements and trajectories across the United States and eventually north into Alberta. His father, Harlan, was born a slave in Georgia, and after his Civil War emancipation he dragged his family through several states (Kansas, Utah, Oklahoma), everywhere finding that "things weren't any easier. Good for nothing but barbers and bootblacks—if your luck was buttered, you became a porter" (164). In Canada (the old "Canaan" for runaway slaves) they thought they would be finally free from segregation and multifarious systemic racism in the United States: "It was not being able to read that kept the vote from us in Oklahoma, sent us north in the first place. We always been the bottom of the pecking order. No respect" (163). Sadly, their hopes were not fulfilled. As mentioned above, they found instead very poor farm land, an unforgiving climate, and neighbours who despised them and actively joined ranks against them. Interestingly, while the author is faithful to the archival history of the region, she also imaginatively depicts through Saul Porter an idealized, closely knit all-black community that the character still clings to and pines for all these many years later, very possibly due to his current isolation from other black people.

The arrival of the Tynes would seem to be an opportunity to rekindle that nostalgic dream, but contrary to our expectations, animosity soon develops between the two black families living in similar-looking old neglected houses that, though standing very close, are separated by some fields. Frictions stem from several sources. First of all, the Ghanaian characters clash on their differing attitudes towards their colonial histories. Saul Porter's second wife, Akosia, is a Ghanaian with strong anticolonial views, who expresses outrage at the Tynes' refusal to speak any Ghanaian language to their Canadian-born children, and at their complete rejection of their culture (except for cooking habits, due to Samuel's dislike of Western food). On the contrary, the older Tynes (Samuel and his wife, Maud) have fully interiorized the old colonial values they grew up with, most clearly conveyed in their always thinking of and referring to their native land by the old pre-independence name, "Gold Coast." Canada was not Samuel's first Western destination, for he spent several years in the UK as a student.

He lost his connection to his homeland very soon—a connection reduced now to a regular stream of family letters requesting money and a clock always set on Ghanaian time that suggests at the very least the trace of a double consciousness. Maud Tyne's is an even stronger assimilationist position, having cut off all connections to her native land due to the violence she endured during her childhood at the hands of an overbearing, abusive father. Arriving in Canada as a nanny, Maud embraced the West and Western values, hiding the tribal marks on her face under face powder and enunciating for hours until she lost her accent.

If the first reason for dissent between the two families is the colonial past they all share in some measure, the second and perhaps even more important is the "postcolonial" Canadian present they live in. Due to their "continuing aspiration to acquire a supposedly authentic, natural, and stable 'rooted' identity" (Gilroy 30), the Tynes resent the sense of entitlement displayed by the older black inhabitants, the Porters, in relation to the Albertan land and the town of Aster. It rankles Samuel as the issue of his inheritance remains unsolved and he is thwarted in his attempts to regain possession over the lands around the house. Jacob Tyne's will, allegedly deposited with town officials, is missing, which makes Samuel unable to fight against Saul Porter's claim that Jacob gave him his lands in gratitude for the care the Porters provided him with in his old age. Saul's small acts of possession, like cutting trees or mowing the lawn around the Tynes' house, trigger Samuel's irritation because for him, these are acts of trespass on his private property. As a result, the plot of this novel rests largely on the politics of belonging, rootedness, and entitlement to the land, evidencing what Karina Vernon has described as "the difficulty of finding an adequate 'home' for prairie Blackness" ("Writing" 67). Edugyan's representation of these black Canadian constituencies stresses their heterogeneity in terms of gender, class, language, and so on, thus building for readers an experiential map of Gilroy's black Atlantic as a crisscrossing of historical arrivals and departures—a flowing network of cultural influences within the framework of the black diasporas in the West.

Likewise, Edugyan's fiction emphasizes the differences between first- and second-generation black Canadians in her portrait of the Tynes children, Yvette and Chloe. The fact that they are twins underlines the migrant's dual condition, while the fact that they are Canadian born and deprived of contact with their parents' homeland sets them apart, inhabiting a world of their own that only they can fully understand.[12] Samuel and Maud are puzzled by and occasionally afraid of their children's strangeness and closeness, and their initial feelings are compounded as the narrative unfolds, because through them most of all, Edugyan conveys the trauma of displacement and the pains produced by systemic racism. It is the twins who, feeding on the aggressive ambience surrounding them, engage in increasingly violent little acts of aggression that come to a head when they set the Porter house on fire. The white community closes ranks behind the Porters, and when reparation does not appear to be forthcoming, the Tynes find themselves increasingly ostracized (the pharmacist does not carry Samuel's medication any longer; cafés refuse to serve him; shopkeepers do not accept Maud's money; a bag of burning fertilizer is thrown at their front door; his shop is vandalized). Eventually, this protracted harassment takes an economic and psychological toll on Samuel and Maud that compels them to surrender to the community's demands.

Interestingly, their ordeal is explicitly likened to the former plight of the Porters as they travelled north from the United States. At this point, Edugyan's story veers towards an exploration of the complex topic of reparation and reconciliation between the two black constituencies in an important epistemological shift that has been bypassed by critical readings to date. The most important requirement exacted of the Tynes is the removal of Yvette and Chloe. Acting as spokesperson for the Aster community, Ray Frank threatens Samuel: "'You figure things out for yourself. But you've got two days for your children to leave Aster before I'm forced to tell the authorities what I know. I'm sorry.' He left without looking back" (239). Samuel then feels that he has to give up the twins, that they have been lost for a long time, and they are sent to a facility for distressed children. Their institutionalization is a painful reminder of the way that socially "undesirable" subjects (whether they were black, Aboriginal, or other racialized peoples) have historically been put away, sometimes for life, on spurious claims. In fact, in a scene that was excerpted from the paperback edition of the novel, the Tynes waited for the twins' test results in the company of a Native couple, "those other inconsolables" (296). Nevertheless, I believe that the novel also symbolically conveys a necessary (though traumatic and nearly surgical) obliteration of the double. The Porters and Tynes can only find their way towards reconciliation once the twins—visible reminders of their othering as well as of their past confrontation—have been sent away.

Related to this painful experience is the crucial decision not to leave Aster as Maud pleads, but for the Porters to be housed with the Tynes at Samuel's invitation, acting on the principle that "for what you cannot change, you make amends" (246), so that the novel's last chapters focus on the progress from enmity to conviviality, and from strife to reconciliation. At first, the last standing black pioneer home is a claustrophobic space in which both families are thrown together in resentful poverty. Nevertheless, little by little, small acts of kindness and "re-memory"[13] bring them closer over the years. This happens first between Samuel and Maud, who are finally united in their grief and guilt over the twins. Eventually, it comes to happen as well between the Tynes and Porters, but before that may occur the Tynes have to learn to forgive themselves and to repair as best they can the psychological rift of diaspora. As Maud and Akosia cook together, Maud gives in to using their mother tongue, which she had rejected out of hurt. Samuel blames himself for neglecting his uncle in his final years, especially considering how much he owed Jacob Tyne, who had supported him for many years by working hard at all sorts of menial jobs. He also bears the blame of having failed to perform the proper funeral rituals for his uncle, a sin for which Akosia Porter, the black character more in touch with her African past, upbraids him: "Moving to another country does not exempt you from a proper burial and the forty days' libation. Your uncle was a good, good man, deserving of his final rest. Do you think you are not bringing punishment against yourselves? Do you think we sleep in comfort knowing he has not received his proper rest?" (122). The rift is repaired towards the end of the novel, when Samuel performs the ceremonial libation for Maud as well as for Jacob, so the ghosts of diaspora can be laid to rest. Once effected, reparation ushers in reconciliation, and Samuel helps Akosia raise her children after the death of their spouses. In a way, they have merged into a single family, recomposing once more the close-knit community Saul Porter was so nostalgic for. With the re-establishment of tradition and these acts of re-memory, the tear in the fabric of collective memory caused by diaspora is repaired, and its disruption sutured. Likewise, the damage and fissures with the larger white community also eventually heal, knitting them all closely together. At the death of Ray Frank, his wife, Eudora (formerly a close friend of Maud's), restores full property of the farm to the Tynes. They are then able to acknowledge each other's losses and grieve together: "Samuel stood clutching his hat...and said, 'I am sorry for your loss.' Eudora gave him a desperate look, as though she'd been waiting for that gesture. 'And I'm sorry for yours,' she said, taking a gentle step forward. 'I'm sorry for yours'" (261–62).

Like his uncle Jacob before him, Samuel ends up aging alone in the old decaying house. But in a significant turn of events, in his final days he experiences the generous care of Ama Oillet, the white friend of the twins who lived through the events of that first summer in Aster. For some obscure reason, Ama feels she too owes Samuel her own act of reparation, thus sealing the reconciliation of the white and black populations of Aster. Arguably, however, these harmonious tidings happen at the cost of the continued institutionalization of the twins. There may be no true reconciliation if it requires the removal of part of the community. In the hardback edition, Edugyan's text emphasizes those loose ends. More details are given about the facility where the twins have been taken, about their parents' unsuccessful efforts to see them over the years until they stop fighting and learn to accept that the twins' absence from their lives is irreversible, and even about Ama's own qualms over the role she played in her friends' fate. Yet in the paperback edition those sections have been streamlined, so that emphasis is displaced towards reparation, Samuel's and Maud's separately and also towards each other. In both versions, however, the author has chosen to provide the seed of a fruitful new beginning, as the closing scene foresees a "lone twin returned to reclaim the home where all had changed for her...burdened with her past and the dead sister she carries like a conscience inside of her, she sits where Ama sat, trying to endure her first night of freedom, waiting for the sight of dawn to believe she is strong enough to begin again" (277). This is a bittersweet ending, suggesting that there is indeed a future for the Tynes in Aster despite the terrible past, but also stressing the loneliness of one that used to be double and the painful encumbrance of decades of incarceration. In her book *Dreaming of Elsewhere: Observations on Home*, Edugyan has observed that there is "no aloneness quite so stark as genuine unbelonging" (5), a declaration that aptly describes this ending. The writer does not minimize the damage of systemic racism; she leaves her character in those dark hours before renewal is even possible. The lone twin is thus the picture of utter unbelonging, sitting on the ledge of the bay window, not quite within but neither completely without.

Conclusion

Esi Edugyan's *The Second Life of Samuel Tyne* paints a complex picture of black Albertans, torn apart not only by the different chronologies of migration and their own transnational trajectories, but also by diverse identity features, thus inserting the province into Gilroy's black Atlantic as one of its destinations. As Edugyan states, "Each farewell carries the promise of a return" (*Dreaming of Elsewhere* 31). In paying such close attention both to the material conditions of rooted black subjectivity as well as to the fissured spaces of pain devolving from the convoluted trajectories of the black diasporas, this novel balances out the opposing drives of diasporic and essentialized black consciousness described in black Canadian literary studies.[14]

Such remarkable balance is largely attained by underscoring the topic of reparation and reconciliation. In other words, the author does not simply pay tribute to the politics of difference, but she also shows the perilous process of bridging differences and reaching conviviality. As mentioned above, memory plays a key role in Gilroy's geography of the black Atlantic, for it is the slave ship that connects the different places of this wide space, implicating its black subjects in its long-reaching legacy. Although not necessarily nor always so intimately connected to the history of slavery, memory and forgetting are likewise remarkably important to an understanding of this novel. Mirroring the complex interplay of roots and routes within it, close consideration has been given to imagining and recreating a collective memory that is "multidirectional" in the terms defined by Michael Rothberg, that is, based on the interaction of different historical memories in dynamic intercultural relation instead of a competitive model of memory based on "a struggle for recognition in which there can only be winners and losers" (3). Weaving together the multifarious threads of the memory of Albertans, black and white, Edugyan has managed to replace an emphasis on erasure with an investment in relations, which, in my view, stands out as an elegant and productive appropriation and concretization of the geography of the black Atlantic.

Notes

1. See Lucy Evans's review essay "*The Black Atlantic*: Exploring Gilroy's legacy" for an account of critical responses to the book spanning fifteen years (1994 to 2008).
2. See Joan Dayan's "Paul Gilroy's Slaves, Ships, and Routes: The Middle Passage as Metaphor" and Kathleen Gyssels's "The 'barque ouverte' (Glissant) or *The Black Atlantic* (Gilroy): Erasure and Errantry."

3. See Lorraine York's perceptive account of the critical reception and marketplace fortunes of Esi Edugyan's two novels in "'How a Girl from Canada Break the Bigtime.'"
4. On the subject and import of Angélique, see Afua Cooper, *The Hanging of Angélique*.
5. George Elliott Clarke's "Select Bibliography of Literature by African-Canadian Authors" in *Odysseys Home* is an excellent resource to trace the rise and evolution of the literature.
6. First published in *Canadian Ethnic Studies*, vol. 28, no. 3, 1996, and later collected in *Odysseys Home* (2002).
7. The acknowledgements section in Walcott's *Black Like Who?* lists essays that may in fact have preceded G.E. Clarke's abovementioned article. I believe, however, that Walcott's theses and his adaptation of Gilroy's paradigm to Canada matured in the book and gained more currency *after* its publication in 1997.
8. Gilroy mentions several times, always in passing, that Delany wrote *Blake* in Canada, but he never truly considers it may be a black Atlantic location, perhaps because in the Western imagination, Canada is still very much a "white" country.
9. They have also been the object of less critical contestation. For instance, one can see some continuity with Godard's approach in Katherine McKittrick's *Demonic Grounds* and Sharon Morgan Beckford's *Naturally Woman*.
10. For instance, the city of Edmonton banned black people altogether in 1911 (Mensah 52).
11. I am grateful to Daniel Coleman for pointing this out.
12. See my essay "Transnational Memory and Haunted Black Geographies: Esi Edugyan's *The Second Life of Samuel Tyne*" on the significance of the twins and their psychosis.
13. I am using Toni Morrison's concept of "re-memory" as defined in her essay "The Site of Memory."
14. Although I lack the space to further develop my argument here, I believe that this new direction can be confirmed if one examines other twenty-first-century black Canadian novels. A case in point is Dionne Brand's *What We All Long For* (2006), whose plural viewpoints belong to second generation firmly rooted in Toronto.

III

Mapping Bodies, Place, and Time

7

"Off the Highway"
Margins, Centres, Modernisms

KATALIN KÜRTÖSI

> The best things are off the highway.
> —Emily Carr, June 11, 1934, *Opposite Contraries*

GROWING UP IN PROVINCIAL TOWNS (Kecskemét, Szeged) in a Central European country (Hungary) that, due to the uniqueness of the language, is viewed in many respects as a periphery of the continent, I have long held a personal interest in the workings of culture on the margins. This interest has stretched into my academic work and main field of research on culture in Canada. Specifically, I am curious about how the margin/centre dichotomy is perceived from widely different geographical (and cultural) locations. How are cultural manifestations in the margins related to the shaping of national cultures? The following pages will consider these questions, and in the process question and destabilize categories that have previously been thought of as secure.

Modernisms

In his book on modernism, Steven Matthews finds it necessary to challenge the notion of "a single, monolithic, literary movement which might be called *modernism*" and proposes the plural form as "a more indicative term for the many competing modes and impulses which govern the diverse writings...from this era of literature" (1). For Peter Childs, modernism was "both a provincial phenomenon...and a global one in which migrants, exiles and émigrés brought difference to bear on and militate against literary dominants" (2). As Charles Taylor puts it, "the ways of modernism are many" (*Sources* 479). Frederic Jameson speaks about "various modernisms" as attempts "to *recode* the...decoded flux of the realistic, middle-class, secular era" (183). Peter Faulkner also mentions the "plural vision (as) one of the central recognitions of Modernism" (13). Andreas Huyssen proposes that "modernism as an adversary culture cannot be discussed without introducing the concept of alternative modernities to which the multiple modernisms and their different trajectories remain tied in complex mediated ways," adding that the "politics of alternative modernisms are deeply embedded in colonial and postcolonial contexts" (7, 15). These views are shared by several other authors (Levenson, Lehan, Virágos) who deal with modernisms in general or with their regional manifestations. The mid-1920s are generally seen as the peak period of modernisms. The plural here clearly indicates the local or regional varieties that can modify our image of modernist art. This plural form also contests the previously held hierarchical classification of works based on geographical location, and on language in the case of literary works.

In Canada, modernism appeared at a time when many artists and thinkers were preoccupied with the idea of a national culture and were convinced that culture could play a vital role in this process of self-definition. The general features of modernism and the modernist artist, therefore, interestingly blended with the specific situation of modernist artists in cultural centres and margins. Referring to the McGill group of poets, Dean Irvine suggests that—in accordance

with F.R. Scott's locating the modernist poet in a "far corner"—
"modernism in Canada is...among the marginal modernisms outside
the Anglo-American canons" (4). Irvine adds, "the study of marginal
modernisms not only performs a critique of canonical modernism's
exclusionary practices but also provides insight into the historical marginality of its avant-garde aesthetics" (4). These perspectives can serve
as general guidelines for a study of modernism in Canada and so they
are not limited exclusively to that group.

Emily Carr, Modernist Artist on the Margin in Canada

Like many modernist artists in Canada and elsewhere in the world, Emily Carr complained of isolation, loneliness, and financial difficulties, even if, as later research has shown, her perception and self-dramatization as the neglected and misunderstood artist were not always supported by reviews and critical responses to her work. Born in Victoria, British Columbia in 1871, Carr decided to study painting abroad. Leaving the familiar environment, however, produced unusual symptoms: bigger towns, particularly cities, repelled Carr. In her late twenties, she went to study in London, England, where she stayed from 1899 to 1904. She found the capital of the Empire unbearable. There the conflict between the two major forces in her life—the pursuit of art and her love for nature—resulted in health problems. She made an effort to know the city, went to museums and theatres, and had good friends, but still she was simply unable to live in the city. She wrote, "London had instructed, amazed, inspired, disgusted me. The little corners that I had poked into by myself interested me most" (*Growing Pains* 390).

After more than five years in England, she returned to her beloved British Columbia in 1904:

> The coast called and Vancouver Island, that *one step more Western than the West*. I went to her, longing yet dreading. Never had her forests looked so

solemn, never her mountains so high, never her drift-laden beaches so vast. Oh, the gladness of my West again! Immense Canada! Oh, her Pacific edge, her Western limit! I blessed my luck in being born Western. (*Growing Pains* 421, emphasis added)

While the art schools in San Francisco and London had improved her technical skills, it was in Paris that her general viewpoint changed and she could start to synthesize her thematic preferences and the new colour schemes of the Fauves. Carr described her situation to Mr. Gibb, her art instructor in Paris in 1910: "Our far West has complete art isolation...no exhibitions, no artists, no art talk." Gibb responded not as Carr expected: "So much the better!...Your silent Indian will teach you more than all the art jargon" (*Growing Pains* 432).

Sharyn Udall argues that "an important aspect of Carr's artistic and personal relationship with native peoples relied on her own 'outsider' status. For Carr, to be an artist was to be 'different'—marginalized from society in ways akin (at least in her mind) to the cultural isolation of indigenous peoples" (35). One of Carr's biographers, Stephanie Walker, also finds these traits of great importance when analyzing her work:

> Native art and spirituality inspired her; the boundary between her Western Self and the indigenous Other offered freedoms available only at the periphery of order. Interest in the lives of other women artists on similar margins, like Georgia O'Keeffe and Frida Kahlo, suggest a societal urge to come to terms with the links between women, art and nature...Emily Carr's experience of the world, lived on *geographic and cultural boundaries* has invited interpretation... She challenged religious, social and artistic conventions. Marginalization by geography on the west coast of Canada had given her an exceptional view of the world. Marginalization by gender deprived her of easy access to the practices of art. (6, 10, 11, emphasis added)

Back in Vancouver, Carr felt that her first exhibitions were not well received. She particularly regretted the complete indifference toward her paintings in France and in the French style at exhibitions in 1912 and 1913; after all, it was in France that "Emily Carr became a modernist...[and] she was determined to apply what she had learned in France to the landscape and indigenous culture of the West Coast" (R. Laurence 14). A crisis of almost a decade and a half followed when she hardly painted at all (although she produced pottery and rugs with Indigenous motifs). Thirty years later, in a letter to Ira Dilworth, the BC regional director for CBC and a close friend of Carr's later in her life, she wrote of these years, "I was *so far off* [emphasis added] from *all* [emphasis original] the workers so totally on my own & rather bewildered I had been through a period somewhere around 15 years dormant all the art smashed out of me flat" (15 Feb. 1942, qtd. in Morra 110). While critics generally emphasize Carr's lack of creativity between 1913 and 1927, Charles Taylor thinks that "it may well have been that she found her new strength and inner vitality, not despite the barren years, but *because* of them" ("Emily Carr" 177).

The turning point arrived when she was asked to send pictures to Ottawa, where the National Gallery organized an exhibition called *Canadian West Coast Art: Native and Modern* in December 1927. Carr travelled from Victoria, British Columbia, to Ontario, and met several Group of Seven artists in Toronto before the exhibition. Seeing the paintings of Lawren Harris was like an epiphany for her: at long last, she could talk about art with someone whom she highly respected. Although Harris was fourteen years younger than Carr, she considered him almost her master: "His work and example did more to influence my outlook upon Art than any school or any master" (*Growing Pains* 452). The visual experience was soon accompanied by a verbal exchange of ideas through an intensive correspondence that lasted with more or less regularity until the end of her life: "When I returned from the East in 1927, Lawren Harris and I exchanged a few letters about work. They were the first real exchanges of thought in regard to work I had ever experienced" (23 Nov. 1930, *Hundreds* 668). As her journals reveal, Carr considered her new connection to Toronto artists and the exhibition at the National Gallery milestones in her life as an artist. The positive attitudes toward her painting that emerged from these events were all the more important since she had felt that her pictures in the new style were not well received in Vancouver in 1913. Toronto and Ottawa, then, were perceived by her as meaningful alternatives to European centres such as London or Paris. Although she sent pictures to West Coast cities such as San Francisco during the "barren years," she did not find those exhibitions of great value for her artistic development.

Despite the fact that Carr felt inferior intellectually to Harris and the other Toronto artists, she appreciated their warm welcome: "one week and two days have passed. Every minute has been splendid, too full of living to be written down....I'm glad, glad, glad that I have these rare privileges and that I am able to talk straight and unafraid....I was one of them. They accepted me....They made me feel one of them and not a stranger from the far off West" (17 Nov. 1933, *Hundreds* 710, 711). After so many efforts to overcome the spatial gap (studies in San Francisco, London, France), Carr needed more than a decade and a half to be accepted in her own country. All through her life, however, she was often hesitant about her position in Canadian art.

In my view, Emily Carr can be considered a modernist in Canada, even if hers is not "pure" modernism. As with many other Canadian artists (e.g., F.R. Scott, A.J.M. Smith—see Trehearne), elements of romanticism and aestheticism alike can be detected in both her painting and her writings. On the other hand, her very early endeavour to depict Indigenous life and art, which can be related to modernists' admiration of "primitive" cultures, and her constant search for showing both the totem poles before the First World War and the thick British Columbia forests in the late 1920s using cubist and expressionist methods, make her an important representative of modernist art in Canada. Being a female artist in the mainly male domain of painting produced further barriers—she was always conscious of the ways her gender acted as a "handicap," which contributed to her experience of multiple marginalizations.

Carr's marginalization and isolation only partly resulted from her geographical situation and gender, however. Her extraordinary character and inclination to not only shock people around her but be self-consciously eccentric also contributed greatly to deepening the gap between herself, a declared artist, and the everyday world, including her sisters (Crean 66–67). I agree with Doris Shadbolt, who says that "her art was too deeply lodged within herself for discussion. That is the real essence of Carr's isolation" (*Emily Carr* 24). She was often suffering from loneliness—and as often from being in company that did not understand her. Carr wrote, "we all stand so *utterly alone* and our only real critic and judge is our own soul." "Oh better a million lonelinesses than an uncongenial companion!" (22 and 24 Apr. 1934, *Hundreds* 736).

She was aware of the blessings and disadvantages of "margin" and "centre" alike: conscious of her own marginal location, she did not hesitate to devote time, energy, and her little savings to studying art in "centres" such as London and Paris. From the second half of the 1920s on, she systematically kept in touch with "centres" in North America; she visited Toronto, Ottawa, Montreal, New York, and Chicago, where she met artists including members of the Group of Seven, art historian Fred Housser, Katherine Dreier, Georgia O'Keeffe, and she continued to correspond with some of these artists from her home in Victoria. Her visits and discussions with artists very often strengthened her feeling isolated in times of frustration—personal or artistic. Her achievements and success later in her lifetime are all the more remarkable if we consider these conditions.

As Walker argues,

> Without postmodern insight to decode her predicament, excluded from full participation in the institutions of her era, Carr had prescient skills for living on the margins of social, economic, political and religious systems...She continued to be perceived as an eccentric and indomitable woman, only domesticable by her own standards...This particular life...remains marginal and sensitive

> to dualisms that easily discount female experience: mind/body, spirituality/carnality, truth/appearance, life/death. (S. Walker 147)

After being integrated in the Group of Seven's exhibitions in the late 1920s and becoming a founding member of the Canadian Group of Painters, geographical isolation hurt Carr less. In fact, she saw it as an advantage: "I stopped grieving about the isolation of the West. I believe now I was glad we were cut off" (*Growing Pains* 444). She reproduces a short dialogue with influential art collector Harold Mortimer Lamb: "'It's a shame to think of you stuck out here in this corner of the world unnoticed and unknown,' says he. 'It's exactly where I want to be,' says I. And it is, too. This is my country. What I want to express is *here* and I love it. Amen!'" (7 Mar. 1934, *Hundreds* 727). Joy Coghill, author of a play about Carr, was also profoundly intrigued by this dichotomy in Carr's life. For Coghill, the key question was "'how in hell did she do it?' How did she manage to overcome the isolation and alienation of this edge-of-the-world Western place? I know what helped. It helped to swear and smoke and push a monkey in a pram up Government Street!" (316).

Isolation, being far from centres, solitude, the sensation of the periphery are recurrent themes in various art forms in the Canada of the 1920s and subsequent years: most visibly in paintings by members of the Group of Seven, but also in the poetry, plays, and novels of the interwar period (e.g., *Wilderness: A Play of the North*, a one-act play by Herman Voaden, which was greatly influenced by J.E.H. MacDonald's *The Solemn Land* and Harris's *Above Lake Superior* [Wagner 85]; *Think of the Earth* [1936], Bertram Brooker's Governor General's Award–winning novel, or *As for Me and My House* [1942] by Sinclair Ross, the best-known literary example of marginal existence).

Discussions of the Margin by Canadian Theorists

As Douglas Coupland remarks, "in a single city (Toronto—what the hell?) over a clear period of time, a small group of men revolutionized the way the world understands and uses communications" (*Marshall McLuhan* 104). Indeed, the work of Harold Innis, Marshall McLuhan, and Northrop Frye focused significantly on margins and centres.

Elaborating on the "dependency relationship between the centre and the margins" (Heyer and Crowley xiii), Harold Innis wrote three basic books in the interwar period: *The History of the Canadian Pacific Railway* (1923), *The Fur Trade in Canada* (1930), and *The Cod Fisheries: A History of an International Economy* (1940). Innis, like several other modernist thinkers and even artists, was influenced by European thinkers and historians such as Oswald Spengler, Arnold Toynbee, Theodor Adorno, and Walter Benjamin, among others. As his first three books show, he started out with the analysis of commerce and transportation in Canada, claiming that "Canada, a country on the margin of Europe...had to be examined in its own context" and that "Canada's evolution as a nation was...a microcosm for an understanding of the paradoxes of modernity in the Western world" (Francis 214, 215). In *The Fur Trade in Canada*, he concluded that "fundamentally the civilization of North America is the civilization of Europe" (Innis qtd. in Francis 217) and argued that "this association of North America with Europe—what he called a relationship 'between the centre and the margin of western civilization'—was...one of inequality and discrepancy," adding that "upon initial contact of the Europeans with the indigenous population this inequality did not exist" (Francis 217). He was convinced that "the truly creative thinking and the indomitable human spirit always surfaced from the margins of civilization." For him, "the center and the margin—the source of power and creativity respectively—were polar opposites"; therefore "Canada, a country on the margin of power, had something positive to contribute to the modern world" (Francis 223, 225). Innis exercised a strong influence on many of his contemporaries (particularly Marshall McLuhan) and subsequent generations of artists, thinkers, and writers. David Staines sums up Innis's academic contribution to knowledge in his native country: he "considered his writings as an ongoing attempt to explain Canada to Canadians" (339).

In his early career, McLuhan published several articles on English and American literature, including essays on Joyce, Eliot, Pound, Dos Passos, and Wyndham Lewis. He was strongly influenced by New Criticism, the views of I.A. Richards and F.R. Leavis, his instructor in Cambridge in the mid-1930s. After teaching in the United States for some years, McLuhan became a professor at St. Michael's College in Toronto in 1946. Soon after his arrival, he started to work with Innis, applying his views about the dichotomy of centres and margins to literature, too. In 1948, McLuhan visited Ezra Pound in St. Elizabeths hospital and a correspondence of almost a whole decade started. McLuhan's letters to Pound tell us a lot about his understanding of modernism. In July 1948, McLuhan was discussing the question of centre and margin:

> In a merely historical perspective should not something be said of the fact that the job of getting English poetry into the central European current (the work you did in 1908–14 with Gaudier, Lewis and others) could not have been done by the English? That Yeats and Joyce, Pound and Eliot, two Irishmen and two Americans, were obviously more aware and more receptive of what had fallen out of the English mind? (Molinaro, McLuhan, and Toye 196–97)

This viewpoint is close to what Innis wrote about the general historical role of peripheries as far as new approaches were concerned. According to Tony Tremblay, McLuhan's "new authority to speak about popular and mass culture from such an engaged periphery became Canada's own, finally privileging our position on the edge of two titanic cultures" (164). The problem area around the centre and the margin receives a new dimension in McLuhan's well-known coinage of the "global village."

In *Understanding Media* McLuhan argues that historically "Sea powers...tend to create centres without margins, and land empires favor the center-margin structure. Electric speeds create centers everywhere. Margins cease to exist on this planet" (92). The case of Canada combines the features of the two groups: on the one hand, in the early decades of the twentieth century the country was functioning as the colony of a sea power; then gradually it changed into a "land country" with centres (Montreal, Toronto, later Winnipeg and Vancouver), to give way to the electronic age in which—thanks to highly developed technology and communications facilities—huge distances can easily be overcome. Concerning the approach to the problematic of margin and centre in Innis's writings and those of McLuhan, David Williams thinks that the difference is "between a man writing in the age of radio and one writing in an age of television" (39).

In *Divisions on a Ground*, Northrop Frye, McLuhan's colleague at the University of Toronto, deals with the central issues of this chapter—namely, the relationship of the centre and the margin—putting them in the wider context of the relationship between society and culture. Frye writes,

> As long as I have been a literary critic, I have been interested in the relations between a culture and the social conditions under which it is produced...I feel that Canada is perhaps as interesting and valuable a place as any to study such a question...To centralize is to create a hierarchy. The top of the hierarchy is the central city, London or Paris, which is where all the cultural action is...It is also possible, in modern times, for the centrifugal movement from the main centres to reverse itself, for works of culture to be export goods coming out of a small community. (15–17)

Frye's example of the decisive influence of a non-centre on centres is Dublin, mythicized by Joyce. By negating the exceptional role of the centre and establishing cultural hierarchies, Frye was approaching postmodernism.

In "Culture and Interpretation," Frye concludes that "political and economic organization tends to centralize and unify....Literature and painting do appear to depend on decentralization in a very subtle way. The artist seems to draw strength from a very limited community...but the community itself is not their market" (*Divisions* 24). In reference to Faulkner's fictional world, he crystallizes his argument: "This is where the principle of interpenetration operates: the more intensely Faulkner concentrates on his unpronounceable county in Mississippi, the more intelligible he becomes to readers all over the world" (24). This interpenetration is one of the features that make modernism not only a practically inexhaustable terrain for the researcher but also an artistic phenomenon that manifests a dynamism between small communities, regions, and centres of Western art. Frye was fully aware of the movement between the local and the universal: he admitted that "no muse can function...outside geography and history," but immediately added,

> In an "instant world" of communication, there is no reason for cultural lag or for a difference between sophisticated writers in large centres and naive writers in smaller ones. A world like ours produces a single international style of which all existing literatures are regional developments. This international style is...a way of seeing and thinking in a world controlled by uniform patterns of technology, and the regional development is a way of escaping from that uniformity. (*Divisions* 31)

Frye himself offered a convincing example of these views in a short personal discussion in his Toronto office on May 16, 1989: he was asking me about the importance of the symbolist poet Endre Ady (1877–1919) in the matrix of Hungarian culture. Ady grew up in Northern Transylvania, studied in several provincial towns before going to the centre, Budapest. With his espousal of symbolism and decadence, he could be considered a poet breaking the ground before the advent of modernism in Hungary.

I explained to Frye that modernism in Ady's period was embedded in a very complex historical and social context: after the First World

War, Hungary became an independent country (i.e., no longer part of the Austro-Hungarian monarchy), but lost two-thirds of its former territory in the redesignation of its territory, and millions of previously mainstream Hungarians became minorities in the surrounding states that succeeded the former empire. These radical changes were necessarily reflected in Hungarian culture, as well—thus modernism in the country was accompanied by a redefinition of the nation and its culture. What used to be the periphery during the monarchy years, no longer formed part of the country—on the other hand, new border-regions appeared, changing the role of some provincial towns into regional centres (e.g., Debrecen, Szeged, Pécs, Miskolc), which were inviting to experimental artists by offering a thriving cultural life away from the capital. Thus, I explained to Frye, the advent of modernism for Hungarians is closely tied to the re-mapping of centre and periphery in the national imagination, and it seemed natural to me, then, to attend to what was happening to these categories in the context of Canadian modernism.

Conclusion

Although Robert Kroetsch downplays the existence of modernism in Canada ("Canadian Writing"), it did appear in various art forms and was a topic of theoretical discussions for several decades in the twentieth century. In my view, Canadian artists and scholars significantly contributed to our present understanding of this complex cultural process in various degrees. Dean Irvine, in his introduction to *The Canadian Modernists Meet*, does not "deny the fact that the formation of American and European 'high' modernisms antedates and influences the emergence of Canada's modernisms;" rather, he ascertains Canada's "medial position between dominant modernisms" (6–7):

> Canada's modernists are always enmeshed by and, at the same time, peripheral to these canonical modernisms. Modernisms in Canada therefore represent

> transnational cultural formations among the matrices of European and American modernisms—and, simultaneously, marginal modernisms on the edges of principal cultural modernities....
>
> The recovery of neglected modernists is a constituent element in the formulation of Canadian modernism's marginality. (Irvine 7, 10)

With true respect for Irvine's remarkable contribution to a better understanding of modernism in Canada, I propose that his last statement might be modified if we take into consideration the work of other artists (particularly painters) and not limit our observations to literature, implying that modernism does have a strong canonical position in these forms of artistic expression.

8

Canadian Photography and the Exhaustion of Landscape

CLAIRE OMHOVÈRE

> Landscape is an exhausted medium, no longer viable as a mode of artistic expression. Like life, landscape is boring; we must not say so.
> —W.T.J. Mitchell, *Landscape and Power*

PROPOSING TO LOOK AT LANDSCAPE in a book project that addresses the achievements of the Understanding Canada program is likely to trigger a feeling of déjà vu, even perhaps plain boredom. After all, the genre was pronounced dead by all the thinkers who were beginning to make a difference in the field of cultural studies back in the 1980s. Yet, exhausted as landscape conventions may be, landscape continued to feature prominently everywhere in Canadian literature and visual culture far beyond the age of the picturesque and the first-established criteria of documentary photography. The question is why? This chapter searches for possible answers in the works of William McFarlane Notman (1857–1913), Edward Burtynsky (b. 1955), and Douglas Coupland (b. 1961), and the inter-iconicity informing their otherwise very distinct ways of seeing.[1] Turning to photography and its relation with pictorial conventions is a way of exploring the silent yet insistent claim these photographers make to simultaneously preserving a certain vision of the land and documenting its exhaustion. We commonly regard "images as devices of memory and tools of preservation" (Schwartz 205). Taking our fascination with photography's "funereal enigma" (Barthes, *Grain* 331) one step further, Susan Sontag has problematized the relationship of photography to the past by arguing that photography's true magic lies in its invention of reality: "As photographs give people an imaginary possession of a past that is unreal, they also help people to take possession of a space in which they are insecure" (*On Photography* 9). This chapter, however, questions the function of memory-keeper we attribute to photography, and the historical role it has played in the recording, production, and preservation of a certain vision of the land, from the late days of the exploration of the Canadian West to the post-industrial present. Its approach is therefore genealogical in the sense that it attempts to delineate the ruptures and continuities in the representation of the land as landscape that the photographs of Notman, Burtynsky, and Coupland preserve and transmit, even when the landscapes they capture on film are caught in the very process of disappearing, as evinced by the pictorial tension informing Notman's photography, the residual aesthetic found in Burtynsky's pictures, and the provocative kitsch of Coupland's still lifes.

When the demise of landscape was heralded in the wake of the 1980s cultural turn, the news was greeted with a mix of relief and dismay reminiscent of earlier responses to the death of the author (Barthes, "Mort") and the exhaustion of literature (Barth). Today, however, memoirs and literary biographies are read with a curiosity that is only matched in its intensity by the popularity of ubiquitous coffee-table books showing more of Canada's spectacular landscapes. Meanwhile, scholars have queried the endurance of the idea of landscape beyond the obsolescence of the genre, proceeding to a thorough redefinition of landscape as "a way of seeing" (Cosgrove 20) or "a medium" (Mitchell 5–30). These terms point to a shift from landscape as object to landscape as process, or event. This shift, in turn, has caused scholarly analysis to reorient its focus from aesthetics to the wide array of cultural transactions—the circulation of artistic, symbolic but also social, political, and economic values—that occur between the viewer and the viewed when a portion of the environment is "taken in at a glance from one point of view."[2]

Recalling the unmooring of landscape studies from art history, and their subsequent revision through the interdisciplinary lenses of cultural geography and media studies, Denis Cosgrove admits to his lack of foresight when he claimed, in the first edition of *Social Formation and Symbolic Landscape*, that "after the last flourish of romanticism, landscape as an active concern for progressive art died in the second half of the nineteenth century, and that its ideological function of harmonizing social environmental relations through visual pleasure was appropriated by the discipline of geography" (Cosgrove 28).[3] Cosgrove goes on to attribute the renaissance of landscape in later years to two main factors. He identifies the first one as the interest of postmodern culture "in the referential capacities of art, but now with a much freer attitude toward references and iconographic meanings than at the time of modernism" (Cosgrove 29). The second factor lies in the adaptation of landscape to recent technologies such as speed, the aerial view, and photography "in explicit dialogue with the picturesque tradition inherited from eighteenth-century theory and practice" (Cosgrove 30). This leads Cosgrove to conclude that "twentieth-century technologies of vision and representation have been coupled with other technical achievements, transforming, but not extinguishing, the appeal of landscape and its power to articulate moral and social concerns" (Cosgrove 31).

The transformations landscape photography underwent in Canada in the course of the last hundred years participate in the dialectic between endurance and exhaustion characteristic of the Western history of the genre, but they acquire a particular poignancy in Canada on account of the role landscape has traditionally played in the rhetoric of national identifications. Cultural geographer Jonathan Bordo once drew an important difference between what he regards as the textual and verbal assertiveness of American identity and the essentially visual and silent nature of its Canadian counterpart (151–52). The latter found its inception in the images of the wilderness captured in sketches and watercolours by the artists or the officers with artistic inclinations—names such as William Hind, Robert Hood, or George Back readily come to mind—who travelled with the many expeditions sent to the Western interior and the Arctic in the course of the nineteenth century, and who were later succeeded by documentary photographers in the waning years of the expedition age. In the 1920s, during a period when the camera rendered the testimonial function of painting secondary and freed it from figurative constraints, the Group of Seven reclaimed the European genre of landscape painting, renewing it through bold experimentations with colour and design that expressed a sense of belonging steeped in their reverence for the wilderness. It is no wonder that their paintings and the geography that inspired them should have engaged artists and critics alike during the cultural boom of the Centennial decade, when the second act of Canadian independence played itself out.

The Notman family has their own history enmeshed with that of the Dominion of Canada. The founder of the line was forced to leave Glasgow in 1856, and seek refuge in Canada after the family dry goods business had gone bankrupt and unsound financial decisions made an outlaw of him. Once in Montreal, he turned photography, a favourite hobby of his, into his new profession with the creation of the William Notman photographic studio. At the peak of his career, William Notman (1826–1891) ran seven studios in Canada and nineteen in the whole of North America. He founded one of the mighty Scottish dynasties upon which the economy and the reputation of the young country came to rest: he proclaimed himself Queen Victoria's personal photographer in 1860, and subsequently associated his name with the transformation of Canada from fledgling Dominion into the daughter of the Empire.[4] The Notman dynasty gives us a striking example of a Canadian rags-to-riches story, a real-life counterpart to the character of the enterprising Scottish orphan rising to the opportunities of imperial expansion in the novels of John Galt and Ralph Connor.⁵ But the Notmans' success story also shows that the emergence of an English Canadian elite cannot be separated from the development of the media and the arts in a country where national sentiment was never a given but the result of culturally fostered identifications, an aspect to which the mini-videos available on the McCord Museum website bear strong evidence. When Notman photographs his eldest son, William McFarlane Notman, posing in full winter attire and a howling blizzard for *Young Canada* (1867), the father is activating clichés such as the nordicity of the national character that was gaining definition in these years of formation (Coleman, *White Civility* 137–38). He is also making a visual contribution to the rhetoric of the family allegory that was emerging in the popular literature of the same period (37).

A century later, Douglas Coupland acknowledges the longevity of the *topos* with "Young Country"—one of the essays included in *Souvenir of Canada* (131)—as well as with the frontispiece he chose for the same volume—namely, the book cover of Bruce Hutchinson's *Canada: Tomorrow's Giant*, which received the Governor General's Award for creative non-fiction in 1957. The design of Hutchinson's original cover gives a visual answer to postwar challenges. It is neatly divided in two halves, the top one showing a generic illustration of the wilderness complete with spruce, lake, and snowy mountain tops, whereas the bottom half features the steel works and slag heaps that evoke the industrial sites of southern Ontario and the wastelands Edward Burtynsky will photograph in the 1990s. The flaming emblem of the maple leaf embossed on an orange title banner effects the mediation between these two, barely compatible profiles of the nation. The visual composition thus inscribes the promise of an organic growth naturalizing the transformation of the country into an industrial giant.

Back in 1882, at a time when only a handful of Montreal tycoons were beginning to conceive of such transformations, William McFarlane Notman was made a partner in his father's business. He subsequently played an important part in the documentation of the territorial growth of the dominion. Starting in 1884, he travelled the northwest interior for fifteen years, taking photographs of regions largely unknown to settler Canadians and, in some cases, reluctantly associated with the Confederation process, as evinced by the Red River Resistance that urged Ottawa to include Manitoba as a full-fledged province instead of an annexed territory in 1870 (Thompson 40). On the eve of further discontent with the outbreak of the North-West Rebellion in 1885, the Canadian Pacific Railway (CPR) supplied William McFarlane Notman with a railroad car fully equipped with a darkroom to take, develop, and print the kind of pictures likely to attract passengers and prospective tourists, enticing them to buy a transcontinental ticket to discover the wonders of the hinterland for themselves.

In "Territorial Photography," Joel Snyder explains that "the first generation of landscape photographers—those who worked with paper negative systems from the early 1840s through the early 1850s—were almost completely dependent upon the pictorial conventions of the genre" (Snyder 177). By the 1860s, however, photography had won a technological and documentary legitimacy among the public that eclipsed its value as *landscape* photography, and liberated it from the limitations of pictorialism. Snyder selects photographs by the American explorers Watkins and O'Sullivan to show how aesthetic conventions nevertheless went on informing the implicit relation these photographs supposed between nature and the human eye. This interplay of the documentary and the aesthetic is also what interests me in Notman's photography. Notman salvaged from the northwest interior and the Pacific coast the images of a fast-changing world somewhat at odds with the stillness and the long duration of the exposures required in early photography.

The photographs collected by William McFarlane Notman in the course of these fifteen years document the development of modern means of transportation, as Notman's journey was dependent on the emerging companies that were opening the distant interior to Eastern entrepreneurship and vigilance. The CPR yards Notman photographed in 1884 would within a year's time teem with the Canadian troops rushed from Ontario to Winnipeg when the North-West Rebellion broke out. Also about the same year, Notman captured on print the gleaming interior of the dining room in a Canadian Pacific Line steamer, intimating that one need not forsake safety, comfort, or even refinement when undertaking long-distance journeys.[6] These pictures show us a northwest and a Pacific region that are both within reach and modern, in sharp contrast with the American *Far* West, which, half a century earlier, could only be reached by covered wagons pulled by oxen. In his photographs, Notman foregrounds the technology that was altering the appeal of the sublime favoured by the travelling artists who first depicted these regions (Raban 42). His landscapes turn the traveller into a spectator whose attention, distracted as it is from the discomfort of travelling, can be fully devoted to the contemplation of the spectacular yet accessible grandeur of the interior. *Scuzzie Falls, near North Bend, BC, 1887*[7] is quite representative of a series of photographs meant to reorient the dynamic of the sublime by shifting its focus from the landscape to the technology that makes it available. Instead of gazing down into the abyss, the photograph is taken from the bottom of a mountainous gorge where it looks up to the foaming water cascading down the granite face. Because of the low angle shot, the precipice is far less impressive than the trestle bridge, which, in the top right-hand corner, reinforces the perspectival construction of the photograph and creates the illusion that its iron beams hold the mountains together.

Like most of the artists who preceded him in the Pacific Northwest, Notman was overwhelmed by a geography that "perfectly fit the reigning conception of how a Romantic landscape ought to look. British Columbia conveniently combined, within a single view, the essential iconic features of the Swiss Alps, the German forests, and the English Lake District" (Raban 42). Notman's photography, however, expresses a sense of bewilderment in front of such an abundance of riches, as if the sheer size and vitality of the natural environment somehow resisted its capture through the camera's eye. As a result, his pictures frequently feature an intriguing tension between code and content, between the photographic medium and its message. *Douglas Pine Trees, Vancouver, BC, 1887*,[8] for instance, displays a strong contrast between its factual content and the "rhetoric of the frame" (Duro 8) that transforms the site into a landscape. If this photograph deserves to be regarded as landscape and not as a topographical portrait, it is because it contains a strong injunction to "look at the view" much more than at any of its discrete, visual components (Mitchell, Preface viii). In *Douglas Pine Trees*, the landscape imperative is quite manifest in its reliance upon the picturesque convention of the side-screen or *repoussoir*. This function is performed by the two massive tree trunks that frame the visual field and guide the gaze from the underbrush in the foreground to the man sitting on the edge of the forest and, finally, to the house in the foggy depths of the picture. Yet the relationship between the three constitutive planes of fore- middle- and background is fraught with tensions that disrupt the naturalizing effect of the topographical portrait. To begin with, the two trunks make a paradoxical frame: they simultaneously assert the boldness of the perspectival construction and the impossibility of beholding and containing the sheer bulk of the natural world. The human figure no longer serves as "a yardstick for the conveying of information about size relationships" (Snyder 196). Instead, the seated figure indexes both disproportion and dislocation, although one has to admit that, for all his incongruous attire, the man in the bowler hat somehow looks like an offshoot of the rainforest. In fact, if we fail to register the presence of his elf-like figure, barely distinguishable as it is from the undergrowth, it is probably because the pine trees get all the attention. The duplication of the "convenient tree" traditionally used by painters as an appropriate *repoussoir* (Mitchell, "Imperial" 24) creates an intrusive, uncanny effect. The photograph, as opposed to what its caption asserts, does not record the existence of specimens of Douglas pine in British Columbia. Rather, it indexes the phenomenal impact of an encounter

Douglas Pine Trees, Vancouver, BC, 1887. William McFarlane Notman photograph, glass lantern slide, copied ca. 1902. © McCord Museum. [N-0000.25.1071]

with the treeness of trees. In contradiction with its caption, the photograph says something like, "if you think you know what a tree is, now look." Here is tree as event. Here is the kind of treeness that questions the centrality of the human subject in representation along with the classical assumption that Man is the measure of all things.

"The traditional system of planes of shadow alternating with planes of light" found in picturesque paintings (Mitchell, "Imperial" 24) is also taken up and given unprecedented contrast in the opposition between the dark foreground and a lighter background shrouded in fog. Dwarfed as it is by the *repoussoir*, the huge, garrison-like mansion causes the eye to consider the distance between the edge of the forest and the emptiness of the central intermediate zone. In this space—this field or perhaps garden—the negativity of the photographic medium plays itself out in the luminosity that fills and saturates the middle distance where the gaze ventures, hesitates, and searches for vertical landmarks—the absent shadows of trees in the now clear-cut expanse of land. The tension between this photograph's constitutive planes adumbrates the emptying-out informing Tom Thomson's *The Jack Pine* (1916), where it bespeaks the genealogical anxiety of a postcolonial condition in which "the originary occasion has gone blank" (Kroetsch, "Reciting" 37), and the representation of nature has turned into a querying of its generic protocols. To their self-conscious use of pictorial codes, Notman's photographs, however, add a dimension that is specific to the indexical nature of the photographic medium,[9] insofar as it is through the exposure to light that the contours of absence, what was never there but also what has vanished, detach themselves on the negative print. In Notman's pictures, the world changes in shades of white and grey wherever the light flows in to suffuse the spaces where the tangible absents itself along the vertiginous vistas that have just been carved through the Rocky Mountains, and into the Pacific rainforest where they herald the transformation of the kingdom of fur and feather into a modern, industrial nation.

When one compares Notman's portraits of Young Canada at the turn of the twentieth century and their counterpart on the eve of the new millennium, what is perhaps most striking is the sudden realization that what the land seemed to have in abundance—its wild, open spaces, its pristine nature and infinite resources—is suddenly gone. A similar recognition found its expression in the United States in the myth of the frontier. In Canada, however, the frontier could never quite gather momentum in a Western interior where the transfer of Rupert's Land to the Confederation was managed under the careful supervision of the Northwest Mounted Police (Stegner 100–10). It is rather the motif of boom and bust that came to embody the dialectic of exploitation and exhaustion fundamental to the Canadian restlessness, from the age of the fur trade to the transformations that are now affecting the Arctic. The fascination of artists with exhaustion and loss—with "what remains of what does not remain" to recall the poet's quest in *The Hornbooks of Rita K* (Kroetsch 8)—is ubiquitous in Canadian culture. But so is the difficulty of attending to the memory of what has been erased because it jeopardizes the assumptions upon which Canada's fictive ethnicity came to rest (Coleman, *White Civility* 34), a preoccupation that recurs in Canadian literature, from the historiographic metafictions of the 1970s to 1990s to the geological tropism characteristic of the neo-Victorian novels of Jane Urquhart and Joan Thomas (Omhovère 281–86).

Contemporary Canadian photographers participate in the same memorial obsession. Among them, the work of Edward Burtynsky is most remarkable in the way it engages with the postmodern question: "How does one quote nature?" (Kroetsch, "Reciting" 38). Like Notman, Burtynsky's first tentative answer is to explore the pictorial possibilities of inter-iconicity. Many of his photographs of the 1990s cite the painting tradition of the Group of Seven, mimicking the Group's nationalistic rhetoric and displacing it onto territories beyond the national boundaries. *Vermont Marble Company #5, Abandoned Marble Quarry, Rochester, Vermont* (1991) and *Abandoned Marble Quarries #1, near Rutland, Vermont* (1991)[10] all conjure up the lake setting of Lawren Harris's *Shimmering Water, Algonquin Park* (1922) with its tremulous birches and tonal harmony of green, russet, and fawn. Likewise, *Rock of Ages #2, Granite Quarry, Bebee, Quebec* (1991) refers inter-iconically to Lawren Harris's *Isolation Peak* (c. 1930).

Because they are pictorial compositions as well as photographs, Burtynsky's residual landscapes rest upon two distinct semiotic regimes. They partake of the iconic through their references to schools of painting among which the Group of Seven and the landscapists of the Hudson River School feature prominently. In addition, they are doubly indexical since they reproduce mechanically the photographic print of an imprint—namely, the visible and tangible traces left by the impact of human activities upon the ecumene. In a radical sense, Burtynsky's photographs present us with traces of traces. The viewer cannot fail to respond to the familiar likeness between the photographs and the landscapes whose colour, volumes, and design the former overtly mimic. But the moment of recognition rapidly shades into unease when the viewer realizes his delusion, and perceives, beneath the simulacrum of a pristine nature, the quarries, the gutted rock faces, and oozing tailings that now enshrine the memory of a wilderness that, perhaps, never existed except in the imagination of these artists. Burtynsky's manufactured landscapes turn away from the age of innocence: "We have left the Garden, an acknowledgement that the landscape is not immutable virgin terrain, but a hybrid of nature modified by human restlessness, aspiration and lust" (Burtynsky 7–8). In the same interview, Burtynsky elaborates on his gradual understanding, after visiting Toronto as a young boy and, later, the bust towns of Pennsylvania, that the architectural magnificence of North American cities required the extraction and transformation of fuel and raw materials, all of which processes necessarily left an imprint on the environment (Baker 43–44). There is an environmental awareness in Burtynsky's postmodern art that could not reach the same level of expression with Notman, in an age when the value of progress remained unquestioned by most. The idea of a reciprocity between nature and the human industry that informs Burtynsky's photography also upsets modern assumptions regarding economic growth and prospects for a sustainable development. In this respect, it is remarkable that the perspectival construction characteristic of Notman's CPR iconography disappears from the series *Railcuts* (Pauli 57–63) where the composition is strictly horizontal and follows the thin scar the railway has left across a mountain face where stitch-like electric poles mark the prodigious graft of the technology onto the landscape.

If Burtynsky's residual landscapes are so resonant with contemporary anxieties about the environment, it is probably because the economy of subtraction and addition that produced them is apprehended through a medium defined by its indexical operations. The efficacy of Burtynsky's aesthetics rests upon a strong adhesion between the object he documents and his medium of documentation, insofar as both partake of the ambivalence constitutive of the indexical trace. Residual landscape and photographic print both proceed from the negativity that carves out the contours of loss. Yet, as such, they are also endowed with the generative potency of a matrix yielding impressions:

> I'll go out and uncover an interesting place and find that it can be read as a geological event, as evidence of our knowledge and ability to extract resources, or finding things that exist as a reference to art history. Out in the landscape you can see the elements of field painting or abstract expressionism or constructivism. To take a cue from Marcel Duchamp, the world is the ultimate "ready made." (Torosian 50)

Burtynsky's nod to Marcel Duchamp inscribes his own work as a photographer within the aesthetic paradigm of the imprint. As shown by Georges Didi-Huberman in his study of Duchamp, the imprint produces resemblance through contact rather than through visual likeness. That is why the regime of the imprint is non-mimetic. In this sense, the impression created through contact challenges the requirements of classical *imitatio* and the supremacy of the eye in the appreciation of art. Whatever technique of transference produced it, the fossil, the handprint, or the sculptor's cast is a negative matrix encasing the enigma of its reference. Paradoxical as it may seem, resemblance through contact therefore frequently entails a reluctance to be recognized (Didi-Huberman 259).

The imprint's enigmatic reference, and the delay this entails in terms of recognition, are central to the effect of *Nickel Tailings*, a series of pictures Burtynsky took in the industrial region of Sudbury, Ontario, in the late 1990s. The ensemble makes a bold inter-iconic use of the romantic motifs of the cataract and the ruin for which Burtynsky chose colours reminiscent of the lustrous, velvety dark, and scarlet favoured by Thomas Cole in *Falls of the Kaaterskill* (1826), a painting of which *Nickel Tailings #31* proposes the uncanny negative. In *Nickel Tailings #31*, it is as if the incandescence that suffuses the autumn foliage in Cole's famous allegory of the Wild had finally consumed the remains of the primeval forest, contaminating the tumbling cataract in the centre of the picture with mephitic effluents. In the photograph, the absence of a horizon and of a human tally makes it difficult for the viewer to assess size. Contrary to Cole's painting, there is no tiny Indian warrior standing in (dis)proportion to the wilderness to give us an idea of scale. That is the reason why it takes some time for the viewer to recognize, even as s/he moves closer to take in all the details, that what s/he initially mistook for an apocalyptic disaster merely shows a few square inches of scorched grass traversed by a fluorescent ripple of toxic fluids. But this dubious relief barely lasts, for in the next set of pictures—diptych *#34* and *#35*—the presence of a horizon restores its proportions to the transformation of the wilderness into a wasteland: "Burtynsky as the contemporary heir to the metaphysical picture of the wilderness has made himself the photographic witness to the disaster, as if he were the last one at the scene of the disaster at closing time" (Bordo 169). But one could equally contend that the erasure of the human figure in Burtynsky's photographs necessarily endows the spectator with an ethical responsibility impossible to shrug off as s/he remains the ultimate custodian to the memory of nature enshrined in these pictures.

Burtynsky's elegy for lost landscapes acquires grotesque overtones in Douglas Coupland's *Souvenir of Canada* (2002) and its sequel, *Souvenir of Canada 2* (2004). The two volumes combine vignettes in Coupland's hand, some of his own creative photographs along with others taken by contemporary photographers. Burtynsky's *Nickel Tailings #34* and *#35* are given pride of place in *Souvenir of Canada 2* with a double-page reproduction that preserves the panoramic scale of the diptych (96–97). The titles of the two volumes allude to Canada's international image as the ultimate destination for urban tourists ready for a bit of roughing it in what remains of the North American wilderness. Coupland's choice of iconography does not, however, readily submit to the memorial recognition and appropriation encapsulated in the word *souvenir*:

> This book contains eleven still life photographs I made for several reasons, the simplest one being that I wanted to create images understandable only to Canadians. Americans should look at these photos and think: "Huh? Everything looks familiar, and yet nothing is familiar." To accomplish this insider-only goal, I used the nearly extinct visual mode of the still life. I wanted the formal beauty of the still life to draw in the viewer, and then confront him or her with icons and forms which draw on our nation's shared memories, both humble and noble. (Coupland, *Souvenir* n.p.)

The nationalist dig at the assumption that Canada is a mere territorial appendix to the United States includes Coupland within a long line of Canadian writers. Less expected, though, is the choice of the still life as a form likely to foster a sense of belonging through the recognition of collective memories in the bric-a-brac of the past. Like the other ten pictures that compose the series, *Canada Picture No. 3, 2001* was taken in the electric-lit space of what looks like a basement corner.[11] On the walls and the plywood countertop is arranged a collection of objects—flyswatter, sundry posters, toys, musical instruments, tinned food, insect repellent, deer antlers, paperbacks, fishing tackle, empty hunting cartridges, cord telephone, etc.—around the central piece and focus of the composition: a stuffed coyote howling under the neon glare of the basement light. The assemblage invokes the displays of the ethnographic museum and the department store alike, their glass cases exhibiting forms of consumption that had their inception in the trading posts of the Hudson's Bay Company. With the development of such retail giants as the Bay, Simpsons, and Eaton's, the consumer society that soared in the nineteenth and the twentieth centuries asserted to the face of the nation that its prosperity went on a par with its economic self-sufficiency in pre-NAFTA days (Belisle 45–80). And indeed, the homely clutter shown in these pictures is imbued with the nostalgia aroused by the vintage labels and quaint designs of goods that once reflected to the nation a remarkably homogenous image of itself as massively consumerist, white, and middle-class (Belisle 7).

The chastising lesson incipient in the aesthetics of the still life, from the Baroque *vanitas* to the *natures mortes* of French Impressionism, makes it impossible, however, to view Coupland's still lifes as merely bemoaning the passing away of a fantasized Golden Age. These pictures also suggest that Canada's past, glorious as it may seem in retrospect, was premised on a less than romantic exploitation of the land and its resources leading to decay and exhaustion, and ultimately ruling out the possibility of a rejuvenation. In addition to Burtynsky's *Polyfoam Resurrections*,[12] all of the eleven still lifes collected in *Souvenir of Canada* display a taxidermization of nature whose remains, its charismatic wildlife and more discrete flora, have now been drawn indoors. Immortalized in spectacular poses, they decorate our homes and offices, but most of all, they endure in the warehouses of the collective imagination.

What is ultimately at stake in Burtynsky's residual aesthetics and in Coupland's still lifes, what is already incipient in William McFarlane Notman's documentary style, is the way their photographs explore the entanglement of nature and culture through their self-conscious use of painterly prisms—perspective, the inter-iconic citation of pictorial schools and genres, for example, the picturesque or the still life. Because they foreground the exhaustion of landscape as a set of conventions as well as a repository for usable resources, these photographs question the role landscape has traditionally played in the Canadian rhetoric of national identifications. At their core lies the possibility that the viewer may fail to recognize the landscapes they represent for what they are—namely, traces of an ongoing disappearance. These pictures, therefore, revert the logic of the trompe l'oeil to suggest that the eye can indeed be fooled or teased, and hesitate between the recognition of a visual convention and the concomitant retraction of the real in the medium that retains its imprint. They dramatize the encounter with the land as a delayed recognition, sometimes even as a misapprehension of its very nature, in accordance with the non-mimetic, anachronistic regime of the imprint (Didi-Huberman 324–25). The photographs analyzed in this chapter evince a lasting preoccupation with the reading of traces and the insistence of the past in the present. The inter-iconicity and the delayed recognition fundamental to their aesthetic effect suggest alternative responses to the belatedness many have detected in Canadian culture in its successive formative periods as colonial, postmodern, or even postnational, a question Smaro Kamboureli teases out in her own essay in this volume. The exhaustion of landscape operating in Notman's, Burtynsky's, and Coupland's photography is fraught with a creative ambivalence and an irony that bespeak an epochal sense of lateness.[13] Far from being unproductive or even sterilizing, the processes of exhaustion they make visible take the viewers beyond their immediate reference and national relevance, and urge us to query our ethical involvement with the ecumene.

Notes

1. Inter-iconicity is modelled on the concept of intertextuality as initially defined by Julia Kristeva and later elaborated by Gérard Genette. Like its textual analogue, inter-iconicity draws attention to the generative propensity of images, "their processual and processional nature," as Mathilde Arrivé aptly puts it, querying notions of originality and authenticity.
2. Such is the narrow definition of the word *landscape* given by the OED.

3. First published in 1998, Cosgrove's influential introduction was chosen as one of the opening essays in DeLue and Elkins's discussion of recent trends in landscape theory.
4. Detailed information is available from the online exhibition *The Photographic Studio of William Notman*. The photographs by William McFarlane Notman discussed in this chapter are part of the Notman Photographic Archives accessible on the McCord Museum website (http://www.mccord-museum.qc.ca/en/exhibitions/notman-2/).
5. Although William Notman was not actually an orphan—his aging father joined him in Montreal as soon as the new business picked up—his itinerary has much in common with those of the characters analyzed by Daniel Coleman, particularly in the chapter in *White Civility* that he devotes to "The Enterprising Scottish Orphan: Inventing the Properties of English-Canadian Character" (81–127).
6. William McFarlane Notman, *Dining Room "Athabasca," Canadian Pacific Line, about 1884*, McCord Museum, www.musee-mccord.qc.ca/en/collection/artifacts/VIEW-1405?Lang=1&accessnumber=VIEW-1405.
7. William McFarlane Notman, *Scuzzie Falls, near North Bend, BC, 1887*, McCord Museum, www.mccord-museum.qc.ca/en/collection/artifacts/VIEW-1757.
8. William McFarlane Notman, *Douglas Pine Trees, Vancouver, BC, 1887*, McCord Museum, www.mccord-museum.qc.ca/en/collection/artifacts/N-0000.25.1071.
9. Linguist C.S. Peirce distinguishes between three types of signs: the icon, which bears a relation of similarity with what it signifies; the index, which bears a causal reaction to what it signifies; and the symbol (or sign strictly speaking), where the relation is determined by convention (Abrams 170). In her influential two-part essay, "Notes on the Index," Rosalind Krauss takes up Pierce's semiotic system to argue that, as the photographical print proceeds from the exposure of a sensitive surface to light, it is indexical by nature, thus disengaging photography from mimesis and the author's intentionality.
10. Most of the photographs of Edward Burtynsky cited in this article can be consulted on the photographer's personal website: edwardburtynsky.com. In addition, an excellent selection is available in *Manufactured Landscapes*, the catalogue of the retrospective organized by the National Gallery of Canada in 2003.
11. The photograph can be consulted in an archive of Coupland's *New York Times* column, where it illustrates "What Is CanLit?," one of the opinion pieces Coupland wrote for his 2006 column (see www.nytimes.com/slideshow/2006/08/22/opinion/20060823_COUPLAND_SLIDESHOW_1.html). "What Is CanLit?" explicates the links Coupland perceives between the exhaustion of the still life genre, which he relates to landscape, and the ossification of Canadian literature into CanLit: "One could say that CanLit is the literary equivalent of representational landscape painting, with small forays into waterfowl depiction

and still lifes. It is not a modern art form, nor does it want to be" (22 August 2006, *New York Times, Time Capsules* [Coupland blog]).

12. Burtynsky's *Show Room and Office* (Hanover, Ontario, 1982) and *Workbench* (Hundred Mile House, BC, 1983) are both reproduced in *Souvenir of Canada 2* (30–31).

13. For a far-reaching discussion of the hermeneutics of lateness, and a detailed contextualization of the philosophical debates around this question, see Ben Hutchinson's essay "Entre littérature et Histoire."

9

Posthuman Affect in the Global Empire
Queer Speculative Fictions of Canada

BELÉN MARTÍN-LUCAS

> Revolution is not for the faint of heart. It is for monsters.
> You have to lose who you are to discover what you can become.
> —Michael Hardt and Antonio Negri, *Commonwealth*

> A monster is a monster is a monster.
> —Suzette Mayr, *Venous Hum*

AN OLD INTEREST OF MINE HAS BEEN the analysis of literary genres and their relation to the politics in a given text, by which I mean the evaluation of how the characteristics of a certain literary form may contribute to the feminist, queer, postcolonial, anti-racist struggle, and how authors may innovate and reinvigorate traditional genres. Speculative fiction seems to me a most suitable genre for the search for alternatives in the postmodern era of global empire. It is not by mere coincidence that philosophers of our neoliberal age, such as Donna Haraway, Rosi Braidotti, Michael Hardt, and Antonio Negri, all turn to literature to find the mutant monsters that embody their conceptualizations of the posthuman. Thus, Braidotti has pointed out that

> One needs to turn to "minor," not to say marginal and hybrid genres, such as science fiction, science fiction horror and cyber punk, to find fitting cultural illustrations of the changes and transformations that are taking place in the forms of relations available in our post-human present. Low cultural genres, like science fiction...end up being a more accurate and honest depiction of contemporary culture than other, more self-consciously "representational" genres. ("Posthuman" 203)

Their descriptions of the postmodern world heavily rely on the figure of the queer monster that inhabits speculative fictions. This chapter will pay attention to this booming genre in Canada to examine a number of "queer monsters" imagined by Hiromi Goto, Nalo Hopkinson, Larissa Lai, and Suzette Mayr. The hybrid creatures who take centre stage in their narratives may be considered, I will argue, representative examples of what Braidotti has coined (most notably in *The Posthuman*) "the posthuman predicament" of our times. I am studying these four authors as a distinct collective among other authors of speculative fiction in Canada, focusing on their shared politics and poetics. While each of them draws on different cultural backgrounds and folklore for the creation of their fantastic mutant characters—Japanese, Chinese, black Caribbean, Western, and their mixture[1]—the four authors together enable their readers to imagine new figures of queer posthuman hybridity, embodied by "impure" mythological and/or cyborgian shapeshifters. Among other figures, I would foreground as significant examples the various "skin folk" in Hopkinson's stories (collected in a volume with that title) and the hybrid cyborgians in her novel *Midnight Robber*; Goto's recurrent kappa (appearing in *The Water of Possibility*, *The Kappa Child*, and *Hopeful Monsters*); Lai's Fox (in *When Fox Is a Thousand*) and the female protagonists of *Salt Fish Girl* (goddess Nu Wa, cyborg Evie, goddess-cyborg Miranda); or the late twentieth-century version of Ovid's

Metamorphoses in Mayr's *Moon Honey* together with the vegetarian vampires in her *Venous Hum*. I maintain that they all, in diverse ways, participate in a common project that can be described as postcolonial, posthumanist, feminist, queer, anti-racist, and anti-imperialist (of the sort of radical anti-imperialism of "the multitude" that Hardt and Negri have theorized in their famous trilogy *Empire, Multitude*, and *Commonwealth*).[2]

To clarify the main theoretical concepts I am employing here, I will first indicate what kind of narratives I am including as "speculative fiction" to then describe queer posthuman subjectivity as depicted in the chosen novels. A third section will gather my theoretical reflections on the contribution these novels make to the conceptualization of the posthuman in the Canadian context, in relation to multiculturalism and transnationalism.

Queer Speculative Fiction

Much critical discussion has been dedicated to the definitions of and distinctions between speculative fiction and science fiction. The most widely accepted distinction is that authors of speculative fiction are "more interested in philosophies of time and communal organization" (Thaler 9) than in technology and science, which would be a priority for science fiction writers. Canada's most famous speculative fiction writer, Margaret Atwood, has insisted that a distinction must be made between the two genres according to their genealogies—science fiction descends from H.G. Wells, speculative fiction from Jules Verne, she proposes—and this distinction is marked, in Atwood's view, by the possibility or impossibility that the speculations could happen in the "real" world (*In Other Worlds* 6): speculative fiction may happen, science fiction will not. Another Canadian author, Nalo Hopkinson, on the other hand, has defined speculative fiction as "fiction that starts from the principle of making the impossible possible" (Nelson 98), thus envisioning this genre as a tool for social change. This is the kind of speculative writing that I find has a more inclusive politics.

I use *speculative fiction*, as many other critics do, as an umbrella term that encompasses science fiction, fantasy, and their fusion into what has often been defined as a "hybrid blend of generic features" (Cuder-Domínguez, "Politics" 117); this broad category includes diverse modes such as "science fiction, fantasy, gothic, horror, utopian, and dystopian fiction" (Thaler 9), and their combination, which is most often the case in the works that I am considering here. Given its flexibility and, most especially, its "unrealistic" character, speculative fiction constitutes a privileged space for social critique that offers us cautionary tales, as "it shows us our nightmares and therefore contributes to our efforts to avoid them" (Urbanski 1). In *Black Atlantic Speculative Fictions*,[3] Ingrid Thaler argues that this term foregrounds the politics and aesthetics of texts in their relation to time and history (9), and this is also my own position regarding the fiction of the four authors surveyed here, Goto, Hopkinson, Lai, and Mayr.[4] In the face of the current political despair under rampant neoliberalism and the apparent lack of alternatives to "the domination of transnational capital, the failures of the nation-state, of identity politics, of popular revolution" (I am quoting Daniel Coleman's thoughtful editorial comments offered during revisions of this chapter), these authors choose affirmative politics of the kind that Braidotti associates with the posthuman (*Posthuman* 5) when they speculate about their social context taking into account the histories of the dispossessed, the displaced, the exiled, the migrant, the multitude. By choosing this genre, they also make a significant break from the almost compulsory autoethnographic mode demanded of racialized authors by globalized cultural markets,[5] while inserting new subversive perspectives into a long tradition of feminist speculative fiction; in the English language, this tradition has been traced back to Margaret Cavendish's *A Blazing World* (1666), though Mary Shelley's *Frankenstein* (1818) is more frequently credited with its invention.

Speculative fiction has become a trendy topic in Canadian literary studies in the twenty-first century due in part to Margaret Atwood's intensive dedication to this genre since 2003 and the undeniable influence of her public profile. Given her international stature, an important number of recent studies on the genre have focused on her novels *Oryx and Crake* (2003), *The Year of the Flood* (2009), and *MaddAddam* (2013). Atwood has also contributed to the critical study of this genre with her collection of essays *In Other Worlds* (2011), which surprisingly (or not) does not recognize other Canadian authors who have greatly contributed to this form. Among them, the aforementioned quartet composed by Goto, Hopkinson, Lai, and Mayr, all of whom have also produced influential critical essays on the genre plus an outstanding body of speculative fiction from posthumanist queer perspectives. Some representative examples of their speculative novels are Goto's *The Kappa Child*, Lai's *When Fox Is a Thousand* and *Salt Fish Girl*, Hopkinson's *Midnight Robber*, *The Salt Roads*, *The New Moon's Arms*, *Sister Mine*, and *Falling in Love with Hominids*, or Mayr's *Moon Honey* and *Venous Hum*, among other works.[6] Their imaginative and innovative narratives have in many aspects preceded most of the issues addressed in Atwood's novels that are characteristic of this genre in the postmodern era, such as organ donations, cloning, environmental degradation, and the fierce exploitation of girls and women in ultra-capitalist societies. However, a very clear divergence can be easily identified when comparing the more radical sexual and racial politics in these queer racialized authors' texts with the more conservative heterosexual and white-centred approach predominant in Atwood's trilogy.[7]

In previous essays, I have studied these four authors' texts focusing on their anti-racist and anti-capitalist aspects, always in relation to their literary poetics (see Martín-Lucas 2012, for instance); here, in contrast, I intend to approach primarily their queer politics by putting in relation the queer (post)identities and affect modes represented in selected narratives by these four authors, the queerness of speculative fiction as a genre, and the alleged "queerness" of the Canadian postcolonial nation.[8] None of these political coordinates—racism, capitalism, sexism, homophobia—operates in isolation, and it is precisely the "interlocking systems of oppressions," in Patricia Hill Collins's phrasing—or rather, the "intertwined relations of intersectionality and assemblages" in Jasbir Puar's—that they present that makes these texts so relevant to contemporary theorizations of the queer posthuman/posthuman queer. Among them, Braidotti's pedagogical revision of Enlightenment humanism and contemporary subjectivity in *The Posthuman* is particularly relevant to my critical reading of these figures.

Queer Posthumans

In my essay "Of Aliens, Monsters, and Vampires," I contextualized the speculative fiction of this group as part of a more general critique of the official discourses of multiculturalism in Canada that gained full force in the 1990s, the moment when these authors were first emerging in the literary sphere. Those were days of important cultural identity struggles, and I have argued in that essay that the mutant and alien characters they portray may be strategically read as imaginative resistance to the labelling and cataloguing in ethnic and racial terms characteristic of official multiculturalism in Canada.[9] Their emphasis on the morphing body offers a conceptualization of identity that is, literally, fluid, transsexual, transgender, often trans-species, and it creatively contributes to the theorizing of what Braidotti has defined, in relation to Haraway's theories, as "high post-humanism" ("Posthuman" 197). This term signals the twofold dimension of posthumanism: "the first concerns the philosophical posthumanism that is the trademark of the post-structuralist generation; the second is a more targeted form of post-anthropocentrism that is not as widespread" ("Posthuman" 197). In *The Posthuman*, Braidotti explains that

> The human of Humanism is neither an ideal nor an objective statistical average or middle ground. It rather spells out a systematized standard of recognizability—of Sameness—by which all others can be assessed, regulated and allotted to a designated social location. The human is a normative

> convention, which does not make it inherently negative, just highly regulatory and hence instrumental to practices of exclusion and discrimination. The human norm stands for normality, normalcy and normativity. It functions by transposing a specific mode of being human as the universalized format of humanity. This standard is posited as categorically and qualitatively distinct from the sexualized, racialized, naturalized others and also in opposition to the technological artefact. The human is a historical construction that became a social convention. (26)

The unitary subject of humanism—visually represented by the Vitruvian Man—reduces all its others to sub-human status, and this has been fiercely criticized from anti-humanist positions (postcolonial and feminist). But as Braidotti points out in the same work, there are positive aspects in humanism that not even anti-humanists wish to get rid of, for example: emancipation, solidarity, community-bonding, social justice, or secularism, among others (29). To escape this paradox, the posthuman is born: "Posthumanism is the historical moment that marks the end of the opposition between Humanism and anti-humanism and traces a different discursive framework, looking more affirmatively towards new alternatives...towards elaborating alternative ways of conceptualizing the human subject" (37). This new subject is "the posthuman," and posthuman subjectivity as conceptualized by Braidotti is "materialist and vitalist, embodied and embedded, firmly located somewhere, according to feminist 'politics of location'" (51).[10] The posthuman is an ethical subject with "an enlarged sense of community, which includes one's own territorial or environmental inter-connections" (Braidotti, *The Posthuman* 190).

In her final conclusions to *The Posthuman*, Braidotti affirms that "human embodiment and subjectivity are currently undergoing a profound mutation" (196), and speculative fiction is an optimum mode for exploring such new forms of subjectivity. The trope of the mutant hybrid offers an obvious resistance to normative categorization that brilliantly illustrates queer posthumanism's re-vision of identity. Like Braidotti, Hardt and Negri defend in *Commonwealth* the value of identity politics against the fierce attacks of postmodernity, in their case as a pedagogical tool that teaches us strategies of resistance and creativity for a new world of non-identities, since the ultimate goal of any revolutionary identity politics is its self-abolition (326). They point to radical feminism, queer politics, and black radicalism as exemplary post-identity projects that link identity politics to a critique of identity (334–36). A crucial point that most theorists agree upon is that these post-identitarian projects will not bring a world of sameness, a world without difference. As Eve Sedgwick incisively pointed out, the denaturalizing of body categories that feminist, queer, and anti-racist theories have so extensively and intensively developed has not managed to *eradicate* the binary logics of the oppressive ideologies they oppose because, as she affirms employing a Deleuzian image, "they're rhizomatic—they can't be killed by pulling up one root" (22). An effective solution must come, necessarily, from escaping binarism via an emphasis on the interrelation of multiplicity and singularity.

In the speculative fiction of Lai, Goto, Hopkinson, and Mayr, hybrid characters embody an excessive (abjectively overflowing) proliferation of *differences*, in the plural; they accumulate differences—in terms of race, culture, gender, sex, class—in an "exaggerated ethnoscape [where] to be hybrid means more than taking on bicultural practices; instead hybridity is used at the physical genetic or biological level" (Ty 94). Eleanor Ty is referring here to Larissa Lai's Sonias in the novel *Salt Fish Girl*, a patented new cyborg species cloned from a mixture of carpian and human biomaterials, who epitomize the neoliberal exploitation of Asian female flexible workers (in Aiwha Ong's terminology) and organized resistance to it. The Sonias speak a hybrid language that mixes Chinese, English, Spanish, and French (*Salt Fish Girl* 222), that is, a language of colonial roots that serves Lai to link the new forms of globalized neoliberal imperialism to their colonial foundations.[11] Sonia 113, who prefers to be called Evie, has a love relationship with Miranda, the protagonist of the futuristic sections of the novel (set between 2044 and 2062) who becomes pregnant from eating a genetically engineered durian fruit. Genetic hybridity relates "humans" and "clones" in the novel into a common interspecies "kinship," complicating any definition of "family" in a way that seems directly inspired by Haraway's famous questions in her *Modest_ Witness@Second_Millennium*:

> Who are my kin in this odd world of promising monsters, vampires, surrogates, living tools, and aliens? How are natural kinds identified in the realms of technoscience? What kinds of crossings and offspring count as legitimate and illegitimate, to whom and at what cost? Who are my familiars, my siblings, and what kind of livable world are we trying to build? (52)

For Haraway, kinship in the posthuman era is a relation based not on blood, but on choice, and it generates politics founded on "affinity, not identity" (*Simians* 155). The definition of the family is a very important theme in Lai's two novels. *When Fox Is a Thousand* complicates the heteronormative nuclear family by introducing transracial adoption, while in *Salt Fish Girl* cloning and "pregnancy by fruit ingestion" make it impossible to clearly define family origins: Miranda wants to tell her lover Evie, "I am your grandmother,...the maker of your maker" (253), while Dr. Flowers, the evil representative of neoliberal Life manipulation (I'm echoing here Braidotti's phrasing in *The Posthuman*), is first claimed as a father by Evie—"I'm here to see my father" (254)—just to be renounced a few paragraphs later: "You got rid of me. You put me back in the factories. I am not your daughter any more" (255). Since "heterosexuality is a script that binds the familial with the global" (Ahmed, *Cultural Politics* 144) in order to contest globalization, as *Salt Fish Girl* does, the heteronormative family must be put under suspicion, at the very least. Commenting on Lai's disruption of the narrative of origins, Sharlee Reimer emphasizes that "if most political movements are built upon a sense of shared identity categories—many of which are linked to biologized categories (or shared origins)—then a disruption of the centrality of shared origins to political movements affords the possibility of considering shared experience as a basis for political action" (5). Nicholas Birns proposes the term "transfeminism" to describe the deep emotional ties between hybrid figures in *Salt Fish Girl*, where it signals the possibility of political coalition based on "reciprocal, mutual acceptance" (10) of differences.

Although Lai's Sonias are perhaps the example—among the ones I am studying here—that has been more often studied in relation to Haraway's cyborgian politics (e.g., Birns, Lee, Mansbridge, R. Morris, Reimer), they are not the only genetic hybrids to develop such politics of affect. The kappa child in Goto's novel of the same title is the hybrid progeny of a Stranger with an "oddly shaped head" (88) and "a strangely formed hand" (120), first identified as a female and later referred to as a "person of questionable gender and racial origin" (121), and the narrator, who becomes abnormally pregnant during a night of "queer" sex under the stars which is described as sumo wrestling (123–24). Despite the bad press in Japanese folktales of the kappa as the evil figure "who drowned children and livestock, who caressed the bottoms of beautiful women" (*Kappa Child* 229), the novel recurrently portrays interspecies affect in positive terms and the novel closes on a most hopeful note when "humans and kappas dance together, our lives unfurling before us" (275). These final lines are followed by a brief epilogue that can be read as the novel's final call to, if not celebrate, at least accept posthuman hybridity, when the voice of the kappa child directly addresses the reader with the following request: "I am a creature of water. I am a kappa child. Come, embrace me" (276).

Hopkinson similarly draws on folklore—black Caribbean in her case—to create the douen people in *Midnight Robber*, or the shape-shifting sea people in *The New Moon's Arms*, to mention just a couple of examples of her many becoming-animal hybrids, all of whom are closely related by Hopkinson to colonial oppression in the Caribbean and its ongoing effects on a transnational level. Chichibud, the protagonist "creature"/"douen" in *Midnight Robber* is described as a sort of hybrid with a bird-like head, four-finger hands, goat-like feet, and "something looking like a pocket of flesh at its crotch" for genitalia (92). This becoming-animal figure gives voice to a posthuman critique of anthropocentric humanism and its obsession with hierarchical taxonomy;[12] during his very first encounter with Tan Tan (the heroine in the novel) and Antonio (her abusive father) when Antonio refers to "the creature" as "the beast," Chichibud replies, "Beast that could talk and know it own mind. Oonuh tall people quick to name what is people and what is beast" (92). The posthuman douen's ethics will prove to be more compassionate and protective of the dispossessed than those of the exiled humans colonizing their planet.[13] The douen people in *Midnight Robber* clearly represent the colonized indigenous peoples of the Caribbean, with frequent allusions to the violent encounter of "newcomers" and indigenous communities. This first meeting of Chichibud with Antonio and Tan-Tan refers to the colonization of the Caribbean through Chichibud's sarcastic criticism of the exchange of pens and beads for vital resources like water and food, and, as in the case of the Sonias that I mentioned earlier, his knowledge of the languages of "the tallpeople"—"Anglopatwa, Francopatwa, Hispanopatwa, and Papiamento" (95)—which the douens have learned "for oonu don't learn we own" (95). Even the fact that the douens call themselves by that name because this is what the newcomers called them replicates the Europeans' labelling of the indigenous as "Indians" in the Caribbean.

After Tan-Tan kills her father while he's raping her, Chichibud offers her shelter in the secret home of the douens, where they have kept themselves apart from "the tallpeople" "even though we sharing the same soil, same water, same air" (173). The interspecies hostility between "humans" and "beasts" is bridged in the act of hospitality offered by Chichibud despite the high risk for the future survival of the douens this entails: "Come in peace to my home, Tan-Tan. And when you go, go in friendship" (179). For me, the positive interspecies affects developed in *Midnight Robber*, as with those in *The Kappa Child* or *Salt Fish Girl*, reflect Braidotti's and Haraway's similar understanding of affectivity, where

> the emphasis falls on a cognitive brand of empathy, or intense affinity: it is the capacity for compassion, which combines the power of understanding with

the force to endure in sympathy with a people, all of humanity, the planet and civilization as a whole. It is an extra-personal and a trans-personal capacity, which should be driven away from any universalism and grounded instead in the radical immanence of a sense of belonging to and being accountable for a community, a people and a territory. (Braidotti, "Posthuman" 205)

In Mayr's novels, hybridity is associated with sudden transformations of the human body, and it has been critically read as expressing a concern for the status of mixed-race citizens in a multicultural society regulated by ethnicity into neat identity compartments (Vernon, "Suzette Mayr") In *Moon Honey*, "metamorphosis always signals a happy alternative" (Mayr, *Moon Honey* 113). The main mutation is that of its protagonist, Carmen, a white-middle-class-good-civic Canadian who, during a discussion over racism with her boss, a South Asian Canadian woman, reproduces the liberal discourse of official multiculturalism in an idyllic appeal to common universal humanness as she demands of Rama: "Educate me, says Carmen. Show me where all this racism is, why you are so angry and bitchy all the time. Show me. If I cut you you bleed, if I cut me I bleed, we're all the same underneath. Show me the difference. Show me the difference!" (21). It is at this moment that Carmen's skin turns darker, her hair "curls and frizzes, shortens" (23) and she becomes a black woman. From this moment on she will inhabit a new (dark) skin to experience how dramatically skin-colour change affects her social status, life standards, and emotional life, especially when her white boyfriend abandons her. At one point she considers trespassing the line of heteronormativity, when she first meets some lesbian friends, though she finds this a bit too much to deal with because "she's not prepared to become a lesbian. She's finally gotten her life together" (86). She is speaking from a normative white heterosexual stance which she resists abandoning, one that sees "race" and "sexuality" as separate layers of identity that, like Tetris blocks, are piling up onto her body to crash her to the very bottom of the social scale. Since the sudden darkening of her skin seems irreversible, she chooses to suppress her homoerotic desires in order to conform, at least sexually, to social expectations.

Venous Hum, Mayr's novel about migrant vegetarian vampires turned cannibals, opens with Trudeau's famous promises of multicultural conviviality and sexual freedom:

> In December 1967...Trudeau said, "The state has no place in the bedrooms of the nation," and the beds of many nations promptly spun out of control.
>
> In 1971, Pierre Elliott Trudeau, as Prime Minister of Canada, brought in an official Policy of Multiculturalism that proclaimed, Bonjour, You are invited, Hello, Vous êtes invités, to the thousands of non-European immigrants who had been flooding the country since the early 1960s. Those who never felt comfortable suddenly were *home*. At the time, Trudeau sported a long, flowing haircut.
>
> Canada's hair has been disheveled ever since. (*Venous Hum* 11)

This novel offers a hilarious and profound critique of the interlocking oppressions operating in post-Trudeau multicultural Canada: homophobia, racism, sexism, and classism are "unpalatable" and difficult to "digest." To represent this, Mayr has Louve, a hardworking migrant mother, feel "sicker and sicker...fully nauseated" (Mayr, *Venous Hum* 222) after having sucked all the blood off the drunken heteronormative married (unfaithful) white man who happened to be the lover of her lesbian married (unfaithful) daughter, Lai Fun.

As in the case of *Moon Honey*, racial hybridity and sexual deviance from the heterosexual norm are a source of social ostracism for the main character in *Venous Hum*, Lai Fun, who carries both marks of monstrosity, as she is both queer and the mixed-race daughter of immigrants to Canada: Fritz-Peter and Louve. In her acute analysis of this novel as an "Albertan revenge comedy" (subtitle of her essay), Nicole Markotić reminds us that "the monster in folklore has traditionally represented mixed-race characters, whom readers abhor because the very idea of mixing up bodily binaries both terrifies and exhilarates" (73) and she observes that "the monster as hybrid identity threatens stability in that it cannot be only one thing, but manifestly embodies a corporeal mix" (70). Apparently, Lai Fun has reached a certain social "stability" via her same-sex marriage and motherhood, as she insisted on getting married "to stop their child from being a bastard" (18) and the sperm donor is her wife's brother "so they could both be blood related to the baby" (19).[14] While achieving this status of social respectability in an allegedly post-Trudeauian "disheveled" Canada, however, Lai Fun seems to be suffering from a sort of "feminine mystique" syndrome in her role as the expectant wife of a workaholic woman who is often too tired to make love to her. She not only embarks in the organizing of a high school reunion to gather a group of former classmates she had never liked—a quest that will, literally, "unearth" the ghosts of her past, embodied by the vampiric Mrs. Blake—but she also "enters an adulterous relationship with her friend's husband rather than uphold her own sexuality and heritage" (Markotić 72). Lai Fun's domestic situation thus mirrors heterosexual traditional family patterns; her need to fit into "normal" society (via marriage, pregnancy, and even adultery) may be interpreted as a comment on the pressure for "happiness" that heterosexual society associates with "a good life," one that makes of the family something good and desirable "not because it causes happiness, or not even because it affects us in a good way, but if we share an orientation toward the family as being good, as being what promises happiness in return for loyalty" (Ahmed, "Happiness" 4). Lai Fun summarizes this illusion as follows: "What is her purpose, really? Good wife, good mother, good employee? These are words they use in movies and magazines, but how do you verb the adjective 'good'?" (30). Lai Fun's "failure" to be satisfied with this normative happiness may be read as an illustrative example of the "queer unhappiness" theorized by Sara Ahmed as a form of political dissidence. Resisting a notion of heteronormative "happiness" that functions as a potent instrument of social control, Ahmed proposes that "the unhappiness of the deviant performs a claim for justice" ("Happiness" 11). In the novel, Lai Fun's identitarian anxiety leads the narrative towards its excessive, gory final banquet where all "monsters" leave aside their social masks (and prudent vegetarianism) to have their own "reunion dinner," hosted by Louve and Fritz-Peter (227–29). Lai Fun "tries not to look at the table strewn with the roasted and fried and fricassed parts of her ex-lover" (228) and focuses instead on recovering Jenniffer's love. This cannibalistic extravaganza where the white, middle-class, male Canadian is consumed constitutes a grotesque satirical exaggeration of the "fear of immigrants" that Mrs. Blake had previously voiced when confronting Louve:

> You've been feeding on children, says Louve....
> I am just doing my job, says Mrs. Blake. Assimilating them. You parading around here like this is your home, like you were born here, like you own the rules. Who gets to feed on whom! Taking jobs away from people who deserve them and were here first. You are an invader. You're not only a creep and a bum, you're a monster and a freak. (219)

In the face of such a racist discourse, still too familiar even in globalized multicultural societies, the cannibalist banquet becomes a literal act of poetic justice.

Posthuman Singularities in the Multitude

The intersection of a multiplicity of differences constitutes the singularity of the posthuman body, which is in constant metamorphosis. Singularity is one of the key concepts in Hardt and Negri's trilogy, which they define as a "social subject whose difference cannot be reduced to sameness, a difference that remains different" (*Multitude* 99); the multitude is then composed of plural singularities, versus the unity of "the people," who share a common identity. Reiichi Miura further explains Hardt and Negri's concept by pointing out that "a singular subject is irreplaceable even if there were to exist precisely the same human being, or even a clone, identical in every possible way" (64); Larissa Lai's "more human than human's" cyborg Evie stands for this idea. I find useful Hardt and Negri's concept of the multitude and its living social flesh: an elusive shapeshifting monster "from the perspective of political order and control" (*Multitude* 192), which can be translated—in the Canadian multiculturalist jargon—as simply "unmanageable." Identity is therefore not denied, but conceived of as a political strategy that allows diverse, even contradictory, alliances among singular members of the multitude. The narratives reflect the ambivalent desire for identification of marginalized individuals who, even in postmodernity, continue de facto to be grouped according to their skin colour, gender, sexuality, and/or ethnicity. As Thaler has pointed out, "reaffirming the persistence of identity, the texts seek to transcend these accepted categories in search of de-essentialized affiliations in literary-speculative imaginary spaces and tropes" (131). In relation to this, it is important to keep in mind that the posthuman figures in those novels bring different cosmologies and epistemologies that are often "foreign" to Western anthropocentrism and correspond with what Braidotti defined as the "new conceptual style that refuses to engage in negative criticism for its own sake and acts instead from positive and empowering relationships" ("Posthuman" 205). And in most of the cases analyzed, these relationships are "posthumanly queer."

Judith Halberstam and Ira Livingston's definition of the posthuman underlines the resistance to categorization at the core of its very ontology; while "the human functions to domesticate and hierarchize difference within the human (whether according to race, class, gender [or sexuality]) and to absolutize difference between the human and the nonhuman" (Halberstam and Livingston 10), the posthuman, on the other hand, "participates in re-distributions of difference and identity" (10). In this radical resistance to taxonomy, the posthuman is implicitly queer, "a (non)identity category that, like the category of 'queer' in analyses of human sexual identities, can fold into itself a wide range of potential significations, including bodies that are redolent of difference and perversity" (Hollinger 270). This is not an abstract or metaphorical abuse of the catch word *queer* as a mere symbolic signifier of ambivalence or plurality, but a whole reconceptualization of sexual politics from a perspective where the human body is itself reconfigured, as Hardt and Negri explain when they observe that "conventional norms of corporeal and sexual relations between and within genders are increasingly open to challenge and transformation. Bodies themselves transform and mutate to create new posthuman bodies" (*Empire* 215). New medical improvements that contribute to the redefinition of gender and sexual identities by altering naturalistic assignation of gender and sex onto bodies, together with "technological advances—cloning, gene manipulation, etc.—[that] erode the biological imperative for heterosexuality as a means of procreation, making the social stigma against same-sex relations even less relevant" (Schimel 14) led Richard Labanté and Lawrence Schimel to optimistically proclaim that *The Future Is Queer* (title of the science fiction anthology they co-edited, published by Arsenal Pulp Press in 2006). Still, although many of the narratives we have examined above explore and celebrate such new paths towards a "happily queer" future (Ahmed's cautions notwithstanding), their engagement in queer politics remains firm in their denunciation of the staunch resistance to change of a yet strong heteronormative and homophobic society and of the many forms of symbolic and material violence, from insults and harassment of gay students in the horrific high school portrayed by Mayr in *Venous Hum* to the crimes of gay bashing and murder in Larissa Lai's *When Fox Is a Thousand*. These narratives thus constitute good examples of queer speculative fiction, examples that "remind us that the subject of queer theory—the role of normativity and Cartesian thinking on human sexualities, both as actual practices and as epistemologies—exists within a field of conflicting discourses, each of which has material effects on the everyday lives of real people" (Pearson, Hollinger, and Gordon, 3).

Conclusion

Speculative fiction is a fertile ground for the growth of the posthuman and a good source of metaphors for the philosophers of our days, as we have seen. As Wendy Pearson has pointed out, speculative fiction is a perfect genre "to imagine alternative possibilities for the ways in which we live, and love, in the world" (307); she considers it especially important to portray non-normative sexualities and invites authors to "bring on the lesbian, gay, and bisexual vampires, and the queer blue aliens" (307). However, I think it is important to remind us all that the four authors who have imagined the posthuman affects I am describing here are cultural activists engaged in anti-racist, queer, and feminist politics. Commenting on her choice of speculative fiction in relation to her queer politics, Hopkinson calls our attention to how "the people who are courageously non-normative in their sexualities are doing in the real world some of the work that speculative fiction can do in the world of imagination, that is, exploring a wider range of possibilities for living" (Johnston 203). The exercise in speculation at work in these narratives is, I would argue, solid "historically-informed extrapolation from current tendencies" (499), a phrase that Nick Dyer-Witheford employed in reference to the catastrophic futures engendered by current economic globalization but that I find perfectly describes the kind of vision these four authors offer us. Now that "The monsters begin to form new, alternative networks of affection and social organization" (Hardt and Negri, *Multitude* 193) it is perhaps time to fully join them in their struggle towards a new form of posthumanity because, again following Hardt and Negri, "when love is conceived politically, then, this creation of a new humanity is the ultimate act of love" (*Multitude* 356).

Notes

1. While Hopkinson, Goto, and Lai are first-generation migrants to Canada, born elsewhere, Suzette Mayr was born in Canada, of mixed racial origins.

2. At the risk of oversimplification, given the extensive analysis of this concept in their trilogy, we could define the *multitude* as a neo-Marxist term referring to a new form of social subjectivity different from the people, the masses, and the working class, all of which cancel differences and depend on unity, indifference, or exclusivity, respectively. In the Preface to *Multitude,* Hardt and Negri describe it in the following terms: "The multitude is composed of innumerable internal differences that can never be reduced to a unity or a single identity—different cultures, races, ethnicities, genders, and sexual orientations; different forms of labor; different ways of living; different views of the world; and different desires. The multitude is a multiplicity of all these singular differences....The challenge posed by the concept of multitude is for a social multiplicity to manage to communicate and act in common while remaining internally different" (*Multitude* xiv). The speculative texts to be analyzed here provide, I think, interesting examples of this social subject.

3. Thaler's book includes a chapter dedicated to Nalo Hopkinson's *Midnight Robber,* a novel Thaler describes as "a postcolonial dream of a better world that embraces the technotropes of cyberpunk and science fiction" (98). Thaler contextualizes Hopkinson primarily as a black Caribbean within the black Atlantic.

4. Although the four authors under review are deeply concerned with the link of history to contemporary injustices, Lai's strategy of having a shapeshifter—the Fox and Nu Wa, in *When Fox Is a Thousand* and *Salt Fish Girl,* respectively—moving across diverse chronological moments makes this connection most explicit. Commenting on Lai's second novel, Eleanor Ty emphasizes this political goal, that I would make extensive to the rest of the speculative works by this group: "Instead of seeing a break between the myths, histories, and traditions of the past and the postindustrial, scientific, fragmented, and sanitized world of the postmodern, Lai stresses the parallels between them and shows the value of remembrance and unforgetfulness at the same time that she seeks to rework a past that effaces the histories of the dispossessed" (91).

5. See Graham Huggan's very influential *The Postcolonial Exotic* (2001) for a more general approach to autoethnography in the global market, and Ty and Verduyn's edited collection *Asian Canadian Writing beyond Autoethnography* (2008) for a more specific study in the Canadian context.

6. The four of them have also published speculative short stories, some of which will be employed here for the analysis of queer affect, especially those in Goto's *Hopeful Monsters* and Hopkinson's *Skin Folk.* Hopkinson and Goto have published speculative fiction for youth; although I am not using these youth novels here, I find their contribution to youth literature a major and important form of social activism. Goto, Lai, and Mayr have also produced poetry that addresses similar issues.

7. A full comparative analysis is beyond the scope of this chapter. Suffice it here to notice there is an obvious majority of white protagonists in Atwood's speculative novels, and sexual relationships are all heterosexual, with the exception of the bioengineered Crackers, who become polysexual during the mating season; these posthuman creatures are presented as naive children in need of guidance, and a source of humour.

8. In her study of Canadian queer literary and visual cultures, Wendy Pearson examines "both the inherent Canadian-ness of queer culture, the potentially ineluctable queerness of Canadian culture" (68), which she attributes to the "queer" postcolonial position of Canada as an ex-colony of European powers, a colonizer of its Indigenous nations, and a nation currently subservient to the United States. Other pioneer analyses of the "queering Canada" project are Peter Dickinson's *Here Is Queer: Nationalisms, Sexualities and the Literatures of Canada* and Terry Goldie's *Pink Snow: Homotextual Possibilities in Canadian Fiction*. Libe García Zarranz's *TransCanadian Feminist Fictions: New Cross-Border Ethics*, in a great part coincides in its theoretical framework with my own approach here. This book studies, among other texts, youth fiction by Hiromi Goto.

9. Despite this resistance, critical studies of their works—mine included—tend to categorize these authors in terms of their ethnicity. Thus, Goto and Lai are often framed within Asian North American literary studies (e.g., Cuder-Domínguez, Martín-Lucas, and Villegas-López's *Transnational Poetics* or Ty's *Unfastened*); Hopkinson is generally reviewed as a black author or, more specifically, as black Caribbean (e.g., Barr's *Afro-Futures*, Thaler's *Black Atlantic Speculative Fictions*, Thomas's *Dark Matter*), and Suzette Mayr is included in studies of black Canadian and, more often, of mixed-race "zebra" poetics (e.g., Bast's *"The Quiltings of Human Flesh": Constructions of Racial Hybridity in Contemporary African-Canadian Literature*, G.E. Clarke's "Canadian Biraciality and its Zebra Poetics," or Petersen's "Defying Categorization," among others).

10. Braidotti distinguishes the posthuman—embodied and material—from the transhuman, which she describes as a "delirium of transcendence from the corporeal frame of the contemporary human" (*The Posthuman* 197).

11. A similar strategy can be found in Hopkinson's fiction, to which I will return.

12. On the becoming-animal trope and its relation to diverse indigenous philosophies in Hopkinson's novels, see Dubey, "Becoming Animal in Black Women's Science Fiction," and Dillon, "Indigenous Scientific Literacies in Nalo Hopkinson's Ceremonial Worlds," and "Totemic Human-Animal Relationships in Recent SF."

13. In *The New Moon's Arms* the sea people are descendants of shipwrecked slaves who were transformed by Uhamiri, a water divinity, into shapeshifters who alternate between human and seal forms. In *The Salt Roads*, colonial slavery is a predominant theme explicitly addressed by setting a large part of the novel in a Caribbean plantation.

14. In a novel on vampires, allusions to blood are of course doubly meaningful, and the tension between "full-blood" and "mixed-race" categories emerges recurrently in the novel. See Markotić, "Reunion: An Albertan Revenge Comedy," for a more detailed analysis of hemophobia and homophobia in relation to racial hybridity in *Venous Hum*.

IV

Border Zones

10

Unexpected Dialogical Space in David Albahari's Immigrant Writing

VESNA LOPIČIĆ AND MILENA KALIČANIN

"ARE YOU FROM GREECE?" a drunken Indigenous man asks the main protagonist of Serbian writer David Albahari's story "An Indian at Olympic Plaza." "No, I am from the country that is no more," he answers. "That's why you so easily get lost," the Indian responds (Albahari, "Indian" 82). This short exchange says a lot about three different cultures—Indigenous, diasporic, and settler—that meet in Calgary, or modern-day Canada in general. The two characters—representative of Indigenous people and the immigrant population, respectively—make a deal against the cultural backdrop of Calgary, the site of 1988 Olympic Games. Focusing on three of Albahari's works—"An Indian at Olympic Plaza," *Snow Man*, and "Learning Cyrillic"—this chapter explores how Albahari creates a dialogical space between characters, often between Indigenous people in Canada and Serbian immigrants, between Indigeneity and diaspora. We argue that the exchange of stories helps to create this dialogical space and that one of the consequences of this dialogical space is the implementation of a better kind of multiculturalism or, to borrow from Daniel

Coleman, the growth of "wry civility." Coleman explains, "My sense is that a 'wry' or critical inhabitation of civility requires a multiple, decentred consciousness, one that is aware of a whole range of contending civilities—that is, of competing, contemporaneous conceptions of what constitutes the polity, of the different conceptions in any given collective of who 'we' are, how 'we' got here, what the protocols for constructive dialogue should be" (Coleman, "Contented Civility" 230). The three "contending civilities" engaged in intercultural communication and constructive dialogue in Albahari's immigrant writing are Indigenous,[1] immigrant, and mainstream Canadian.

The phrase "a country that is no more" has an elegiac ring to it, with a twinge of regret or balladic nostalgia that can create an illusion of referring to bygone times, or to imaginary fairytale lands, safely removed from present-day reality. However, the hero of Albahari's story is in fact hinting at Yugoslavia, now so often referred to as the former Yugoslavia, as if there were the possibility of a future Yugoslavia. Evidently a recent immigrant to Canada, this character is still attentive to the presence of Indigenous people in the streets of Calgary, though they have become all but invisible to some Canadian nationals since normative Canadianness is taken to be white and British. They are "Indians" to him, which in Yugoslavia was a commonly accepted term for Indigenous people, without any derogatory connotations, contrary to the common practice in Canada where the word *Indian* is considered politically incorrect.

As an author of Jewish origin, Albahari is acutely aware that he is playing with volatile stereotypes that demand careful framing. His most critically acclaimed work is *Götz and Meyer*, a novel about the extermination of the Jews in a concentration camp in Belgrade during the Second World War. *Götz and Meyer* explores the banality of evil as reinforced by negative stereotypes. Albahari understands the effect that oversimplified and often misleading images and conceptions can have on individuals and whole nations, but he refuses to offer his readers alternative interpretations. By putting the unacceptable term "Indian" in the title of his story, he risks being misunderstood but

leaves it to the reader to reconsider the stereotypes that persist due to the lack
of dialogical interaction between ethnicities.

In the introductory chapter of *Exalted Subjects: Studies in the Making of Race and Nation in Canada*, Sunera Thobani explores the fabrications of nationhood by emphasizing the idea of the outsider. The outsider, most commonly perceived as "the stranger who wants what nationals have" (Thobani 4), provokes anxiety and hostility in the supposedly responsible, caring, compassionate, and law-abiding citizen, who is also presumably devoted to the values of diversity. In Albahari's novel *Snow Man*, this latter figure is represented by two characters, the Canadian political history teacher and the dean. "The nation of citizens," as Thobani terms it, has been menaced by various interlopers throughout history—Indigenous people, immigrants, and refugees—who have represented a threat to collective welfare and national stability with their "virulent, chaotic, criminal, and sometimes, even deadly menaces" (4). Thus, the master narrative of the nation has been necessarily separated from its idealized vision and corrupted by what are perceived to be the unreasonable practices of the "outsiders," including Indigenous people's relentless demands for "special treatment" in their claims to land and state funding and the implementation of diverse, "backward" cultural practices into the country, along with diseases and criminal groups, brought by immigrants.

Thobani's point about the relationship between the groups that constitute the notion of the Canadian Other (Indigenous people and immigrants) is relevant here. More specifically, Thobani deals with the issue of the colonial violence against the Indigenous population as a regrettable necessity in the formation of the Canadian nation. Viewed as being of national interest, criminal acts of murder, enslavement, and torture of the Indigenous population were given legal sanction that was central to "the constitution of nationals as 'law-abiding' even in their most murderous actions" (Thobani 10). In addition to the figure of heathen Native, essentially primal in nature, the figure of the immigrant has been constituted as "incommensurable with nationality"

(10). However, concentrated solely on gaining equality with nationals, immigrants have mostly ignored their own subordinate position in Canadian society and its implications as it relates to Indigenous peoples. Thobani writes,

> Most have largely forsaken the possibilities of building alliances with Aboriginal peoples, failing to imagine a future of sovereignty for them and what their own location within such a future might be...Relating to Aboriginal peoples largely through the national symbolic, upholding its imagining of the self-determination of Aboriginal peoples to be an impossible political objective, most immigrants continue to articulate their own interests only with regard to the status and interests of nationals. (17–18)

As one of these immigrants, the protagonist of Albahari's "An Indian at Olympic Plaza" would have most likely turned a blind eye to a drunken Roma in his hometown, but it seems that being an immigrant in Calgary has sensitized him to the position of the Other. When approached by the drunk man, the main character does not hurry past or ignore him; instead, he has a conversation with the stranger, intuitively opening an "ethical space of engagement" between Indigeneity and diaspora (Ermine 193). As an obviously recent immigrant—still confused, curious, and easily lost—he appreciates even chance encounters for the possibility of communication they may offer. An indication of loneliness and alienation, his readiness to get involved with the stranger leads to an unexpected cultural insight. He first asks the Indigenous man for his name, and then offers him twenty dollars for a heritage story that the Indian has heard from his elders. What the immigrant gives the Indigenous man in return, besides the promised money, is his own name and a vague allusion to his country of origin, the country that is no more: Yugoslavia.

Yugoslavia was formed in the Balkans in 1918 after the First World War as the Kingdom of Serbs, Croats, and Slovenes, as one of the Versailles states. In 1929 it was given the name of Yugoslavia by its king, Aleksandar, but after the Second World War the name was changed to the Federal People's Republic of Yugoslavia. We were born in that country, but by then, the name had evolved into the Socialist Federal Republic of Yugoslavia, which existed from 1946 to 1992. Since the beginning of the breakup of Yugoslavia, the part of the country we were born in changed its name a few more times: the Republic of Yugoslavia (1992–2003), Serbia and Montenegro (2003–2006), and finally the Republic of Serbia, which is its official name at the moment.

In its short history of eighty-eight years, the homeland of Albahari's hero (as well as Albahari and ourselves) experienced turbulent transformations and, like some kind of shapeshifter, changed its form and name seven times, which is probably the reason why the protagonist of the story cannot name his country. He knows that none of the names he could use would do justice to the history of that place or to his personal memories of it. A political history teacher in Albahari's 2005 novel *Snow Man* articulates this dilemma precisely: "If my figures are correct," he said, "there is not a single border here that has lasted for fifty years, not counting the ones imposed by natural features. During one century alone, every town became several, no language stood firm, people went to bed at night without knowing what place they would wake up in the next morning" (96). Each political transmogrification drew the borders along different lines, caused tragic migrations of the people, and produced extremes in group or personal identity formation, ranging from self-assured nationalistic zealots to insecure, bewildered, and indecisive persons.

Albahari's hero in *Snow Man* is an uncivil, disillusioned Yugoslav who cannot reasonably deal with the brutality of political transitions, especially those that include civil wars and humanitarian bombing. He is not simply nostalgic for his former country; rather, he feels utterly lost in the pattern of ever new beginnings, newly created political entities, the same old parties taking turns at governing the same new countries, the pattern of constant change but no real progress. He needs the maps on his walls to get oriented, to recover the meaning buried under the debris of political breakups and human slaughter. The maps temporarily provide him with the lost sense of stability, order, and safety that one commonly associates with home. For this reason, the Canadian political history teacher is probably right when he epigrammatically claims, "Nostalgia kills" (*Snow Man* 38).

Indeed, the Yugo-nostalgia that appeared in the wake of the civil wars is a defining characteristic of Albahari's disillusioned hero, although, for the Canadian teacher, "a country that is no more" is just a failed experiment. This is a judgement he delivers matter-of-factly, as if the man he is speaking to did not live this "experiment," as if the twenty-three million people of Yugoslavia could be the subjects of a political experiment. This remark stabs at the anarchist heart of the Yugoslavian writer-in-residence just as it would hurt the Serbian immigrant who was talking to the Indigenous person at Olympic Plaza, or many other citizens of Yugoslavia. In his frankness, the political history teacher is quite heartless, not realizing that one's country of birth, whether an experiment or not, whether it now exists or not, is still one's homeland. The writer-in-residence from Albahari's *Snow Man* is an older and more experienced man. He is, therefore, better aware of the complexity of political systems and social contexts and, owing to his historical consciousness, more appreciative of their positive aspects even though he does not forget the negative ones. His comprehensive understanding of the present moment makes him angry with the laconic conclusions of the political history teacher.

Just as the bitter feeling of homelessness due to political upheavals in their countries remains with some immigrants, Indigenous people may similarly harbour resentment for their treatment and displacement by the early invader-settlers and later by the Canadian government. It seems this is the reason why the Indigenous person and the immigrant in "An Indian at Olympic Plaza" can easily talk to each other: they share similar personal and collective experiences of dispossession and marginalization.

While the Indigenous and immigrant characters may share a moral vocabulary, Willie Ermine warns against universalizing; because world views are so disparate, societies so diverse, and political agendas so divergent, mutual understanding cannot be taken for granted, even in the case of underprivileged minority populations such as diaspora or Indigenous groups in Canada. Acknowledgement of difference, or affirmation of human diversity, is a necessary step towards dialogue: "the idea of the ethical space, produced by contrasting perspectives of the world, entertains the notion of a meeting place, or initial thinking about a neutral zone between entities or cultures" (Ermine 202).

In "An Indian at Olympic Plaza," Albahari provides space for "the poetics of relation" (Lai 124) by creating a meeting place for his characters that shows them not only how different they are but also that their encounter is meaningful. The scene of their meeting and exchange of names is charged with bitter irony. The immigrant's name is Ljubomir, which in Serbian and Croatian denotes the person who loves peace. Knowing a few things about the traditions of Indigenous people, Ljubomir expects the Indigenous man to produce a highly individualized personal name, something like "She Sees Deer" or "He Catches the Leaves."[2] Ljubomir is surprised to learn that the man's name is simply John. This detail hints at the history of colonization of the North American continent by European settlers—at the appropriation of the land inhabited by Indigenous peoples, the obstruction of their way of life, the devastation of their culture and customs, and the legal kidnapping of their children, who were put in residential schools to be assimilated. The colonial imposition of foreign names on Indigenous people symbolically dispossessed them of their original identity.[3]

For some critics, practices of colonialism continue in Canada's official policy of multiculturalism. For example, Himani Bannerji, a contemporary Bengali Canadian author, is among those who perceive multiculturalism as "a vehicle for racialization" (Bannerji 78). Her interpretation of Canadian multiculturalism rests on the dualism between the dominant "white" centre and oppressed "visible" margins or minorities. Theoretically, a diverse and pluralistic gathering of Canadian identities is a multicultural ideal to strive for; in practice, European whiteness is set as a standard for hegemonic Canadian identity:

> As long as "multiculturalism" only skims the surface of society, expressing itself as traditional ethics, such as arranged marriages, and ethnic food, clothes, songs and dances (thus facilitating tourism), it is tolerated by the state and "Canadians" as non-threatening. But if demands go a little deeper than that (e.g., teaching "other" religions or languages), they produce violent reaction, indicating a deep resentment. (Bannerji 79)

Justly integrating diverse ethnic groups under the concept of multiculturalism is a difficult task; however, while the differences between these groups seem to be huge, similar patterns in their historical backgrounds may unexpectedly knit them together in the fabric of Canadian identities if the power of exchanging stories is recognized. Listening to the other person's story is a sign of respect and acknowledgement, which are necessary if a productive alliance is to be made between Indigeneity and diaspora to turn the world to respectful balance (Lai 102).

Another story by Albahari, "Learning Cyrillic," provides a good example of bonding between representatives of Indigenous and immigrant populations. A Serbian teacher in a cold Canadian city who teaches the second- and third-generation children how to write the alphabet of the homeland meets Thunder Cloud in front of his Orthodox church and starts a friendly relationship with him. The point is that these two marginalized individuals, who should have been integrated through the strategies of multiculturalism, find a common language between themselves more easily than in mainstream society. It seems that the policy of multiculturalism has not failed: the teacher has a job at a local Orthodox church, and the Siksika man's band is well represented at a local museum. However, Thunder Cloud is visible only to the teacher, and the teacher is misunderstood both by the Serbian priest and his young students. The comforts of a high standard of living are there, just like in Albahari's *Snow Man*, but what is missing is the cohesive agent, the cultural glue that keeps people together in lasting relationships. The two characters achieve this cohesion by exchanging their stories after disclosing their names to each other.

Thunder Cloud reveals to the teacher that his whole family died from drink. He explains the origin of his great-grandfather's name, Black Otter; the destiny of Crowfoot, the greatest Siksika chief; the customs related to unfaithful husbands and wives; and the story of Napi, their deity. Thunder Cloud takes the teacher to the museum to show him his culture, and the teacher takes Thunder Cloud to a patron saint's day party to show him Serbian customs that have been preserved by the diaspora in Canada, and teaches him the basics of Christianity. While everybody else has prejudices regarding these two men and their social and ethnic backgrounds, the two of them develop a bond, a sort of "kinship in difference" (Lai 102) through the stories they exchange. Thunder Cloud in fact instructs both the teacher and his students on the value of storytelling: "'When we want to learn about a thing,' says Thunder Cloud, 'they tell us the story of how it came into the world. Everything has its own story,' he says, 'every living and non-living thing, and when you know its story, then you know the thing the story is about'" (101).

This is how Thunder Cloud makes the teacher tell his students and Thunder Cloud himself the story of Cyrillic letters, which finally makes the Serbian-descended students pay attention in their heritage class. Bridging the gap between cultures cannot be achieved by sharing a common history, since their pasts are not the same, but by learning each other's stories. To the children in the class, stories of the Serbian past are as remote as the stories of the past of Indigenous people. Still, if they are to be among those who develop the idea of multiculturalism in modern Canada, they need to know as many of these stories as possible to avoid the pitfalls of master discourses, which tend to blur the borders between ethnic groups and downplay significant historical and cultural differences.

Creating the character of Thunder Cloud as a storyteller, Albahari seems to share the views of Niigonwedom James Sinclair, an Anishinaabe academic who discusses the roles of storytelling in Indigenous cultures in his article "Trickster Reflections":

> Native storytellers of the Americas are not interested in giving up their own, nor their nations' creative and critical sovereignties. In fact, many seem to privilege their specific Indigenous identities, cultures, and communities. Even if stories are told about acquiescing to colonialism, giving up local identities, and "cultural death," they most often teach about the importance, responsibilities, and relevance of family, community, nationhood—not that they must be cast away. (Sinclair 42)

This is exactly why Thunder Cloud shares his culturally specific stories, which are "very much dynamic, complex, and alive today" (Sinclair 47), with the Serbian teacher. He teaches the teacher about historical Siksika personages as well as about everyday experiences of his people, showing them in all their human power and frailty as individual human beings who, by that determinant, deserve respect. That is how he exercises what Larissa Lai calls "the politics and practice of respect," which is achieved by placing "racialized settlers in conversation with Indigenous people" (Lai 108) to the effect that their differences, or "opposed and at times mutually hostile political and cultural values" (Coleman, "Indigenous Place," 62), are acknowledged and the space for dialogue is created. The stories of Thunder Cloud resist assimilation and help tribal members participate in communal knowledge, which is the best way to preserve it. Communal knowledge is "a fundamental affirmation of the Indian nationhood of a specific community that expresses a tribal-specific identity that's rooted somewhere in a tribal-specific language, sacred history, ceremonial cycle, and geography" (214), Daniel Heath Justice explains in his Cherokee literary history. It is no less important that members of other communities, a Serbian diaspora in this case, also hear these culturally specific stories, which further help to dismantle stereotypes produced by imperial dangerous discourses that, through multicultural policies, aim either at assimilation or othering. Thunder Cloud effectively does "memory work on knowledge" (Ermine 202), which Ermine believes is the task of the community intent on preserving its values.

With this idea in mind, in "An Indian at Olympic Plaza" Albahari casts John, by imbuing him with storytelling skill, as another typical representative of Indigenous people who does memory work on knowledge for the sake of his community. Albahari takes the view that ethnicity and nationhood are preserved in narrative knowledge (Bhabha, "Narrating" 360), which is John's case because, despite his low social and economic status, he still knows and tells the stories of his ancestors. Although John's Indigenous heritage is not specified, and although he is not individualized but rather stereotyped, Albahari manages to shape him as an interesting character who becomes a repository of some qualities that are important to many Indigenous communities. For example, in an interesting plot turn, instead of buying some pot or giving spare change to John, Ljubomir offers him twenty dollars in exchange for a story. This is how this immigrant taps into what is most significant to Indigenous people—their rootedness in the land through the stories they tell about it, or through "the emplaced knowledges," to use a phrase from Coleman ("Indigenous Place" 65). John readily tells Ljubomir the myth of the Corn Woman, grabs the money, and disappears. Two details in this scene merit special attention: the choice of the story and the fact that John seems to be a disappearing figure.

It is relevant that John, who the story suggests is victimized by social ills that accompany the stereotypical marginalized modern-day Indigenous person, proves to be still connected to an oral tradition that characterizes Indigenous cultures. His willingness to tell a story to a stranger shows that he still shares a cultural understanding of stories as meaningful. At the beginning of his book *If This Is Your Land, Where Are Your Stories?*, Edward Chamberlin recounts a meeting between a Native American community and some government officials about land rights. His description of this encounter reflects the values of stories that John, too, retains:

> Finally one of the elders put what was bothering them in the form of a question. "If this is your land," he asked, "where are your stories?" He spoke in English,

but then moved into Gitksan, the Tsimshian language of his people—and told a story. All of a sudden everyone understood...even though the government foresters didn't know a word of Gitksan, and neither did some of his Gitksan companions. But what they understood was more important: how stories give meaning and value to the places we call home; how they bring us close to the world we live in by taking us into a world of words; how they hold us together and at the same time keep us apart. (1)

Chamberlin's words echo with Albahari's ideas in *Snow Man*, "An Indian at Olympic Plaza," and "Learning Cyrillic." Stories are indispensable for the creation and preservation of one's identity, and their exchange can allow for a successful intercultural communication. As Sinclair explains in his discussion of storytelling among the Anishinaabeg, storytelling is "a complex historical, social, and political process embedded in the continuance of our collective presence, knowledge, and peoplehood" (23) whose aim is "to honour, maintain, and critically strengthen relationships between themselves, their communities, and the universe" (26). The emphasis is on the living, modern voices of the storytellers who create and disseminate culturally significant knowledge, as opposed to the idea of "de-historicised Indigenous artists" (Fagan 9) as vague shamanistic figures of the past, or the presumption that Indigenous heritage is archaic and quickly disappearing.

In relation to the significance of "voice," Rey Chow demonstrates the pitfalls of "privileged speech": "What one can do without is the illusion that, through privileged speech, one is helping to save the wretched of the earth" (Chow, "Against the Lures" 42). Instead of having their voice appropriated as the voice of the underprivileged, marginalized, and suppressed, Indigenous cultures should be free to articulate their past history and present problems, and thus come to terms with the historical conditions that have shaped their identities. In the words of Margery Fee, "what they needed was political solidarity and support, not to be spoken for but to be heard" (69). Albahari attempts to reach this goal by allowing John to tell the story of the

Corn Woman to an immigrant, though a Serbian author dealing with Indigenous heritage can be construed as trespassing onto the territory of spiritual and cultural authority of Indigenous communities. Lenore Keeshig-Tobias, a poet and storyteller from the Chippewas of Nawash First Nation, explains, "You know, in our culture, people own stories. Individuals own stories. Families own stories. Tribes own stories. Nations own stories. And there is a protocol if you want to tell those stories: you go to the storyteller. And if you don't and you start telling those stories, then you are *stealing*" (Keeshig-Tobias 85). Thus, there is a complex issue at stake here. First, Indigenous writing itself shows, among other things, that there are more ways to be Canadian than "a normative *Canadian*-Canadianness" (Coleman, "From Canadian Trance" 34). Second, by having John tell an important Indigenous story, culturally sensitive author Albahari allows Serbian readership to partake of the rich oral tradition of North American bands and learn of these other ways to be Canadian. After all, Albahari keeps writing in Serbian, so the story was originally meant for the Serbian public.[4]

The second significant point in the Corn Woman storytelling scene of "An Indian at Olympic Plaza" is that John seems to be a very mysterious figure. Besides the fact that he selects the myth of the Corn Woman, which is not native to the area around Calgary where he lives, John manifests some strange behaviour that may allow the reader to see him as a mythical trickster figure. Trickster criticism has been on the rise in recent years; Deanna Reder and Linda M. Morra's 2010 collection *Troubling Tricksters: Revisioning Critical Conversations* ultimately brings tricksters' cultural and historical specificity into sharp focus.

John has many typical trickster qualities. For one, he may be deceiving Ljubomir by claiming his name is John and telling him a story that is not part of his native heritage, which Ljubomir naively accepts as authentic. John also seems to be capable of moving imperceptibly, approaching Ljubomir at unexpected moments and angles, reading his thoughts, disappearing and reappearing, slightly changed or maybe not, in a manner of a shapeshifter. He also approximates a divine creature when he tells the story of the fertility goddess, sharing the powers man exercised in the bygone times and possessing a sort of ancient intuitive wisdom that are all characteristics assigned to the positive Native stereotype embodied in the trickster figure. When Ljubomir complains that John keeps disappearing, John tells him the truth that it is Ljubomir, not John, who is lost: "That is quite common...most people constantly get lost, and many never find themselves" (Albahari, "Indian" 80). As an immigrant, Ljubomir indeed feels lost and incapable of establishing and maintaining close contact with Canadian citizens. John senses his existential condition and offers a metaphorical explanation for it: "This world is a devilishly slippery place...and if you lose your foothold, who knows where you will end up" (80). It is evident that Ljubomir, like many of his people, lost his foothold and slipped dangerously in the existential sense when his country disintegrated and he became part of the Yugoslav diaspora. On the other hand, this lost footing is also a familiar experience for John, who lost his territory and was pushed into a diasporic existence in his own country. The fact that John possesses some trickster traits probably proves that all is not lost, and that he intrinsically belongs in the North American continent, despite a long history of marginalization. Not even by telling the immigrant a sacred story does John betray the binding conventions of his culture. In fact, as a trickster, John does not tell Ljubomir a true story; he tricks him by sharing a typical story that satisfies Ljubomir's needs, but he does not actually share a story that would have been true of his band or territory. The Corn Woman story he relates is widespread across many Indigenous story traditions and does some work towards validating Indigenous histories, but John holds back what would have been the truly sacred, individual aspects of a story from his own territory. John shares enough to make a connection with Ljubomir but not enough to steal from or dishonour his people. The trickster takes a special place in the imaginary of the Indigenous people, and sometimes even becomes a saviour. In the story, Ljubomir for a moment transcends his lost state and in his imagination enters a field of corn, which miraculously covers Calgary's Olympic Plaza. John's power of storytelling heals

Ljubomir's immigrant soul and makes him feel at home in the land of Indigenous people.

This last point is in fact a nod to the most important issue—"the question of how and why the trickster figure is actually used," as Kristina Fagan puts it (9). Although not created by an Indigenous author, John as a trickster figure signifies that the ethical space of the Indigenous people is being challenged. Albahari's story was published in 2012, a year that witnessed a record-breaking number of immigrants entering Canada, as CIC News reports: 2012 "continued a 7-year trend of successive record-breaking, welcoming over 257,000 new permanent residents alone." As an alternative to a possible tension and hostility between these two outsider segments of population (Indigenous groups and recently immigrated Canadians), Albahari offers an option of co-operation and complementarity preceded by and grounded in Ermine's affirmation of human diversity. Although differently positioned in relation to the nation, diaspora and Indigeneity can develop opportunities for alliances and allegiances due to similar experiences of displacement and marginality. As an alternative to institutionalized monoculture, the ethical space thus created offers itself as "the theatre for cross-cultural conversation in pursuit of ethically engaging diversity and disperses claims to the human order" (Ermine 202). Instead, the profound opportunities for more productive dialogue in the meeting of these two outsider positions, different in many respects but similarly positioned in terms of multiculturalism discourse, may provide a fresh model for Canadian society. Canada missed its opportunity to disengage from the mentality of Old Europe and enter a reciprocal, human-to-human dialogue with the Indigenous groups. It cost the Indigenous peoples many lives but it also affected the ethical space created in the new world, which did not turn out to be "a meeting place" (Ermine 202). The influx of modern-day immigrants calls for this issue to be reconsidered. Being in outsider positions, Indigeneity and diaspora can build alliances, as Sunera Thobani suggests, rather than get into conflict as they strive for what the nationals have. Their responsible political action may be effective if it is preceded by mutual understanding of differences and consequent bonding through cultural communication represented in this case as sharing stories.

Furthermore, Albahari indeed has his characters bond, however briefly. Ljubomir enters the North American Indian imaginary and feels what it is like to believe in the Corn Woman. John has an advantage here because, trickster or not, he is connected to his tradition and the heritage of his people. Believing in the myths such as the one of the Corn Woman makes the centre hold, despite the intrusions of foreign cultures or other disruptive influences of immigrants, which Coleman bluntly refers to as a situation in which "abstract diaspora space runs the risk of colonizing literal Indigenous place" (Coleman, "Indigenous Place" 8). Instead of "colonizing" him, Ljubomir learns from John. In a very similar manner, this is what Thunder Cloud from "Learning Cyrillic" teaches the Serbian teacher. By showing him what is left of his own Siksika culture and tradition, Thunder Cloud draws the attention of the narrator to the Serbian heritage that he brought to Canada and the need to preserve it by telling stories about its various aspects. Thunder Cloud is also a deft trickster figure, capable of showing up simultaneously in different places and reading the narrator's thoughts and knowing his feelings. He assumes the role of a shamanistic guide who directs the immigrant newcomer, though they do not share the same cultural background. History indeed seems to repeat itself: just as in the early periods of exploration and colonization of the continent the local Indigenous peoples guided the European newcomers, so now in times of global movements and migrations modern-day Indigenous people may be equally ready to guide a willing immigrant listener. However, the mistakes of the past should not be repeated, as Coleman warns: "Indigeneity and diaspora are proximate cultural formations, having in common the experiences of displacement from a homeland and marginalization in the metropolitan settler state, but the differences in their histories of displacement have given them such different political trajectories that the distance between them cannot simply be got across" (Coleman, "Indigenous Place" 13). Blurring the differences through the policy of multiculturalism has not brought the desired engagement or progress in Indigenous–newcomer relations. Entrenched power structures still preclude what Ermine calls clear rules of engagement between First Nations, the settler nationals, and immigrant ethnicities, which, as contending civilities, need to build a different moral architecture in Canada.

This is the reason why the work of David Albahari is exceptional: the dialogue between immigrants and Indigenous peoples that many Canadian nationals as well as immigrants in Canada have been trying to avoid is potently dramatized in his stories and novels. Albahari's characters in *Snow Man*, "An Indian at Olympic Plaza," and "Learning Cyrillic" engage in conversations with Canadian nationals and thereby learn important things about them. Whether these are the stories and attitudes of university elites or the myths of Indigenous people, Serbian immigrants are given an opportunity to challenge their own prejudices and dislodge stereotypes about Canada, whether positive or negative. At the same time, telling their own stories about the remote world of the former Yugoslavia and the present-day Serbia, these characters show the potential of narrative strategies to build bridges between communities negatively affected by politics and propaganda. The fact that their cultural locations are different can only contribute to Canada's cultural diversity, while a potentially constructive encounter of two alternatives to the political mainstream can possibly move from "an asymmetrical social order to a partnership model," as Ermine suggests (203).

Lai begins her essay "Epistemologies of Respect: A Poetics of Asian/Indigenous Relation" by emphasizing the role an individual can play in changing power relations by taking personal responsibility: "That personal ethics also includes the sense of responsibility to participate in the remaking of contemporary culture and an imagining of the nation to address the injustices of the past and present, in order to produce the future differently" (99). We also believe that without respect, a corrective to the current political practices cannot be realized. It is one's personal responsibility to contribute to actions that will turn the political pendulum to respectful balance instead of communal imbalance. In this spirit, Albahari engages his characters in cross-cultural conversations by creating unexpected dialogical spaces between Indigeneity and diaspora in the urban places of contemporary Canada.

Author's Note

Research for this chapter was supported by the project 178014 granted by the Ministry of Education, Science and Technological Development of the Republic of Serbia.

Notes

1. Though genuinely interested and concerned, we as authors are acutely aware of our outsider position in relation to Indigenous traditions we are trying to inform ourselves about.
2. The names used in Beth Brant's "A Long Story."
3. In 2015, Canada's Truth and Reconciliation Commission put forward ninety-four recommendations based on six years of testimony from nearly seven thousand witnesses enjoining all levels of government—federal, provincial, territorial and Aboriginal—to redress many wrongs done to Indigenous peoples and trace a path to reconciliation through new policies and financial support. Recommendation 17 needs to be quoted here: "We call upon all levels of governments to enable residential school Survivors and their families to reclaim names changed by the residential school system by waiving administrative costs for a period of five years for the name change process and the revision of official identity documents, such as birth certificates, passports, driver's licenses, health cards, status cards, and social insurance numbers."
4. The last two recommendations of the Truth and Reconciliation Commission, Recommendations 93 and 94, are especially significant for this chapter. Recommendation 93 calls for the federal government to include information about treaties and the history of residential schools in newcomers' kits and citizenship tests. Recommendation 94 calls for the government to add observance to Treaties with Indigenous Peoples in the Oath of Citizenship. Indeed, immigrants may not be aware of the history of Indigenous peoples in Canada, and these kinds of efforts may lay the ground for a more informed intercultural dialogue between immigrant and Indigenous groups.

11

The Politics of Art and Affect in Michael Helm's Cities of Refuge

ANA MARÍA FRAILE-MARCOS

> As an act of language, a novel should be set into the culture to make it see differently.
> —Michael Helm, "Putting the Strange in the Stranger"

FROM ITS INCEPTION, Michael Helm's 2010 novel *Cities of Refuge* challenges the mythos of Canada as a peaceful, compassionate, humanitarian, and protective nation set aside from the atrocities of the world, as it asks the reader to look unflinchingly (or flinchingly) to all sorts of past and present human violence and trauma within the Canadian borders. This witnessing begins with the prefatory narration of the disappearance of a foreign girl in the city and the gruesomely detailed account of the brutal attack that almost kills Kim Lystrander, the twenty-seven-year-old Canadian protagonist, and continues with the narratives of fear of various asylum seekers in Toronto. Gendered and sexual violence against women in present-day Canada is thus linked to global atrocities, and connected to a violent legacy of colonial history that continues into the present, for example, with the disturbing figure of nearly 1,200 missing and murdered Indigenous women in Canada over the last three decades, according to recent police records.[1]

Kim's vicious assault takes place one night as she walks to the Royal Ontario Museum, where she works as a night-shift security guard. With its accretion of history and art, the heterotopian space of the museum hints at the importance of both (history and art) in the construction of Kim's subjectivity and in the novel at large. As a dropout PHD student of History, Kim eschews the detached scholarly approach adopted by her father, the professor of Latin American History Harold Lystrander. Instead, she defends an empathetic approach to history (in lower case) that focuses on people's suffering. This affective approach leads her to engage in historical developments through her volunteer work for an NGO called GROUND—the Group for the Undocumented—that helps rejected refugees and asylum seekers. In addition to history, Kim's interest in art is instrumental in her attempts to overcome not just her present trauma caused by the assault, but also the grief caused by her ailing mother's terminal cancer, and the estrangement from her father, which derives from his erratic behaviour before and after he deserted the family when she was thirteen. Kim's attack torments Harold, who suspects that his past blunders are somehow connected to it. Among them, one stands out: his unwitting complicity with the tortures and murders that took place during the first stages of Pinochet's 1973 military coup in Santiago de Chile, where he was a young student at the time. Once Kim accidentally finds out about this period in his life, which he has kept secret, Harold tries to acquit himself by finding Kim's assailant, who he figures is one of the rejected asylum seekers that she may have come across in her work at GROUND. When he learns about a Colombian undocumented young man called Rodrigo Cantero who is hiding in the basement of the Anglican social worker Rosemary Yates, Harold provokes his deportation in what he sees as a heroic act to rid his city and nation of undesirable criminals. However, his actions may just unchain more violence and death by putting Rodrigo's life at risk once he is back in Colombia. All in all, the novel's characters appear caught up in the midst of the turbulent events they try to understand *a posteriori*, just as Klee's *Angelus Novus*, a central work of art in Harold's mental universe, portrays "the angel of history blown forward through time, looking back at the piling wreckage at his feet" (Helm, *Cities* 215). Like this "new angel," the characters are not simply observers, but part and parcel of the ever-present violence that saturates their daily lives as much as it does the media.

Concurrently, the novel revels in a profusion of art references concerned with the representation of atrocity. Thus, the various characters' perceptions of reality as chaotic and threatening are intertwined with a plethora of artworks, ranging from music, to literature, sculpture, installations, architecture, painting and drawing, photography, dance, and performance that invest in violence. However, rather than considering artworks primarily as ways of seeing, artistic expressions seem to respond to Jürgen Habermas's understanding that they are structures of feeling, "feeling complexes whose truthfulness involves a distinct sort of non-cognitive—but certainly not irrational—claim" (Boucher 63).

Drawing on the critical thinking about the connection between art and affect offered by Susan Sontag, Gilles Deleuze and Félix Guattari, Raymond Williams, Jürgen Habermas, Geoff Boucher, and Simon O'Sullivan, among others, this chapter foregrounds the ways in which art is used in Helm's *Cities of Refuge* to enact affect, self-estrangement, and (non-conscious) understanding of the Other—and of oneself as Other—in a world saturated with violence at the personal, local, national, and global levels. I suggest that Helm's aesthetic engagement with violence, through his own creative performance as a novelist and his weaving of a rich and complex tapestry of works of art into the narrative, seeks to shock the reader into pondering the limits of knowledge as well as the ethics of representation, thus connecting aesthetics with affect, epistemology, and agency. In addition, I aim to address the novel's important question: Can art lead us through affect to ethical positions of understanding and reconciliation that other more factual representations of reality cannot easily offer?

The prominence of the visual in *Cities of Refuge* reflects the privileged position that sight occupies in the hierarchy of the senses in Western culture, as John Urry reminds us (389). From its inception, the novel registers the repetitive broadcasting of news about the disappearance of women in the city of Toronto, as well as in Canada at large, about casualties of war abroad, totalitarian regimes, global terrorism, and global warming. In the preface, for example, the reader is forced into the position of a watcher "we" haunted by the latent violence implicit in the disappearance of a familiar "foreign girl" whose elusive existence has been reduced to her everyday movements, recorded by surveillance cameras in different parts of the city. Yet the collective "we" confronting the multicultural, multiracial city, though disturbed by the awareness of nearby violence, is not prompted to action: "*We wake in the night and the foreign girl's name is with us…Here beneath the whisper, we consign her to the dark*" (2). The iteration of images of atrocity mediated by the various electronic screens produces in the viewer a sort of "stupidity" and numbness whereby individual memory and introspection are supplanted "by collective technologies of storage and screening" (Massumi 25). Such desensitizing equals a voyeurism that precludes any affective response. As it appears in the novel, the media's use of the image is "part of the normality of a culture in which shock has become a leading stimulus of consumption and source of value" (Sontag, *Regarding* 20). However, the incessant repetition of images of atrocity no longer guarantees shock. Rather, the observers become impervious to the suffering of others due to their inability to do something about it or to learn from it. From Kim's perspective, the pervasiveness of violence in the city is such that the bad news no longer registers, "that thinking of local sudden deaths was like staring at the rain" (151). Whereas media or electronic representations of atrocity usually have a paralyzing effect that curtails action, artistic renditions of violence that provoke estrangement, a different way of perceiving reality, mobilize affect. As a result, affect appears as a potentially enabling politico-ethical asset prompting the characters to action.

Art and the Politics of Affect

Turning the familiar into the strange is a recent development in understanding the work of art in the West. As Susan Sontag reminds us, if in the past art was considered "as an expression of human consciousness, consciousness seeking to know itself," the later version of the myth "posits a more complex, tragic relation of art to consciousness": "Denying that art is mere expression, the newer myth, ours, rather relates art to the mind's need or capacity for self-estrangement. Art is no longer understood as consciousness expressing and therefore, implicitly, affirming itself. Art is not consciousness per se, but rather its antidote—evolved from within consciousness itself" ("The Aesthetics of Silence" 1).

Kim's approach to art evolves in two different phases that parallel the modern shift from an understanding of art as an expression of consciousness to the current consideration of art as an expression of the mind's need for self-estrangement. Thus, in a first phase Kim seeks to connect with her estranged father by sending him over the years postcards that represent Harold's ambiguous personality: the cubist perspectives of Picasso's *Brick Factory at Tortosa*, or Klee's *Angelus Novus*. Besides evoking the privilege of travellers and tourists visiting far off places and observing other cultures, postcards usually constitute an interesting meeting point for the politics of visual arts and the politics of creative writing and affect. However, Kim does away with words, and relies only on the postcard images in her attempt to reach out to Harold and let him know that he is not a stranger to her. Like in her relationship to Harold, after the assault she finds solace in art as an expression of her consciousness of grief, pain, loss, and disorientation. Thus, if for her the messiness, pain, circularity, and ambiguity of the world "is an Escher sketch" (44), her mood in the aftermath of the attack is attuned to Góreki's music (45). His commemoration of the trauma of the Holocaust—his "Symphony of Sorrowful Songs" particularly laments the separation of a girl from a parent—reverberates with her own apocalyptic experience of vulnerability and loss. Art similarly functions as a reflection of her consciousness when, during one of her visits to the Art Gallery of Ontario, she identifies with the representation of Helga Matura, the murdered prostitute that inspired a painting with her name. The realistic painting, which evokes a blurry photograph, leads her to reflect on the sly violence implicit in male artistic renditions of women's bodies. In this case, Helga's abused body is made to appear "falsely romantic" (263). Kim realizes that the painting resembles the image of the beautiful woman that, as a girl, she had imagined she would become. Ironically, that beautiful woman who was sexually exploited and murdered now appears to Kim as ominously foreshadowing her own destiny.

However, Kim does not really make any progress in her way to recovery until, shifting from an understanding of art as an expression of consciousness to one of art as inciting self-estrangement, she enters a second phase in which she takes an empathetic approach to the violence in her life (the attack, but also her traumatic abandonment by her father when she was a young girl) through creative writing. Perhaps this is so because, as Sontag points out, "narratives can make us understand," whereas visual artworks "do something else: they haunt us" (*Regarding* 71). The empathy required to inhabit some other consciousness or subjectivity in creative writing also demands a degree of self-estrangement that allows for a different perspective on reality, leading Kim to the awareness of a perpetual ontological becoming.

Art emerges then as a "function of *transformation*" whereby it appears directly related to affect and the senses. In this way, as Simon O'Sullivan explains, "Art is less involved in making sense of the world and more involved in exploring the possibilities of being, of becoming, in the world. Less involved in knowledge and more involved in experience, in pushing forward the boundaries of what can be experienced" (130). Similar understandings of art are propounded by Gilles Deleuze and Félix Guattari when they posit art as "a bloc of sensations, that is to say, a compound of percepts and affects" (164) whose autonomy and agency turn them into "*beings* whose validity lies in themselves and exceeds any lived [experience] (164). Raymond Williams similarly holds that artworks, and more specifically literary works, are "structures of feeling" rather than pictures of reality (128–35). He draws attention to the capacity of art to move individuals through affect, understanding affect as "an event or happening," immanent to experience (O'Sullivan 127). Jürgen Habermas's take on art theory equally relies on the notion that autonomous artworks provide a kind of "knowledge that is affective and non-propositional, but has the power to catalyse a shift in the motivational structures of individuals" (Boucher 62). Identifying a distinct aesthetic rationality reasserts the idea that artworks "promote the maturation of the person's subjectivity and provide the motivational structures necessary for moral autonomy and scientific thinking" (62).

From Kim's perspective, writing appears as a highly intuitive hermeneutics that relies to a large extent on empathy. In contrast with sympathy, which refers to the recognition of the Other's emotional state of suffering, empathy, Richard Ashby Wilson and Richard D. Brown argue, "inhabits a site further along on the emotional register and refers to a projection of one's own mental state into that of another. Whereas in a state of sympathy one says 'I recognize your pain,' in empathy one says 'I feel your pain'" (2). Thus, Kim uses writing as a creative tool that helps her inhabit an antithetical other, and as a result understand a different point of view, opening the possibility of resolving conflict. Her strategy can be seen in the light of Keats's notion of *negative capability*, or "the idea of not forever searching after reason—residing in doubt" (Helm, "Putting" 319). If doubting—*dubitare* in Latin—etymologically refers to the conflict of being of two minds, for Keats such an opposition is open to the imagination and to creativity, and true poetry emerges from these states of conflict that leave doubt and uncertainty unresolved. In this sense, negative capability is a sublime expression of supreme empathy that Kim undertakes when she tentatively explores her assaulter's life through writing. In a long computer file she calls "R.doc." she creates "short scenes, and half scenes, descriptions of the city from *R*'s point of view" (159), until from her imaginings he turns up as one of the asylum seekers that she knows, his mind "full of the whole history of his witnessing, what he's seen first-hand, what he's seen on TV" (160). By inhabiting the fictional life of R, Kim does not just feel "a great weight for him" (160), but she is brought back "to the plural, present world" (218).

In the process, Kim also ends up fictionally inhabiting her father's mind in a related quest to understand his nature, which she intuits is determined by some secret event that took place in his past as a student in Santiago de Chile. Believing in the healing effect of telling one's story, Kim is willing to assume the role of Truth and Reconciliation Commissions—"All I've ever wanted to be is a truth commission" (215), Kim tells her father. Her personal endeavour to bear witness to the plight and suffering of others so as to facilitate reconciliation evokes other truth-telling and reconciliation processes, including the one under way in Canada regarding the individual and collective recognition and condemnation of the Indian residential school abuses suffered by Indigenous children and their families during the state-sponsored attempt to colonize (or *civilize*) First Nations, which lasted until the mid-1990s. Thus, Kim prompts Harold to tell her his story and voice his own hidden trauma. When he refuses to do so, Kim pretentiously adopts Harold's narrative voice to write a story in which she imagines him sending an explanatory email letter to her: "Her hope now is to know her father as no one knows him. He is entirely undiscovered, even to himself" (218). The story reminds us again of Escher's complex self-referentiality, a trope Kim used at the beginning of the novel to explain the world (44). To Kim, creative writing is revealed as an epistemological exercise in empathy, compassion, and forgiveness by means of which she can inhabit somebody else's subjectivity and share his or her burden. Writing emerges then as a performative act, deeply invested in affect and aimed at reconciliation and redemption. Kim's methodology combines Harold's empirical research with the cognition she derives from affect, to astonishingly empathetic results:

She'd described the world as he saw it, an evil world guided by an evil god, but in doing so found a way to penetrate confusion, guilt, anger, even evil itself. And yes, she held to this word, *penetrate*, to mean what she wanted it to mean—she had put herself lovingly inside another. And writing in his voice, she understood that Harold was someone else from the inside. In the time it took to truly imagine her father, to inhabit him, language and thought, the anger gave way to something like forgiveness, something she didn't, finally, have words for. A place to rest, to stay, so that a soul might find itself. (290–91)

Kim believes that her affective approach to writing can distill the necessary emotion in Harold to move him closer to her. To her, the imagination has a performative power that can produce positive results. For instance, she has been led to believe in writing as a therapeutics of sorts, which she is encouraged to use as a means of overcoming the psychological trauma resulting from the assault (356). Above all, Kim sees creative writing as redemptive art of estrangement that can put both Harold and herself back in touch with reality and allow for a connecting ground between them. Harold reluctantly admits the story's success, elucubrating that Kim must have inferred from his attitude, deportment, and facial gestures he was unaware of (310–11) what it felt like for him to be in Santiago de Chile during the coup. As she expected, her narrative provides a sort of estrangement that forces Harold to look at himself from a distance and see the essence of who he is, beyond the deception of words and his artful self-image. Harold recognizes that though the persona she creates is not him exactly, she manages to capture his self with an accuracy that does not allow for any further hiding or self-deception, changing his own relation with her, with the world and with himself (305). The estrangement Kim's creative letter enacts strikes Harold with its intuitive truth about him, and prompts a genuine emotional response that sets him adrift, "beyond language or control" (304).

Despite the story's success in capturing Harold's essence, he eschews the empathy derived from aesthetics, and disarticulates Keats's romantic equation that holds that "Beauty is truth, truth beauty,"[2] arguing that fiction cannot equate the experience of the suffering, that trauma is unrepresentable and beyond language, and that storytelling does not constitute an epistemological source: "We know only ourselves, and ourselves thinly" (339). Intriguingly, Harold's position is best articulated by the protagonist of Helm's second novel, *In the Place of Last Things*, where Russ, a Classics instructor, confesses that "he himself didn't believe the seeming truths of art. Even in its most refined forms, imaginative literature indulged in a kind of emotionalism, like religion, and engaged us mostly at the level of, if not superstition, then intuition" (*In the Place* 93). However, even if concluding that "nothing that existed only in language or its imagery could ever be more than half true" (94), Russ admits that art "can make us see clearly, too, or make us experience honest feelings" (94). Kim, for her part, reclaims the transformative agency of writing when she says, "You don't believe in talking cures. I do believe in telling ones" (Helm, *Cities* 237), while Harold retorts, "Fiction, no matter its scope, will always fail history" (342). He thus engages in a critique of the politics of representation, arguing that "Good aesthetics don't promote good ethics" and calling Kim's fictional story about his experience in Santiago de Chile an "abomination, all the more vile... for its believability" (339). This passage brings to the forefront "a question about whether the act of writing can be understood as one way of performing acts of justice or empathy" (Helm, "Putting the Strange" 316), as Smaro Kamboureli perceptively notes in her interview with Helm. Harold's answer to this would be that the mobilization of affect through aesthetics does not necessarily lead either to knowledge or to ethics, as it appears as a dubious act of witnessing. His view is that no matter how empathetic and compassionate the witness of violence may be, witnessing can never equate being the victim. Consequently, the insights reached by the victims of evil are barred for those who stand at a distance from it as witnesses: "If we acknowledge this solemnly, we won't live in ignorance, and we won't make the mistake of thinking we can pretend our way into knowing" (339). Father André concurs with Harold's perspective, but trusts in love as the alternative to compassion when at the end of the novel he tells Rosemary, the Anglican social worker hosting Rodrigo, that compassion is not enough to get to know the other: "though the weight we bear is the weight of all, and though we cannot truly know the pain we witness, any pain greater than our own, we can nevertheless know love" (385).

Harold's point fulfills itself when, horrified by Kim's perceptive fictional representation of his inner self, he is moved to commit suicide. His death cancels out Kim's ethical effort and achieves the opposite of what she set out to do with her story, as she is transformed into both Harold's victim and his executioner. Through Harold, Helm discards any facile understanding of writing as inherently ethical, expressing the idea that "writing as a furthering of perception is a moral act if it works, and if it doesn't work it's a kind of abomination" (Helm, "Putting" 316). The novel therefore reasserts the ethical neutrality, or even ambiguity, of aesthetics, while underlining its capability to mobilize affect and its performative power.

One of the novel's central passages for the analysis of how affect is mobilized through images of violence in art is the scene where Harold has asked his assistant, Drew, to scan a series of paintings, photographs, and engravings that he uses in his popular yearly lecture "on physical coercion." Here, Harold makes the connection between past and present acts of violence by focusing on "the thematic elements of images of suffering in Western art, from the crucifixion, to Goya, to the World War I sketching of Otto Dix" (134). The idea, he explains, is to make his students not just witnesses of the violence that has driven human history, but aware that they partake of the same fascination with violence that shapes history and popular art from the Middle Ages to the present (134). The artworks Harold presents in class seek to effect changes on the spectator, both at the physical and the mental levels, through the mobilization of affect. Thus, of Goya's print series *Los desastres de la guerra*, for example, Sontag writes, "The ghoulish cruelties in *The Disasters of War* are meant to awaken, shock, wound the viewer. Goya's art, like Dostoyevsky's, seems a turning point in the history of moral feelings and of sorrow—as deep, as original, as demanding. With Goya, a new standard for responsiveness to suffering enters art" (*Regarding* 36). Accordingly, Harold's assistant, Drew, is shaken by the representations of torture that she digitizes for Harold's classes (Helm, *Cities* 136). Yet, year after year, Harold remains impervious to the effects of the paintings, even though he recognizes their power in stirring some dormant memories that link the past of humanity to our present condition (137).

Harold's unperturbed contemplation of images of the atrocious could be misunderstood as the voyeurism of a cynic. Instead, Harold has simply acquired a knowledge that Sontag identifies as "moral adulthood": "Someone who is perennially surprised that depravity exists, who continues to feel disillusioned (even incredulous) when confronted with evidence of what humans are capable of inflicting in the way of gruesome, hands-on cruelties upon other humans, has not reached moral or psychological adulthood. No one after a certain age has the right to this kind of innocence, of superficiality, to this degree of ignorance, or amnesia" (*Regarding* 89). Harold, for one, does not allow himself this nefarious innocence, and seems to subscribe Plautus's dictum that man is a wolf to man. His enhancing of rational knowledge over the non-rational has, so far, made him impervious to either the media's iteration of images of violence or to art's arousal of affects. Yet at this point in the novel he is feeling irrationally guilty for the assault on Kim and troubled by the image she has created of him in her story. With the irrational now taking over the rational, Harold begins to believe that it is possible that his own sins are revisited upon his daughter. Thus, he suspects that the attack Kim suffered, as well as her disclosure of his terrible secret, are but two acts of the angel of history seeking to punish him through her for the tortures and murders he unwittingly contributed to in the past when he handed in a group of people to the Chilean military. As a result of this shift from rational to affective paradigms in his search for meaning and understanding of the world, Harold becomes vulnerable to the renditions of torture with which he has been illustrating his lecture for years, unperturbed.

This affective opening occurs when Drew is digitizing Titian's painting *The Flaying of Marsyas*. Noticing her discomfort, Harold attempts to explain the painting in terms of resolving "Thinking, Feeling, and Will in a contemplation of suffering" (136), which is pretty much the main quest of the characters in the novel, and Harold's in particular. However, Drew rejects his offer to understand it conceptually, and with it, the possibility of not being upset by the painting. Arguing that Titian "probably didn't do it just to get us all talking" (136), Drew eschews Harold's offer of a rationalizing numbness. This scene brings to the fore the idea that affects are extradiscursive and extratextual, that they occur on a different, *asignifying* register from that of language. "In fact," O'Sullivan argues, "this is what differentiates art from language—although language, too, can and does have an affective register" (126). In a world so saturated by scenes of violence and death that we may become impervious to them, Drew's yielding to art's affective and effective agency moves Harold in turn to look at Titian's painting "as she had, as if for the first time" (136). In a clear example of "affective resonance" (Tomkins) or "emotional contagion" (Hatfield et al.) acting as the original basis for all human communication, Harold's body reacts in an uncharacteristically empathetic way to the violence portrayed and he unwittingly breaks into tears (136–37). In an email he sends Drew thanking her for her work, Harold insists on the importance of rationalizing the affect elicited by the artworks representing torture as, he contends, art intends to make us think (138). In this, he coincides with Sontag's assessment that art should elicit not sympathy, but *thought*. Nevertheless, Harold valorizes the political function of art when he praises Drew for her capability to be shocked by painting (138).

In *Cities of Refuge* Helm grapples with what Stephen Henighan identifies as "The Victory of Metaphor over History" in the quintessential Canadian novels of the 1990s, as he controversially deplores that writers such as Michael Ondaatje and Anne Michaels produced "self-consciously artistic artifacts" (134) whose "metaphor-saturated aesthetic" (138) appeals to the elitist aspirations of a Canadian bourgeoisie

(155). Far from elitist, Helm's use of artworks and creative writing in the novel to re-inscribe the atrocities of history through aesthetics mobilizes affect at a visceral level from which no subjectivity can be immune. The novel, itself an aesthetic construct, manages to make an imprint on the reader as "something that stands outside of the white noise of the culture," as Helm puts it ("Putting" 324). This imprint is achieved through the combined strategy of, on the one hand, depicting violence through a focus that does *"not seek to make it less monstrous,"* to use John Updike's words cited in the novel (Helm, *Cities* 241). The iteration of representations of violence eschews any attempt to diminish its impact through aesthetics, as the other line in Updike's poem seems to convey: *"Let us not mock God with metaphor"* (240). On the other hand, the novel's complex and nuanced use of affects through literary language and artworks manages to convey estrangement in a way that makes the reader see violence and otherness anew, as if for the first time, as Harold did, and shock us into reconnection, recognition, and understanding.

Nonetheless, the novel insists on pointing out the limits of trying to achieve knowledge and find meaning, either rationally, or through the more intuitive or sensorial epistemological approaches provided by art. As Rosemary once told Harold, "it's very hard to accept the randomness of violence. We'd rather that the world made sense somehow, and that's what you're trying to come up with. Sense. Meaning. Sometimes, Harold, there is no meaning" (104).

Author's Note

I wish to thank Daniel Coleman, Lorraine York, my fellow participants in the Understanding Canada Conference (McMaster University, September 27–29, 2013), as well as the various readers of early drafts for their thoughtful comments and suggestions.

Notes

1. This specifically Canadian situation needs to be inscribed in the global history of colonization and its vestiges, as similar violence against Indigenous women and their communities occurs all over the American continent. The connections between Canada and the hemispheric violence against Indigenous women goes beyond the recognition of a shared global colonial history to the present-day transnational synergies and alliances aiming to combat it. Thus, Deena Rymhs points out, "the forms of activism that have emerged in response to the missing and murdered women in Canada have been inspired by similar organizing in Mexico, Argentina, and El Salvador, where astounding numbers of young women have also gone missing." Similarly, "The memorials that have appeared along highways in Canada might be likened to the work of Las Madres, a group of mothers in Latin America who have created public memorials to their disappeared daughters" (35n7).
2. I am indebted to Vesna Lopičić for this insight.

V

Reading Publics

12

Canada through the Lens of the Communist Censor
The Translation of CanLit under an Authoritarian Regime

LUCIA OTRÍSALOVÁ

ALTHOUGH FOR MOST SLOVAKS Canada is a distant country beyond the scope of their daily concerns, it has penetrated the Slovak consciousness in ways that even the United States has not. While "amerika" has taken up residence in colloquial Slovak as an expression of being well and at ease, "kanada" has become synonymous with ice hockey and good fun and amusement. Our grandfathers used to play "kanada" wearing hockey skates that came to be known as "kanadky" and maybe making "kanada" (fun) of each other. The phrase "kanadský žartík" (a Canadian joke), although imported from Czech,[1] has become established in the Slovak language to refer to a cleverly devised practical joke whose purpose is to throw its object off balance. The origin of this phrase can allegedly be traced back to the first Czechoslovak Republic when a vivid tramp culture developed in the Czech lands inspired by the organized Boy Scout and Woodcraft movements that had emerged shortly before the First World War.[2] Canada had a powerful symbolism for these groups. It was imagined as a beautiful, mysterious, forest-covered country inhabited by tough guys, mostly lumberjacks, who had not only rough manners but also a coarse sense of humour. Czech tramps used to relate anecdotes (probably not based on real-life incidents) about rough "Canadian jokes" that these men played on each other. This infiltration of Canada into the basic wordstock of the Slovak language not only proves the presence of Canada in the minds of Slovaks, but also reaffirms its traditional stereotypical representations as a land of ice hockey and hardy, tenacious men.

Besides vocabulary, a certain vision of Canada has also been created through translations of its literature. Although these have not been as numerous as translations from other literatures written in English (see Otrísalová and Gazdík), these works, and their reception in the target culture, convey significant images of this northern country to Slovak readers. After all, literary texts and their authors are ambassadors of the culture from which they come. Because texts originate in a certain place, time, and context, they are carriers of information about the place and articulations of the values and beliefs of the culture. However, when transferred from one place and time to another—for example, when translated—texts also change their values so that they are intelligible to different readers. In turn, these new readers try to engage with these translated texts in a way that approximates how they would be read in their original language, and through this process, according to Lawrence Venuti, the texts convey "representations of foreign cultures" (67). This means that what is selected for translation determines what people from a given target culture can read and what images are conveyed to them of a source culture. Mária Kusá, a prominent Slovak translation studies scholar, writes that the choice of texts for translation is dependent on a target country's political system, reigning ideology, social situation, cultural character, and existing literary system (16–17). However, as Don Sparling points out in his contribution in the present volume, there are other factors at work here, such as the international reputation of the author to be translated, the support of a source country's agencies, and the personal initiative of academics or translators. All these criteria have an impact on what canons are established for foreign literatures in a target culture. Venuti brings attention to the fact that these canons may sometimes "conform to domestic aesthetic values and therefore reveal exclusions and admissions, centers and peripheries that deviate from those current in the foreign language" (67).

However, how a source culture is perceived and imagined in a target culture depends not only on the selection of its texts for translation but also on the translation strategies employed. Translation is never impartial, as ideology affects it in subtle and sometimes overt ways. By ideology I mean not only a political doctrine—although this plays a significant role in totalitarian regimes, one of which is the subject of my chapter—but also "the set of beliefs and values which inform an individual's or institution's view of the world and assist their interpretation of events, facts, etc." (Mason 25). Like any other readers, translators always read through their own lenses and make choices, conscious or subconscious, "selecting aspects or parts of a text to transpose and emphasize" (Tymoczko 24) based on their assumptions, inclinations, experience, and world view. As a result, their translations usually offer a very particular and oftentimes considerably narrowed or, in Maria Tymoczko's words, "overdetermined" reading of a source text (24). In consequence, translations are merely representations of the source texts, and rather than introducing a culture in its complexity to the reader, they participate in the creation of mental constructs about the culture. Sometimes these may be simplified and stereotypical, and like media images, they may lack "the ability to represent a place's complex social reality" (Barrer 6).

This was particularly true for Slovak translations of Canadian literature between 1948 and 1989. At that time, Slovakia was part of the re-established state of Czechoslovakia. While the first Czechoslovak Republic in the interwar period had displayed a pro-Western orientation, after the trials and tribulations of the Second World War the renewed republic faced a dilemma as to whether its reconstruction should follow the example of the Soviet Union, as was championed by the Communists, who were becoming a dominant political force in the country, or whether it should return to its pre-war democratic heritage (Brenkusová 178). When the Communist Party seized power in February 1948, Czechoslovakia came under the Soviet sphere of influence and disappeared behind the Iron Curtain for several decades. A system of absolute control by one party was imposed upon political, economic, cultural, and civil life in the country, a system that, as Karel Kaplan notes, "ran counter to [its] traditions, interests, needs and will" (vii). The totalitarian regime that was grafted on to Czechoslovakia put the society into political and cultural isolation. Despite a certain historic affinity and sympathy with which Canada regarded Czechoslovakia, "the most 'Western' of the Eastern European states" (Madokoro 163), the countries ended up on the opposite sides of the ideological gulf, which also affected the translation culture. The Communist censor only allowed cultural transfer that did not jeopardize the Party's objectives and was compliant with proletarian aesthetics as formulated by the Soviet theoretician Andrei Zhdanov. His doctrine saw the world divided into two antagonistic camps—imperialist and capitalist (headed by the United States); and Communist and progressive (led by the Soviet Union). Zhdanov believed that for the Soviet Union to achieve its inevitable victory over the imperialists, the world of art was required to serve the Party and its totalitarian goals. Individualistic, critical, or abstract art was therefore condemned as contradicting the Party's ideology and was suppressed. As Canada was too closely allied to the Soviet Union's chief political and ideological enemy, the United States, it was seen as part of the "corrupt" Western Bloc and its literature as "a product of the late-bourgeois system" (Korte 37). Hence, very little was translated from Canadian literature between 1948 and 1989. Most books that got past the Communist censors during the early years of the regime were either politically left-leaning (see also Javorčíková 55), portraying Canada as a capitalist country rife with social and economic inequalities (see the pro-Soviet writings of Herbert Dyson Carter discussed below[3]), or they were set in Canada's wilderness and drew an ideologically neutral but one-dimensional and slightly romanticized picture of Canada (for example, L.M.

Montgomery's Anne series or E.T. Seton's books). It was not until the 1970s that the first works of "bourgeois realism" started appearing accompanied by "paratexts" that usually presented them as "reflection[s] of a capitalist world in decay" (Korte 37) and thus highlighted their conformity with at least some aspects of socialist dogma.[4]

Due to the severe political persecution and unscrupulous censorship by Communists in the first decade after the onset of totalitarianism in Czechoslovakia, the only Canadian book published in Slovak was Carter's *Zajtrajšok je náš* (1952; *Tomorrow Is with Us*). And not surprisingly, its author, a Sovietophile and active member of the Communist Party of Canada, although absent from the Canadian literary canon and from most Canadian literary histories, was deemed a "progressive" writer who "[put] his pen in the service of the most beautiful idea"—the fight for peace (Drug 7), which, in translation, meant that he produced pro-Soviet propaganda.[5] In addition, his social-realist novel had been translated into Russian a year before, which in itself was a sufficient credential for an author at that time. The Slovak translation of the book was, moreover, equipped with an afterword by the Soviet literary critic Anna Yelistratova, as was the custom. Even though normally a well-written afterword enriches the reader's cultural context by situating the book both historically and culturally (cf. Bieliková), between 1948 and 1989 afterwords such as this one were meant to provide potential readers with guidelines on how to consume a book in an ideologically profitable fashion. As a result, Yelistratova's afterword to Carter's novel is replete with ideology-laden Cold War rhetoric. Canada is presented as a prey in the clutches of the American eagle hatching a criminal plot of aggression against the Soviet "camp of peace." As Yelistratova writes,

> American monopolists have set their sights upon Canada due to its natural and human resources and military strategic position. Canada's ruling circles, controlled by fear and hatred for their own nation, betray their country's interests. In an effort to win a share of war profits they submissively let Wall Street assume control of the Canadian national economy...[and are blind to] the

fact that in recent documents issued by the US Department of War the territory of Canada features as part of "the northeastern military zone of the United States." (295, my translation)

It is possible that ordinary Canadians desired to remain neutral in the conflict between their southern neighbour and the USSR, as Yelistratova suggests, but due to Canada's geographical position, neutrality was not an option. General Foulkes confirms in his 1961 article "Canadian Defence Policy in a Nuclear Age" that "Canada cannot negate geography. Canada is physically joined to the United States just like Siamese twins. If one of the twins gets hurt the other one suffers" (10). However, even this obvious fact does not prevent Yelistratova from criticizing Prime Minister Louis St. Laurent for his declaration that should a third world war break out, Canada could not stay out of it even if "11,999,999 of her 12,000,000 citizens wanted to remain neutral" (qtd. in Conant 73). Yelistratova calls this statement of his "impudent" and inconsiderate of his people and attributes it to his treacherous loyalty to "his Washington bosses" (295).

However, it is not only the afterword that is marked with Cold War anxieties. Carter's novel itself, centred on the false indictment of a young talented scientist Alan Baird for allegedly dealing in nuclear bomb secrets for the Soviet Union, resonates with overtones of the Gouzenko and Rosenberg cases. Failing to break through with his invention of a physiotherapeutic device in Canada, the idealist Baird decides to send his project as a gift to a state institute for balneotherapy in the Soviet Union. His attempt at establishing contact with a Soviet institution is almost automatically interpreted by the press and the government as an act of espionage and triggers a libel campaign against him. In the end he is accused of stealing confidential technical drawings from the military plane plant where he used to work. Carter's Canada thus appears steeped in the same anti-Communist hysteria as its neighbour to the south. It is a country where representatives of intelligentsia can only "dream of peaceful creative work for the good of humanity" (Yelistratova 298) and where human life no longer presents the ultimate value. No one seems to be interested in Baird's invention, which is meant to improve or prolong human life, and Canadian companies could not care less for medical advancement. They want inventions that have the potential to kill, as Baird is told by his cynically honest boss, McMahon.

Fortunately, there seems to be an organized network of Communist activists ready to help Baird elude the police. They are depicted as "decent committed people, sacrificing their domestic tranquility to their political obligations" (J. Doyle 18). Baird finds in them friends and allies whom he can trust or, as Yelistratova puts it, "the best representatives of his nation" (299). Carter's novel emphasizes the massiveness of the workers' movement and praises the courage and heroism of individuals in the movement. Yelistratova finds particularly moving the characters of the Dunns, elderly people from the working class who, despite their lack of interest in politics and frail health, end up involved in a public fight against the "warmongers" who are behind the arrest of their daughter (299).

The fate of Calvin Finley's father, a priest, further contributes to the unflattering picture that Carter paints of Canada. Following the arrest of his son, the father is also scrutinized and, when he is caught preaching in defence of peace supporters and Canada's friendship with the nations of the Soviet Union in an overcrowded church, he is prohibited from serving masses. In Carter's rendering, the country acquires the features of a totalitarian regime, suppressing freedom of speech and persecuting those whose views differ from that of the ruling class, which contradicts its usual association with the traditions of democracy, freedom, and tolerance. This portrayal of Canada is, of course, biased, but its tendentiousness must have suited Communist leaders who deliberately hyperbolized (and even distorted) the crimes that Western countries committed against their citizens to divert public attention from the atrocities that they inflicted on political dissenters at home.

It was not until the late 1950s that Slovak readers were introduced to a different face of Canada that was just as reductive as Carter's, but with a much more positive spin. This image was promoted through children's books by L.M. Montgomery and E.T. Seton. These authors enjoyed great popularity in socialist Czechoslovakia, which is attested to by the number of Slovak translations of their works that appeared in the period under survey,[6] and thus had the most significant impact on the perception of Canada in this Central European country.

Anne of Green Gables by L.M. Montgomery was first translated in 1959. It may have been part of a larger endeavour in the publishing business to systematically introduce the world's greatest classics to a Slovak readership (cf. Gazdík, "Recepcia anglickej" 130). While previously publishers had focused mainly on ideologically relevant Soviet literature, towards the end of the 1950s they sought to restore the continuity with the early postwar years and as a result started printing hitherto unpublished (even Western) authors (Kusá 56). This change in publishing policies was an accompanying sign of a socio-political thaw that set in after the Twentieth Congress of the Communist Party of the Soviet Union in February 1956, where Nikita Khrushchev exposed the brutality of Joseph Stalin's dictatorship and denounced his personality cult. Even though the Congress of Czechoslovak Writers that was held only two months later called for its abolition, censorship continued, albeit in a softened form.

This slightly relaxed atmosphere appears to have allowed the publication of *Anne of Green Gables*. However, since the regime still had not parted ways with political dogma, its translation was affected by the intensification of atheist propaganda and religious persecution in the late 1950s. As most mentions of religion and God fell victim to Communist censorship, Anne from the Slovak translation is not the pagan becoming Christian that some literary critics (for example, John R. Sorfleet) believe the Anne Shirley of the original to be. On the contrary, as a result of the censor's interventions, the translation makes Anne come across as an independently minded child resisting religious indoctrination (Otrísalová 174).

This suppression of its religious content, together with its celebration of family life and cohesion that interestingly spoke to the values of a collectivist socialist society, probably allowed the publication of Montgomery's novel in Czechoslovakia. Communist ideologues valued community, family, and fellowship. One was expected to renounce one's individual desires if they were in conflict with the will of the majority or threatened the common good. Conformity was the social norm. The story of the unruly Anne who, in the end, conforms to social and cultural norms regarding female behaviour and even sacrifices her individual dreams to take care of the woman who has looked after her since she was a child, thus corresponded with the requirements that the socialist society placed on women. One reviewer in 1959 praised the increasing prudence and self-possession that Anne displays as she grows up, the sense of responsibility with which she approaches her school and household duties as well as the great enthusiasm that she shows for her teacher training ("Nové knihy" 4). However, Slovak readers have probably always preferred the rebellious and unconventional Anne Shirley, who "can assert her emotions, opinions, attitudes and her ideas of love in an extremely conventional environment" ("Anna zo Zeleného domu"), as Jana Juráňová, a contemporary Slovak feminist, remarked in a 2010 TV show, the Slovak version of the BBC's *The Big Read* or the CBC's *Canada Reads* program.

Thanks to *Anne of Green Gables*, Canada became associated with the pastoral in the eyes of the Slovak reading public, at least those who have been aware of the novel's setting. Despite the fact that the censor did not omit local references, some readers are always surprised when they are told that the book is set in Canada. The reason may be that the book has never been explicitly marketed as a Canadian product, nor have the reviewers emphasized its Canadianness. In addition, Montgomery's considerably romanticized version of her native Prince Edward Island lifts the story of the orphaned redhead into the realm of the mythical—and it thus becomes somewhat timeless and placeless. Consider Anne's first glimpse of her new home:

> They had driven over the crest of a hill. Below them was a pond, looking almost like a river so long and winding was it. A bridge spanned it midway and from

there to its lower end, where an amber-hued belt of sand hills shut it in from the dark blue gulf beyond, the water was a glory of many shifting hues—the most spiritual shadings of crocus and rose and ethereal green, with other elusive tintings for which no name has ever been found. Above the bridge the pond ran up into fringing groves of fir and maple and lay all darkly translucent in their wavering shadows....There was a little gray house peering around a white apple orchard on a slope beyond and, although it was not yet quite dark, a light was shining from one of its windows. (Montgomery 19)

Montgomery's language, rich in evocative sensory imagery, lends the landscape of Avonlea the aura of a dreamscape. It is evident that in her writing "the real Prince Edward Island countryside is integrated with a landscape of the mind" as Shelagh J. Squire aptly puts it (141). Montgomery's descriptions of pastoral idyll reflect her nostalgic longing for the ideal world of childhood memory as well as "[her] intense emotional attachment to her native province" (Squire 141).

While L.M. Montgomery's arcadian gardens of Avonlea appealed to Slovak girls and young women in socialist Czechoslovakia, E.T. Seton's adventures in the northern wilderness fascinated a younger male readership. His popularity in socialist Czechoslovakia can be explained by its people's close relationship to rural areas and nature. Despite being urban nations now (with more than half of the population living and working in towns and cities), both Czechs and Slovaks have preserved close ties to the countryside and like to get out of the city on weekends. Both nations also like to actively enjoy the countryside: as Don Sparling writes, few European countries can boast of "such a dense network of hiking trails" ("'Canada'" 42). It is therefore not surprising that Czechs and Slovaks have a predilection for stories set in the wilderness, and Seton's popularity is part of a trend. It coincided with that of Jack London,[7] who, though not a Canadian, was instrumental in constructing stereotypical representations of the "true north," and with that of Karl May, a popular German writer known for his Vinnetou series, whose fictional world, as Sparling and Tomáš Pospíšil write, "has become for Czechs [and Slovaks] the ultimate

American myth" (74). Even though May never visited the places where his stories are set, he was read as a principal authority on America and Native Americans from the nineteenth century to the 1980s when Czechs and Slovaks could not access the real America either due to physical distance or due to "the fierce travel restrictions imposed by the Communist regime" (Sparling and Pospíšil 74). Most young readers in socialist Czechoslovakia thus derived their idea of the American West, the North American wilderness, and Indigenous peoples from adventure stories by Seton, London, and May, as well as a few others. As Sparling and Pospíšil further argue, their fictional worlds were a source of fascination for Czechs—and I believe that it is also applicable to Slovaks—because they constituted "an exotic 'other'" to the world that they were so intimately familiar with: "ancient cities with highly developed industries and a countryside thickly dotted with villages and chateaux, artificial ponds and carefully managed forests" (74). Although Slovakia's mountainous regions make the country "wilder" than the Czech lands, still, they are too settled and civilized to compete with the allure of the "unspoiled" and "empty" North American spaces that, according to Sparling and Pospíšil, offer freedom—"freedom from a society bound by bureaucracies and regulations, freedom from the weight of centuries of high cultural traditions, freedom from a society trapped within the narrow bounds of its limited physical space" (74).

Although it may seem that E.T. Seton did not become popular in Slovakia until after the Second World War, this is not true. The first selection of his *Animal Stories* was published in 1936, the second book by a Canadian author to appear in Slovak.[8] However, it is quite possible that Slovak readers had access to Seton's work much earlier as most of them could understand Czech, thanks to its linguistic proximity to Slovak, and his books were available in Czech as early as 1909.[9] Seton was also popular with young people's movements in the interwar period. As Sparling points out, his works were canonical for the Woodcraft and Boy Scout movements that developed and had a strong presence in both parts of Czechoslovakia as well as for the unorganized young tramps who would flood the countryside on weekends or during the summer ("'Canada,'" 42–43).[10] Even Seton's first book in Slovak might have been published on the occasion of his visit to Czechoslovakia in 1936.[11] The publication of Seton's *Zálesák Rolf* (*Rolf in the Woods*) in 1959 followed by *Dvaja divosi* (1967; *Two Little Savages*), and *Medveď monarcha* (1972; *Monarch, the Big Bear of Tallac*) can thus be viewed as a return to a tradition established before the Second World War.

E.T. Seton, together with authors such as Allen Roy Evans, James Houston, and Farley Mowat, whose works were published later in the 1970s and 1980s, promoted the image of Canada as a country of endless, virginal, untamed wilderness inhabited almost exclusively by wild animals and a handful of Native Canadians and tough white men, an image that was fully in line with how Canada was conceived by some colonizing Europeans—as an empty and essentially unpeopled land. This image made Canada appear to the average Slovak reader as a premodern country, untouched by the urbanization and industrialization that had been a social reality in Canada for almost a hundred years by that time.

Although in the Judeo-Christian tradition, wilderness was viewed as the antithesis of the Garden of Eden, Canada's northern wilderness stands in marked contrast to the corruption and decay of civilization and appears to be a haven of morality in the Canadian adventure novels translated into Slovak under the totalitarian regime. In all of them, morality is embodied either in the figure of the Indian or in wild animals. Rolf Kittering, the abandoned orphan in Seton's *Rolf in the Woods*, is taught the true way of life by the highly moral and friendly Indian Quonab. Yan and Sam in *Two Little Savages* are not guided by any particular Native figure, but they attain maturity and wisdom through imitating Indian manners and customs. His Monarch is a truly noble and dignified animal rising above the purely instinctive and reaching towards the spiritual, and his capture is, in Seton's view, the herald of humanity's self-destruction. Similarly, Mowat's wolf from *Never Cry Wolf* is portrayed as an accomplished wilderness hunter with an independent spirit. Allen Roy Evans's *Reindeer Trek* celebrates the incredible persistence, courage, and willpower of Lapp and Inuit herders who trek three thousand reindeer from Alaska to a reserve in Canada's Northwest Territories to save the people there from famine. James Houston contrasts the chastity and simplicity of Inuit people with "the self-interest, cynicism, misguided morality, cowardice and violence" of white men "coming from the 'civilized' and most powerful capitalist country in the world," as one Slovak reviewer summarizes the central conflict of his novel *White Dawn* (AJK 15). He is obviously critical of what he perceives as the oppression of indigenous minorities in imperialist societies. As can be seen, in all of these novels wilderness is a place of moral goodness, and as Canada was perceived as primarily defined by its wilderness in Czechoslovakia in the decades following the Second World War, the country had a positive image. It was regarded sentimentally as a site of boyhood dreams come true, a place of escape where one could live free from the constraints of one's social and cultural environment (Hykisch, "Návod").

Canada's positive image was slightly dented in the 1970s when the first novels of "bourgeois realism" started appearing. Brian Moore's *Ginger Coffey má šťastie* (*The Luck of Ginger Coffey*, 1978) was hailed as conclusive evidence that Canada was not "the promised land" that potential immigrants worldwide believed it to be. Although the novel is usually appreciated for its comic aspects, its Slovak reception has unexpectedly serious undertones. Reviewer Darina Šimečková interpreted the novel as depicting the lives of average people "in a capitalist society," who, "disadvantaged by their imperfect language skills and their unfamiliarity with local customs and laws," have to fight for daily survival (136). Despite being advertised as a land of opportunities, as the reviewer further writes, Canada seems to be offering none, especially to the poor and the socially disadvantaged. Moneyless people have no chance to complete their education, and as a result, they are condemned to do unqualified jobs until the end of their productive lives (Šimečková 136). Canadian society is portrayed as a typical capitalist country controlled by "the cruel laws of profit and power" (Babín), bereft of human emotion and understanding and indifferent to the ordinary man if it can no longer profit from his work (Šimečková). Šimečková does not hesitate to call Canada "immoral" and "inhumane" (137). However, because Moore's book never achieved the kind of popularity with Slovak readers as Montgomery and Seton did, this negative image of Canada did not stand a chance to prevail over the positive image conveyed by the more popular works. Moreover, reviews and other similar paratexts are usually ignored by the general reading public, as Barbara Korte points out in her study of the reception of Anglo-Canadian literature in the German Democratic Republic (34). Šimečková's simplistic reading of Moore's novel is thus unlikely to have had any significant impact on how the book was read and received by the common Slovak reader.

While Marxist-Leninist interpretation still dominated literary criticism in the 1970s, the 1980s provided more space for thinking in different directions and brought the first attempts at introducing Canada's complex social reality to the Slovak readership. 1984 saw the publication of Hugh MacLennan's *Dve samoty* (*Two Solitudes*). This canonical work was proposed for publication by Jarmila Samcová, editor-in-chief of *Revue svetovej literatúry*, a Slovak quarterly specializing in the promotion of foreign literature. At that time she worked as an editor for the Pravda publishing house and felt that the time had come for a representative Canadian author to be translated (Samcová). In the 1980s Canadian literature was slowly penetrating English studies curricula. Works by Canadian authors were commonly included in courses on Commonwealth literatures taught by Danuša Brenčičová and Mária Huttová at Comenius University in Bratislava, literary scholars who also played a key role in popularizing Canadian literature with Slovak readers. Samcová thus wanted to give a helping hand to the promotion of Canadian literature. In her opinion, MacLennan was a good choice because, both as a personality and as a writer, he was not likely to irritate Communist ideologues (Samcová). Despite the Christian humanist ideas that permeate his novel, to which the author of the afterword, Mária Huttová, raises objections in line with political dogma, it was the general humanistic appeal and antimilitarist message, also underlined by Huttová, that probably helped the book to get approval from censors (402).

MacLennan's description of the geography of Canada in the introductory part of the novel, specifically of the Ottawa and the St. Lawrence Rivers that meet at the island of Montreal, is immediately interpreted as symbolic of the long-standing inner tension that marks Canada's national unity. Canada is portrayed as a country of "two old races," the English and the French, that are divided by insurmountable differences and mutual antagonism and living "their separate legends, side by side" (MacLennan 2). The search for national unity and identity is identified as one of the primary concerns of postwar Canadian literature both by Huttová (397) and Brenčičová (21). The latter explains in a 1988 article that because the two founding nations did not merge to form "a universal Canadian," descendants of immigrants keep looking for an answer to the questions about who they are and who they become in the adopted country. As a result, Canadian literature is, in her view, "marked with nostalgia and sorrow, eternal searching and groping around, insecurity and pessimism" (Brenčičová 21). Huttová, however, insists that the vision that MacLennan presents in his *Two Solitudes* is essentially an optimistic one. His idea of "a modern Canadian" drawing on the heritage of both English and French cultures is not a utopian ideal, but finds personification in the character of Paul Tallard, who, as Huttová writes, represents the perfect synthesis of both cultures (401).

Although, according to Huttová, Canadian literature "achieved maturity" in the work of Hugh MacLennan and his like (397),[12] Brenčičová still speaks of Canadian literature as "the literary newborn" (21). She blames its rather belated development on the peculiarities of the country's socioeconomic development and, rather reductively, on its harsh environment. She presents Canada as a country that was for centuries too busy fighting the elements and trying to "survive" to be able to afford such a "luxury" as producing literature. In addition, it was plagued by a shortage of educated people who would possess the talents to write books and those who would read them (Brenčičová 21).

However simplistic and uninformed this is, the essence of Brenčičová's view is that Canada is an immature country with an underdeveloped literary tradition. Her opinion is in no way isolated. Northrop Frye's 1965 view of Canadian literature was also rather unflattering. He thought that it was the expression of an immature culture, there being "no Canadian writer of whom we can say what we can say of the world's major writers, that their readers can grow up inside their work without ever being aware of a circumference" (*The Bush Garden* 215–16). Although Frye was to change his opinion of Canadian literature by the 1980s, when he recognized that Canadian culture had after all awakened "from its sleeping beauty isolation" (*On Education* 7), Slovak literary scholars and critics only acknowledged the positive qualities of Canadian literature after 1989. One of the turning points was a 1989 review of Ted Wood's detective novel *Živá návnada* (*Live Bait*) in which the reviewer queried why so few Canadian books were translated into Slovak and came to the conclusion that it had nothing to do with the inferior quality of Canadian literature. In his opinion, Slovak publishers were to blame for the inadequate representation of Canadian literature on the Slovak book market because they were not making a sufficient effort to expand the selection of foreign literature available in Slovak (vh 3).

A quantitative analysis shows that, between 1948 and 1989, Slovak publishers, despite a politically unfavourable climate for the reception of literatures in English, brought out about twenty Canadian book titles. As books by E.T. Seton and L.M. Montgomery accounted for more than one-third of these titles and went through several editions, although they were not given sufficient critical attention, it may be assumed that they had the most decisive influence on the images Slovak readers constructed of Canada through reading its literature. Unlike in colloquial Slovak, these images were unrelated to hockey or Canadian humour because no hockey stories or Canadian humourists were translated in the surveyed period.[13] Rather than through its most popular sport, Canada came to be represented through its landscapes in socialist Slovakia, be they idealized pastoral ones or landscapes of savage beauty. As the natural environment of Canada is often identified as a force influencing and motivating Canadian writing, this is not surprising.

However, for Slovak readers, the Canadian landscapes featured in the texts translated into Slovak acquired a different meaning: they invited them to let go and leave behind the oppressive social conventions and norms. Although paratexts accompanying the publication of some books attempted to cast negative light on Canada, nothing could have detracted from the allure of this country's boundless spaces that promised what Slovaks under the authoritarian regime could only dream of—freedom. They were physically trapped in a country that denied them freedom of movement and restricted their access to basic rights. However, their minds could not be confined, and books about Canada's pristine forests inhabited by "wild animals" and "noble Indians" allowed them to wander freely.

Notes

1. Since Slovaks and Czechs shared a common state for most of the twentieth century, there was a lot of linguistic and cultural exchange between their languages. Although they have always possessed the status of independent languages, they have been similar enough to be mutually intelligible.
2. Tramping, as understood in the Czech lands, is an unorganized movement of people who like to spend their leisure time backpacking in the Czech countryside and sleeping outdoors.
3. Born Herbert Dyson Carter, he published under the name "Dyson Carter."
4. Gérard Genette employs the term *paratexts* to refer to all textual and non-textual elements that accompany a literary text and thus form "a *threshold*, or...a 'vestibule' that offers the world at large the possibility of either stepping in or turning back" (qtd. in Korte 33). The notion therefore comprises not only texts like titles, blurbs, forewords, afterwords, but also an author's comments on his or her work in private correspondence or during his or her public appearances.
5. Although Dyson Carter believed that he brought "an inside view of the enlightened and altruistic Soviet experiment" (Anderson 180), an alternative view to the purposefully distorted and censored information about the USSR spread by Western media and governments, in reality he put his name in the service of Soviet authorities. In 1950 he received an invitation to spend three weeks in the

USSR. As J.L. Black writes in *Canada in the Soviet Mirror: Ideology and Perception in Soviet Foreign Affairs, 1917–1991* (1998), his visit was "carefully orchestrated" (212). Besides planning what he was to be told at various host institutions, Soviet puppeteers also selected with special care what he would be shown.

6. Out of the twenty Canadian books that were published in Slovak translation between 1948 and 1989, three titles (*Anne of Green Gables*, *Anne of the Island*, and *Anne of Avonlea*) were authored by L.M. Montgomery and three (*Rolf in the Woods*, *Two Little Savages*, and *Animal Stories*) by E.T. Seton. Montgomery's novels, moreover, went through at least three editions each (*Anne of Green Gables* through an unbelievable five). See the database compiled within CEACS's translation research project and available at http://korel.savana-hosting.cz/cecanstud/www/sign/in?backlink=87hth (Login and Password: guest).

7. Jack London was one of the most widely published Western authors in socialist Czechoslovakia. He was acceptable because many of his novels are steeped in a socialist ideology, and he was said to be one of Vladimir Ilyich Lenin's favourite authors.

8. The first Canadian book ever published in Slovak translation was Martha Ostenso's lesser-known novel, *The Young May Moon*, which appeared in 1931.

9. E.T. Seton is probably the most translated Canadian writer in the Czech lands. In the interwar period alone, he was published seventy-six times (see Sparling, "'Canada'").

10. Slovak scouting celebrated its centennial in 2013.

11. Seton came upon the invitation of Miloš Seifert, Czech high school teacher, translator, amateur naturalist, and founder of the Woodcraft movement in the Czech lands, who also helped to bring it to Slovakia in the 1920s.

12. According to Huttová, after the Second World War the Canadian novel found its language as the authors were capable of deeper insight into the depicted reality, improved the formal aspects of their works, and focused on being good writers in the first place (397).

13. The only exception is Stephen Leacock. Although none of his books were translated into Slovak, quite a significant number of his sketches and short stories found their way into Slovak dailies, weekly magazines, and literary journals in the surveyed period (Otrísalová and Gazdík 116).

13

Economies of Export
Translating Laurence, Atwood, and Munro in Eastern Europe (1960–1989)

CRISTINA IVANOVICI

THE SUCCESSFUL EXPORT OF CONTEMPORARY Canadian literature abroad has been accompanied by feminist, postcolonial, and postmodernist approaches to English-Canadian writers, coupled with a growing scholarly interest in their reception in both Western and Eastern European contexts. Within these larger theoretical frameworks, biographical, text interpretation, and reader-response-oriented perspectives have prevailed, but these approaches have rarely questioned the material conditions that have often constricted or facilitated translation and publication strategies, and subsequently have excluded a corresponding discussion of translation practices with respect to the demands of different European publishing markets.[1] The neglect of these material factors have often resulted in misrepresentations of international readerships and limited understandings of the crucial role that cultural agents played in how translations of various contemporary Canadian writers appeared in pre-1989 politically different European contexts. With few recent exceptions—such as Lucia Otrísalová's and Don Sparling's analyses included in this collection, the translation research project conducted by the Central European Association for Canadian Studies (CEACS) from 2010 to 2012, and several essays published in *Translating Canada* (2007) and *Canada in Eight Tongues* (2012)—studies of the dissemination of contemporary English-Canadian literature internationally tend to disregard how translation operates as a key issue in the cultural export of these writers' fiction to non-Western European countries, and, intriguingly, seldom engage with archival materials related to specific translations.[2] Drawing primarily upon archived correspondence between Margaret Laurence, Margaret Atwood, Alice Munro, and European publishers, literary agents, editors, and translators, which is held in manuscript collections in Canada[3] but has not yet attracted significant scholarly attention, this chapter critiques a number of delayed and abandoned translation projects that discouraged a prompt cultural export of the three writers' fiction to Eastern Europe at what was a crucial moment for both the promotion of contemporary English-Canadian literature abroad and the development of Eastern European publishing industries between the 1960s and 1989.[4] My examination of the material conditions that facilitated these cultural transfers, therefore, highlights that pre-1989 Eastern European translations of contemporary English-Canadian women's writings were not published according to commercially driven criteria, but either as a result of passing censors' assessment of the writers' alignment with state-imposed imperatives or of succeeding in subverting socialist party ideology, editorial control, and financial censorship. More broadly, an analysis of ideological interventions in a series of translation projects that were often represented as non-lucrative or culturally insignificant interrogates to what extent the writings of these contemporary English-Canadian women were perceived as translatable across several political and cultural borders and how they were affected by the dynamics of cultural exchanges, (mis)representations of Eastern European publishing industries, and the values of cultural institutions.[5]

In the export of literature, translation typically functions as "soft diplomacy," or as "cultural or public diplomacy...[employed] in gaining 'soft power'" (von Flotow 9), in that it effectively brands a nation abroad, and so it also enables an evaluative assessment of the interrelationship between funding, publishing, reviewing, and marketing writers across borders. Viewed as instrumental in the promotion of contemporary English-Canadian writers as cultural brands, translations have been produced under a spectrum of political, economic, and cultural circumstances, often articulating a site of negotiation between national and global forces. Material conditions (e.g., policies and legislation pertaining to cultural production, external and publishers' translation funds, foreign currency regulations, ideologically marked editorial interference, market-driven pursuits of literary agents, publishers' interests in foreign rights, prestigious literary awards, and media presence) directly influenced what pre-1989 Eastern European publishing houses focused on, and how the writers' literary success has been translated in culturally and ideologically distinct environments. The correspondence examined in the following pages highlights the fact that Eastern European cultural agents consistently drew these writers' attention primarily to the economic pressures exerted upon national presses that initiated and centred on publishing translations of contemporary (foreign) literature. These pre-1989 translation projects also specifically indicate differences in the prestige and symbolic power assigned to Western and Eastern European publishers that mediated the cultural transfer of contemporary English-Canadian writers to Europe. Particularly before 1989, Western European and Eastern European publishing industries were placed in a binary opposition, due to state, economic, and cultural policies that accommodated or discouraged translations, the available funding, resources, and collaborative networks, writers' own involvement in promoting their work in translation, cultural agents' access to publishers' networks, and because of representations of these publishing markets as financially profitable or as unproductive.

The most evident connection between various pre-1989 Eastern European publishing industries and literary markets is that, in these countries, ideological imperatives subjected state publishers to regularly monitored thematic production plans, politically controlled networks, and prescribed economic resources, and negatively shaped publishing, translation, and marketing strategies, in order to predominantly advance ideological outputs. Despite being central to the production and enforcement of socialist propaganda, both cultural and educational institutions consistently experienced drastic budget cuts and registered declines in the quality of their services because pre-1989 Eastern European political regimes considered cultural industries to be non-lucrative compared to other sectors. With respect to economic aspects, financial restrictions over annual budgets allocated to national publishing houses resulted in the unavailability of printing resources, state-prescribed print-runs and paper quotas, poor paper quality standards, publishers' inability to transfer foreign currency abroad, fewer foreign titles issued annually, and limited contacts with Western European and North American presses. Coupled with ineffective copyright legislation, these strict ideological and economic imperatives primarily enabled the publication of out-of-copyright classics in translation, whereas translations of contemporary foreign writers' fiction occurred under exceptional circumstances.

Similar to the cultural export of contemporary English-Canadian literature to East Germany, which was briefly discussed in *Gaining Ground* (Nischik, "New Horizons" 258) and more broadly in *Translating Canada* (e.g., Ferguson 99–108; Korte 27–46; Oeding and von Flotow 81–82),[6] Eastern European translations constituted a gateway for readers under restrictive political regimes to access forbidden (fictional) worlds and Western cultures. Whereas East German translations of contemporary English-Canadian literature registered low production costs and became profitable for publishers in the German Democratic Republic (GDR) because of their export to other German-speaking countries,[7] or because East German publishers could also be granted export rights,[8] Eastern European translations were confined to small literary markets, partly due to linguistic diversity, but mainly due to both ideological imperatives and state-imposed regulations over the production, distribution, and circulation of translated texts and foreign currency transfers. The latter negatively affected the cultural export, as pre-1989 Eastern European currencies were not transferable and convertible abroad and were less economically powerful compared to Western European and North American currencies. Nevertheless, successful Eastern European translation projects frequently capitalized on informal book circulation networks and readers' demand for contemporary foreign literature. While book distribution, circulation, and prices remained under state control across pre-1989 Eastern Europe, publishers, translators, editors, academics, and readers succeeded in establishing informal collaborative networks with writers, cultural agents, and readers from outside of the Eastern Bloc, who provided access to otherwise forbidden texts that were produced in the so-called capitalist West. Upon their publication, since these informal book circulation networks valued the writers' non-alignment with socialist ideology as well as their political stances on freedom of expression, translations conferred a prestigious status to Eastern European cultural agents who exploited gaps in state-control mechanisms, passed censors' screening and subsequently contributed to the institutionalization of the work of contemporary foreign literature in translation. Usually included in "universal" or world literature collections of state-monitored publishing houses, most pre-1989 Eastern European translations of Atwood's, Laurence's, and Munro's fiction were accompanied by ideologically marked paratexts, such as forewords, afterwords, and book covers, that underlined the charged themes of anti-Americanism, feminism, nationalism, humanism, and motherhood, emphasized a capitalist world in decay (as opposed to the political goal of a successful "construction of a socialist society"), and underlined collectivism. In an attempt to politically control readers' responses, these paratexts represented contemporary English-Canadian writers as committed to gender equality and as cultural informants who remained socially responsible, outspoken about environmental issues, and highly critical of capitalism, elements that were advanced by party ideology and also stressed in academic readers' reports in an attempt to to legitimize translations of foreign literature. Although such paratexts repeatedly led to reductive representations of these writers' literary production, cultural activism, political stances, and gender politics, Laurence, Atwood, and Munro gained popularity among pre-1989 Eastern European academic and non-academic readerships, due to their critique of ideology and because their fiction centred on and subverted the taboo topics of censorship, abortion, lack of freedom of speech, and issues related to national identity, ethnic diversity, and political control. Their depictions of countries and intertextual references to contemporary (foreign) literatures to which common readers were denied access also contributed to their increased popularity in these countries. In this sense, the material conditions shaping the publication of their work in translation also point to the opposition between a commercially oriented Western capitalist evaluation and an Eastern European ideological or thematic assessment of what was worth publishing, or to different valuations of capitalist capital versus cultural capital.

Between 1960 and 1989, Atwood, Munro, and Laurence were the most successful contemporary English-Canadian women writers in Eastern Europe, generating interest in their work in translation in countries such as Bulgaria, Hungary, Poland, Romania, and the former Yugoslavia and Czechoslovakia (e.g., Kürtösi, *Canada in Eight Tongues*). According to the essays included in *Canada in Eight Tongues*, Eastern European translations of Atwood's fiction have currently registered an average of thirteen titles,[9] compared to one to only three translations of Munro's and Laurence's writings per Eastern European country. However, in each case, within the same decades, the majority of the Eastern European translations were published only after the early or the mid-2000s, when the Canadian government granted funding for publishers' translation projects, and recorded a typical print run of between 1,500 and 3,000 copies per translated title, compared to figures of over 30,000 copies for pre-1989 editions. Whereas a number of Western European translations of these writers' works were promptly initiated in the 1960s, the 1970s, or the mid-1980s,[10] most pre-1989 Eastern European translations were issued decades after the original Canadian publications,[11] often following editorial interventions, ideological censorship, and a restricted circulation in libraries and bookshops. Or they were abandoned mainly owing to restraining foreign currency regulations. In several Eastern European countries, Atwood's writings were first translated in the 1970s: a selection of poems from *The Animals in That Country* (1968) were included in *Panorama novije kanadske poezije* (1972), an anthology of Canadian poetry in Croato-Serbian translation, and also published in an anthology of English-Canadian poetry in Romanian translation called *Înțelegând zăpada* (1977).[12] Between the 1970s and 1989, *The Edible Woman* (1969), *Surfacing* (1972), and *Bodily Harm* (1981) were translated in most Eastern European countries, whereas translations of *The Handmaid's Tale* (1985) rarely passed censors' screening. In this sense, *Sluškinjina priča* (1988), the Croato-Serbian translation of the 1985 dystopian novel, represented a notable exception. Coupled with the paratexts of *Strömung* (1979)—the East German translation of *Surfacing*—the accompanying afterwords and forewords that legitimized the Eastern European translations of Atwood's early novels aimed to thematically inscribe her fiction within socialist propaganda by placing an emphasis on feminism, anti-Americanism, nationalism, humanism, daily life, idealistic depictions of nature, drawbacks of consumerism, and negative representations of capitalism.

As required by the main institution controlling printing and publishing at the time in the GDR, it was typically necessary that two academic recommendations or "Gutachten" (i.e., reports) accompany a publication's licence application. For example, in her report on *Surfacing*, which was submitted to Hauptverwaltung Verlage und Buchhandel—the censoring body responsible for publishing in the GDR—by the Leipzig-based publishing house in 1978, Gabriele Bock acclaimed the text as "Atwood's most influential so far," and accentuated the thematic discussion of the legal equality between women and men, identity search, the influence of the United States on Canada, pollution, and "short-sighted decisions of industrialization," coupled with the heroine's attempts to "become a consciously acting member of society" (Bundesarchiv DR1/2212.f.35, my translation) as central to the novel. In a second "Gutachten," submitted in July 1978, academic Eva Manske pointed out that *Surfacing* pursued the topic of anti-consumerism that Atwood had previously explored in *The Edible Woman* but was combined with the main character's search for identity (ibid., my translation).[13] With the aim of suggesting that the 1972 novel urged readers to develop "a sense of moral and social responsibility," Manske's academic recommendation further claimed that *Surfacing* sharply critiqued "the foreign infiltration of Canada by American capital, the thoughtless or profit-oriented destruction of the environment" and also "the brutal foreign policy of the United States" (ibid., my translation). In their thematic approach to ideologically charged topics, both reports thus attempted to inscribe Atwood's novel within socialist propaganda and, therefore, succeeded in legitimizing the publication of the East German translation, after the Leipzig-based publishing house complied with prescriptive regulations over production and export. Furthermore, these two East German academics' critical perspectives were subsequently reiterated in Bock's 1979 afterword to *Strömung*, not only in its emphasis on how Atwood's novel critiqued Americanism, but also in the details that this paratext provided. For example, Bock wrote, "in the 1970s, in Canada, the USA controlled 60 per cent of the industrial production, 60 per cent of the raw material production and 75 per cent of the oil and gas production" (196, my translation). Under these complex circumstances, Atwood was the first contemporary Canadian writer to secure a contract with a German publisher in 1978 (Müller 66), followed by the publication of *Surfacing* as *Strömung* ["Current"] in the GDR, with an approved print run of twenty thousand, and as *Der lange Traum* ["The Long Dream"] in the FRG in 1979, both translated by Reinhild Böhnke.

This initial tandem publication of Atwood's novel in translation in these two German contexts, qualified by Atwood's (West) Berlin-based editor and publisher as "another indirect compliment to the novel" (Conradi 27 July 1978, MS Coll.335.138.1), not only ensured a symbolic transnational project that capitalized on the West German publisher's capitalist evaluations and East German academics' thematic assessments, but also "continued with the enormous subsequent production, translation and enthusiastic reception of her works [in Germany]" (Oeding and von Flotow 81).[14] As Brita Oeding and Luise von Flotow note, Atwood significantly contributed to the promotion of contemporary Canadian women writers' fiction mainly in the late 1980s and 1990s, when German readers "could easily have got the impression that virtually all Canadian writers were women" (80). Such representations also resonated with feminist stances that were regularly adopted by German reviews of these English-Canadian novels as feminist. In this sense, the Canadian women writers published in German translation since the 1970s filled in a gap in the East and West German literary markets that were invaded by semi-autobiographical and radical feminist writings of national authors who aimed to redefine postwar German identity but tended to be viewed either as "too introspective" or as "aggressive, programmatic, and far too politicized" (84). Furthermore, German translations of English-Canadian women's writings met readers' demand for both entertaining stories and foreign literature in translation (Pausch 45), and were supported by funding as well as by publishers' belief in these texts as lucrative investments (39). What distinguishes Atwood from other contemporary Canadian women writers in how translations of her fiction became available in Germany, and, more broadly, in other European contexts, also lies in her consistent interventions in foreign and media representations of her literary persona as a cultural ambassador and anti-censorship campaigner, her regular participation at marketing and academic events organized in Western Europe, and a manifest awareness of the culturally symbolic values that Eastern European translations were afforded.

In Margaret Laurence's case, although foreign rights requests from both East and West German publishers were received in the early 1960s, translations of her novels and short stories were issued predominantly in West Germany before 1989. Similar to the translation of her fiction in Scandinavian countries and Italy, this cultural transfer was mainly facilitated by Western European publishers that made her first novels and short story collections available primarily to academic audiences, despite Laurence's limited attendance of promotional events organized in European countries and her limited involvement in most European translation projects. Whereas Western European publishing houses have issued Munro's short stories in translation and typically followed a chronological order predominantly since the mid-1980s (e.g., Balestra et al.; Müller 71), the majority of the Eastern European translations of Munro's fiction have been published only since the early 2000s, when external translation funds became accessible to Eastern European publishers, revisions of copyright legislation started being enforced, and national economies stabilized after having experienced not only extremely high inflation rates of between 100 per cent and 300 per cent but also drastic currency devaluations recorded in the mid- and late 1990s, particularly 1995 and 1997. What becomes evident in these three cases is that Laurence, Atwood, and Munro were translated in pre-1989 Eastern European contexts thanks to academic communities, informal book circulation networks, gaps in state-control mechanisms, and cultural agents' personal involvement in translation initiatives. However, these latter factors might explain why the majority of these Eastern European translations have not been issued chronologically. Furthermore, when compared to the financially profitable cases of their Western European counterparts, pre-1989 Eastern European translation projects tend to be represented in the Laurence, Atwood, and Munro papers and in their publishers' archived correspondence as culturally symbolic but financially insignificant, as limited by a poor management of financial or academic resources, and as often infringing copyright law, thus placing European publishers in a "West"/"East" binary divide.

Laurence was largely marketed by well-established North American and Western European presses and literary agencies as a Canadian woman writer who registered a significant success in North America and the UK. Although translations of her work did not represent a central issue for her Canadian, American, and British publishers, these publishers and Laurence had been approached for European translations of her fiction since the early 1960s.[15] Well-established German publishing houses' attempts to translate Laurence's debut novel, *This Side Jordan* (1960), in the GDR and the FRG shortly after its original publication, coupled with foreign rights requests from literary agents Celina Wieniewska[16] and Nanette Butler that McClelland & Stewart Ltd. had received by November 1960 (McClelland & Stewart Ltd. Fonds, First Accrual 35.37), constitute an intriguing case in terms of Laurence's and her Canadian publisher's limited agency in promptly exporting her fiction to Europe. Between March and November 1960, seven East and West German presses eagerly contacted McClelland & Stewart Ltd., which at that time dealt with the writer's translation rights, with hopes of publishing *This Side Jordan*.[17] In addition, Zurich-based Rascher Verlag requested permission for German translation rights, which McClelland & Stewart Ltd. eventually ignored, mainly owing to miscommunication problems and because the rights held in Canada, the United States, and the UK were prioritized (ibid.). Although correspondence between Piper Verlag, Wolfgang Krueger, Kurt Desch, Rutten & Loening, F.A. Brockhaus, Kreuz-Verlag, Verlagsbuchhandlung, and McClelland & Stewart Ltd. was established within the same year as the novel's original publication in English, the cultural agents involved in these prospective translation projects failed to bring these initiatives to fruition and to capitalize on the interest from both East and West Germany, and therefore did not build on thematic and commercially driven evaluations of her work, or on the potential exports to other European countries.[18]

This early correspondence reveals several issues that might not only account for the fact that *This Side Jordan* has not yet been translated into German but also explain why Laurence's fiction has rarely been translated in Eastern European countries.[19] First, since Macmillan of London was also considering the publication of *This Side Jordan*, miscommunication between European publishers and foreign rights representatives soon appeared; several European publishers sent their requests to both McClelland & Stewart Ltd. and Macmillan of London. Second, after "be[ing] inundated with translation option requests" (J.G. McClelland 18 Oct. 1960, McClelland & Stewart Ltd. Fonds, First Accrual 35.43), the Canadian publisher eventually waived responsibility for foreign rights to Laurence's American literary agent, Willis K. Wing, who ceased to represent the writer in 1968 when his agency closed (Lennox and Panofsky 5) and Laurence decided to work with the John Cushman Literary Agency instead. Third, when considering prospective profits generated from translation projects, the John Cushman Literary Agency did support French-Canadian, Italian, and Scandinavian translations of Laurence's novels and short stories, but, particularly in the 1970s, generally prioritized the promotion of her fiction in North America and Britain.[20] Furthermore, although Munich-based Droemer Knaur published *The Stone Angel* (1964) in Herbert Schlüter's translation under the title *Der steinerne Engel* in 1965, the economic value of other potential German translations failed to be acknowledged. In 1966, which appears to be a crucial point in how the promotion of her novels and short stories in European countries was managed, while suggesting the cultural value of German translations, Laurence herself questioned her own understanding of publishers' rights in German translations of her work as well as whether this cultural transfer would make "a lot of a difference" (Laurence 31 May 1966, Adele Wiseman Fonds, F0447, Accession 1991-012/043.14). Although in 1969 Droemer Knaur issued *Die Stimmen von Adamo*, the translation of *The Tomorrow-Tamer* (1963), the Laurence papers only briefly document this publisher's interest in introducing her fiction to (West) German readerships. Finally, the majority of Eastern European presses were confronted with restrictive legislation regarding the payment of royalties in foreign currency and academic translators' limited access to Laurence's work in the original. In 1978, East German academic Karla El-Hassan, for instance, in her second letter to Laurence, reminded the writer about "the currency situation and a lack of possibilities of information [leading to] serious obstacles in the GDR to get the material necessary,"[21] and kindly asked to be sent copies of short stories "because [she] didn't know any other way out" (El-Hassan 6 May 1978, F0341, Accession 1980-001/015.32). A second edition of *Der steinerne Engel*, with a foreword by Kaila El-Hassan, was issued by East German publishing house Philipp Reclam in its "universal literature" collection in 1988, after the two required academic recommendations, signed by Gabriele Bock and Marianne Müller in 1987, had legitimized the translation and the publication plan for a print run of twenty thousand copies had been approved (Bundesarchiv, DR1/2221.f.225). However, neither El-Hassan's 1978 correspondence with Laurence, nor her foreword to the 1988 edition of *Der steinerne Engel* mentioned the West German translations of Laurence's fiction that were issued in the 1960s, thus indicating restrictive circumstances shaping both the formation of academic networks and book circulation in the GDR. Taken together, the 1965, 1969, and the 1988 German translations of her fiction also indicate a missed opportunity for Laurence, her agents, and her publishers to capitalize on both West and East German publishing houses' and academics' interest in her work, although the practice of exporting East German translations to German-speaking countries and beyond foregrounded the formation of collaborative cultural networks that could be employed in compiling publication lists or promoting anthologies of contemporary English-Canadian authors.

Miscommunication between Laurence's Canadian, American, and British publishers and European publishing houses persisted from the late 1960s onwards. For example, when two Polish cultural agents approached McClelland & Stewart Ltd., as well as Macmillan of London, and suggested a translation of *This Side Jordan* into Polish (Lason n.d.; Michalski n.d., McClelland & Stewart Ltd. Fonds, First Accrual 35.37),[22] their enthusiasm was not reciprocated and the projects did not eventually materialize. By 1974, McClelland & Stewart Ltd. had transferred the foreign rights management to A.P. Watt Ltd., which mainly focused on permission requests to translate Laurence's fiction in Western Europe, particularly in Scandinavian countries. In 1982, when A.P. Watt received a foreign rights request from Bulgarian publisher Hristo Dnov who planned to publish *A Jest of God* (1966) in translation and offered an advance of four hundred dollars against a royalty of 6 per cent (Shaughnessy 18 Jan. 1982, F0341, Accession 1984-004/002.76), Laurence promptly expressed her delight and amazement, even if "how the novel w[ould] translate into Bulgarian [wa]s anyone's guess" (Laurence 1 Feb. 1982, F0341, Accession 1984-004/002.76), and agreed to sign the contract despite "the modest offer" (Shaughnessy 18 Jan. 1982, F0341, Accession 1984-004/002.76). About a month later, the Bulgarian translation project was abandoned, most likely because "the problem was getting hold of the foreign currency" (Shaughnessy 4 Mar. 1982, F0341, Accession 1984-004/002.76). Despite this publisher's hope "to be able to publish [*A Jest of God*] 'in the next few years'" (ibid.), projects of translating Margaret Laurence's fiction into Bulgarian have not yet materialized.

In Atwood's case, the impressive number of translations suggests that her fiction has appealed to academic as well as informal reading communities in addition to underlining her recognition of both economic and symbolic values attached to translation.[23] The 1970s constituted a turning point in Atwood's career: her work gained critical acclaim in North America; permission requests for translation of her poetry and fiction were received from Western and Eastern European (academic) translators and publishers; and the early and often well-received translations contributed to the successful representation of the writer as a cultural brand of Canada. Nevertheless, these early translations did not always generate profits for either Atwood or her Eastern European publishers. Whereas in West Germany and Scandinavian countries, translations of Atwood's fiction did demonstrate their economic value, in pre-1989 Eastern European countries, the impact of her fiction, mainly due to how a thematic discussion of her novels focused on anti-Americanism, nationalism, feminism, and censorship, for instance, was more politically subversive rather than financially profitable. In the latter contexts, translations enabled Atwood to achieve recognition among academic and informal reading communities, in that her work was perceived as translatable across multiple geographical, cultural, and ideological barriers.

In several files tracing her correspondence related to pre-1989 Eastern European translation projects, Atwood acknowledges forms of institutionalized censorship as practices that particularly affected the production and the circulation of her fiction in translation in the region. Although allusions to financial censorship do occur in the pre-1989 business correspondence between Atwood and her foreign rights representatives, the writer herself explicitly refers mainly to ideologically imposed editorial censorship and state-controlled foreign currency regulations that Eastern European publishers had to abide by under restrictive political regimes as well as during the early 1990s, when key legislation had yet to be enforced. In addition, various cultural agents also drew Atwood's attention to the economic pressures imposed upon Eastern European presses with respect to publishing pre-1989 translations of her fiction. As a form of financial censorship, this set of economic regulations often affected the prestige of the Eastern European publishing house that aimed to promote Atwood's work to large audiences, in that whereas the press was highly recognized by pre-1989 Eastern European readerships, its economic power was perceived abroad as insignificant. Such circumstances also resulted in an un-chronological or random publication of Atwood's writings in translation in Eastern Europe. For instance, although her Polish publisher before 1989, Książka i Wiedza, did plan to translate her early novels, the projects were often not financially profitable for the Canadian author, since "the Poles frequently ha[d] difficulty in purchasing foreign currency and therefore often ask[ed] to pay royalties in local currency, *zlotys*, to be retained in Poland for the use of the author" and "any monies transferred [were] subject to a 40% withholding tax" (Fisher 16 Mar. 1979, MS Coll.335.140.3). What further complicated the initiative to publish the translation of *Surfacing* into Polish, with a planned print run of ten thousand copies (ibid.), was that "there [was] very little likelihood of this money [in *zlotys*] being available to [Atwood's] use for a further two and a half years" and that the Polish publishing house retained money "payable on publication" and thus seemed "notoriously slow" in transferring it (Fisher 11 Apr. 1979, MS Coll.335.140.3). Furthermore, in her correspondence regarding cultural exchanges with Eastern Bloc countries in the 1980s, Atwood alluded to both financial and editorial censorship that Polish publishers had been exposed to, and rendered the publication of her work in Polish translation as financially insignificant while recognizing the translation's role in promoting her as non-compliant with ideological imperatives:

> I have a Polish publisher, as you know, and *zlotys have apparently accumulated*, but lord knows how many or what they're worth....*Doubt that the zlotys would finance such a trip* [to Warsaw], or that the poor *beleaguered* publishers have any spare cash. Interested?...
>
> I would be well enough behaved, I think, and try not to make a huge crashing faux pas; though of course I would be meeting writers informally. I would also like to avoid situations in which one would be blatantly used by govts in question as some kind of *propaganda boost*. As I know people in both places, I don't think they could put any glaring *mistranslations* of what I say over on me, though there are always *edited versions*. (Atwood 16 Feb. 1982, MS Coll.335.140.1; emphasis added)

Coupled with the correspondence between Atwood and John Farquharson Ltd., which dealt with European translation rights at that time, these letters show that, in the case of several pre-1989 Polish translation projects, the royalty payments could not be made available to the writer, due to the restrictive law on the transfer of foreign currency outside of Poland and because of the taxes that the Polish state would have applied, should such a transfer of either national or foreign currency have been attempted. In this project and similar pre-1989 Eastern European translation projects, cultural agents often indicated their belief that translations of Atwood's fiction "would not be a waste of time" and acknowledged that there was "a great interest in Canada and all things Canadian all over Eastern Europe and an ever growing interest in 'Western' literature" (Durrant 8 Oct. 1984,

MS Coll.335.140.3), but they also found royalty payment arrangements extremely limiting and confusing, since at that time Eastern European publishers could pay in non-transferable national currencies only. For instance, even though a project to translate selections from *Bluebeard's Egg* (1983) was suggested by the Polish publishing house Czytelnik in 1984 (ibid.),[24] the literary agency did not grant permission, in case a translation planned by Książka i Wiedza might have also been issued (MS Coll.335.140.3). Unlike other pre-1989 Eastern European publishers, Książka i Wiedza did manage to publish *Surfacing* under the title *Wynurzenie* in 1987,[25] soon after the Polish translation of *The Edible Woman* under the title *Kobieta do zjedzenia* in 1986, which was then followed by *Pani wyrocznia* (1989),[26] the Polish translation of *Lady Oracle* (1976).

Politically imposed financial regulations also affected Atwood's work in Romanian translation before the early 1990s. As discussed elsewhere (Ivanovici, "A Courageous Project" 85–89), Bucharest-based Romanian publisher Univers issued the translation of *The Edible Woman* under the title *O femeie obişnuită* ["An Ordinary Woman"] in 1989, after Romanian academic and translator Margareta Petruţ was also granted translation rights by André Deutsch Ltd. in 1986. However, the original title was subjected to editorial censorship, since a title faithful to the original would have jeopardized the translation's chances for publication (Petruţ qtd. in Ivanovici, "A Courageous Project") by alluding to the taboo topics of cannibalism and famine. Because of the national legislation prohibiting payment in foreign currency, Univers press failed to transfer the money outside the country (MS Coll.335.137.3; MS Coll.335.137.11:3; MS Coll.335.138.9; MS Coll.335.140.3) and therefore suggested that it could be spent by Atwood in Romania (Larmore 23 Aug. 1989, MS Coll.335.137.11:3), thus rendering the entire translation project as non-lucrative for the writer. Although this latter correspondence also testified to Atwood's interest in having *Survival* published in Romanian translation by Margareta Petruţ in 1989 and, therefore, engaged with the politically and culturally symbolic capital that the Romanian edition might have represented, such a translation has not yet been issued in Romania. In turn, the Romanian translations of Atwood's fiction were interrupted until 1995, when *The Handmaid's Tale* was published under the title *Galaad 2195* ["Gilead 2195"], which focused on inscribing the novel to speculative fiction or science fiction, arguably in an attempt to respond to the publisher's commercially driven criteria. Similar to paratexts to other pre-1989 and post-1990 Eastern European translations of the novel, and to her own afterword to the 1995 translation, Monica Bottez's afterword to *Povestirea cameristei*, the 2006 Romanian translation of *The Handmaid's Tale*—issued under a title faithful to the original—did not draw any comparisons between the created fictional world and the restrictive regimes, policies, and ideologies that Romanian readerships experienced before 1990. Instead, it outlined the mainstream Western academic critical approaches to the acclaimed dystopian novel. The subsequent delayed publications of translations of Atwood's novels were partly due to the fact that December 1989 unexpectedly brought the fall of the Communist regime in Romania, and also because, in the early 1990s, the majority of the consecrated state-owned and state-controlled Romanian publishing houses became privatized, had to face national currency reforms, dealt with fierce competition caused by an unprecedented editorial boom, and were forced to grapple with the collapse of state monopoly over the national book distribution system.

A keen interest in Alice Munro's fiction was also evident in several Eastern European countries from the late 1970s onwards, despite a constant disempowering lack of resources available to these publishers, editors, translators, and readers.[27] Both academic and non-academic readers often approached McGraw-Hill Ryerson, Macmillan of Canada, and Munro's literary agency to request copies of her short story collections, suggest the writer's presence at literary events organized in Eastern Europe, initiate translation projects, and contribute to the promotion of English-Canadian literature in the region. However, Eastern European publishers encountered problems such as poor academic networks beyond the Eastern Bloc and nonexistent or limited translation funds. Moreover, shifting pre-1989 Eastern European publishing markets and their devaluation and disadvantageous positioning compared to German, Norwegian, Danish, and Italian presses, for instance, also negatively affected Eastern European publishers. Both West and East German academics have been interested in translating and teaching Munro's fiction since the late 1970s. Approximately thirteen of her short story collections have been translated into German, and reviews of her work appear regularly in mainstream German literary magazines and daily newspapers.

One illustration of how economies of translation resulted in a delayed export of Munro's short story collections in Eastern Europe is the case of permission requests to translate the writer's fiction into Romanian.[28] A letter from Ileana Galea, an academic who translated and taught modern English literature at the Babeş-Bolyai University (located in Cluj-Napoca), to Alice Munro's North American literary agent, Virginia Barber, acknowledged both Munro's international recognition and a series of politically and culturally symbolic values that were conferred upon translations within the Romanian literary market:

> Unfortunately *few Canadian novels are available here*. But I am sure the novels [sic] of Alice Munro will be widely read and appreciated in Romania....
>
> My wish is to translate some novels by Alice Munro into Romanian and also to write about her work in our literary journals. The novel that I've read is entitled "Who Do You Think You Are?" and I'd like to translate it. *Unfortunately we cannot pay royalties in hard currency or any other currency because of the difficulties involved in the great economic changes after the Revolution we had three years ago.* I wrote to Alice Munro and I enclose a Xeroxed copy of her letter. I have her permission to translate her novels....
>
> I'd be very happy if I could contribute to this *noble aim* [of publishing world literature] with my translations from the books of Alice Munro. (Galea 16 Dec. 1992, Alice Munro Fonds, Accession 883/11.5.1.2; emphasis added)

Although the marginalia mentions "told her no, 2/3/93" (Alice Munro Fonds, Accession 883/11.5.1.2), the correspondence generated by this initial proposal illustrates conflicting values assigned to the Romanian translation of Munro's fiction: an insignificant economic value, according to Munro's literary agent; and a culturally symbolic one, according to Munro. Despite the problematic repetition of "novel"/"novels," which indicates Romanian readers' limited access to both Munro's fiction and critical studies of her work in the early 1990s, Galea's initial letter to Virginia Barber poignantly signals not only academic interest in the Canadian writer's work but also high market demand—both before and after 1989—for translations to which large Romanian readerships ascribed new cultural and political values. Even though the first correspondence exchange between the Romanian academic translator and Munro is incomplete in the manuscript collections deposited at the University of Calgary, a letter from Munro did grant Galea permission to translate *Who Do You Think You Are?* and confirmed Munro's interest in having her fiction translated into Romanian (Munro 20 Oct. 1992, Alice Munro Fonds, Accession 883/11.5.1.2). At the end of her reply to Galea's first letter, Munro mentioned that she did not make such decisions herself and suggested that Galea could contact her agent, Virginia Barber, whose business address she enclosed. Nevertheless, several months later, permission to translate *Who Do You Think You Are?* into Romanian was refused. It was only in 2011 that Litera publishing house issued the Romanian translation of *Too Much Happiness*, under the title *Prea multă fericire*,[29] followed in 2013 by a second edition that acclaims Munro as the winner of the Man Booker International Prize in 2009 and of the Nobel Prize for Literature in 2013, a marketing strategy that also facilitated the publication of four of her other short story collections in Romanian translation in 2014.[30] Therefore, the 1992 translation initiative counteracts assumptions that no attempts to translate Munro's fiction into Romanian had been made prior to the 2000s. Furthermore, the impacts of the translation project initiated in 1992 and abandoned in 1993 point to a situation similar to the case studies of Slovakia, Poland, and

Bulgaria, among other Eastern European countries, thus contradicting Jason Blake's claim that "which book or author gets translated [in Eastern European countries] is an eclectic mix of personal initiative, market concerns and pure chance" (177–78).

With the collapse of socialist ideology in the 1990s, Eastern European publishing houses and cultural agents were given a much-needed freedom of which they had been previously deprived, particularly with respect to how they contributed to the formation of reading communities for literary genres banned under totalitarian regimes, how they engaged with the expectations of large readerships for literatures in English, and how they responded to post-1989 shifts to market-oriented translation and commercially driven publishing strategies. The newly gained freedom of speech and the political paradigm shifts occurring across Eastern Europe in the early 1990s also meant that publishing industries faced multiple changes in structure and operation, which required them to re-evaluate practices of translation, publishing, writing, and reading. Since the late 1990s, Eastern European presses have freely published English-Canadian writers in translation, addressed readers' expectations, employed capitalist-oriented marketing strategies, and extended their participation at international book fairs and networking events. Because in the mid-1990s most Eastern European countries experienced a series of economic crises, it was only in the early 2000s that national policies, economic measures, and external funding allowed for capitalist-oriented promotion strategies and also enabled a re-evaluation of Eastern European publishing industries as lucrative markets. Despite a persistent interest in translating contemporary English-Canadian literature and an increasing number of titles published annually, numerous post-1989 Eastern European translations still raise issues related to quality,[31] copyright, availability of funding, and Canadian writers' own involvement in the formation of readerships for their work.

The examined correspondence files, coupled with the gaps in the cultural export of these three writers' works, highlight that although Eastern European translators did approach Laurence, Atwood, and Munro shortly after their recognition in Canada, most Eastern

European translation projects failed or were discontinued due to restrictive material conditions, the market-driven pursuits of North American literary agents, and Canadian publishers' interests in investing in profitable European literary markets, as well as the writers' own involvement in the process of cultural transfer. Although this chapter does not claim to be exhaustive, it has suggested that restrictive material conditions, assessments of European translations as economic capital and/or cultural capital, and these contemporary Canadian women writers' types of interventions in the production of their work in translation have affected Eastern European readers' access to these writers' fiction. The delayed publications of contemporary English-Canadian women's fiction in translation, coupled with a series of abandoned projects that infringed upon the texts' prompt availability within pre-1989 Eastern European literary markets, therefore, resulted in an underrepresentation of readerships for English-Canadian women's fiction in Eastern Europe.

Author's Note

Permission to use the correspondence cited in this chapter has been kindly granted by Margaret Laurence's estate, Margaret Atwood, Linda Shaughnessy, United Agents LLP, Anne Louise Fisher, Karla El-Hassan, and Eva Manske. All these permissions were granted in early and mid-2016.

Notes

1. For instance, the methodologies employed in exploring contemporary writers' literary archives have tended to chiefly consider how drafts of literary manuscripts can be scrutinized (e.g., McGill 2006, 2009; McWilliams 2009), focused exclusively on a Canadian writer's correspondence or professional relationship with North-American authors, publishers, and cultural agents (e.g., Lennox 1993; Lennox and Panofsky 1997; Thacker 2005), investigated the organization and cultural value of manuscript collections (e.g., Gerson 2001; McCaig 1997, 1998, 2002; McGill 2009); analyzed representations of literary celebrity in the archives (e.g., Nischik 2009; Slettedahl Macpherson 2010; York 2013); or prioritized biographical and historiographical perspectives on writers' and/or publishers'

fonds (e.g., Gillies 2007; King 1997, 1999; Morley 1991; Morra and Schagerl 2012; Paňotsky 2012).

2. In her investigation of English-Canadian literature in translation in the GDR and the FRG, Barbara Korte (28) briefly discusses the official print-licence form, now catalogued in the Bundesarchiv (DR1/2221, f.225), that allowed for the 1988 East German publication of Margaret Laurence's *The Stone Angel* under the title *Der steinerne Engel*. Neither the academic reports leading to this translation, nor Korte's study referred to the 1965 edition of *Der steinerne Engel*, and thus indicated unawareness of previous German publishers' permission requests that are currently deposited in the McClelland & Stewart Ltd. Fonds.

3. My access to manuscript collections that include Laurence's, Atwood's, and Munro's correspondence files with publishers, editors, and translators was enabled by an Independent Scholar Award from the Canada-UK Foundation (2015), an International Council for Canadian Studies Postdoctoral Fellowship (2012), a *Universitas 21* travel grant (2008), and a research travel grant from the British Association for Canadian Studies (2008). The examined print licences and academic recommendations for the analyzed East German translations (currently deposited at the Bundesarchiv) were accessed during a John F. Kennedy Institute for North American Studies library research grant (2007).

4. Most book history studies of Eastern European publishing industries (e.g., Billiani 2006; Schöpflin, 1983; Smejkalová 2001) also emphasize the 1960s as a decade when the state's control of national presses, publishing practices, and the availability of foreign literature to large readerships was secured, and explore fruitful comparisons between pre-1989 and post-1990 cultural environments.

5. Conversely, particularly since the early 2000s, Eastern European publishers have consistently demonstrated interest in translating contemporary writers who received literary awards, a selective practice that perhaps explains the association of Canadian literature awards with foreign markets.

6. These studies, however, enforce Gaby Thomson-Wohlgemuth's claim that censorship constituted a silenced area of GDR's society (62), a critical approach applicable to both most pre-1989 Eastern European contexts and Eastern European translations of contemporary Canadian literature.

7. Print licence forms authorizing East German translations of foreign literature also specified the percentage of copies for export (most often to the Federal Republic of Germany and Switzerland).

8. For instance, Philipp Reclam Verlag was also granted rights to export *Strömung* (Bundesarchiv, DR1/2212.f.35) and *Der steinerne Engel* (DR1/2221.f.225).

9. The majority of these titles, however, were published after the mid-1990s or the early 2000s, not before the collapse of socialist regimes.

10. In Atwood's case, for instance, the German translations of *Good Bones* (1992) and *Alias Grace* (1996) were initiated simultaneously with the original Canadian

publications, indicating that her work was "assigned a pioneering role" (Oeding and von Flotow 88). In this respect, Atwood exemplifies how contemporary English-Canadian writers gain symbolic capital through their consecration in non-English-speaking countries, which can put publishers under pressure to publish translations in tandem with the originals.

11. See the CEACS online database (http://www.cecanstud.cz/en/translation-research-project-database), for instance, which lists a total of approximately 2,500 translations of Canadian literature that have been so far published in Eastern Europe, a small figure compared to over 6,500 literary translations from English into German that were issued in 2015 alone (Börsenverein des Deutschen Buchhandles 2015).

12. The publication of a selection of Atwood's poems in these Romanian anthologies was discussed in my previous studies (Ivanovici, "A Courageous Project" 85; *In Search of Utopia* 143–50).

13. It was not until 1985 that West German publishing house Claassen issued *Die eßbare Frau*, the first German translation of *The Edible Woman*. In 1989, Aufbau-Verlag issued the translation in the GDR.

14. Stefan Ferguson (101–08) discusses aspects regarding textual and cultural differences between the two German translations of *Surfacing*, whereas a section of my doctoral dissertation (*In Search of Utopia* 175–90) explores forms of financial censorship and economic aspects related to *Strömung*.

15. What complicates the reading of the Laurence papers is also the fact that the writer herself destroyed her business letters before leaving England in 1973 (Laurence, n.d., F0341, Accession 1980-001/019: 132a). This situation also explains several gaps in Laurence's correspondence with regard to translation projects planned by both East and West German publishers in the 1960s and by Eastern European presses in the 1970s, thus rendering Eastern European interest in translations of her fiction as rather inconsistent.

16. By December 1960, literary agent and translator Celina Wieniewska had not been sent a copy of the manuscript, even though permission for Italian, Norwegian, and German translation rights had been requested, as indicated in a list of translation requests (McClelland & Stewart Ltd. Fonds, First Accrual 35.37).

17. Within this time frame, requests from German, Swiss, French, Swedish, Danish, Dutch, and Italian publishing houses were received by McClelland & Stewart Ltd., while the original edition of *This Side Jordan* was issued in the fall of the same year.

18. Intriguingly, the correspondence initiated by Kurt Desch, and dated August 9, 1960, was in the German language; upon receipt, the letter includes a handwritten English translation of the publisher's request for a sample copy for the German rights to be sent (McClelland & Stewart Ltd. Fonds, First Accrual 35.37).

19. The CEACS online database includes only four titles—namely, the 1991 Croatian and the 2000 Slovak translations of "The Loons," *Hledači pramenů* (1993),

the Czech translation of *The Diviners*, and *Kameni anđeo* (2007), the Serbian translation of *The Stone Angel*. None of her novels have yet been published in Hungary, Romania, and Bulgaria, for example.

20. In her private correspondence with Al Purdy, for instance, Laurence stated that most of her income came from either Canada or the United States (Laurence 31 Aug. 1967, Lennox, *Margaret Laurence—Al Purdy* 49).

21. In most cases, foreign currency regulations also resulted in East German publishers buying the rights from West German publishers, since the latter had capital in a currency with a higher purchase power and also typically secured rights for all German-speaking countries (Thomson-Wohlgemuth, 89).

22. Both letters are highly damaged. However, most correspondence included in the same file was dated in the 1960s.

23. Margaret Atwood has often been hailed as a Canadian writer whose work has been translated into over thirty-five languages. The Atwood literary archive, in its current arrangement of six manuscript collections and inclusion of over 250 European translations of her fiction, places both literary translation and literary celebrity as central cultural values, in addition to touching upon abandoned translation projects that aimed to introduce her work to Eastern European audiences, despite pre-1989 restrictive policies.

24. *Bluebeard's Egg* has not yet been translated into Polish.

25. The novel was re-issued in Polish translation by different publishers in 1998 and in 2004.

26. The CEACS online database does not list *Pani wyrocznia* (1989) and *Kobieta do zjedzenia* (2004). The Thomas Fisher Rare Book Library holds the 1997 and the 2008 editions of *Pani wyrocznia*.

27. For a discussion of how Alice Munro's fiction is taught at various European universities, see, for instance, the interviews included in part three of *Alice Munro: Understanding, Adapting and Teaching* (2016), edited by Mirosława Buchholtz.

28. The majority of Munro's short story collections have been published in Eastern European countries only since 2003. In Poland, for instance, translation projects have materialized since 2009, most probably due to the translation funding programs available.

29. Since 2010, translations of *Too Much Happiness* have been issued in most Eastern European countries.

30. These two editions do not include prefaces, forewords, or afterwords. Both the 2013 and 2014 editions were published by Litera but with different translators.

31. In their study of translation of Canadian literature in Bulgaria, Andrei Andreev and Diana Yankova underline issues pertaining to the quality of translations published after the early 1990s (25).

14

Canadian Literature and Canadian Studies in the Czech Republic

DON SPARLING

IN 2010 THE CENTRAL EUROPEAN ASSOCIATION for Canadian Studies (CEACS) embarked on a two-year project aimed at tracking down and recording all translations made into the eight languages spoken in its members' countries of literary works by Canadian authors or authors dealing with Canada. In doing so, it opted for a broad definition of the word *literary*—in practice, that used by the editors of the *Literary History of Canada* (1965), as explained by Northrop Frye in his "Conclusion":

> We have asked for chapters on political, historical, religious, scholarly, philosophical, scientific, and other non-literary writing, to show how the verbal imagination operates as a ferment in all cultural life. We have included the writings of foreigners, of travellers, of immigrants, of emigrants—even of emigrants whose most articulate literary emotion was their thankfulness at getting the hell out of Canada. (214)

The project brought many surprises. One was the final number of entries in the project database—slightly over 2,700.[1] Another was the time span: the oldest entry in the database, for a Czech translation of Frederick Marryat's *The Settlers of Canada*, dates from 1875, while the first translation of a book by a Canadian author—May Agnes Fleming—appeared in 1900 (this was also into Czech). But perhaps most surprising—for me, at any rate—was that well over 1,000 of the entries were for translations into Czech, representing almost 40 per cent of the total.

This is not the place to explore the reasons for this remarkable fascination for things Canadian among Czech readers.[2] Instead, in this chapter I wish to look at the explosion of Canadian and Canada-related texts in Czechoslovakia and the Czech Republic in the period since the end of the Communist regime in 1989 against the broader background of Canadian public diplomacy and suggest some of the main factors that have fed the expansion of the Canadian literary presence in the country in recent years.

Canadian Studies and Czech Universities

Before 1989, options for Canadian cultural diplomacy in Czechoslovakia were severely limited. Canada did not have a government program such as the Fulbright program, let alone privately funded NGOs such as the International Research & Exchanges Board that enabled American scholars to do research in countries of the Communist Bloc. Nor did it have its own cultural agency along the lines of the UK's British Council. Thus, any support from Canada in the area of cultural diplomacy was of necessity ad hoc, dependent on the momentary situation in Canada or the personal commitment of an individual. As an example of the former, twice in the 1970s, as part of a program originating within the Canada Council, the Canadian Embassy in Prague made gifts of large numbers of Canadian books (in this case, Canadian literature and literary criticism) to the English

Department of Charles University in Prague. As an example of the latter, more than one Canadian diplomat (to the best of my knowledge on their own initiative, not as part of embassy policy) quietly distributed to Czechs copies of books published in Canada that were on the official blacklist in Czechoslovakia.

Both types of initiative, though praiseworthy, had severe limitations. In the case of the book donations to Charles University, university administrators were initially unwilling to say "yes" for fear of possible political repercussions. In the end the books were reluctantly accepted, but only after political pressure at the highest level. However, only books by internationally known authors (for example Margaret Atwood and Robertson Davies) were actually added to the departmental library; the rest, uncatalogued, were locked in cupboards. In the case of the "libri prohibiti," the impact was also limited, owing to the small numbers involved and the problem of safe distribution.

With so few tools available for the support of Canadian culture and academic development, it is no surprise that Canadian studies was virtually non-existent in Czechoslovakia before the end of the Communist regime in 1989. The first Canadian studies course in the country dates to as late as 1985: this was a one-semester elective Canadian literature course that I managed to introduce within the degree program in English and American studies at Jan Evangelista Purkyně University (now Masaryk University) in Brno. Additional courses were created in subsequent years, but only one could be offered per year. Interest among students was great, but the available materials were extremely limited: books came from my personal library, and because of the total ban on photocopying facilities in the country, any material needed for distribution to the students had to be typed.

With the collapse of the Communist system in 1989, the context in which Canadian studies could be pursued changed radically. However, there was no framework for promoting Canadian studies: neither Czechoslovakia nor the Central European region as a whole was yet eligible to take part in official Canadian government programs for the support of Canadian studies (this came towards the end of the 1990s), nor were there any teachers with a knowledge of the field. In this situation, the Canadian Embassy in Prague opted to jump-start the discipline. Substantial financial support was offered directly to Charles University in Prague and to Komenský University in Bratislava as an incentive to introduce Canadian studies. In each case this support amounted to C$10,000 and was to be used for two purposes: first, to enable a teacher to travel to Canada for a month, familiarize himself or herself with the Canadian studies scene, meet Canadianists there, and obtain materials for courses; and second, to permit the purchase of Canadian books. At Masaryk University a similar sum was donated solely for the purchase of books, the aim being to create the nucleus of an important regional library collection.

Though extremely generous financially, these contributions had varying impacts. In Prague, where the member of the English Department chosen to introduce Canadian studies was a highly regarded teacher and one of the country's most respected translators, the initiative took root and launched a Canadian studies tradition within the English Department that continues to this day. In Bratislava, however, the individual selected used the opportunity to travel to Canada, but never followed through with any teaching of Canadian-related courses; the initiative thus died on the vine. It was only five years later, thanks to another teacher in the English Department there, that the teaching of Canadian literature began; this has continued into the present. In both cases, however, the status of Canadian studies has been precarious, depending as it does on the personal interest of a very few, at times only one, teacher, and largely restricted to the English Department.

In Brno—owing partly to the slightly older tradition and partly to structural reforms at the university that favoured innovation—Canadian studies flourished. Very soon it expanded beyond the English Department, first to the Department of Romance Languages and Literatures, then to others. As of 2016, Canada-related courses are offered in Anglo- and Franco-Canadian literatures (children's literature included), Canadian English and French, folk and popular music, film, history, political science, geography, Native studies, and queer studies. Of the twelve teachers involved, two-thirds visited Canada on Faculty Research Program (FRP) or Faculty Enrichment Program (FEP) grants, and in fact were first drawn into the field of Canadian studies thanks to these grants.

Much research has also been produced by scholars at Masaryk University, most notably a massive (534-page) history (in Czech) of francophone literature in Quebec and the rest of Canada (*Dějiny francouzsko-kanadské a quebecké literatury*, 2005) by the chair of the Department of Romance Languages and Literatures, Petr Kyloušek, and a collection of essays on the search for Canadian identity in Canadian literature and film that appeared in both Czech (*My— Oni—Já*) and English (*Us—Them—Me*) versions in 2009. The library collection has grown to almost six thousand volumes, and covers a wide range of disciplines, in both English and French. It serves as a research library for the broader Central European region, reflecting the fact that the CEACS has its Secretariat in Brno.

The factors influencing the emergence of Canadian studies in the Czech Republic were similar all across Central Europe. In Czechoslovakia/the Czech Republic, the first impetus, coming from the Canadian Embassy in Prague in 1990, was decisive in the sense that it put Canadian studies on the map, making academics aware of the discipline and providing funding that allowed Canadian books to be purchased for university libraries. But this was not sufficient to ensure continuity. The key component in ensuring the continuing development of these programs was and still is teachers, and here it must be pointed out that Canadian studies everywhere (Canada included) is a precarious discipline. This is because very seldom, when university positions are advertised, is expertise in the field of Canadian studies being sought, since only in a very few cases are Canada-related courses compulsory. Universities are looking, for example, for teachers of American, British, or French literature, American history, or cultural studies, since these are the fields where they have core courses. Where

Canada-related courses are offered, they are usually electives or at best form part of some module—for example within the "new literatures." This means that the presence of a Canadian studies course almost always indicates the presence of a teacher with some kind of personal, individual interest in Canada: Canadian studies courses are "extras," and do not reflect departmental policy. As such, they are vulnerable to general trends in higher education and the momentary needs of departments, and more than one Canadian studies "centre" or "program" has vanished with the retirement of a particular professor.

By encouraging teachers to take an interest in Canada, the FRP and FEP grants were therefore crucial; they provided an incentive that was lacking within the higher education system itself. It might be suspected that many teachers were in Canadian studies simply because it gave them a chance to travel to Canada. Based on personal knowledge and experience, I would strongly disagree. Rather, it was precisely the opportunity for teachers to discover Canada, as well as their experiences there, that turned them into very committed Canadianists. In the Czech Republic, the spread of Canadian studies has been closely linked to the opportunities offered by the FRP and FEP grants. As of 2016, courses related to Canada are offered at six universities, with academics at a further two doing research in the field. Of the twenty-eight Czech academics who are currently members of the CEACS, eighteen were introduced to Canadian studies thanks to FRP or FEP grants; all continue to devote themselves to the field, both in teaching and in research.

It is also important to stress the role of Canadian embassy staff in encouraging Canadian studies. Certainly in the Czech case, this meant more than merely sending out information bulletins or posting calls for grant applications on the embassy website. Rather, the Canadian Embassy played a proactive role in two key ways. First, embassy staff made systematic enquiries at, and visits to, universities throughout the country with the aim of singling out individuals who could be encouraged to take an interest in Canadian studies; many of the Canadianists outside Brno and Prague first learned about the field and the opportunities it offered in this way. And second, the embassy launched a tradition of organizing annual meetings of all Czech and Slovak Canadianists. These take the form of a general informative session on developments in the field as well as a mini-seminar, and have proved of great benefit to Canadian studies in both countries, not least by strengthening interuniversity links and deepening personal and collegial ties, both of which have become a distinctive feature of Canadian studies throughout the world.

Finally, there is the wider European and Central European context in which the growth of Canadian studies in the Czech Republic has taken place. The European Network for Canadian Studies (ENCS) groups together all the national and regional Canadian studies organizations in Europe with the aim of developing continent-wide co-operation in the field. One of its early concerns was promoting Canadian studies in the countries of the former Communist Bloc, and with funding from Canada's Department of Foreign Affairs and International Trade it organized the first meeting of Canadianists from the Central European region at Budmerice in Slovakia in 1995. Subsequently, an outreach program was developed to promote Canadian studies in the region, with the Association for Canadian Studies in the German-speaking Countries (GKS) being assigned the key role. The program provided generous support to GKS members that enabled them to travel to Central European universities, where they gave lectures and taught intensive courses on Canadian topics, and funded the presence of Central European Canadianists at German universities. In addition, for many years the GKS invited scholars from the Central European region to participate in its annual conference at Grainau (in Bavaria), where they were able to hold meetings among themselves as well as become part of the broader Canadian studies community.[3] It was at Grainau that many Central European Canadianists first met each other, and there that they took the initial steps leading to the organization of the first Central European regional conference in Brno in 1998 and, ultimately, the creation of the CEACS in 2004.

Canadian Literary Texts in the Czech Republic

The early translation of Canadian and Canada-related texts into Czech, as well as the sheer volume of such texts over the past century reflect a keen, long-time interest in Canada on the part of Czechs. It is difficult to pinpoint precisely the factors behind this, though certainly their perception of the country as a place of vast spaces and great natural beauty plays a major role.[4] In addition, at all crucial moments in recent Czech history—the Second World War, the Communist takeover in 1948, the invasion by troops of the Warsaw Pact in 1968—Canada was quick to accept Czech refugees. This means that many Czechs have personal links to the country and that Canada enjoys the reputation of being an open and welcoming society. As a result, there is a ready audience in the Czech Republic for things Canadian, translations included. If one examines those that have appeared since 1989, three things stand out. First, a very large proportion of them comprise authors of best-selling fiction. Second, for the first time a broad range of more critically acclaimed writers of fiction is represented. And third, several other genres are also present. Let us look at these three aspects in turn.[5]

It is not surprising that there is much popular commercial fiction—such fiction makes up a large portion of the market everywhere, and ever since the nineteenth century many Canadians have been counted among internationally successful writers of this kind. What *is* surprising—at least to me—is the very wide range of popular fiction translated into Czech and the sheer numbers of works translated since the fall of communism. With her thrillers and mystery novels, Joy Fielding accounts for twenty-one titles (fifty entries), closely followed by David Morrell, with thirty-two titles (forty-one entries) in the field of violent, action-packed cliffhangers (the best known being *First Blood*). Czech readers can now choose from eleven titles (thirty-seven entries) by Arthur Hailey, twenty titles by A.E. van Vogt, one of the founding fathers of science fiction, and twelve titles by Eric Wright, whose quirky, modest detective stories are set in a very recognizable Toronto.

Pauline Gedge, known for her historical fiction trilogies, has seen ten titles translated. Two of the leading fantasy writers on the international scene, Steven Erikson and Guy Gavriel Kay, have had twelve and nine titles, respectively, appear in Czech. And then there are numerous writers of romantic fiction, headed by Mary Balogh with ten titles, and several authors of fiction for children and young people, among them Angela Dorsey and Sharon Siamon with twenty-two and nine titles, respectively. (Dorsey's and Siamon's special niche is novels about horses for young girls.) Few if any areas of popular fiction are unrepresented, reflecting both the great international popularity of these kinds of Canadian authors (something most Canadians are unaware of) and the relative dearth of Czech authors in these genres.

With regard to writers of more critically acclaimed fiction, of those translated in the Communist years even the most generous definition would be unlikely to encompass more than Stephen Leacock, Ernest Thompson Seton, Farley Mowat, Brian Moore, Malcolm Lowry, and Margaret Atwood. However, the situation since the end of the Communist regime has been radically different. Not surprisingly—aside from the ever-popular (at least with Czechs) Stephen Leacock and Ernest Thompson Seton—Atwood heads the list, with fourteen titles,[6] followed by William Gibson with ten, Leonard Cohen with eight, Alice Munro and Michael Ondaatje with six each, Lucy Maud Montgomery with five, Mordecai Richler with four, and Yann Martel with three titles. But many other significant Canadian writers have been represented by one or two titles, among them Matt Cohen, Douglas Coupland, Robertson Davies, Timothy Findley, Barbara Gowdy, Janette Turner Hospital, Thomas King, Margaret Laurence, Ann-Marie MacDonald, Anne Michaels, Rohinton Mistry, and Carol Shields. When one adds Brad Fraser, Tomson Highway, Daniel MacIvor, Daniel David Moses, and Drew Hayden Taylor, it can be seen that all the classical literary genres—the novel, the short story, life writing, poetry, and drama—are represented.

But beyond these texts, the Canadian books translated into Czech in the last twenty odd years have also included a number of other genres. Literary criticism has been represented by Northrop Frye, communications theory by Marshall McLuhan. The distinguished political philosopher Charles Taylor has been translated, as has the popularizer of the social sciences Malcolm Gladwell. History has also been reflected, with Margaret MacMillan's widely praised account of the post–First World War peace negotiations (*Paris 1919: Six Months that Changed the World*) and two books by Gordon Skilling dealing with the Communist era in Czechoslovakia—all three of them publications that hold a special interest for Czech readers. One area that would perhaps surprise many Canadians is that of religion: nineteen titles by the Dutch-born Catholic priest Henri Nouwen, and five by Jean Vanier, founder of L'Arche, an international network of homes and support facilities for those with intellectual (learning) disabilities. Though the overall total of these kinds of texts is modest, they attest to a new appreciation in the Czech milieu of the richness of Canadian contributions to modern thought.

Canadian Authors in the Czech Republic

An awareness of Canadian literature and Canadian literary texts has also developed in the Czech Republic since 1989 in other ways, most notably through the presence of Canadian authors themselves. With the growth of Canadian studies, they have been invited in small numbers to give lectures or even courses at the country's universities: such writers have included Barry Callaghan, Aritha van Herk, Myrna Kostash, and a number of others. More visible to the public as a whole have been those who have appeared at the country's main annual literary extravaganza, the Prague Writers' Festival, where several Canadians have been "featured authors": Margaret Atwood (2000, 2008), Graeme Gibson (2008), Irving Layton (2000), Yann Martel (2003), and Anne Michaels (1999, 2000, 2009). A more concentrated dose of Canadian authors came in 2007 with the book launch of a collection of six plays by Canadian Native authors—*Čekání na Kojota:*

Současné drama kanadských Indiánů (Waiting for coyote: Contemporary drama of Canadian Indians); four of the playwrights whose work was included in the publication—Tomson Highway, Daniel David Moses, Ian Ross, and Drew Hayden Taylor—came to Prague for the occasion. The high point of the physical presence of Canadian authors in the Czech Republic so far, however, came in 2008 at the annual Month of Authors' Readings in Brno, where Canada was that year's "guest of honour." Every evening in July a different author read from his or her work. The event included both anglophone and francophone authors, thirty-two in all (one evening included a pair of authors). Among the anglophones were George Elliott Clarke, Jason Sherman, Eden Robinson, Lee Maracle, Aritha van Herk, Robert Bringhurst, Lynn Coady, Sharon Butala, Madeleine Thien, and Michael Crummey. The readings themselves were filmed, with simultaneous live transmission online; after the event, the texts read by the authors and additional material that had been translated were posted online, along with the sessions themselves.

Factors Promoting the Canadian Literary Presence

There have been many reasons for this enhanced presence of Canadian literature in the Czech Republic since 1989, but three factors stand out as paramount: the role of various cultural phenomena both outside and within the Czech Republic; the role of official Canadian agencies and bodies; and the role of Czech academics.

Cultural phenomena

It is clear that in the broadest sense the international reputations of various writers have been a significant factor in their works being translated into Czech. The best example of this is—almost inevitably—Margaret Atwood. As of 2016, fourteen of her works have appeared in Czech. However, it is worth noting that in the wake of her first translation in 1989 others followed rather sluggishly—a second in

1995 and two more in 1998. The bulk of translations only began a few years later, in 2001, with subsequent translations coming out at the rate of more than one a year: between 2001 and 2009 ten further titles appeared in Czech. Though there is no definitive explanation for this particular time line, in my view it is no accident that in 2000 Atwood received the Booker Prize for *The Blind Assassin*, that this same year she was guest of honour at the Prague Writers' Festival, where she read from her prize-winning novel, and that the next year the string of translations began (with *The Blind Assassin*). A similar phenomenon can be noticed in the case of Yann Martel: recipient of the Man Booker Prize in 2002 for *The Life of Pi* and a guest of honour at the Prague Writers' Festival in 2003, he saw the same novel translated into Czech in 2004, the first of his works to appear in this country. This translation was followed the next year by *The Facts behind the Helsinki Roccamatios*—not a book that one would expect a publisher to risk promoting had its author not already been familiar to Czech readers. A variation on this process can be seen in the case of Michael Ondaatje. Though *The English Patient* received the Booker Prize in 1992, it only appeared in Czech in 1997. The impetus here, however, was clearly the phenomenal success of the film version of the novel, which came out in 1996 and swept the awards at the Oscars and at all the major international film festivals. *The English Patient*'s success was then followed by translations into Czech of four more works within five years.

It would seem, then, that being the recipient of a major international book prize or some other clear form of international recognition may well influence the decision to initiate a translation into Czech. What the role of local, Czech publicity may be is less clear, though at the very least the appearance of Atwood and Martel at the Prague Writers' Festival added further luster to reputations created elsewhere. And in all likelihood, Anne Michaels's three appearances in Prague help explain the translations of her works (*Fugitive Pieces*—2000; *The Winter Vault*—2009). On the other hand, none of the thirty-two Canadian writers at the Month of Authors' Readings in Brno in 2008 were subsequently translated into Czech, probably at least to some extent a result of the overwhelming dominance of Prague in all areas of culture in the Czech Republic.

Canadian agencies

When it comes to the role of official bodies and agencies in promoting Canadian literature, the two most important are the Canada Council and the Canadian Embassy in Prague. The Canada Council has essentially two tools: its International Translation Grants program and the Travel Grants for Professional Writers program, both of which have proved very effective in the Czech context. The translation grants go to the publishers themselves, covering half the cost of the translation into the local language. When it comes to more demanding fiction in the Czech Republic, where the majority of publishers are small and a good print run might be 1,000 to 1,500 copies, the availability of this grant is in many cases a key factor in the decision to publish a Canadian text. It is hard to get a specific figure here; however, my estimate is that something around 25 per cent of the more serious Canadian fiction published in the Czech Republic since 1990 has benefitted from Canada Council support. To receive such support, the applicant must, among other things, be an established publisher with a clear track record in the field of literary translations, and be able to guarantee adequate distribution of the translated work. However, the Czech publishing scene is still fluid, characterized by a multitude of small companies, some having relatively short lives. This means that, in all likelihood, only a minority of publishing firms would be eligible to receive Canada Council translation grants, making it all the more remarkable that so many publishers have been willing to take the risk involved in publishing Canadian fiction with no supplementary funding.

As mentioned above, the Canada Council also offers support for writers within its Travel Grants for Professional Writers program; certainly the great majority of writers who have appeared in the Czech Republic, whether at universities, book launches, or festivals, were able to do so thanks to support from this program. In the case of the Month of Authors' Readings in Brno in 2008, virtually all the anglophone writers received such a grant (the francophone writers were funded by the Conseil des arts et des lettres du Québec). And in some cases support is given for an author's appearance at the launching of a book that has also itself been the recipient of support in the form of a translation grant—this was the case, for example, of *Waiting for Coyote*, mentioned above.

The role of the Canadian Embassy in Prague in promoting Canadian literature (in the broadest sense) has been complex and changing. In general one can say that its contribution has been twofold: disseminating information and offering support, both material and non-material. However, its ability, and indeed mandate, to do so have varied greatly over the past two decades. The general trajectory is clear: Canadian government commitment to all aspects of cultural diplomacy increased gradually during the 1990s and beyond, in the case of the embassy in Prague reaching a peak in 2002, when it was included among twenty-odd embassies receiving special funding for the purposes of cultural diplomacy. For a few years embassy staff were very active in a broad range of activities promoting Canadian culture (Canadian literature and Canadian studies included), but their ability to do so was sharply reduced in succeeding years, through radical staff cuts, reduced budgets for specific activities, and restrictions on what funds could be used for. These were all accompanied by a general realignment of priorities in Canadian foreign policy, in particular the virtually complete elimination of cultural diplomacy as an element in the government's foreign policy.[7] With the squeeze on funds and increasing limitations on the areas in which embassy staff can make independent decisions, the embassy's role in this area is more or less limited to publicizing Canadian-related cultural and academic activities through its weekly electronic newsletter.

Czech academics

There remains the role of Czech academics—above and beyond their professional lives as teachers and researchers in the area of Canadian studies—as intermediaries and interpreters of Canada. Though there is widespread sympathy for Canada among Czechs, their specific knowledge of the country is very limited. Compared to Britain and the United States, whose history, society, life, culture, and institutions are reasonably familiar to Czechs thanks to their inclusion in school curricula or through various cultural channels and the media, Canada is largely a blank. So it falls to Czech Canadianists to help fill this gap. When it comes to the translation of Canadian literature in the Czech Republic, Czech Canadianists have played a crucial role. At the most obvious level, many translations of Canadian fiction, poetry, and drama have been done by academics involved in Canadian studies, several of whom are experienced translators in their own right. Here the outstanding example is Miroslav Jindra, the Charles University teacher who introduced Canadian studies at that university in the early 1990s. Widely known as a leading translator of American and British literature—Heller, Malamud, Updike, Kingsley Amis—he turned to Canadian literature in the 1990s; since then he has translated works by Margaret Atwood, Farley Mowat, and Leonard Cohen. In 2009 he was awarded the State Prize for Translation in recognition of his achievements in the course of fifty-five years of active literary service; the award also marked the occasion of his translation of Cohen's *The Book of Longing*. In addition, he has been responsible for encouraging other translators to take on Canadian texts: in this way works by Timothy Findley, Susanna Moodie, Catharine Parr Traill, and Thomas Chandler Haliburton have come to be published.

The role of teachers in fostering translations of Canadian works can be seen in other ways. Several translators of Canadian literary texts first acquired their interest in Canadian literature, and even in specific texts, while taking Canadian studies courses as undergraduates, and they often turn to their former teachers to help solve particular problems related to the specific Canadian social, political, and cultural context when working on their translations.

Many forewords and afterwords found in literary translations have been the work of Czech Canadianists, reflecting their close links not only with the translators but with the publishing houses. Very few Czech publishing houses are in a position to carry out research for the purpose of preparing a publishing schedule that includes specific authors or books for which they would commission translations. Instead, within whatever areas they specialize in, they depend very much on suggestions from friends and friends of friends who come to them with proposals for books to translate. So, for example, Canadianists at Masaryk University were approached by the organizer of the Month of Authors' Readings at the very beginning of the project, when all he had was the idea that Canada should be the guest country. It was the teachers who undertook the first task in the process of making this a reality by compiling a list of authors to be invited.

Academics can also play another role in the translation process, and that is by involving students. At Masaryk University, to give one such instance, teachers of American and Canadian literature selected a set of contemporary short stories by North American Indigenous authors, both Canadian and American (the Canadians included Beth Brant, Thomas King, Lee Maracle, Eden Robinson, Ruby Slipperjack, Jeannette Armstrong, and others), which were then translated by students, working in teams, as part of a semester-long translation course. The final products were then published as *Vinnetou tady nebydlí : antologie sou˘casných povídek severoamerických indián˚u* (Vinnetou doesn't live here: An anthology of contemporary North American Indian short stories, 2003). This book was a particularly good example of the importance of translations in enabling the Czech public to understand Canada and Canadian society in a more complex and contemporary fashion, reflecting as it did a reality completely at odds with the stereotypical Romantic picture of North American Native peoples Czechs were accustomed to. Something similar could be said of the texts at the Month of Authors' Readings—texts that were translated by students from the English and Romance languages departments of Masaryk University, supervised by their teachers.

To complete this account of the role of teachers as experts, mention must also be made of their position vis-à-vis the wider public, for whom they act as a resource in many situations. Czech television, radio stations, and newspapers have turned to Canadianists on many occasions, whether for commentary on immediate events—elections, controversial statements by government officials—or for background information and advice when they are preparing programs where they believe that the Canadian experience is relevant, for example in the area of multiculturalism.[8]

Conclusion

In 1865, two years before the creation of Austria-Hungary, in which the Germans and Hungarians were to share power within the empire as "master nations" at the expense of its Slavic peoples, the great Czech historian František Palacký wrote, "We Slavs will look upon this [creation of a dualistic state] with genuine sorrow, but without fear. We were here before Austria, and we will be here after it is gone." To paraphrase Palacký, we Canadianists look upon the end of government support for Canadian studies with genuine sorrow, but without fear. Canadian studies was here before Understanding Canada began, and it will be here now that it is gone. Undoubtedly it will be harder for foreign Canadianists to pursue their interest in Canada, and encouraging younger scholars to enter the field will be particularly challenging. But the beginnings of scholarly interest in Canada internationally predated the first coherent program of official Canadian government support,[9] and will undoubtedly continue now, though in all likelihood in reduced form.

The real loser, of course, will be Canada itself, both internally and externally. One of the most surprising and commendable aspects of Canadian government support for Canadian studies since the mid-1970s has been its largely disinterested character. Of course all cultural diplomacy has as its ultimate aim the promotion of the country in question and its values. However, my own personal experience over the past twenty years of working in the field of Canadian studies has been that those running the support programs were genuinely interested in knowing how outsiders viewed Canada, that academic excellence was the primary criterion in awarding grants and not conformity to some government agenda. This immensely important mirror has now been clouded over. And on top of that, Canada is depriving itself of much expertise throughout the world—the knowledge and experience of Canadianists, allies in matters of cultural diplomacy (once considered the "third pillar" of Canadian foreign policy), able to explain and interpret Canadian society to their countries and their local communities. The elimination of support for Canadian studies, then, could be seen as yet another step in the growing isolation of Canada internationally, a trend that became increasing marked in the last years of the Stephen Harper government. In many areas, the Liberal government of Justin Trudeau has reversed that trend, but whether this will also prove true when it comes to public diplomacy in general, and support for Canadian studies in particular, remains to be seen.

Notes

1. Each edition of a particular title is listed in the CEACS Translation Research Project database as a separate entry. The database itself can be accessed at http://korel.savana-hosting.cz/cecanstud/www/sign/in?backlink=87hth (Login and Password: guest).
2. I have treated this subject in "'Canada' in the Czech Lands."
3. A similar outreach role for the Baltic countries (Latvia, Lithuania, Estonia) was played by the Nordic Association for Canadian Studies (grouping Finland, Sweden, Denmark, Norway, and Iceland).
4. Interestingly, one of the most densely forested and unspoiled areas in the Czech Republic, in southern Bohemia, has been known as "Czech Canada" since at least the 1920s.
5. Here, as elsewhere in this chapter, I deal only with anglophone Canadian texts; considerably smaller numbers of francophone Canadian writers have also been translated.
6. It should be noted that writers of this kind seldom see their books go into second, let alone further, editions.
7. For a comprehensive study of the development of Canadian public diplomacy in the past twenty years, see Polachová, *Cultural Diplomacy of Canada (1993–2012)*. Insofar as cultural diplomacy still remains, it takes the form of a rather vague

concern for promoting Canadian "values and principles," which seem to comprise general concepts such as freedom, democracy, human rights, and the rule of law. However, there is no explicit mention of Canadian culture, or its importance for promoting the country abroad, in connection with these Canadian values and principles.

8. For an extremely detailed record of activities by Canadianists in Central Europe (the Czech Republic included) since 2000 see the website of the Central European Association for Canadian Studies (www.cecanstud.cz); under Documents, see Country Reports.

9. Canadian studies centres had already begun springing up abroad (at Johns Hopkins University in 1969 and the University of Bordeaux in 1970), while in 1971 the first association grouping academics in the field of Canadian studies had been established, the Association for Canadian Studies in the United States (ACSUS) (Jaumain 17).

Works Cited

Abrams, M.H. *A Glossary of Literary Terms*. New York: Holt, Rinehart & Winston, 1981.
Aciman, Andre. *Letters of Transit: Reflections on Exile, Identity, Language, and Loss*. New York: The New Press, 2000.
Ahmed, Sara. *The Cultural Politics of Emotion*. New York: Routledge, 2004.
———. "Happiness and Queer Politics." *World Picture Journal*, vol. 3, 2009, pp. 1–20, http://www.worldpicturejournal.com/WP_3/PDFs/Ahmed.pdf.
AJK. "Pre nášho čitateľa je svet Eskimákov stále pomerne málo známy..." *Nové slovo*, vol. 18, no. 18, 1976, p. 15.
Albahari, David. *Götz and Meyer*. Translated by Ellen Elias-Bursac. London: Vintage, 2005.
———. "An Indian at Olympic Plaza." *Selected Stories*. Beograd: Vreme knjige, 1994, pp. 82–92.
———. *Learning Cyrillic*. Beograd: Geopoetika, 2012.
———. *Snow Man*. Translated by Ellen Elias-Bursać. Vancouver: Douglas & McIntyre, 2005.
Algoo-Baksh, Stella. *Austin C. Clarke: A Biography*. Toronto: ECW P, 1994.
Almonte, Richard. "'Treason in the Fort': Blackness and Canadian Literature." Walcott, *Rude*, pp. 13–25.

Anderson, Jennifer. "The Pro-Soviet Message in Words and Images: Dyson Carter and Canadian 'Friends' of the USSR." *Journal of the Canadian Historical Association*, vol. 18, no. 1, 2007, pp. 179–206.

Andreev, Andrei, and Diana Yankova. "Translation of Canadian Literature in Bulgaria: Changes in Editor's Choices." Kürtösi, pp. 23–30.

"Anna zo Zeleného domu." *Moja naj kniha*, written and directed by Yvonne Vavrová. Slovak Television, 2010, DVD.

Antwi, Phanuel. "Dub Poetry as Black Atlantic Body-Archive." *Small Axe*, vol. 19, no. 3, 2015, pp. 65–83.

Antwi, Phanuel, Sarah Brophy, Helene Strauss, and Y-Dang Troeung. "Introduction: Postcolonial Intimacies: Gatherings, Disruptions, Departures." *Interventions: International Journal of Postcolonial Studies*, vol. 15, no. 1, 2013, pp. 1–9.

Appadurai, Arjun. "Grassroots Globalization and the Research Imagination." *Globalization*, edited by Arjun Appadurai. Durham, NC: Duke UP, 2001, pp. 1–21.

Arrivé, Mathilde. "La question de l'inter-iconicité: Trajectoires des images, circulations des codes, relance des imaginaires." Geographies of Displacement seminar, oral presentation, 12 Oct. 2012, University of Montpellier 3.

Atwood, Margaret. *Alias Grace*. Toronto: McClelland & Stewart, 1996.

———. *The Animals in That Country*. Toronto: Oxford UP, 1968.

———. *Bluebeard's Egg*. Toronto: McClelland & Stewart, 1983.

———. *Bodily Harm*. Toronto: McClelland & Stewart, 1981.

———. *Der lange Traum*. Translated by Reinhild Böhnke. Düsseldorf: Claassen, 1979.

———. *The Edible Woman*. Toronto: McClelland & Stewart, 1969.

———. *Die eßbare Frau*. Translated by Werner Waldhoff. Düsseldorf: Claassen, 1985.

———. *Die eßbare Frau*. Translated by Werner Waldhoff. Berlin and Weimar: Aufbau-Verlag, 1989.

———. *Galaad 2195*. Translated Monica Bottez. Bucharest: Univers, 1995.

———. *Good Bones*. Toronto: McClelland & Stewart, 1992.

———. *Guten Knochen*. Translated by Brigitte Walitzek. Munich: Goldmann, 1997.

———. *The Handmaid's Tale*. Toronto: McClelland & Stewart, 1985.

———. *In Other Worlds: SF and the Human Imagination*. New York: Nan A. Talese/Doubleday, 2011.

———. *Kobieta do zjedzenia*. 1986. Translated by Małgorzata Golewska-Stafiej. Warsaw: Książka i Wiedza, 2004.

———. *Lady Oracle*. Toronto: McClelland & Stewart, 1976.

———. *MaddAddam*. Toronto: McClelland & Stewart, 2013.

———. *O femeie obișnuită*. Translated by Margareta Petruț. Bucharest: Univers, 1989.

———. *Oryx and Crake*. Toronto: McClelland & Stewart, 2003.

———. *Pani wyrocznia*. Translated by. Zofia Uhrynowska-Hanasz. Warsaw: Państ. Instytut Wydawniczy, 1989.

———. *Povestirea cameristei*. Translated by Monica Bottez. Bucharest: Leda, 2006.
———. *Sluškinjina priča*. Translated by Nedjeljka Paravić. Zagreb: Globus, 1988.
———. *Surfacing*. Toronto: Anansi, 1972.
———. *Survival: A Thematic Guide to Canadian Literature*. Toronto: Anansi, 1972.
———. *Strömung*. Translated by Reinhild Böhnke. Leipzig: Reclam, 1979.
———. *The Year of the Flood*. Toronto: McClelland & Stewart, 2009.
———. *Wynurzenie*. Translated by Jolanta Plakwicz and Teresa Poniatowska. Warsaw: Książka i Wiedza, 1987.
Atwood, Margaret, et al. "Understanding Canada No More." *The Globe and Mail*. 19 June 2012.
Babín, Emil. "Román o írskych vyst'ahovalcoch." *Nové knihy*, vol. 50, 1979, p. 4.
Bailey, Nancy. "Identity in *The Fire-Dwellers*." *Critical Approaches to the Fiction of Margaret Laurence*, edited by Colin Nicholson. London: Macmillan, 1990, pp. 107–18.
Baker, Kenneth. "Form versus Portent: Edward Burtynsky's Endangered Lanscapes." Pauli, pp. 40–45.
Balestra, Gianfranca, Laura Ferri, Caterina Ricciardi, editors. *Reading Alice Munro in Italy*. Toronto: Frank Iacobucci Centre for Italian Canadian Studies, 2008.
Ball, John Clement. *Imagining London: Postcolonial Fiction and the Transnational Metropolis*. Toronto: U of Toronto P, 2007.
Bannerji, Himani. *The Dark Side of the Nation: Essays on Multiculturalism, Nationalism and Gender*. Toronto: Canadian Scholars' Press, 2000.
Barr, Marlene S., editor. *Afro-Future Females: Black Writers Chart Science Fiction's Newest New-Wave Trajectory*. Columbus: Ohio State UP, 2008.
Barrer, Peter. "A Necessarily Better Place: Images of New Zealand in the Slovak Mass Media." *Journal of New Zealand & Pacific Studies*, vol. 1, no. 1, 2013, pp. 5–21.
Barth, John. "The Literature of Exhaustion." *The Friday Book: Essays and Other Fiction*. Baltimore, MD: Johns Hopkins UP, 1984, pp. 62–76.
Barthes, Roland. "La mort de l'auteur." *Le Bruissement de la langue*. Paris: Seuil, 1984, pp. 61–67.
———. *Le Grain de la voix: Entretiens 1962–1983*. Paris: Seuil, 1999.
Bast, Heike. *"The Quiltings of Human Flesh": Constructions of Racial Hybridity in Contemporary African-Canadian Literature*. Dissertation. Universität Greifswald, 2010, http://d-nb.info/1043328947/34.
Batcos, Stephanie. "Lessons from the Writer: Olive Senior's *Over the Roofs of the World* and the Interface of the Caribbean-Canadian Reader." *Beyond the Canebrakes: Caribbean Women Writers in Canada*, edited by Emily Allen Williams. Trenton, NJ: Africa World Press, 2008, pp. 57–78.
Baugh, Edward. "Epilogue: Coming of Age in the Fifties." *Beyond Windrush: Rethinking Postwar Anglophone Caribbean Literature*, edited by J. Dillon Brown and Leah Reade Rosenberg. Jackson: UP of Mississippi, 2015, pp. 239–47.

Beckford, Sharon Morgan. *Naturally Woman: The Search for Self in Black Canadian Women's Literature*. Toronto: Inanna, 2011.
Belisle, Donica. *Retail Nation: Department Stores and the Making of Modern Canada*. Vancouver: UBCP, 2011.
Bhabha, Homi K. *The Location of Culture*. London: Routledge, 1994.
———. "Narrating the Nation." *Nations and Identities*, edited by Vincent P. Pecora. Oxford: Blackwell Publishers, 2001, pp. 359–63.
Bieliková, Mária. "Funkcia doslovu v preklade umeleckých textov v recipujúcej literatúre." *35 rokov výučby prekladateľstva a tlmočníctva na Slovensku, 1970–2005: Minulosť, súčasnosť a budúcnosť prekxladateľstva a tlmočníctva na Slovensku*, edited by Alojz Keníž. Bratislava: Letra, 2006, pp. 107–10.
Billiani, Francesca, editor. *Modes of Censorship and Translation: National Contexts and Diverse Media*. Manchester: St. Jerome Publishing, 2006.
Binder, Wolfgang. "An Interview with Olive Senior." *Commonwealth Essays and Studies*, vol. 18, no. 1, 1995, pp. 106–14.
Birns, Nicolas. "'The Earth's Revenge': Nature, Diaspora and Transfeminism in Larissa Lai's *Salt Fish Girl*." *Australian Critical Race and Whiteness Studies Association e-Journal*, vol. 2, no. 2, 2006, pp. 1–15, http://www.acrawsa.org.au/files/ejournalfiles/83NicholasBirns.pdf.
Black, J.L. *Canada in the Soviet Mirror: Ideology and Perception in Soviet Foreign Affairs, 1917–1991*. Ottawa: Carleton UP, 1998.
Blake, Jason. "Late for the Party: Alice Munro in Slovenian Translation." Kürtösi, pp. 177–88.
Blanchfield, Mike. "Canada Axes Foreign Studies Program Despite Being Told of Economic Spinoffs." *The Globe and Mail*, 16 May 2012, http://www.theglobeandmail.com/news/politics/canada-axes-foreign-studies-program-despite-being-told-of-economic-spinoffs/article4184581/.
———. "Foreign Affairs Cuts Canadian Studies Abroad Program Despite Millions Generated for Economy." *Huffington Post*, 16 May 2012, http://www.huffingtonpost.ca/2012/05/16/foreignstudies-program-cut_n_1522632.html.
Bloom, Harold. "The Dialectics of Literary Tradition." *boundary 2*, vol. 2, no. 3, 1974, pp. 528–38.
Bock, Gabriele. Afterword, *Strömung*, by Margaret Atwood. Translated by Reinhild Böhnke. Leipzig: Reclam, 1979.
Bordo, Jonathan. "The Wilderness as Symbolic Form—Thoreau, Grünewald and the Group of Seven." *Reflective Landscapes of the Anglophone Countries*, edited by Pascale Guibert. Amsterdam: Rodopi, 2011, pp. 149–71.
Börsenverein des Deutschen Buchhandles. "Der Buchmarkt in Deutschland: Zahlen & Fakten." 2015, http://www.boersenverein.de/.

Bottez, Monica. "Postfață la *Guluud 2195*" [Afterword to *Guluud 2195*]. Bucharest. Univers, 1995, pp. 289–99.

———. "Postfață" [Afterword to *Povestireacameristei*]. Bucharest: Leda, 2006, pp. 418–36.

Boucher, Geoff. "The Politics of Aesthetic Affect: A Reconstruction of Habermas' Art Theory." *Parrhesia*, vol. 13, 2011, pp. 62–78.

Braidotti, Rosi. *The Posthuman*. Malden, MA: Polity, 2013.

———. "Posthuman, All Too Human: Towards a New Process Ontology." *Theory, Culture & Society*, vol. 23, no. 7–8, 2006, pp. 197–208.

Branach-Kallas, Anna, Agnieszka Rzepa, and Eugenia Sojka, editors. *Essays in Red and White/Essais en rouge et blanc*, *TransCanadiana*, vol. 1, 2008.

Branach-Kallas, Anna, Dagmara Drewniak, Renata Jarzebowska-Sadkowska, and Piotr Sadkowski, editors. *Canada and its Utopias/Canada et ses utopies*. *TransCanadiana*, vol. 2, 2009.

Brand, Dionne. "Bread Out of Stone." 1990. *Grammar of Dissent: Poetry and Prose by Claire Harris, M. Nourbese Philip, Dionne Brand*, edited by Carol Morell. Fredericton: Goose Lane, 1994, pp. 171–80.

Brant, Beth. "A Long Story." *The Oxford Book of Stories by Canadian Women*, edited by Rosemary Sullivan. Oxford: Oxford UP, 1999, pp. 318–24.

Brathwaite, Edward Kamau. *The History of the Voice: The Development of Nation Language in Anglophone Caribbean Poetry*. London & Port of Spain: New Beacon Books, 1984.

Brenčičová, Danuša. "Kanada rozpráva svoj príbeh." *Nové slovo*, vol. 30, no. 51, 1988, pp. 20–21.

Brenkusová, Ľubica. "Recepcia americkej literatúry na Slovensku v povojnovom období (1945–1956)." *Slovak Studies in English II: Proceedings of the Second Triennial Conference on British, American and Canadian Studies, Dedicated to Ján Vilikovský on the Occasion of his 70th Birthday*, edited by Alojz Keníž. Bratislava: AnaPress, 2009, pp. 177–86.

Brooker, Bertram. *Think of the Earth*. Toronto: Brown Bear Press, 2000.

Brooks, Lisa Tanya. *The Common Pot: The Recovery of Native Space in the Northeast*. Minneapolis: U of Minnesota P, 2008.

Brown, Jarrett H. "The Shadow of Intimacy: Male Bonding and Improvised Masculinity in Claude McKay's *Banjo: A Story Without a Plot*." *Journal of West Indian Literature*, vol. 21, no. 1/2, Nov. 2012/Apr. 2013, pp. 1–22.

Brownstein, Bill. "Mélanie Joly Reading to Reinvest in the Arts as Federal Heritage Minister." *Montreal Gazette*, 5 Dec. 2015.

Brydon, Diana. "Cross-Talk, Postcolonial Pedagogy, and Transnational Literacy." Sugars, pp. 57–74.

———. "Re-Routing the Black Atlantic." *Topia*, vol. 5, spring 2001, pp. 94–100.

Brydon, Diana, and Marta Dvořák, editors. *Crosstalk: Canadian and Global Imaginaries in Dialogue*. Waterloo, ON: Wilfrid Laurier UP, 2012.

Buchholtz, Mirosława, editor. *Alice Munro: Understanding, Adapting and Teaching*. New York: Springer, 2016.

Bucknor, Michael A. "Beyond Windrush and the Original Black Atlantic Routes: Austin Clarke, Race and Canada's Influence on Anglophone Caribbean Literature." *Beyond Windrush: Rethinking Postwar Anglophone Caribbean Literature*, edited by J. Dillon Brown and Leah Reade Rosenberg. Jackson: UP of Mississippi, 2015, pp. 206–21.

———. *Postcolonial Crosses: Body-Memory and Inter-Nationalism in Caribbean-Canadian Writing*. Dissertation, University of Western Ontario, 1998.

Bucknor, Michael A., and Daniel Coleman. "Introduction: Rooting and Routing Caribbean-Canadian Writing." *Rooting and Routing Caribbean-Canadian Writing*, special issue of *Journal of West Indian Literature*, vol. 14, nos. 1/2, 2005, pp. i–xxxv.

Burtynsky, Edward, with an interview by Michael Torosian. *Residual Landscapes: Studies of Industrial Transfiguration*. Toronto: Lumiere Press, 2001.

Canada, Department of Foreign Affairs and International Trade. "DFAIT Launches 'Understanding Canada' Program." 2008. www.iccs-ciec.ca/documents/Understanding%20Canada.pdf.

Caraion, Ion, editor. *Poețicontemporani de limbaengleză*. Bucharest: Albatros, 1978.

Carr, Emily. *Growing Pains* in *The Complete Writings of Emily Carr*, edited by Doris Shadbolt. Vancouver: Douglas & McIntyre, 1997, pp. 293–471.

———. *Hundreds and Thousands: The Journals of an Artist* in *The Complete Writings of Emily Carr*, edited by Doris Shadbolt. Vancouver: Douglas & McIntyre, 1997, pp. 653–893.

Casteel, Sarah Phillips. "Experiences of Arrival: Jewishness and Caribbean-Canadian Identity in Austin Clarke's *The Meeting Point*." *Rooting and Routing Caribbean-Canadian Writing*, special issue of *Journal of West Indian Literature*, vol. 14, no. 1/2, 2005, pp. 113–40, http://www.jstor.org/stable/23020015.

Chamberlin, J. Edward. *If This Is Your Land, Where Are Your Stories?: Re-Imagining Home and Sacred Space*. Cleveland, OH: Pilgrim Press, 2004.

Chariandy, David. "Black Canadas and the Question of Diasporic Citizenship." *Narratives of Citizenship: Indigenous and Diasporic Peoples Unsettle the Nation-State*, edited by Aloys N.M. Fleischmann, Nancy Van Styvendale, and Cody McCarroll. Edmonton: U of Alberta P, 2011, pp. 323–46.

———. "'Canada in Us Now': Locating the Criticism of Black Canadian Writing." *Essays on Canadian Writing*, vol. 75, winter 2002, pp. 196–216.

———. "Postcolonial Diasporas." *Postcolonial Text*, vol. 2, no. 1, 2006, http://www.postcolonial.org/index.php/pct/article/viewArticle/440/839.

———. "'That's What You Want, Isn't It?': Austin Clarke and the New Politics of Recognition." *Rooting and Routing Caribbean-Canadian Writing*, special issue of *Journal of West Indian Literature*, vol. 14, no. 1/2, 2005, pp. 141–65.

Childs, Peter. *Modernism*. London and New York: Routledge, 2000.

Chow, Rey. "Against the Lures of Diaspora: Chinese Women and Intellectual Hegemony." *Gender and Sexuality in Twentieth-Century Chinese Literature and Society*, edited by Tonglin Lu. SUNY P, 1993, pp. 23–45.

———. "Theory, Area Studies, Cultural Studies: Issues of Pedagogy in Multiculturalism." *Learning Places: The Afterlives of Area Studies*, edited by Masao Miyoshi and H.D. Harootunian. Durham, NC: Duke UP, 2002, pp. 103–18.

Chrisman, Laura. "Whose Black World Is This Anyway?: Black Atlantic and Transnational Studies after *The Black Atlantic*." *New Perspectives on the Black Atlantic: Definitions, Readings, Dialogues*, edited by Bénédicte Ledent and Pilar Cuder-Domínguez. Bern: Peter Lang, 2012, pp. 23–57.

CIC News. "2012. Canada's Record-Breaking Year for Immigration." *Canada Immigration Newsletter*, 13 March 2013. www.cicnews.com/2013/03/2012-canadas-recordbreaking-year-immigration-032346.html.

Clarke, Austin. *A Passage Back Home: A Personal Reminiscence of Samuel Selvon*. Toronto: Exile Editions, 1994.

Clarke, George Elliott. "Canadian Biraciality and Its 'Zebra' Poetics." *Intertexts*, vol. 6, no. 2, 2002, pp. 201–31.

———. *Directions Home: Approaches to African-Canadian Literature*. Toronto: U of Toronto P, 2012.

———. "Must All Blackness Be American?: Locating Canada in Borden's 'Tightrope Time,' or Nationalizing Gilroy's *The Black Atlantic*." *Canadian Ethnic Studies*, vol. 28, no. 3, 1996, pp. 56–71.

———. *Odysseys Home: Mapping African-Canadian Literature*. Toronto: U of Toronto P, 2002.

Clarke, George Elliott, editor. *Eyeing the North Star: Directions in African-Canadian Literature*. Toronto: McClelland & Stewart, 1997.

Coghill, Joy. "How in Hell Did She Do It?" *Theatre and AutoBiography: Writing and Performing Lives in Theory and Practice*, edited by Sherrill Grace and Jerry Wasserman. Vancouver: Talonbooks, 2006, pp. 313–16.

Coleman, Daniel. "From Canadian Trance to TransCanada: White Civility to Wry Civility in the CanLit Project." *Trans.Can.Lit: Resituating the Study of Canadian Literature*, edited by Smaro Kamboureli and Roy Miki. Waterloo, ON: Wilfrid Laurier UP, 2007, pp. 25–43.

———. "From Contented Civility to Contending Civilities: Alternatives to Canadian White Civility." *International Journal of Canadian Studies*, vol. 38, 2009, pp. 221–42.

———. "Indigenous Place and Diaspora Space: Of Literalism and Abstraction." *Settler Colonial Studies*, vol. 6, no. 1, 2016, pp. 61–76. http://dx.doi.org/10.1080/2201473X.2014.1000913.

———. *White Civility: The Literary Project of English Canada*. Toronto: U of Toronto P, 2006.

Collins, Patricia Hill. *Black Feminist Thought: Knowledge, Consciousness, and the Politics of Empowerment*. Boston: Unwin Hyman, 1990.

Compton, Wayde. *After Canaan: Essays on Race, Writing, and Region*. Vancouver: Arsenal Pulp Press, 2010.

Compton, Wayde, Esi Edugyan, and Karina Vernon. "Black Writers in Search of Place." *The Tyee*, 28 Feb. 2005, http://thetyee.ca/Life/2005/02/28/BlackWriters/.

Conant, M.A. *The Long Polar Watch: Canada and the Defence of North America*. New York: Harper and Brothers, 1962.

Cooper, Afua. *The Hanging of Angélique: The Untold Story of Canadian Slavery and the Burning of Old Montréal*. Toronto: HarperCollins, 2006.

Cosgrove, Denis E. "Introductory Essay for the Paperback Edition" of *Social Formation and Symbolic Landscape* (1998), rpt. in *Landscape Theory*, edited by Rachael Ziady DeLue and James Elkins. New York: Routledge, 2008, pp. 17–42.

Coupland, Douglas. *Marshall McLuhan: You Know Nothing of My Work!* New York: Atlas & Co., 2010.

———. *Souvenir of Canada 2*. Vancouver: Douglas & McIntyre, 2004.

———. "Young Country." *Souvenir of Canada*. Vancouver: Douglas & McIntyre, 2002, p. 131.

Crean, Susan, editor. *Opposite Contraries: The Unknown Journals of Emily Carr and Other Writings*. Vancouver: Douglas & McIntyre, 2003.

Cuder-Domínguez, Pilar. "African Canadian Writing and the Narration(s) of Slavery." *Essays on Canadian Writing*, vol. 79, spring 2003, pp. 55–75.

———. "The Politics of Gender and Genre in Asian Canadian Women's Speculative Fiction: Hiromi Goto and Larissa Lai." *Asian Canadian Writing beyond Autoethnography*, edited by Eleanor Ty and Christl Verduyn. Waterloo, ON: Wilfrid Laurier UP, 2008, pp. 115–31.

———. "Transnational Memory and Haunted Black Geographies: Esi Edugyan's *The Second Life of Samuel Tyne*." *Canadian Literature and Cultural Memory*, edited by Cynthia Sugars and Eleanor Ty. Toronto: Oxford UP, 2014, pp. 432–43.

Cuder-Domínguez, Pilar, Belén Martín-Lucas, and Sonia Villegas-López, editors. *Transnational Poetics: Asian Canadian Women's Fiction of the 1990s*. Toronto: TSAR Publications, 2011.

Cummings, Bruce. "Boundary Displacement: The State, the Foundations, and Area Studies during and after the Cold War." *Learning Places: The Afterlives of Area Studies*, edited by Masao Miyoshi and H.D. Harootunian. Durham, NC: Duke UP, 2002, pp. 261–302.

Cummings, Ronald. "Jamaican Female Masculinities: Nanny of the Maroons and the Genealogy of the Man-Royal." *Journal of West Indian Literature*, vol. 21, no.1/2, Nov. 2012/Apr. 2013, pp. 129–54.

———. "Queer Theory and Caribbean Writing." *The Routledge Companion to Anglophone Caribbean Literature*, edited by Michael A. Bucknor and Alison Donnell. London: Routledge, 2011, pp. 323–31.

Danov, Madeleine. "Why Michael Ondaatje? Postmodern Trajectories in the Information Society: Twentieth-Century Canadian Literature in Bulgaria." Kürtösi, pp. 139–44.

Darias-Beautell, Eva, editor. *Unruly Penelopes and the Ghosts: Narratives of English Canada*. Waterloo, ON: Wilfrid Laurier UP, 2012.

Davis, Andrea. "Black Canadian Literature as Diaspora Transgression: *The Second Life of Samuel Tyne*." *Topia*, vol. 17, spring 2007, pp. 31–49.

Dayan, Joan. "Paul Gilroy's Slaves, Ships, and Routes: The Middle Passage as Metaphor." *Research on African Literatures*, vol. 27, no. 4, 1996, pp. 7–14.

Deleuze, Gilles, and Félix Guattari. *What Is Philosophy?* Translated by Hugh Tomlinson and Graham Burchill. London: Verso, 1994.

Dickinson, Peter. *Here is Queer: Nationalisms, Sexualities and the Literatures of Canada*. Toronto: U of Toronto P, 1999.

Didi-Huberman, Georges. *La Ressemblance par contact: Archéologie, anachronisme et modernité de l'empreinte*. Paris: Minuit, 2008.

Dillon, Grace L. "Indigenous Scientific Literacies in Nalo Hopkinson's Ceremonial Worlds." *Journal of the Fantastic in the Arts*, vol. 18, no. 1, 2007, pp. 23–41.

———. "Totemic Human-Animal Relationships in Recent SF." *Extrapolation*, vol. 49, no. 1, 2008, pp. 70–96.

Dobson, Kit. *Transnational Canadas: Anglo-Canadian Literature and Globalization*. Waterloo, ON: Wilfrid Laurier UP, 2009.

Dowler, Kevin. "The Cultural Industries Policy Apparatus." *The Cultural Industries in Canada: Problems, Policies, and Prospects*, edited by Michael Dorland. Toronto: James Lorimer & Co., 1996, pp. 328–46.

Doyle, James. "Science, Literature and Revolution: The Life and Writings of Dyson Carter." *Left History: An Interdisciplinary Journal of Historical Inquiry and Debate*, vol. 5, no. 2, 1997, pp. 7–29.

Drug, Št. "Zajtrajšok je náš." *Sloboda*, 25 Jan. 1953, p. 7.

Dubey, Madhu. "Becoming Animal in Black Women's Science Fiction." *Afro-Future Females: Black Writers Chart Science Fiction's Newest New-Wave Trajectory*, edited by Marleene S. Barr. Columbus: Ohio State UP, 2008, pp. 31–49.

Duro, Paul, editor. *The Rhetoric of the Frame*. Cambridge: Cambridge UP, 1996.

Dyer-Witheford, Nick. "Digital Labour, Species-Becoming and the Global Worker." *Ephemera: Theory and Politics in Organization*, vol. 10, nos. 3/4, 2011, pp. 484–503.

Edugyan, Esi. *Dreaming of Elsewhere: Observations on Home*. Edmonton: U of Alberta P and Canadian Literature Centre/Centre de littérature candienne, 2014.

———. *The Second Life of Samuel Tyne*. London: Virago, 2004.

Edwards, Brent Hayes. *The Practice of Diaspora: Literature, Translation, and the Rise of Black Internationalism*. Cambridge, MA: Harvard UP, 2003.

Edwards, Whitney Bly. "Psychoanalysis in Caribbean Literature." *The Routledge Companion to Anglophone Caribbean Literature*, edited by Michael A. Bucknor and Alison Donnell. London: Routledge, 2011, pp. 314–22.

Edwardson, Ryan. *Canadian Content: Culture and the Quest for Nationhood*. Toronto: U of Toronto P, 2008.

Ermine, Willie. "The Ethical Space of Engagement." *Indigenous Law Journal*, vol. 6, 2007, pp. 193–203, http://hdl.handle.net/1807/17129.

Ertler, Klaus-Dieter, and Patrick Imbert, editors. *Cultural Challenges of Migration in Canada/Les défis culturels de la migration au Canada*. Frankfurt: Peter Lang, 2013.

Evans, Lucy. "*The Black Atlantic*: Exploring Gilroy's Legacy." *Atlantic Studies*, vol. 6, no. 2, 2009, pp. 255–68.

Fagan, Kristina. "What's the Trouble with the Trickster?: An Introduction." *Troubling Tricksters: Revisioning Critical Conversations*, edited by Deanna Reder and Linda M. Morra. Waterloo, ON: Wilfrid Laurier UP, 2010.

Faulkner, Peter. *Modernism*. New York: Methuen, 1985.

Fee, Marjory. "The Trickster Moment, Cultural Appropriation, and the Liberal Imagination in Canada." *Troubling Tricksters: Revisioning Critical Conversations*, edited by Deanna Reder and Linda M. Morra. Waterloo, ON: Wilfrid Laurier UP, 2010, pp. 59–76.

Ferguson, Stefan. "Margaret Atwood in German/y: A Case Study." von Flotow and Nischik, pp. 93–110.

Foulkes, Charles. "Canadian Defence Policy in a Nuclear Age." *Behind the Headlines*, vol. 21, no. 1, 1961, pp. 1–10.

Francis, R. Douglas. "Modernity and Canadian Civilization: The Ideas of Harold A. Innis." *Globality and Multiple Modernities Comparative North American and Latin American Perspectives*, edited by Luis Roniger and Carlos H. Waisman. Brighton and Portland: Sussex Academic Press, 2002, pp. 213–29.

Frankenberg, Ruth. *White Women, Race Matters: The Social Construction of Whiteness*. Minneapolis: U of Minnesota P, 1993.

Frye, Northrop. *The Bush Garden: Essays on the Canadian Imagination*. Concord, ON: Anansi, 1995.

———. "Conclusion to a *Literary History of Canada*." 1965. *The Bush Garden: Essays on the Canadian Imagination*. Concord, ON: House of Anansi, 1971, pp. 213–52.

———. *Divisions on a Ground: Essays on Canadian Literature*, edited by James Polk. Toronto: Anansi, 1982.

———. *On Education*. Markham, ON: Fitzhenry, 1988.

Gandhi, Leela. *Affective Communities: Anticolonial Thought, Fin-de Siècle Radicalism, and the Politics of Friendship*. Durham, NC: Duke UP, 2006.

Gazdík, Marián. "Recepcia anglickej prózy na Slovensku v rokoch 1945–1989." *35 rokov výučby prekladateľstva a tlmočníctva na Slovensku, 1970–2005: Minulosť, súčasnosť a budúcnosť prekladateľstva a tlmočníctva na Slovensku*, edited by Alojz Keníž. Bratislava: Letra, 2006, pp. 127–42.

———. "The Reception of Works by Margaret Atwood in Slovakia." Kürtösi, pp. 155–68.

Gerson, Carole. "Locating Female Subjects in the Archives." *Working in Women's Archives: Researching Women's Private Literature and Archival Documents*, edited by Helen M. Buss and Marlene Kadar. Waterloo, ON: Wilfrid Laurier UP, 2001, pp. 7–22.

Gibson, James A. Review of *To Know Ourselves: The Report of the Commission on Canadian Studies*, by Thomas H.B. Symons. *Canadian Journal of Higher Education/La revue canadienne d'enseignement supérieur*, vol. 7, no. 1, 1977, pp. 64–67.

Gikandi, Simon. "Introduction: Africa, Diaspora, and the Discourse of Modernity." *Research on African Literatures*, vol. 27, no. 4, 1996, pp. 1–6.

Gillies, Mary Ann. *The Professional Literary Agent in Britain, 1880–1920*. Toronto: U of Toronto P, 2007.

Gilroy, Paul. *The Black Atlantic: Modernity and Double Consciousness*. Cambridge, MA: Harvard UP, 1993.

Gingell, Susan, and Jill Didur. "Author Meets Critic Forum on Daniel Coleman's *White Civility: The Literary Project of English Canada*." *International Journal of Canadian Studies*, vol. 38, 2008, pp. 183–89.

The Globe and Mail. "Authors, Academics Urge Federal Government to Replace 'Understanding Canada,'" 21 June 2012, http://www.theglobeandmail.com/arts/books-and-media/authorsacademics-urge-federal-government-to-replace-understanding-canada/article4358367/.

Goldie, Terry. *Pink Snow: Homotextual Possibilities in Canadian Fiction*. Peterborough, ON: Broadview Press, 2003.

Goto, Hiromi. *Hopeful Monsters*. Vancouver: Arsenal Pulp, 2004.

———. *The Kappa Child*. Calgary: Red Deer Press, 2001.

———. *The Water of Possibility*. Regina: Coteau Books, 2001.

Government of Canada. "Academic Relations." 4 Apr. 2014, http://www.canadainternational.gc.ca/germany-allemagne/academic_relations_academiques/index.aspx?lang=eng.

Griffith, Glyne. "'This is London Calling the West Indies': The BBC's *Caribbean Voices*." *West Indian Intellectuals in Britain*, edited by Bill Schwarz. Manchester: Manchester UP, 2003, pp. 196–208.

Grossman, Edith. *Why Translation Matters*. New Haven, CT: Yale UP, 2010.

Gruesser, John Cullen. *Confluences: Postcolonialism, African American Literary Studies, and the Black Atlantic.* Athens: U of Georgia P, 2005.

Gyssels, Kathleen. "The 'barque ouverte' (Glissant) or *The Black Atlantic* (Gilroy): Erasure and Errantry." *New Perspectives on the Black Atlantic: Definitions, Readings, Dialogues,* edited by Bénédicte Ledent and Pilar Cuder-Domínguez. Bern: Peter Lang, 2012, pp. 59–82.

Halberstam, Judith, and Ira Livingston, editors. *Posthuman Bodies.* Bloomington: Indiana UP, 1995.

Haraway, Donna J. *Modest_Witness@Second_Millennium.FemaleMan©_Meets_ OncoMouse™: Feminism and Technoscience.* New York: Routledge, 1997.

———. *Simians, Cyborgs, and Women: The Reinvention of Nature.* New York: Routledge, 1991.

Hardt, Michael, and Antonio Negri. *Commonwealth.* Cambridge, MA: Harvard UP, 2009.

———. *Empire.* Cambridge, MA: Harvard UP, 2000.

———. *Multitude: War and Democracy in the Age of Empire.* New York: Penguin, 2004.

Hartmut Lutz, editor. *The Diary of Abraham Ulrikab.* Foreword by Alootook Ipellie. Ottawa: U of Ottawa P, 2005.

Hatfield, Elaine, J.T. Cacioppo, and R.L. Rapson. *Emotional Contagion.* New York: Cambridge UP, 1994.

Head, Harold, editor. *Canada in Us Now: The First Anthology of Black Poetry and Prose in Canada.* Toronto: NC Press, 1976.

Helm, Michael. *Cities of Refuge.* Toronto: McClelland & Stewart, 2010.

———. *In the Place of Last Things.* Toronto: McClelland & Stewart, 2004.

———. "Putting the Strange in the Stranger." Interview with Smaro Kamboureli and Hannah McGregor. *University of Toronto Quarterly,* vol. 82, no. 2, 2013, pp. 313–29.

Henighan, Stephen. *When Words Deny the World: The Reshaping of Canadian Writing.* Erin Mills, ON: Porcupine's Quill, 2002.

Heyer, Paul, and David Crowley. Introduction. *The Bias of Communication.* By Harold A. Innis. Toronto: U of Toronto P, 2006, pp. ix–xxviii.

High Commission of Canada in Australia. "Understanding Canada: Canadian Studies." Government of Canada, 12 Mar. 2013, http://www.canadainternational.gc.ca/australia-australie/academic_relations_academiques/grants-bourses.aspx?lang=eng.

Hodgetts, A.B. *Quelle culture? Quel heritage? / What Culture? What Heritage?* Toronto: OISE, 1968.

Hollinger, Veronica. "Posthumanism and Cyborg Theory." *Routledge Companion to Science Fiction,* edited by Mark Bould, Andrew M. Butler, Adam Roberts, and Sherryl Vint. New York: Routledge, 2009, pp. 267–78.

Hopkinson, Nalo. *Falling in Love with Hominids.* San Francisco: Tachyon, 2015.

———. *Midnight Robber*. New York: Warner Books, 2000.

———. *Skin Folk*. New York: Warner Books, 2001.

Huggan, Graham. *The Postcolonial Exotic: Marketing the Margins*. New York: Routledge, 2001.

Hulme, Peter, et al., editors. *Surveying the American Tropics: A Literary Geography from New York to Rio*. Liverpool: U of Liverpool P, 2013.

Hutchinson, Ben. "Entre littérature et Histoire: La « tardiveté » (Spätheit, lateness) comme modèle herméneutique." *Fabula/Les colloques*, Littérature et histoire en débats, 28 Sept. 2013, http://www.fabula.org/colloques/document2090.php.

Hutchinson, Bruce. *Canada: Tomorrow's Giant*. New York: Knopf, 1957.

Huttová, Mária. "Dve samoty Hugha MacLennana." *Dve samoty* by Hugh MacLennan. Bratislava: Pravda, 1984, pp. 395–403.

Huyssen, Andreas. "Geographies of Modernism in a Globalizing World." *Geographies of Modernism: Literatures, Cultures, Spaces*, edited by Peter Brooker and Andrew Thacker. London: Routledge, 2005, pp. 6–18.

Hykisch, Anton. "Návod na tematiku tentoraz autentickú." *Zlatý máj*, vol. 11, no. 9, 1967, pp. 577–79.

Irvine, Dean, editor. Introduction. *The Canadian Modernists Meet*. Ottawa: U of Ottawa P, 2005, pp. 1–13.

Ivanovici, Cristina. "A Courageous Project: Publishing Margaret Atwood's Work in Romania between 1978 and 1995." *A View from Afar: Canadian Studies in a European Context/Une vision lointaine: Les études canadiennes dans une contexte européen*, edited by Niamh Nestor, Caitriona Ni Chasaide, Isabelle Lemée, and Vera Regan. The European Network for Canadian Studies/Le réseau européen d'études canadiennes, 2010, pp. 79–91.

———. *In Search of Utopia: A Study of the Role of German and Romanian Academic and Literary Communities in the Production and Evaluation of Margaret Atwood's Utopian/Dystopian Fiction*. Dissertation, University of Birmingham, 2011.

James, Carl, and Andrea Davis, editors. *Jamaica in the Canadian Experience*. Halifax: Fernwood, 2012.

Jameson, Frederic. *The Jameson Reader*, edited by Michael Hardt and Kathi Weeks. Oxford: Blackwell Publishers, 2000.

Jaumain, Serge. *The Canadianists: The ICCS/25 Years in the Service of Canadian Studies*. Ottawa: International Council for Canadian Studies, 2006, http://www.iccs-ciec.ca/administration/ckeditor/ckfinder/userfiles/files/CEIC_25_en.pdf.

Javorčíková, Jana. "Kanadská literatúra v preklade na začiatku milénia." *Preklad a tlmočenie 8. Preklad a tlmočenie v interdisciplinárnej praxi*. Banská Bystrica: Fakulta humanitných vied Univerzity Mateja Bela, 2009, pp. 54–59.

Johnston, Nancy. "'Happy That It Is Here': An Interview with Nalo Hopkinson." Pearson, Hollinger, and Gordon, pp. 200–15.

Justice, Daniel Heath. *Our Fire Survives the Storm: A Cherokee Literary History.* Minneapolis: U of Minnesota P, 2006.

Kalliney, Peter J. *Commonwealth of Letters: British Literary Culture and the Emergence of Postcolonial Aesthetics.* New York: Oxford UP, 2013.

Kamboureli, Smaro. "Canadian Ethnic Anthologies: Representations of Ethnicity." *Ariel*, vol. 25, no. 4, 1991, pp. 11–51.

Kamboureli, Smaro, editor. *Writing the Foreign: Canadian Literature and the Politics of Representation and Empathy,* special issue of *University of Toronto Quarterly*, vol. 82, no. 2, 2013.

Kamboureli, Smaro, and Christl Verduyn, editors. *Critical Collaborations: Indigeneity, Diaspora, and Ecology in Canadian Literary Studies.* Waterloo, ON: Wilfrid Laurier UP, 2014.

Kaplan, Karel. *The Short March: The Communist Takeover in Czechoslovakia, 1945–1948.* London: C. Hurst, 1987.

Keeshig-Tobias, Lenore. "Lenore Keeshig-Tobias." *Contemporary Challenges: Conversations with Canadian Native Authors,* edited by Hartmut Lutz. Saskatoon: Fifth House, 1991, pp. 79–88.

Kilgallin, Tony. "The Beaver and the Elephant." *Canadian Writing Today,* special issue of *Times Literary Supplement* vol. 3738, October 1973, p. 1300.

King, Thomas. "Borders." *One Good Story, That One.* 2nd ed. Toronto: Harper Perennial, 1993, pp. 131–47.

Korte, Barbara. "'Two Solitudes'?: Anglo-Canadian Literature in Translation in the Two Germanies." von Flotow and Nischik, pp. 27–51.

Krauss, Rosalind. "Notes on the Index: Seventies Art in America" [part 1]. *October*, vol. 3, spring 1977, pp. 68–81.

———. "Notes on the Index: Seventies Art in America, Part 2." *October*, vol. 4, autumn 1977, pp. 58–67.

Kroetsch, Robert. "Canadian Writing: No Name Is My Name." *The Forty-Ninth and Other Parallels: Contemporary Canadian Perspectives,* edited by David Staines. Amherst: U of Massachusetts P, 1986, pp. 116–28.

———. *The Hornbooks of Rita K.* Edmonton: U of Alberta P, 2001.

———. "Reciting the Emptiness." *The Lovely Treachery of Words.* Toronto: Oxford UP, 1989, pp. 34–40.

Kroetsch, Robert, and Reingard M. Nischik, editors. *Gaining Ground: European Critics on Canadian Literature.* Edmonton: NeWest Press, 1985.

Kurlansky, Mark. *Salt: A World History.* London: Jonathan Cape, 2002.

Kurtin, Petra Sapun, and Mirna Sindičić Sabljo. "Canadian Writing in Croatia." Kürtösi, pp. 49–60.

Kürtösi, Katalin, editor. *Canada in Eight Tongues: Translating Canada in Central Europe/ Le Canada en huit langues: Traduire le Canada en Europe centrale.* Brno: Masaryk University, 2012.

———. Editor's Introduction/Avant-propos de la redactrice. Kürtösi, pp. 7–11.

Kusá, Mária. *Preklad ako súčasť dejín kultúrneho priestoru*. Bratislava: Ústav svetovej literatúry SAV, 2004.

Kyloušek, Petr. *Dějiny francouzsko-kanadské a quebecké literatury* (A history of French-Canadian and Québec literature). Brno: Host, 2005.

Kyloušek, Petr, Klára Kolinská, Kateřina Prajznerová, Tomáš Pospíšil, Eva Voldřichová, and Petr Horák. *My—Oni—Já: Hledání identity v kanadské literatuře a filmu* (Us—Them—Me: The search for identity in Canadian literature and film). Brno: Host, 2009.

———. *Us—Them—Me: The Search for Identity in Canadian Literature and Film*. Brno: Masaryk University, 2009.

Lai, Larissa. "Epistemologies of Respect: A Poetics of Asian/Indigenous Relation." Kamboureli and Verduyn, pp. 99–126.

———. *Salt Fish Girl*. Toronto: Thomas Allen, 2002.

———. *When Fox Is a Thousand*. Vancouver: Press Gang, 1995.

Lamming, George. *The Pleasures of Exile*. Ann Arbor: U of Michigan P, 1960.

Laurence, Margaret. *Der steinerne Engel: Roman*. Translated by Herbert Schlüter. Munich: Droemer Knaur, 1965, 1988.

———. *Die Stimmen von Adamo: 10 Erzählungen*. Translated by Herbert Schlüter. Munich: Droemer Knaur, 1969.

———. *Hledači pramenů*. Translated by Alena Jindrová-Špilarová. Prague: Dita, 1993.

———. *A Jest of God*. Toronto: McClelland & Stewart, 1966.

———. *Kameni anđeo*. Translated by Radmila Ivanov. Belgrade: PortaLibris, 2007.

———. *The Stone Angel*. Toronto: McClelland & Stewart, 1964.

———. *This Side Jordan*. Toronto: McClelland & Stewart, 1960.

———. *The Tomorrow-Tamer: Short Stories*. Montreal and Toronto: McClelland & Stewart, 1963.

Laurence, Robin. *Beloved Land: The World of Emily Carr*. Vancouver: Douglas & McIntyre, 1996.

Lee, Tara. "Mutant Bodies in Larissa Lai's *Salt Fish Girl*: Challenging the Alliance between Science and Capital." *West Coast Line*, vol. 38, no. 2, 2004, pp. 94–109.

Lehan, Richard. *Literary Modernism and Beyond: The Extended Vision and The Realms of the Text*. Baton Rouge: Louisiana State UP, 2009.

Lennox, John, editor. *Margaret Laurence—Al Purdy: A Friendship in Letters: Selected Correspondence*. Toronto: McClelland & Stewart, 1993.

Lennox, John, and Ruth Panofsky, editors. *Selected Letters of Margaret Laurence and Adele Wiseman*. Buffalo, London and Toronto: U of Toronto P, 1997.

Levenson, Michael, editor. *The Cambridge Companion to Modernism*. Cambridge: Cambridge UP, 1999.

Lewis, Justin, and Toby Miller. Introduction to *Critical Cultural Policy Studies: A Reader*. Malden, MA: Blackwell, 2003, pp. 1–9.

Long, Brian. *The Long Report*. Ottawa: ICCS, 2010.
Lorimer, Rowland. "Book Publishing." *The Cultural Industries in Canada: Problems, Policies, and Prospects*, edited by Michael Dorland. Toronto: James Lorimer & Co., 1996, pp. 3–34.
Lowe, Lisa. "The Intimacies of Four Continents." *Haunted by Empire: Geographies of Intimacy in North American History*, edited by Anna Laura Stoler. Durham, NC: Duke UP, 2006, pp. 191–212.
Ludden, David. "Why Area Studies?" *Localizing Knowledge in a Globalizing World: Recasting the Area Studies Debate*, edited by Ali Mirsepassi, Amrita Basu, and Frederick Weaver. Syracuse, NY: Syracuse UP, 2003, pp. 131–36.
MacLennan, Hugh. *Two Solitudes*. New York: Duell, Sloan and Pearce, 1945.
MacLennan, Oriel C.L. "Boundaries, Borders, and Barriers: Marie-Claire Blais and the Archival Adventure." *Journal of Canadian Studies/Revue d'études canadiennes*, vol. 40, no. 2, 2006, pp. 60–78.
Madokoro, Laura. "Good Material: Canada and the Prague Spring Refugees." *Refuge*, vol. 26, no. 1, 2009, pp. 161–71, http://refuge.journals.yorku.ca/index.php/refuge/article/view/30618/28132.
Mansbridge, J. "Abject Origins: Uncanny Strangers and Fetishism in Larissa Lai's *Salt Fish Girl*." *West Coast Line*, vol. 38, no. 2, 2004, pp. 121–33.
Markotić, Nicole. "Reunion: An Albertan Revenge Comedy." *Canada and Beyond: A Journal of Canadian Literary and Cultural Studies*, vol. 1, no. 1, 2011, pp. 64–82, http://www.uhu.es/publicaciones/canada-and-beyond/index.php/canada-and-beyond/article/view/14.
Martin, Paul. "Canada's Image Abroad: Fade to Black." *University Affairs*, 6 June 2012, www.universityaffairs.ca/canadas-image-abroad-fade-to-black.aspx.
Martín-Lucas, Belén. "Of Aliens, Monsters, and Vampires: Speculative Fantasy's Strategies of Dissent (Transnational Feminist Fiction)." *Unruly Penelopes and the Ghosts: Narratives of English Canada*, edited by Eva Darias-Beautell. Waterloo, ON: Wilfrid Laurier UP, 2012, pp. 107–30.
Mason, Ian. "Discourse, Ideology and Translation." *Language, Discourse and Translation in the West and Middle East*, edited by Robert de Beaugrande, Abdullah Shunnaq, and Mohamed Helmy Heliel. Amsterdam: John Benjamins, 1994, pp. 23–35.
Massumi, Brian. *The Politics of Everyday Fear*. Minneapolis: U of Minnesota P, 1993.
Matthews, Steven. *Modernism*. London: Arnold, 2004.
Mayr, Suzette. *Moon Honey*. Edmonton: NeWest, 1995.
———. *Venous Hum*. Vancouver: Arsenal Pulp, 2005.
McCaig, JoAnn. "Alice Munro's Agency: the Virginia Barber Correspondence, 1976–1983." *Essays on Canadian Writing*, vol. 68, 1998, pp. 81–102.
———. *Beggar Maid: Alice Munro's Archives and the Cultural Space of Authorship*. Dissertation, University of Calgary, Calgary, 1997.
———. *Reading in Alice Munro's Archives*. Waterloo, ON: Wilfrid Laurier UP, 2002.

McCall, Sophie. *First Person Plural: Aboriginal Storytelling and the Ethics of Collaborative Authorship*. Vancouver: UBCP, 2011.

McLeod, A.L. Introduction to *The Canon of Commonwealth Literature: Essays in Criticism*, edited by A.L. McLeod. New Delhi: Sterling Publishers, 2003, pp. 1–16.

McGill, Robert. "Biographical Desire and the Archives of Living Authors." *Auto/Biography Studies*, vol. 24, no. 1, 2009, pp. 129–45.

———. "Negotiations with the Living Archive." *Margaret Atwood: The Open Eye*, edited by John Moss and Tobi Kozakewich. Ottawa: U of Ottawa P, 2006, pp. 95–106.

McKittrick, Katherine. *Demonic Grounds: Black Women and the Cartographies of Struggle*. Minneapolis: U of Minnesota P, 2006.

McLuhan, Marshall. *Understanding Media: The Extensions of Man*. New York: Signet Books, 1964.

McWilliams, Ellen. *Margaret Atwood and the Female Bildungsroman*. Burlington and Farnham: Ashgate, 2009.

Meisel, John, and John Graham. "It's Hard to Understand Canadian Studies Cuts." *The Globe and Mail*, 12 July 2012, http://www.theglobeandmail.com/opinion/its-hard-to-understand-canadian-studies-cuts/article4408869/.

Mensah, Joseph. *Black Canadians: History, Experiences, Social Conditions*. 2nd. ed. Halifax: Fernwood Publishing, 2004.

Mirsepassi, Ali, Amrita Basu, and Frederick Weaver. "Introduction: Knowledge, Power, and Culture." *Localizing Knowledge in a Globalizing World: Recasting the Area Studies Debate*, edited by Ali Mirsepassi, Amrita Basu, and Frederick Weaver. Syracuse, NY: Syracuse UP, 2003, pp. 1–24.

Mitchell, W.T.J. "Imperial Landscape." Mitchell, pp. 5–34.

———. Preface to the Second Edition of *Landscape and Power*. Mitchell, pp. vii–xii.

Mitchell, W.T.J., editor. *Landscape and Power*, 2nd ed. Chicago: U of Chicago P, 2002.

Miura, Reiichi. "What Kind of Revolution Do You Want?: Punk, the Contemporary Left, and Singularity." *Mediations*, vol. 25, no. 1, 2010, pp. 61–80, http://www.mediationsjournal.org/files/Mediations25_1_04.pdf.

Molinaro, Matie, Corinne McLuhan, and William Toye, editors. *Letters of Marshall McLuhan*. Toronto: Oxford UP, 1987.

Montgomery, L.M. *Anne of Green Gables*. New York: Bantam Books, 1979.

Morley, Patricia. *Margaret Laurence: The Long Journey Home*. Rev. ed. Montreal and Kingston: McGill-Queen's UP, 1991.

Morra, Linda. "Canadian Art According to Emily Carr: The Search for Indigenous Expression." *Canadian Literature*, vol. 185, summer 2005, pp. 43–57.

Morra, Linda, and Jessica Schagerl, editors. *Basements and Attics, Closets and Cyberspace: Explorations in Canadian Women's Archives*. Waterloo, ON: Wilfrid Laurier UP, 2012.

Morris, Mervyn. "Making West Indian Literature." *Anthurium: A Caribbean Studies Journal*, vol. 10, no. 2, 2013, pp. 1–16, http://scholarlyrepository.miami.edu/cgi/viewcontent.cgi?article=1280&context=anthurium.

Morris, Robyn. "Re-visioning Representations of Difference in Larissa Lai's *When Fox Is a Thousand* and Ridley Scott's *Blade Runner*." *West Coast Line*, vol. 38, no. 2, 2004, pp. 69–86.

Morrison, Toni. "The Site of Memory." *Out There: Marginalization and Contemporary Cultures*, edited by Russell Ferguson, Martha Gever, Trinh T. Minh-ha, and Cornel West. New York: New Museum of Contemporary Art, 1990, pp. 299–305.

Müller, Klaus Peter. "Translating the Canadian Short Story into German." von Flotow and Nischik, pp. 53–78.

Munro, Alice. *Prea multă fericire*. Translated by Ioana Opai. Bucharest: Litera, 2011.

———. *Too Much Happiness*. Toronto: McClelland & Stewart, 2009.

———. *Who Do You Think You Are?* Toronto: Macmillan of Canada, 1978.

Naves, Elaine Kalman. *Robert Weaver: Godfather of Canadian Literature*. Quebec: Véhicule Press, 2007.

Nelson, Alondra. "Making the Impossible Possible: An Interview with Nalo Hopkinson." *Social Text*, vol. 20, no. 2, 2002, pp. 97–113.

Nimijean, Richard. "Harper's Axe Hits Canadian Studies Abroad." *Inroads*, 32, winter/spring 2013, 14–18.

Nischik, Reingard M. *Engendering Genre: The Works of Margaret Atwood*. Ottawa: U of Ottawa P, 2009.

———. "New Horizons: Canadian Literature in Europe." *Gaining Ground: European Critics on Canadian Literature*. Kroetsch and Nischik, pp. 249–76.

Nolette, Nicole. "Partial Translation, Affect and Reception: The Case of *Atanarjuat: The Fast Runner*." *Inquire: Journal of Comparative Literature*, vol. 2, no. 1, 2012.

"Nové knihy pre naše dievčatá." Rev. of *Rozprávky spod Ještěda*, by Karolína Světlá, *Cesta ide ďalej*, by Alexandra Bruštejnová, and *Anna zo Zeleného domu*, by L.M. Montgomery. *Ľud* 28 Nov. 1959, p. 4.

O'Sullivan, Simon. "The Aesthetics of Affect: Thinking Art Beyond Representation." *Angelaki*, vol. 6, no. 3, 2001, pp. 125–35.

Oeding, Brita, and Luise von Flotow. "The 'Other Women': Canadian Women Writers Blazing a Trail into Germany." von Flotow and Nischik, pp. 79–92.

Omhovère, Claire. "The Memory of Landscape: Canadian Explorations on Site." *Re/Membering Place*, edited by Catherine Delmas and André Dodeman. Bern: Peter Lang, 2013, pp. 271–87.

Ong, Aihwa. *Flexible Citizenship: The Cultural Logics of Transnationality*. Durham, NC: Duke UP, 1999.

Otrísalová, Lucia. "Distorted and Misrepresented: The Fate of Anne of Green Gables in Slovakia." Kürtösi, pp. 169–76.

Otrísalová, Lucia, and Marián Gazdík. "English Canadian Literature in Slovak Translation: The Story of Underrepresentation." Kürtösi, pp. 115–28.

Pache, Walter. "*Es gibt eine kanadische Literatur*: Zu zwei Anthologien mit Kurzgeschichten." *Süddeutsche Zeitung*, 17 July 1976.

Paljetak, Luko, editor. *Panorama novije kanadske poezije*. Split: Književni krug, 1972.

Panofsky, Ruth. *The Literary Legacy of the Macmillan Company of Canada: Making Books and Mapping Culture*. Toronto: U of Toronto P, 2012.

Pauli, Lori, editor, with essays by Mark Haworth-Booth and Kenneth Baker, and an Interview by Michael Torosian. *Manufactured Landscapes: The Photographs of Edward Burtynsky*. Ottawa: National Gallery of Canada in association with Yale UP, 2003.

Pausch, Barbara. "Anglo-Canadian Short-Story Anthologies in German(y): 1967–2010." *Theory & Practice in English Studies*, vol. 6, no. 1, 2013, pp. 39–53.

Pearson, Wendy Gay. *Calling Home: Queer Responses to Discourses of Nation and Citizenship in Contemporary Canadian Literary and Visual Culture*. Dissertation, University of Wollongong, 2004, http://ro.uow.edu.au/theses/1961.

Pearson, Wendy Gay, Veronica Hollinger, and Joan Gordon, editors. *Queer Universes: Sexualities in Science Fiction*, Liverpool: Liverpool UP, 2010.

Pearson, Wendy Gay, Veronica Hollinger, and Joan Gordon. "Introduction: Queer Universes." Pearson, Hollinger, and Gordon, pp. 1–11.

Petersen, Katie. "Defying Categorization: The Work of Suzette Mayr." *Canadian Woman Studies/Les Cahiers de la Femme*, vol. 23, no. 2, 2004, pp. 71–75.

Petruț, Margareta. Personal email to Cristina Ivanovici, 2 Sept. 2008.

Pfeiffer, Annette, Director, Argentine Association for Canadian Studies. Email to Patrick James, President ICCS, 3 May 2012.

Pitseolak, Peter, and Dorothy Harley Eber. *People from Our Side: A Life Story with Photographs and Oral Biography*. Manuscript translated by Ann Hanson. Montreal and Kingston: McGill-Queen's UP, 1993.

Polachová, Barbora. *Cultural Diplomacy of Canada (1993–2012)*. MA thesis, Charles University, Prague, 2013, https://is.cuni.cz/webapps/zzp/detail/111789/?lang=en.

Powers, Lyall, H. *Alien Heart: The Life and Work of Margaret Laurence*. East Lansing: Michigan State UP, 2003.

Procter, James. "7th Edward Baugh Lecture" (unpublished), 3 Nov. 2013, University of the West Indies, Mona Campus, Kingston, Jamaica.

Puar, Jasbir. "'I Would Rather Be a Cyborg Than a Goddess': Intersectionality, Assemblage, and Affective Politics." *Transversal: EIPCP Multilingual Webjournal*, 01, 2011, http://eipcp.net/transversal/0811/puar/en.

Raban, Jonathan. "Battle of the Eye." *The Atlantic Monthly*, March 2001, pp. 40–52.

Radford, Tom (Director and co-producer), Peter Raymont (Producer and co-director), and Patrick Reed (co-director). *I, Nuligak: An Inuvialuit History of First Contact.* White Pine Pictures, 2005.

Reimer, Sharlee. "Troubling Origins: Cyborg Politics in Larissa Lai's *Salt Fish Girl.*" *Atlantis: Critical Studies in Gender, Culture & Social Justice*, vol. 35, no. 1, 2010, pp. 4–14, http://journals.msvu.ca/index.php/atlantis/article/viewFile/168/175.

Remi, Cornelius H.W., and Jeanette den Toonder. "Current Developments in Canadian Studies in the Netherlands/Développements récents en Études canadiennes aux Pays-Bas." *Re-exploring Canadian Space / Redécouvrir l'espace canadien*, edited by Jeanette den Toonder and Bettina van Hoven. Groningen, The Netherlands: Barkhuis, 2012, pp. vii–xxii.

Resnick, Philip. *Land of Cain: Class and Nationalism in English Canada, 1945–1975.* Vancouver: New Star Books, 1977.

Roberts, Adam. Review of *MaddAddam*, by Margaret Atwood, with readers' comments. *Strange Horizons*, 25 Nov. 2013, http://www.strangehorizons.com/reviews/2013/11/maddaddam_by_ma-comments.shtml.

Roberts, D.S. "Historicizing the Canon of Commonwealth Literature: Dean Mahomet's *Travels* (1794)." *The Canon of Commonwealth Literature: Essays in Criticism*, edited by A.L. McLeod. New Delhi: Sterling Publishers, 2003, pp. 122–32.

Roberts, Gillian. *Prizing Literature: The Celebration and Circulation of National Culture.* Toronto: U of Toronto P, 2011.

Rodney, Walter. *How Europe Underdeveloped Africa.* London: Bogle-L'Ouverture, 1972.

Ross, Sinclair. *As for Me and My House.* 1942. Toronto: McClelland & Stewart, 1989.

Rothberg, Michael. *Multidirectional Memory: Remembering the Holocaust in the Age of Decolonization.* Stanford: Stanford UP, 2009.

Rowell, Charles H. "An Interview with Olive Senior." *Callaloo* vol. 36, summer 1988, pp. 480–90.

Royal Commission on National Development in the Arts, Letters and Sciences, 1949–1951 (Massey-Lévesque Commission). Ottawa: Government of Canada, 1951.

Rymhs, Deena. "Mobility and its Disenchantments in Marie Clements' *The Unnatural and Accidental Women* and *Burning Vision.*" *Literature and the Glocal City: Reshaping the English Canadian Imaginary*, edited by Ana María Fraile-Marcos. New York: Routledge, 2014, pp. 21–38.

Said, Edward. "Between Worlds." *London Review of Books*, vol. 20, no 9, 7 May 1998, pp. 3–7, www.lrb.co.uk/v20/n09/edward-said/between-worlds.

———. *Culture and Imperialism.* New York: Knopf/Random House, 1993.

Samcová, Jarmila. Personal interview with Lucia Otrísalová, 20 Jan. 2012.

Schimel, Lawrence. "Introduction: Looking in All Directions." *The Future Is Queer: A Science Fiction Anthology*, edited by Richard Labonté and Lawrence Schimel. Vancouver: Arsenal Pulp, 2006, pp. 14–17.

Schöpflin, George. *Censorship and Political Communication in Eastern Europe.* London: Frances Pinter Publishers, 1983.

Schwartz, Joan M. "Agent of Change or Marketing Bait: The Photograph in 100 Photos that Changed Canada." *Journal of Canadian Studies/Revue d'études canadiennes,* vol. 45, no. 2, spring 2011, pp. 205–22.

Schwarz, Bill, editor. *West Indian Intellectuals in Britain.* Manchester: Manchester UP, 2003.

Scott, F.R. "The Canadian Authors Meet." *McGill Fortnightly Review,* 27 Apr. 1927, p. 73.

Sedgwick, Eve Kosofsky. Interview. *La fabrique du genre: (De)constructions du feminine et du masculine dans les arts et la littérature anglphones,* edited by Sophie Marret and Claude Le Fustec. Rennes: Presses Universitaires de Rennes, 2008, pp. 17–28.

Senior, Olive. "At the Slave Museum." *Shell,* p. 63.

———. "Bamboo." *Gardening in the Tropics,* pp. 77–80.

———. "Brief Lives." *Gardening in the Tropics,* p. 83.

———. "Canefield Surprised by Emptiness." *Shell,* p. 55.

———. "Crossing Borders and Negotiating Boundaries." James and Davis, pp. 14–22.

———. *Gardening in the Tropics.* Toronto: McClelland & Stewart, 1994.

———. "Gastropoda." *Shell,* p. 9.

———. "Meditation on Yellow." *Gardening in the Tropics,* pp. 11–18.

———. "My Father's Blue Plantation." *Gardening in the Tropics,* p. 84.

———. "The Poem as Gardening, The Story as Su-Su: Finding a Literary Voice." *Journal of West Indian Literature,* vol. 14, no. 1–2, 2005, pp. 35–48.

———. *Shell.* Toronto: Insomniac Press, 2007.

———. "Shell Blow." *Shell,* pp. 33–40.

———. *Talking of Trees.* Kingston, Jamaica: Calabash, 1985.

———. "Talking of Trees." *Talking of Trees,* pp. 80–85.

———. "'Whirlwinds Coiled at My Heart': Voice and Vision in a Writer's Practice." Brydon and Dvořák, pp. 21–35.

———. "Yemoja: Mother of Waters." *Gardening in the Tropics,* pp. 131–33.

Shadbolt, Doris. *Emily Carr.* Vancouver: Douglas & McIntyre, 1990.

———. Introduction. *The Complete Writings of Emily Carr,* edited by Doris Shadbolt. Vancouver: Douglas & McIntyre, 1997.

Šimečková, Darina. "Brian Moore: Ginger Coffee má šťastie." *Slovenské pohľady,* vol. 96, no. 1, 1980, pp. 136–37.

Simic, Charles. "Refugees." *Letters of Transit: Reflections on Exile, Identity, Language, and Loss,* edited by Andre Aciman. New York: The New Press, 2000, pp. 112–40.

Simpson, Jeffrey. "Making Canada's Past a Slave to Power." *The Globe and Mail,* 4 May 2012, http://www.theglobeandmail.com/opinion/making-canadas-past-a-slave-to-power/article4106937/.

Sinclair, Niigonwedom James. "Trickster Reflections." *Troubling Tricksters: Revisioning Critical Conversations*, edited by Deanna Reder and Linda M. Morra. Waterloo, ON: Wilfrid Laurier UP, 2010, pp. 21–58.

Slettedahl Macpherson, Heidi. *The Cambridge Introduction to Margaret Atwood*. Cambridge: Cambridge UP, 2010.

Smejkalová, Jirina. "Censors and Their Readers: Selling and Silencing Czech Books." *Libraries & Culture*, vol. 36, no. 1, 2001, pp. 87–103.

Snyder, Joel. "Territorial Photography." Mitchell, pp. 175–201.

Sontag, Susan. "The Aesthetics of Silence." *Aspen*, vol. 5/6, item 3, fall/winter 1967, pp. 1–21.

———. *On Photography*. Harmondsworth: Penguin, 1977.

———. *Regarding the Pain of Others*. New York: Picador, 2004.

Sorfleet, John R. "From Pagan to Christian: The Symbolic Journey of *Anne of Green Gables*." *Windows and Words: A Look at Canadian Children's Literature in English*, edited by Aïda Hudson and Susan-Ann Cooper. Ottawa: U of Ottawa P, 2003, pp. 175–83.

Sparling, Don. "'Canada' in the Czech Lands." Kürtösi, pp. 39–48.

Sparling, Don, and Tomáš Pospíšil. "Thirteen Ways of Looking at America." *Brno Studies in English*, vol. 27, 2001, pp. 73–84.

Squire, Shelagh J. "Ways of Seeing, Ways of Being: Literature, Place, and Tourism in L.M. Montgomery's Prince Edward Island." *A Few Acres of Snow: Literary and Artistic Images of Canada*, edited by Glen Norcliffe and Paul Simpson-Housley. Toronto: Dundurn Press, 1992, pp. 137–47.

Stahl, Klaus. "The *New York Times* of Munich—Portrait of the *Süddeutsche Zeitung*." Translated by Marsalie Turner, Goethe Institut, 22 Aug. 2013, http://www.goethe.de/wis/med/pnt/zuz/en 556318.htm.

Staines, David. "Forms of Non-Fiction: Innis, McLuhan, Frye, and Grant." *The Cambridge History of Canadian Literature*, edited by Coral Ann Howells and Eva-Marie Kröller. Cambridge: Cambridge UP, 2009, pp. 335–53.

———. *Margaret Laurence: Critical Reflections*. Ottawa: U of Ottawa P, 2001.

Stegner, Wallace. "Law in a Red Coat." *Wolf Willow: A History, a Story, and a Memory of the Last Plains Frontier*. 1962. Harmondsworth: Penguin, 1990, pp. 110–15.

Stephens, Michelle Ann. *Black Empire: The Masculine Global Imaginary of Caribbean Intellectuals in the United States, 1914–1962*. Durham, NC: Duke UP, 2005.

Stouck, Jordan. "Gardening in the Diaspora: Place and Identity in Olive Senior's Poetry." *Mosaic*, vol. 38, no. 4, 2005, pp. 103–22.

Stryker, Susan, Paisley Currah, and Lisa Jean Moore. "Introduction: Trans-, Trans, or Transgender?" *WSQ: Women's Studies Quarterly*, vol. 36, no. 3/4, 2008, pp. 11–22.

Sugars, Cynthia, editor. *Home-Work: Postcolonialism, Pedagogy and Canadian Literature*. Ottawa: U of Ottawa P, 2004.

Symons, Thomas H.B. *Report on the Commission on Canadian Studies: To Know Ourselves*, vols. 1 and 2. Ottawa: AUCC, 1975.

Szamosi, Gertrud. "Translating Canada into Hungarian." Kürtösi, pp. 71–78.

Szeman, Imre. "Belated or Isochronic?; Canadian Writing, Time and Globalization." *Essays on Canadian Writing*, vol. 71, 2000, pp. 145–53.

Tanna, Laura. "One-on-One with Olive Senior, Part 1." *Jamaica Gleaner*, 17 Oct. 2004, p. F3.

———. "One-on-One with Olive Senior, Part 3." *Jamaica Gleaner*, 7 Nov. 2004, p. F3.

Taylor, Charles. "Emily Carr." *Six Journeys: A Canadian Pattern*. Toronto: Anansi, 1977, pp. 153–87.

———. *Sources of the Self: The Making of Modern Identity*. Cambridge, MA: Harvard UP, 1989.

Teodorescu, Virgil, and Petronela Negoşanu, editors. *Înţelegînd zăpada: 60 poeţi canadieni de limba engleză*. Bucharest: Univers, 1977.

Thacker, Robert. *Alice Munro: Writing Her Lives: A Biography*. Toronto: McClelland & Stewart, 2005.

Thaler, Ingrid. *Black Atlantic Speculative Fictions: Octavia Butler, Jewelle Gomez, and Nalo Hopkinson*. New York: Routledge, 2010.

Thiong'o, Ngũgĩ wa. *Decolonising the Mind: The Politics of Language in African Literature*. London: J. Currey & Heinemann, 1986.

Thobani, Sunera. *Exalted Subjects: Studies in the Making of Race and Nation in Canada*. Toronto: U of Toronto P, 2007.

Thomas, Sheree R. *Dark Matter: A Century of Speculative Fiction from the African Diaspora*. New York: Warner Books, 2000.

Thompson, John Herd. *Forging the Prairie West: The Illustrated History of Canada*. Oxford: Oxford UP, 1998.

Thomson-Wohlgemuth, Gaby. *Translation under State Control: Books for Young People in the German Democratic Republic*. London: Routledge, 2009.

Thorner, Thomas, and Thor Frohn-Nielsen, editors. *A Few Acres of Snow: Documents in Pre-Confederation Canadian History*. 3rd ed. Toronto: U of Toronto P, 2009.

Tinsley, Omise'eke Natasha. "Black Atlantic, Queer Atlantic: Queer Imaginings of the Middle Passage." *GLQ: A Journal of Lesbian and Gay Studies*, vol. 14, no. 2/3, 2008, pp. 191–215.

Tomkins, Silvan S. *Affect Imagery Consciousness: The Complete Edition*. New York: Springer Publishing, 2008.

Torosian, Michael. "The Essential Element: An Interview with Edward Burtynsky." Pauli, pp. 46–55.

Trehearne, Brian. *Aestheticism and the Canadian Modernists: Aspects of a Poetic Influence*. Montreal and Kingston: McGill-Queen's UP, 1989.

Tremblay, Tony. "'a widening of the northern coterie': The Cross-Border Cultural Politics of Ezra Pound, Marshall McLuhan, and Louis Dudek." Irvine, pp. 153–77.

Truth and Reconciliation Commission of Canada. "Truth and Reconciliation Commission of Canada: Calls to Action." Winnipeg, MB, 2015, www.trc.ca/websites/trcinstitution/File/2015/Findings/Calls_to_Action_English2.pdf.

Turner, Victor. *The Ritual Process: Structure and Anti-Structure*. London: Routledge & Kegan Paul, 1969.

Ty, Eleanor. *Unfastened: Globality and Asian North American Narratives*. Minneapolis: U of Minnesota P, 2010.

Ty, Eleanor, and Christl Verduyn, editors. *Asian Canadian Writing beyond Autoethnography*. Waterloo, ON: Wilfrid Laurier UP, 2008.

Tymoczko, Maria. "Translation and Political Engagement: Activism, Social Change and the Role of Translation in Geopolitical Shifts." *The Translator*, vol. 6, no. 1, 2014, pp. 23–47.

Udall, Sharyn Rohlfsen. *Carr, O'Keeffe, Kahlo: Places of Their Own*. New Haven, CT: Yale UP, 2000.

Urbanski, Heather. *Plagues, Apocalypses and Bug-Eyed Monsters: How Speculative Fiction Shows Us Our Nightmares*. Jefferson, NC: McFarland & Co., 2007.

Urry, John. "City Life and the Senses." *A Companion to the City*, edited by Gary Bridge and Sophie Watson. Oxford: Blackwell, 2000, pp. 388–97.

Vanderziel, Jeffrey A., and Jiří Rambousek Jr., editors. *Vinnetou tady nebydlí: antologie současných povídek severoamerických indiánů* (Vinnetou doesn't live here: An anthology of contemporary North American Indian short stories). Brno: Větrné mlýny, 2003.

Van Wyck, Peter C. *The Highway of the Atom*. Montreal and Kingston: McGill-Queen's UP, 2010.

Venuti, Lawrence. *The Scandals of Translation: Towards an Ethics of Difference*. London: Routledge, 1998.

Verduyn, Christl. "Critical Allegiances." Kamboureli and Verduyn, pp. 227–40.

———. "Understanding Canada and International Canadian Literary Studies." Paper presented at Understanding Canada: International Perspectives on Place, Production, and Diversity in the Canadian Literatures, McMaster University, Hamilton, ON, 27–29 Sept. 2013.

Vernon, Karina. "Suzette Mayr in Conversation with Karina Vernon." *Matrix*, vol. 58, 2001, pp. 14–18.

———. "Writing a Home for Prairie Blackness: Addena Sumter Freitag's *Stay Black and Die* and Cheryl Foggo's *Pourin' Down Rain*." *Canadian Literature* vol. 182, 2004, pp. 67–83.

vh. "'Slabí' Kanaďania?" *Nové knihy*, vol. 30, 1989, p. 3.

Virágos, Zsolt. *The Modernists and Others: American Literary Culture in the Age of the Modernist Revolution*. Debrecen: University of Debrecen, 2008.

Voaden, Herman. "Wilderness. A Play of the North." *Canada's Lost Plays*. Vol. 3, *The Developing Mosaic: English-Canadian Drama to Mid-Century*, edited by Anton Wagner. Toronto: CTR Publications, 1980, pp. 84–97.

von Flotow, Luise. "Telling Canada's 'Story' in German: Using Cultural Diplomacy to Achieve Soft Power." von Flotow and Nischik, pp. 9–26.

von Flotow, Luise, and Reingard M. Nischik, editors. *Translating Canada. Charting the Institutions and Influences of Cultural Transfer: Canadian Writing in German/y*. Ottawa: U of Ottawa P, 2007.

Vowles, Andrew. "CBC Radio Show Gave Writers A Voice." *Campus News, University of Guelph*, 16 Apr. 2012, http://news.uoguelph.ca/2012/04/cbc-radio-show-gave-writers-a-voice/.

Wachtel, Andrew B. *Remaining Relevant after Communism: The Role of the Writer in Eastern Europe*. Chicago: U of Chicago P, 2006.

Wagner, Anton, editor. *The Developing Mosaic: English-Canadian Drama to Mid-Century*. Toronto: CTR, 1980.

Walcott, Rinaldo. *Black Like Who?: Writing Black Canada*. Toronto: Insomniac Press, 1997.

———. "By Way of a Brief Introduction—Insubordination: A Demand for a Different Canada." Walcott, *Rude*, pp. 7–10.

———. "'Who Is She and What Is She to You?': Mary Ann Shadd Cary and the (Im)possibility of Black/Canadian Studies." Walcott, *Rude*, pp. 27–48.

Walcott, Rinaldo, editor. *Rude: Contemporary Black Canadian Cultural Criticism*. Toronto: Insomniac Press, 2000.

Walker, Barrington. "Marginality, Interdisciplinarity and Black Canadian History." *New Dawn: The Journal of Black Canadian Studies*, vol. 1, no. 1, 2006, pp. 70–73, http://dawn.library.utoronto.ca/index.php/dawn/article/view/4985/1819.

Walker, James W. St. G. *A History of Blacks in Canada*. Hull, QC: Minister of State Multiculturalism/Canadian Government Publishing Centre, 1980.

Walker, Stephanie Kirkwood. *This Woman in Particular: Contexts for the Biographical Image of Emily Carr*. Waterloo, ON: Wilfrid Laurier UP, 1996.

Walmsley, Anne. *The Caribbean Artists Movement 1966–1972: A Literary and Cultural History*. London: New Beacon, 1992.

Wang, Bing, Association for Canadian Studies in China. Email to Patrick James, 2 May 2012.

Williams, David. "The Politics of Cyborg Communications: Harold Innis, Marshall McLuhan, and *The English Patient*." *Canadian Literature*, vol. 156, 1998, pp. 30–46.

Williams, Raymond. *Marxism and Literature*. Oxford: Oxford UP, 1977.

Wilson, Richard Ashby, and Richard D. Brown, editors. *Humanitarianism and Suffering: The Mobilization of Empathy*. Cambridge: Cambridge UP, 2011.

Winks, Robin W. *The Blacks in Canada: A History*. 2nd ed. Montreal and Kingston: McGill-Queen's UP, 1997.

Xiquez, Donez. *Margaret Laurence: The Making of a Writer*. Toronto: Dundurn Press, 2005.

Yelistratova, Anna. Afterword to *Zajtrajšok je náš*. By Dyson Carter. Bratislava: Slovenský spisovateľ, 1952, pp. 295–301.

York, Lorraine M. "'How a Girl from Canada Break the Bigtime': Esi Edugyan and the Next Generation of Literary Celebrity in Canada." *Canadian Literature*, vol. 217, summer 2013, pp. 18–33.

———. *Literary Celebrity in Canada*. Toronto: U of Toronto P, 2007.

———. Margaret Atwood and the Labour of Literary Celebrity. Toronto: U of Toronto P, 2013.

Yu, L., and Yeoman, E. 双语教育论—加拿大浸入式教育对我国高校双语教育的启示 (Theories of bilingual education: The implications of Canadian immersion education for bilingual instruction in Chinese universities). Beijing: Foreign Language Teaching and Research Press, 2009.

Zarranz, Libe García. *TransCanadian Feminist Fictions: New Cross-Border Ethics*. Montreal and Kingston: McGill-Queen's UP, forthcoming.

Zeleza, Paul Tiyambe. "Diaspora Dialogues: Engagements between Africa and Its Diasporas." *The New African Diaspora*, edited by Isidore Okpewho and Nkiru Nzegwu. Bloomington: Indiana UP, 2009, pp. 31–58.

Contributors

Michael A. Bucknor (University of the West Indies, Mona Campus, Jamaica) CanLit came to me in the late 1980s, all the way to the University of the West Indies, Mona Campus in Jamaica, just as I was completing my undergraduate degree. The literature of Canada came to me first in the form of a graduate seminar that I snuck into when I saw the title, which included the startling words, "Postcolonial Theory." The seminar outlined a new strategy of reading comparatively across different postcolonial societies. A year later, CanLit also came to me through Margaret Laurence's *The Diviners*, which was on the English graduate program at University of the West Indies. It was the only Canadian text I had encountered up to that point. CanLit kept coming and coming: it surfaced at my maiden conference in April 1992, at the University of Guyana, in a paper a Barbadian critic presented on Austin Clarke and narratives of exile, and again at the Association for Commonwealth Literature and Language Studies conference in Jamaica in August 1992—this time in the spectacular personage of Austin Clarke, an invited writer. It was no wonder, then, that I decided to come to CanLit, when I applied to graduate school in Canada and won a CIDA Scholarship to McMaster University and a Canadian Commonwealth Scholarship to the University of Western Ontario. I chose Canadian literature as a concentration at Western; I wanted to be filled with the cool glow of this new writing. By the first year of my PHD studies, I had taken four CanLit courses with major Canadianists: D.M.R. Bentley (early CanLit), Frank Davey (modernist CanLit), Pamela Banting (contemporary

CanLit), and Stan Dragland (CanLit international). In my PHD thesis, "Postcolonial Crosses: Body-Memory and Internationalism in Caribbean/Canadian Writing," I was able to bring the worlds of the Caribbean and Canada into one field of study. As much as I now live in the Caribbean, CanLit is in me now and in my scholarly world!

Daniel Coleman (McMaster University, Hamilton, Ontario, Canada)
I was born and raised the child of Canadians who worked in Addis Ababa, Ethiopia, and when I came to Canada and entered university, I took undergraduate classes that were in the thrall of the British canon, so I didn't clue in to Canadian literature until I read Kristjana Gunnars's *The Prowler* and Michael Ondaatje's *Running in the Family* for a class on Canadian autobiography during my PHD at the University of Alberta. These stories of immigration and cultural in-betweenness resonated with my own "third culture" experience in a way literature never had done previously. So I was introduced to CanLit in its transnational guise, and only learned about its nationalist framing once I was hooked. I've since come to understand more about the institutional machinery that creates and consolidates national literatures and the awkward appropriations and oblivions, as well as the synergies and stimulation, that arise from clustering literatures under various social categories—from nations to diasporas to ethnic or racial or thematic ones. I've become most interested, then, in the reorientations that arise from comparative analysis of the divergent knowledge systems and world views that shape differences in cultural value, intellectual authority, and what we might call the civility in civilization.

Anne Collett (University of Wollongong, Australia)
Despite having completed my secondary school education in British Columbia, my introduction to Canadian literature came through a course I took on postcolonial literature as an undergraduate at the University of Queensland, Australia. Margaret Atwood's novel *Surfacing* (1972) and her critical volume of the same year, *Survival*, gave me a perspective on CanLit that was gendered and bicultural (as opposed to multicultural); and given the course in which it was situated, I was encouraged from the outset to read Canadian literature in the historical context of layered and intersecting colonizations and as always comparative to other literatures. Although Canadian literature is taught in some Australian universities as "CanLit," it is more usual to study and teach it as part of postcolonial studies, and sometimes in particular comparison to Australian literature. This is in part the consequence of the structure of English majors in Australian universities, the notion and attached importance of a literary canon subscribed to by top-ranked institutions, and Australian government research funding that demands relevance to Australia and alignment with government priorities. Canadian funding for "foreign interest" in things Canadian has been generous in the past, but also directed towards Canadian

government priorities and not sufficient to maintain long-term research productivity. Thus, my publications on Canadian literature have been either comparative (most often with Australian literature) or theorized through gendered postcolonialism, and my teaching likewise. *Kunapipi*, the journal I have edited since the early 2000s, has made a significant contribution to research on Canadian literature, but that research sits within a postcolonial framework, the journal being linked to the European Association for Commonwealth Literature and Languages Studies. This is by no means a bad thing, but it provides a very particular lens through which to read the literature.

Pilar Cuder-Domínguez (University of Huelva, Spain)
When I first came to Canada in 1986, Margaret Atwood's *The Handmaid's Tale* had just been awarded the Governor General's Award for Best Fiction written in English. That book changed my life forever: I became a feminist and I started a life-long engagement with Canadian studies. Soon afterwards, in another lucky turn, the Spanish Association for Canadian Studies was founded, and it fast became a dynamic forum supporting young scholars like myself, starting to think "outside the box" and to open up new research areas outside the more canonical British and US studies. Nearly thirty years later, having made countless visits and even more friends, I continue to find in Canadian studies provocative writing, innovative thinking, and modes of academic work that engage with the community's concerns rather than look away from them.

Ana María Fraile-Marcos (University of Salamanca, Spain)
In 1989, when I got my BA in English at the University of Salamanca, Canadian literature was absent from the curriculum. Yet, at the doctoral level, my department was a pioneer in the introduction of Canadian studies in Spain, and I jumped at the opportunity to plunge into this novel field by taking a survey course in Canadian fiction. The successive state-fostered degree reforms of 1997 and 2010 offered us the chance to open up a niche for the teaching of Canadian literature at undergraduate level, alongside the established fields of British and American literatures. This was a reflection of the booming interest in CanLit in Spain during the 1990s, undoubtedly fostered by Canada's international promotion policies, as well as by the epistemological shifts and the revision of critical pedagogies used in the classroom. My career has been shaped by this literary encounter with the imaginary emerging from the Great White North and its contesting narratives. At present I am associate professor of English at my alma mater, and I teach Canadian literature both at undergraduate and graduate levels. My research, too, revolves around CanLit and its multiple intersections with current sociocultural and political concerns. Among my recent publications is the edited collection *Literature and the Glocal City: Reshaping the English Canadian Imaginary* (Routledge 2014). I am also the principal researcher of the research project called Narratives of Resilience: An Intersectional Approach to Literature and Other

Contemporary Cultural Representations, and a member of the Networks of Excellence Project, Transcanadian Research Networks: Excellence and Transversality from Spain about Canada Towards Europe, both funded by the Spanish Ministry of Economy and Competitiveness.

Jeremy Haynes (McMaster University, Hamilton, Ontario, Canada)
I began studying Canadian literature in the final two years of my undergraduate degree at the University of Guelph. During this time I took two courses that have since shaped the way I read and think about Canadian literature; Dionne Brand's poetry seminar led me to do an honours thesis and a master's thesis on African Canadian poetry, and Smaro Kamboureli's course introduced me to the language and politics of Canadian criticism. I met Daniel Coleman and Lorraine York when I arrived at McMaster. At the time I was a somewhat disorganized albeit enthusiastic student who'd really only been thinking in an English critical discourse for a short time. Through their supervision I have encountered new and interesting ways to question the continuously evolving canon of Canadian literature and approach issues of historical and cultural violence through their manifestations in poetry, fiction, and orature. What this particular narrative leaves out is the personal connection I feel with CanLit. I am fascinated by the historical intimacy of storytelling, the legends we circulate in my family—like the mythohistories of the canon—take place in a range of locations, but for the past few generations many have found their way to or been set in Canada. The earliest stories I can remember were told to me by my grandmother, who was trying to make the Prairies exciting to a squirmy little boy by filling them with stories. Gramma's stories, like all stories really, are marbled with our experiences of history—both brutal and beautiful—revealing glimpses of the living tissue of societies and cultures from other times. Ultimately, this land is my home and I am captivated by the way its stories can shift the ground beneath my feet.

Cristina Ivanovici (University of Birmingham, UK)
My interest in Canadian literature was first raised during the final year of my undergraduate studies in English literature at Babeș-Bolyai University, Cluj-Napoca, Romania, when a course on postcolonial literatures in English included several short stories and novels by contemporary Canadian writers. My subsequent postgraduate degrees offered me the opportunity to write a dissertation on the fiction of Margaret Atwood, which further led me to conduct research on the production and dissemination of her dystopian fiction in Germany and Romania. Various research grants that I held at universities and archives in Canada and Germany between 2007 and 2012, while I pursued my doctoral studies and taught at the undergraduate level at the University of Birmingham, further raised my interest not only in factors that prompted Eastern European publishers and academic communities to translate and

promote contemporary Canadian literature since the 1970s, but also in cultural policies that shaped specific projects.

Milena Kaličanin (University of Niš, Serbia)
I became interested in Canadian literature as an undergraduate student in the 1990s. At that time, professor Vesna Lopičić was teaching the only course of this kind in Serbia, still generally believed not to be as relevant for the future graduate philologists in the field of English language and literature as the massive and dominant British literary canon. Twenty years later, a total shift of interest has taken place in this area of study, with new subjects appearing under the large umbrella of Canadian studies (Canadian short fiction, Canadian women writers, literature of the Serbian diaspora in Canada). Bearing in mind the fact that the growing interest in Canadian studies has coincided with my voracious reading and zealous study of Canadian writers, I am immensely honoured to have taken a small part in the implementation of these courses as a teaching assistant at the Faculty of Philosophy in Niš.

Smaro Kamboureli (University of Toronto, Ontario, Canada)
"What brought you to Canada and to Canadian literature, Smaro?" Northrop Frye asked me at a party some thirty-eight years ago. "Lust," I answered, having another sip of wine. "I couldn't think of a better reason," he replied, his eyes smiling. A whimsical, if not rude, answer, with a measure of truth in it, but then after one year in Canada I was already fed up with such questions. As if origins held the key to some kind of unadulterated authenticity. As if there were a single—singular—reason for doing anything. Not to mention "discovering" that, just by virtue of living in another country, one became an "ethnic" (really?!). Canadians are a strange lot, I kept thinking at the time; I must try to figure them out. And so, while refusing to recite Homer at parties upon request—such a Canadian way of engaging my "otherness," a testament to their "civility"—I kept studying Canadian literature and puzzling over the fact that, at that time, many Canadians cared very little for their own literature. In fact I was shocked to discover yet another strange thing about Canadians, that they didn't teach their literature in their schools. Well, I thought, Canada needs a different kind of Canadian… The rest, as they say, is history.

Katalin Kürtösi (University of Szeged, Hungary)
I arrived in Canada on September 1, 1983 (the day Korean Air Lines Flight 007 was shot down) as a postgraduate student at Carleton University with the firm desire to deepen my knowledge of modern drama. I had to take courses in Canadian literature: Professor Robin Mathews's lively lectures opened my eyes to a sort of writing I had not known existed. I was particularly interested in drama and theatre—the study of contemporary drama and theatre made it necessary to visit Canada regularly, which

I did not mind at all. I started to teach courses on culture in Canada in 1985: several students decided to write their theses on Canadian authors. The Gesellschaft für Kanada-Studien played a key role in encouraging Central European scholars to pursue research and teaching related to Canada in various disciplines. Until 2012, the Embassy of Canada in Budapest was also in a position to support events and conferences. On the regional level, we started regular co-operation in the late 1990s and we still do enjoy working together—one testimony to this is the Translation Research Project, a database and collection of papers on the translations and reception of Canadian writing in the languages of the region (*Canada in Eight Tongues/Le Canada en huit langues*).

Vesna Lopičić (University of Niš, Serbia)

The decision to write my PHD thesis, *Human Nature in the Work of W. Golding and M. Atwood*, at the University of Niš, as the first person in Serbian academia to get a degree in Canadian literature, was spurred by reading Margaret Atwood's *The Handmaid's Tale*. This opened a gate for me into the fertile garden of CanLit whose many bifurcating paths I have been walking for twenty years now with many of my students, who joined me at different universities in Serbia, Kosovo, and the Republic of Srpska. A growing interest in Canada and things Canadian finally resulted in the creation of the Yugoslav Association for Canadian Studies in 2001, which was, after the geopolitical changes in that part of the Balkans, renamed the Serbian Association for Canadian Studies in 2011. Despite budget cuts and policy changes, our biennial conferences survive and we publish proceedings with the effective help of the Embassy of Canada in Belgrade. However strange it may seem, close ties between Canada and Serbia are maintained and new opportunities for collaboration arise, challenging like this one.

Belén Martín-Lucas (University of Vigo, Spain)

"Why *Canadian* literature?" In the twenty years I've been teaching CanLit at the University of Vigo many Canadian colleagues have asked me this question. For my PHD I chose CanLit over other postcolonial areas based on erroneous assumptions: I thought it would be "easier" than, say, Asian or African literatures because it was more "European." Of course I soon realized the enormity of my ignorance, faced with the vast variety of transcultural literary productions of Canada and Quebec, including those by Indigenous authors. In 1991–92 I was a visiting grad student at the University of Alberta, where I benefitted from the intellectual and emotional support of a group of inspiring grad students and professors committed to the discussion of ongoing racial and sexual discrimination in the cultural fields. This was the germ for an expanding web of connections with other fellow Canadianists around the world that has recently crystallized around the Canada and Beyond conferences and journal, which I codirect with Pilar Cuder-Domínguez. This informal network focuses on issues of race, gender, sexuality, colonialism, globalization, dissent, and resistance and activism against oppression. These are the guiding lines of my work on transnational women's fiction as well, which examines the intimate relation between poetics and politics, studying their use of underprivileged genres like the short story cycle (which was the topic of my doctoral thesis and first book) and, in more recent years, speculative fiction.

Claire Omhovère (University Paul Valéry, Montpellier 3, France)
Explaining where I stand as a French academic within the field of Canadian studies has frequently led me to dispel the assumption that all French scholars are involved in the study of issues related to French Canada. How can one be French, and be so fickle as to forget to remember the injunction to remember, "Je me souviens"? As a result, my position as a specialist of English Canadian literature has essentially been a marginal one, which, as Canadians well know, has some advantages attached to it. Occupying the margin in the French Association for Canadian Studies created at La Sorbonne in 1976, itself affiliated with the International Council for Canadian Studies, means that I have been participating in conferences where most papers were delivered by French-speaking anthropologists, historians, geographers, lawyers, and political scientists related to the "Belle Province." Since its creation, the Association française d'études canadiennes has repeatedly been confronted with the challenge of creating the conditions for an interdisciplinary dialogue in which the role of the specialist in literary studies—especially if her research lies on the English-speaking side of the Canadian cultural continuum—is to preserve and cultivate a perspective on diversity, no matter how disturbing these plural voices may be in their competitive and contradictory claims. This, to me, is the most appealing aspect of Canadian literature. It is also the one I find most rewarding when teaching students who never suspected, bred as they are on a robust diet of US and British classics, that one could be so creative when tampering with the Western canon.

Lucia Otrísalová (Comenius University, Slovakia)
I came to Canadian literary studies in the late 1990s thanks to the pioneering efforts of Dr. Mária Huttová, a literature instructor in charge of the Canadian Studies Centre at Comenius University, Bratislava. As a student I took some of her Canadian literature courses, and feeling inspired, wrote a thesis about one of the most internationally prominent faces of CanLit, Margaret Atwood. Being fond of challenges, I ventured on an even more adventurous path and explored Caribbean Canadian literature at the doctoral level. As Canadian literature has never been considered of primary interest in Slovak academia, I had to cope with my position as an external PHD student, scribbling my dissertation in the evenings after a full day of teaching English at language schools. Studying Canadian literature thus taught me the ethics of hard work and persistence.

With the same persistence and passion, I am, now in the capacity of a full-time instructor, smuggling some Canadian content courses into the somewhat old-fashioned English studies curriculum at Comenius.

Don Sparling (Masaryk University, Czech Republic)
As a student of English language and literature at Victoria College, the University of Toronto, in the early 1960s, I snobbishly rejected the one elective course on Canadian literature that was offered in the degree program as being neither "serious" nor "demanding." Relatively isolated inside Czechoslovakia, where I had come in 1969 to teach English, I missed the big CanLit boom in the 1970s, and only discovered contemporary Canadian literature for myself in the 1980s. Since then I have devoted increasing time to both Canadian literature and Canadian studies, as a teacher, researcher, and bureaucrat (within Canadian studies organizations at the national, regional, European, and global levels). This has given me the opportunity to offer students an immensely interesting subject of study, to indulge myself in learning more about my native land, to meet hundreds of dedicated Canadianists from around the world, and to make some small return to the country and the culture that so luckily shaped me and my values.

Melissa Tanti (McMaster University, Hamilton, Ontario, Canada)
An undergraduate course in French feminisms revealed to me the world of French Canadian writers. I was instantly absorbed by Monique Proulx's *Sex of the Stars* and Nicole Brossard's *Mauve Desert*. I was compelled to read more and later, on my own, discovered the body of Brossard's work wherein I was tantalized by *Yesterday, at the Hotel Clarendon*. I wanted to devour this book, turning each of its thick pages flowing with equally thick words. I became deeply interested in the relation between bodies, language, and text. This led me to explore the effects of language systems on embodiment and to the work of multilingual women writers such as Erin Mouré and Kathy Acker, and in this pursuit to uncover transnational communities of women writers crossing the Canadian and American border. This has become the focus of my doctoral dissertation, "The 'Translating Subject': Tracing the History of a North American Feminist Literary Avant-Garde." My research shows that a focus on national literatures and poetics has overshadowed important cross-border connections and exchanges between women poets and writers, particularly in the fertile period of the 1980s when much underground feminist writing was coming out of cities such as Montreal, Toronto, Vancouver, New York, Seattle, and San Francisco.

Christl Verduyn (Mount Allison University, Sackville, New Brunswick, Canada)
As many Canadian writers and literary scholars have noted, it was not a given in the early 1970s that universities in Canada offered courses on Canadian literature. At Trent

University where I was an undergraduate student, however, Professor Gordon Roper did teach Canadian literature, and I had the good fortune to take courses with him. I also had the opportunity to take courses on the literature of Quebec and on the new writing coming out of Latin and South America. Studying Canadian, Québécois, and Latin American literatures brought new horizons to more traditional study options of British, French, and Spanish literatures. These horizons widened further with feminist, "multicultural," and Aboriginal writing. These ultimately anchored my teaching and publication career in Canadian literature, understood broadly as literary production in Canada. Canadian literature and Canadian studies have allowed me to read, research, publish on, and teach some of the best writing in the world.

Elizabeth Yeoman (Memorial University, St. John's, Newfoundland, Canada)
I arrived at the work I do in a very roundabout way. I never set out to do Indigenous studies but it seems to draw me in over and over through the places I live and the people I meet. As for Canadian literature, and literature in general, they were my first love and I was fascinated by comparative Canadian literature in French and English as an undergraduate. However, by the time I began to engage seriously with academic work, I had two small children to support and an education degree seemed more practical. After ten years as a teacher and ten more as a professor, I had the opportunity to do some freelance work for CBC Radio—another love—and interviewed Labrador Innu elder and environmental activist Elizabeth Penashue for a documentary about walking. This led to my current collaboration with her on a book based on her diaries, stories, and essays in Innu-aimun, and to my interest in writing in Indigenous languages in general, and also connected me to the wonderful group of people involved in this book and other projects in Canadian studies.

Lorraine York (McMaster University, Hamilton, Ontario, Canada)
I came to Canadian literature via Ireland. As a teenager struggling with nascent disbelief, I was mesmerized by Joyce's *A Portrait of the Artist as a Young Man*. How did this Irish man writing at the beginning of the twentieth century know so intimately a Canadian adolescent's turbulent—frankly, traumatic—experience of Catholicism? A few years later, following the Joycean trail, I found Alice Munro's *Lives of Girls and Women*, and its intertextual rewriting of *Portrait*, and was mesmerized anew. Here was a woman who lived not across the ocean but in my very own community, proof that literature was not something that happened elsewhere. Munro was my "in," and CanLit just came along for the ride—or so I thought. I came to be fascinated by whatever tested the authority of the word (another vestige of my discarded Catholicism?)—first, the visual, the photographic, and then alternative modes of authorship such as women's collaborative writing. Thinking about authorship's others led me to ponder the way it is socially performed as a material practice, and that led me to celebrity. These days, I'm

thinking about the exclusions performed by celebrity authorship, and the way in which the expression of reluctance in relation to celebrity is a privilege that certain classed, raced subjects are able to perform without material risk to their cultural capital.

Index

Page numbers in italics refer to illustrations.

Abandoned Marble Quarries series (Burtynsky), 141
Aboriginal peoples. *See* Indigenous peoples
ACSUS (Association for Canadian Studies in the US), 7, 273n9
Ady, Endre, 128–29
African Canadian, as term, 104
    See also black Atlantic; black Canadians; black Canadian writing; Caribbean Canadian writing
Afroperiphery, as term, 105
After Canaan (Compton), 104–5
Ahmed, Sara, 159, 164, 167
Albahari, David
    about, xix, 175–77
    contending civilities, 176
    dialogical space for immigrants and Indigenous peoples, 175–77, 181–83, 191–92
    nostalgia for former nations, 179–80
    outsiders in national vision, 177–78
    trickster figures, 187–90
Albahari, David, works
    "An Indian at Olympic Plaza," 175–76, 178–81, 185–91
    Götz and Meyer, 176
    "Learning Cyrillic," 175, 182–84, 186, 190–91
    Snow Man, 175, 177, 179–80, 182, 186, 191
Algoo-Baksh, Stella, 66
Alias Grace (Atwood), 251n10
Almonte, Richard, 85
Angilirq, Paul Apak, 41–42
The Animals in That Country (Atwood), 235
Animal Stories (Seton), 221–22, 228n6
Anne of Green Gables series (Montgomery), xx–xxi, 218–20, 228n6
Antwi, Phanuel, 61–62, 70, 75n5
Appadurai, Arjun, 19
area studies, 13–14, 18–19, 46–47, 54

311

See also transnational studies
Argentina, UC program, 29, 34–35
Armstrong, Jeannette, xxiii, 270
arts, visual
    art theory, 195–99, 203–5
    E. Carr as marginal modernist, xviii, 119–24
    expression of consciousness, 197–98
    Group of Seven artists, 121–24, 134, 141–42
    inter-iconicity, 131, 141–42, 144, 146–47, 147n1
    landscape painting, 134
    postcards, 197
    sight in hierarchy of senses, 196
    See also *Cities of Refuge* (Helm); landscape photography
Association for Canadian Studies [in Canada] (ACS), 11, 25–26
Association for Canadian Studies in German-speaking Countries (GKS), 261
Association for Canadian Studies in the US (ACSUS), 7, 273n9
Atanarjuat (film), 41–2, 44
"At the Slave Museum" (Senior), 80
Atwood, Margaret
    awards and prizes, 266
    as a cultural ambassador, 237, 242, 264, 266
    protest against UC termination, 24, 33–34
    speculative fiction, 153–55, 170n7
Atwood, Margaret, translations
    about, xxi, 234–37, 242–46, 249–50
    archives, 230, 238, 243–44, 249–50, 253n23
    censorship, xxi, 235–37, 243–45
    copyright, 238
    cultural agents, 237, 243–44
    currency issues, 243–46
    Czech translations, xxi, 257, 263, 265–66, 269
    history of, 234–37, 249–50
    ideological interventions, 235–37, 242–43
    paratexts added to, 227n4, 233–34, 235, 236, 246
    Polish literary criticism on, 30
    readers, 234–37, 242–44, 251n10
    statistics, xxi, 234, 253n23, 263, 265
    translations delayed or abandoned, 230, 246
Atwood, Margaret, works
    Alias Grace, 251n10
    The Animals in That Country, 235
    The Blind Assassin, 266
    Bluebeard's Egg, 245, 253n24
    Bodily Harm, 235
    The Edible Woman, xxi, 235–36, 245, 252n13
    Good Bones, 251n10
    The Handmaid's Tale, 235, 246
    In Other Worlds, 153, 155
    Lady Oracle, 245
    MaddAddam, 155
    Oryx and Crake, 155
    Surfacing, 235–36, 243–45, 251n8, 252n14
    Survival, 245
    The Year of the Flood, 155
autoethnography, xviii, 154, 169n5
Ayaruaq, John, 45

Babeş-Bolya University, Romania, 247
Bacon, Joséphine, 45
Baird, John, 33, 35
Balogh, Mary, 263
"Bamboo" (Senior), 86
Bannerji, Himani, 181–82
Barbados. *See* Brathwaite, Edward Kamau; Clarke, Austin; West Indies writing
Barber, Virginia, 247–48
Basu, Amrita, 18
Batcos, Stephanie, 86
Baugh, Edward, 66
BBC (British Broadcasting Corporation) Caribbean writers, 65, 66, 67, 68, 70
Besner, Neil, 33–34
"Beyond Windrush and Other Black Atlantic Routes" (Bucknor), 65
Bhabha, Homi, 13, 92–93
Birns, Nicholas, 159–60
Bissoondath, Neil, 24, 33–34

black Atlantic
    about, 52–54
    British and US dominance, 52–53
    broadcast culture, 72–73
    Canada's position, 53–55, 74n3
    maroon intimacy, 53–54, 64–65
    political passion, 53, 61–62, 70, 73
    politics of recognition/erasure, 53, 56–57
    postcolonial intimacy, 61–64, 70–71
    racism, 69–71
    resistance, 63–64
    roots heritage studies, 100, 104–5
    scholarship on, 100
    slavery, 63, 82, 89, 94
    speculative fiction, 154
    terminology, 104–5
    See also *The Black Atlantic* (Gilroy); Caribbean Canadian writing
"Black Atlantic, Queer Atlantic" (Tinsley), 61–62
The Black Atlantic (Gilroy)
    about, 99–103
    Africa's position, 75n7, 100
    British position, 75n4, 75n7, 100, 101
    Canada's position, 75n4, 103
    Caribbean's position, 75n7
    diasporic intimacy, 58–60, 75n8
    nationalism's role, 61
    networks, 55, 60–61
    racial purity, 99, 103
    reception, 75n4, 100–101, 103
    slave ship as chronotope, 99–100, 113
    US's position, 75n4, 75n7, 100, 103
Black Atlantic Speculative Fictions (Thaler), 154
black Canadians
    about, 101–4
    Afroperipheralism vs Afrocentrism, 105
    Alberta settlements, 102, 105–6
    communities in cities, 59, 65, 70, 102
    historical background, 55, 89–90, 101–2
    indigenous vs diasporic subjects, 104
    multiplicities ("black Canadas"), xxii, 101, 103–4
    scholarship on, 102
    statistics, 101, 102
    terminology, 104–5
    women's writing, 104
black Canadian writing
    about, 52–54
    critical questions, 58–59
    diasporic intimacy, 58–62, 65, 75n8
    literary criticism, 104
    maroon intimacy, 53–54, 59–60, 64–65, 70–72, 75n8
    non-white as black, 59–60
    political passion, 53, 61–62, 70, 73
    politics of recognition/erasure, 55–57
    postcolonial intimacy, 61–62
    reception, 103
    rudeness to power, 57–58, 69, 93
    scholarship on, 52–53, 102
    terminology, 104–5
    See also Caribbean Canadian writing; Clarke, Austin; Edugyan, Esi; Hopkinson, Nalo; Senior, Olive; Walcott, Rinaldo
Black Like Who? (R. Walcott), 52–53, 55, 75n15, 102–3, 105, 114n7
The Blacks in Canada (Winks), 102
Blake (Delany), 103, 114n8
Blake, Jason, 249
The Blind Assassin (Atwood), 266
Bluebeard's Egg (Atwood), 245, 253n24
Bock, Gabriele, 235, 236, 241
Bodily Harm (Atwood), 235
Böhnke, Reinhild, 236
The Book of Longing (Cohen), 269
Bordo, Jonathan, 133–34
Bottez, Monica, 246
Bouyoucas, Pan, 30
Bowering, George, 33–34
Boyden, Joseph, 35
Boyle, Harry J., 67, 69
Braidotti, Rosi, 151–52, 154, 156–59, 161–62, 166, 170n10
Brand, Dionne, 24, 30, 33–34, 82, 114n14
Brant, Beth, xxiii, 270
Brathwaite, Edward Kamau, 51–52, 54, 71, 97n1
Brazil, UC grants, 29
"Bread out of Stone" (Brand), 82
Brenčičová, Danuša, 224–26

Bringhurst, Robert, 265
Britain. *See* United Kingdom
British Columbia
    E. Carr as marginal modernist, xviii, 119–24
    interracial communities, 105
    Notman's photography, 137–40, 139
Brno, Czech Republic, 265, 266–67, 268
Brown, Jarrett, 59, 64–65, 75n8
Brown, Richard D., 199
Brydon, Diana, 75n7, 91, 92, 95
Bucknor, Michael A.
    "Beyond Windrush and Other Black Atlantic Routes," 65
    chapter on Caribbean Canadian writing, xvii, 51–78
    on his study of CanLit, 301–2
Bulgaria, translations, 242, 249
Burtynsky, Edward
    about, xviii, 131, 141–46
    elegy for lost landscapes, 144–45
    exhaustion of landscape, 146–47
    genealogical approach to his works, 132
    inter-iconicity, 141–42, 144, 147n1
    manufactured landscapes, 142–44
    online exhibition, 148n10
    residual aesthetics, 132, 143, 146
Burtynsky, Edward, works
    Manufactured Landscapes, 148n10
    Nickel Tailings series, 144–45
    Polyfoam Resurrections, 146
    Railcuts, 143
    Show Room and Office, 149n12
    Souvenir of Canada photos, 145, 146, 149n12
    Workbench, 149n12
Butala, Sharon, 265
Butler, Nanette, 239

Callaghan, Barry, 264
The Cambridge History of English Literature, 7
Canada
    Cold War anxieties, 216
    cultural history in photography, 131–34, 136–37, 140–41
    gendered and sexual violence, 193–94, 196
    history of margins and centres, 125–26
Canada, cultural policy
    about, xi–xii, 10–15
    branding Canada, 38–40, 231, 242
    Canadian Studies Program, 11–12, 25, 37–40
    collaborative approaches, 17–18, 19–20
    critical questions on, 15, 17
    cultural diplomacy, 17, 21n11, 230–31, 256–57, 271–72, 272n7
    economic benefits, 13, 15
    export of culture, 3, 11, 14
    goals, 10–13
    Massey Report, 10–11, 14, 76n23
    mobility and, 19–20
    nationalism, 14–15
    power relations, 18
    priority countries, xiv–xv, xxvi–xxvii
    promotion within and abroad, xxvi, 5–6, 14
    Symons Report, 11–12, 14
    transdisciplinary approaches, 17–18, 19–20
    US cultural relations, 10–11
    See also DFAIT (Department of Foreign Affairs and International Trade); Harper, Stephen, government; multiculturalism; transnational studies; Understanding Canada (UC) program
Canada, writing and literature. *See* black Canadian writing; Canadian literature; Caribbean Canadian writing; Indigenous writing; transnational studies; women's writing
Canada and Its Utopias (Polish Association for Canadian Studies), 26
Canada Council for the Arts
    Caribbean Canadian writing, 68, 73
    funding and grants, 20n6, 41, 267–68
    Indigenous languages, 41
    Symons Report, 11–12, 14

Canada in Eight Tongues (Kürtösi, ed.), 230, 234
Canada in Us Now (Head, ed.), 57–58, 60
"'Canada in Us Now'" (Chariandy), 57–58, 60, 104
Canada Picture No. 3, 2001 (Coupland), 145–46, 148n11
Canada: Tomorrow's Giant (Hutchinson), 135
Canadian Broadcasting Corporation (CBC). *See* CBC (Canadian Broadcasting Corporation)
Canadian literature
  about, 3–10
  Commonwealth studies and, 5–9
  contributors' views on study of, xxiv, 301–10
  critical hierarchy, xxv
  delay in formation, 9–10, 13, 225–26
  international position, 3–10
  multicultural literature, 10, 54–55, 88–89
  national identity, 224–25
  self-knowledge and transnationalism, xxv–xxvi, 14
  See also black Canadian writing; Caribbean Canadian writing; Indigenous writing; translations; transnational studies
Canadian Studies Network–Réseau d'études canadiennes (CSN–REC), 25
Canadian Studies Program (DFAIT), 11–12, 25, 37–40
  See also Understanding Canada (UC) program
Canadian West Coast Art (exhibition), 121–22
Canadian Writing Today (*TLS*), 7–9, 20n9
"Canefield Surprised by Emptiness" (Senior), 81
Carew, Jan, 54, 56–57, 60, 62, 67, 71–72
Caribbean Canadian writing
  about, xvii, 52–54, 66
  Anansi, as symbol, 98n7
  "becoming West Indian," 59–60, 75n14

black Atlantic networks, 53–54, 56–57, 60, 67–68
  Brathwaite's writing, 51–52, 54, 71, 97n1
  broadcast culture, 66–69, 72–73, 76n23
  Carew's writing, 54, 56–57, 60, 62, 67, 71–72
  dub poetry, 73–74, 75n5
  economic struggle of writers, 65–66
  hypervisibility of, 52–54, 56, 103–4
  literary history, 66–67, 73–74
  maroon intimacy, 53–54, 59–60, 64–65, 70–74, 75n8
  nationalism, 54–55
  rudeness to power, 57–58, 69, 93
  Salkey's writing, 54, 62, 70–72, 77n28
  scholarship on, 74n2
  Selvon's writing, 54, 59, 64–67, 70–71
  slavery and sugar plantations, 81–83, 89, 94, 170n13
  speculative fiction, 160–61
  Windrush writers, 65
  See also Clarke, Austin; Hopkinson, Nalo; Senior, Olive
Carr, Emily
  Canadian West Coast Art (exhibition), 121–22
  Group of Seven artists, 121–24
  margins and centres, xviii, 119–24
Carter, Dyson, 215–18, 227n5
Casteel, Sarah Phillips, 54–55
CBC (Canadian Broadcasting Corporation)
  Anthology, 57–58, 76n23
  black global networks, xvii, 53, 67–68
  Brathwaite's role, 51–52
  Caribbean writing, 66–69, 72–73, 76n23
  A. Clarke's role, 52–53, 56–58, 60–63, 66–69, 72–73, 76n23
  cross-racial alliances, 68, 73
  funding cuts, xii
  Ideas, 69
  Weaver's role, 37–38, 62–63, 67–68, 76n23, 76nn25–26

Index 315

CEAC (Central European Association for
    Canadian Studies)
  about, 255–56, 273n8
  database of translations, 228n6,
    252n11, 252n19, 255–56, 272n1
  history and location, 259, 261, 267–68
  members and languages, 255–56, 260
censorship in Eastern Europe (pre-1989)
  about, 214–15
  banned books, 257
  GDR translations, 251n6
  ideological paratexts, 215–16, 227,
    227n4
  publication recommendations
    ("Gutachten"), 235–37, 241, 251n2
  women's writing, xxi, 234–36, 243–45
  See also Eastern and Central Europe,
    translation and publishing
    (pre-1989)
Central Europe. See Eastern and Central
    Europe
Central European Association for
    Canadian Studies. See CEAC
    (Central European Association for
    Canadian Studies)
Chamberlin, Edward, 185–86
Chariandy, David
  black Atlantic paradigm, 53
  "'Canada in Us Now,'" 57–58, 104
  politics of recognition, 54
  positions in literary criticism, 104
  "Postcolonial Diasporas," 61, 75n12,
    76n18
  queer postcolonial intimacy, 64
  rudeness to power, 57–58, 62
Charles University, Prague, 257–58, 267,
    269
Childs, Peter, 118
Chile, historical background, 194,
    200–201, 204
China
  SACS scholars, 28, 36n5
  UC programs, 29, 35, 37–40
Chow, Rey, 186
Choy, Wayson, 24, 33–34
Chrisman, Laura, 100
cinema. See film

Cities of Refuge (Helm)
  about, xix, 193–96, 205–6
  affect and ethical action, 195, 196–97,
    199, 202, 206
  art and affect, 195, 198–202
  creative writing, 199–204, 206
  empathy and sympathy, 199–202, 205
  expression of consciousness, 197–98
  gendered and sexual violence, 193–96,
    198
  music, 197–98
  self-estrangement, xix, 195, 197–98,
    206
  truth and reconciliation, 200
  understanding the Other, xix, 195
  violence in art, 195–96, 198, 202–6
  visual arts, 195–200, 205–6
  witnesses of violence, 202–6
civility, forms of, 92–93, 95, 98n8, 176
Clarke, Austin
  archives, 71, 74n1
  black Atlantic networks, 53–54, 56–57,
    60, 67–68
  CBC connections, 52–53, 56–58,
    60–61, 66–69, 72, 76n23
  economic struggle, 60–61, 65–66,
    69, 71–72
  friendship with Brathwaite, 51–52,
    54, 71
  friendship with Carew, 54, 56–57, 60,
    62, 65, 71–72
  friendship with Salkey, 54, 62, 71–72
  friendship with Selvon, 54, 65–66,
    70–71
  inter-ethnic relationships, 54–55
  life of, 60–61, 65–66
  maroon intimacy, 53–54, 56–57, 59,
    62, 70–72
  The Meeting Point, 54–55
  More, 60, 71–72
  racism, 69–70
  rudeness to power, 57–58, 69
Clarke, George Elliott, 52–53, 103, 104,
    265
class, social, in speculative fiction, 158,
    162–63
Coady, Lynn, 265
Coghill, Joy, 124

Cohen, Leonard, 263, 269
Cohen, Matt, 263
Cold War era in Europe (pre-1989). *See* censorship in Eastern Europe (pre-1989); Czechoslovakia, CanLit studies (pre-1989); Eastern and Central Europe, translation and publishing (pre-1989); Germany, East (GDR) (pre-1989); Germany, West (FRG) (pre-1989)
Cole, Thomas, 144
Coleman, Daniel
    class and political coalitions, 60
    critical intimacy, 95
    diaspora space and Indigenous place, 190
    emplaced knowledges, 185
    "From Canadian Trance," 93, 95
    on his study of CanLit, 302
    "Indigenous Place," 184, 185, 190
    introduction by, xi–xxvii
    "wry civility," 93, 95, 176
Collett, Anne
    chapter on Olive Senior, xvii, xx, 79–98
    on her study of CanLit, 302–3
    identity and career, 81, 84–85, 90–91, 302–3
Collins, Patricia Hill, 155–56
Collymore, Frank, 67
"Colonial Girls School" (Senior), 98n7
Comenius University, Slovakia, 224
comic books, 44–45
Commonwealth (Hardt and Negri), 157–58
Commonwealth Book Fair, 8
Commonwealth of Letters (Kalliney), 68
Commonwealth studies, 5–9, 224
Compton, Wayde, 104–5
conferences
    Canadian Studies Program funding, 38
    conference (2013) on transnational studies, xiv–xvi
    UC funding, 27–28, 36n3
Confluences (Gruesser), 100–101
"Contented Civility" (Coleman), 176
contributors' views on studying CanLit, xxiv, 301–10

Cosgrove, Denis, 132–33, 148n3
Coupland, Douglas
    about, xviii, 131, 135, 145–47
    Canada Picture No. 3, 2001, 145–46, 148n11
    Czech translations, 263
    exhaustion of landscape, 146–47
    genealogical approach to his works, 132
    online archives, 148n11
    Souvenir of Canada 1 & 2, 135, 145–46, 149n12
    still life photos, 132, 145–46, 148n11
CPAJ (Canadian Publishing Awards for Japan), 28, 36n3
"Crossing Borders and Negotiating Boundaries" (Senior), 80–81, 96–97
cross-talk, 91, 95
Crummey, Michael, 265
CSN–REC (Canadian Studies Network–Réseau d'études canadiennes), 25
Cuder-Domínguez, Pilar
    "African Canadian Writing," 53
    on black Atlantic paradigm, 53
    chapter on intra-national black dialogues, xvii–xviii, xxii, 99–114
    on her study of CanLit, 303
cultural capital
    black global capital, 56–57
    mobility of capital, 19
    transnational exchanges, xxv–xxvi
    See also transnational studies
Cultural Challenges of Migration in Canada / Les défis culturels de la migration au Canada (Ertler and Imbert, eds.), 27, 32–33
cultural diplomacy, 17, 21n11, 230–31, 256–57, 271–72, 272n7
    See also Canada, cultural policy
cultural studies and area studies, 18–19, 46–47
    See also transnational studies
"Culture and Interpretation" (Frye), 128
Cummings, Ronald, 59, 64, 75n8
Currah, Paisley, xxiv–xxv
Cushman, John, 240

Index   **317**

Czechoslavakia/the Czech Republic/
    Slovakia
  CEAC database of translations, 255–56
  first Canadian book published, xxi,
    228n8
  historical background, 211–14, 221–22,
    257–58
  images of North America, 219–21
  knowledge of US/UK/Canada, 211–12,
    220–21, 269
  personal connections with Canada,
    xxii, 262
  Slovak and Czech languages, 221,
    227n1
  wilderness culture, 211–12, 221–22,
    227n2, 228n11, 262, 272n4
Czechoslavakia, CanLit studies (pre-1989)
  Canadian cultural diplomacy, 230–31,
    256–57, 259
  censorship, 215, 257
  Commonwealth literature studies,
    224
  fall of communism, 257–58
  London's adventure stories, 220–21,
    228n7
  May's novels on the American West,
    220–21
  university courses, 257
  See also Eastern and Central Europe,
    translation and publishing
    (pre-1989)
Czechoslavakia, CanLit studies (pre-
    1989), Slovak translations
  about, 212–16, 226–27, 228n6
  bourgeois realism, 215, 223–24
  Carter's pro-Soviet novel, 215–18,
    227n5
  censorship, 214–15, 218
  gender issues, 219–20
  ideological interventions, 213–15,
    218–19, 222–25
  images of Canada, xxi, 211–12, 214–15,
    219–20, 222, 226–27
  Indigenous peoples of Canada,
    222–23
  literary criticism, 224–26, 228n12
  morality and freedom in nature,
    222–23, 226–27

  national identity of Canada, 225
  paratexts added to, 215–17, 224–26,
    227, 227n4, 233–34, 236, 246
  publishing industries and markets,
    226, 228n6
  religious content, 218–19
  university courses, 224
  wilderness culture, 211–12, 220–23,
    226–27
  See also Montgomery, Lucy Maud,
    translations; Seton, Ernest
    Thompson, translations
Czech Republic/Slovakia, CanLit studies
    (post-1989)
  about, 256, 257–59, 271–72
  author visits, 264–68
  award-winning authors, 266
  Canada Council support, 267–68
  CEAC database of translations, 255–56
  cultural diplomacy, 256–61, 268,
    271–72, 272n7
  cultural phenomena, 265–67
  Czech academics and courses, 257–61,
    268–71
  fall of communism, 257–58
  francophone writing, 259, 265, 272n5
  genres, 262–64
  Indigenous translations, xxiii, 263,
    264–65, 270
  Month of Authors' Readings, 265,
    266, 267–68, 270
  Prague Writers' Festival, 264, 266,
    267
  publishing industries and markets,
    267, 270
  Slovak and Czech languages, 221,
    227n1
  translations, 262–64, 267–70
  See also Eastern and Central Europe,
    translation and publishing
    (post-1989)

Darias-Beautell, Eva, 31–32
Davies, Robertson, 257, 263
Delany, Martin Robinson, 103, 114n8
Deleuze, Gilles, 158, 198–99
den Toonder, Jeanette, 30–31, 40
Desch, Kurt, 252n18

DFAIT (Department of Foreign Affairs
    and International Trade)
  branding Canada, 38–40
  Canadian Studies Program, 11–12, 25,
    37–40
  conferences funded by, 38
  cultural diplomacy, 21n11, 261, 272n7
  ICCS's administration of programs,
    23, 25–26
  name changes, ix
  operation of UC, xiv
  priority countries, xiv–xv, xxvi–xxvii
  See also Understanding Canada (UC)
    program
dialogue
  dialogical space between
    marginalized peoples, 175–77,
    181–84, 189, 191–92
  intra-national dialogues, 46
  respect for diversity, 180–82
The Diary of Abraham Ulrikabe, 45, 46
diasporic intimacy, 58–62, 65, 70–72,
  75n8
Didi-Huberman, Georges, 143–44
Dion, Stéphane, 35
The Diviners (Laurence), 252n19
Divisions on a Ground (Frye), 127
Dobson, Kit, xxvi
Dorsey, Angela, 263
Douglas Pine Trees (Notman), 138–40, *139*
Dreaming of Elsewhere (Edugyan), 112–13
DSRA (Doctoral Student Research
  Awards), 26–28, 36n3
dub poetry, 73–74, 75n5
Duchamp, Marcel, 143–44
Dyer-Witheford, Nick, 168
dystopian fiction and speculative fiction,
  154
  See also speculative fiction

Eastern and Central Europe
  fall of communism, 246, 249, 257–58
  publishing industries and markets,
    230–33, 238, 249–50
  re-mapping of margins and centres,
    128–29
  translations, xx–xxi, 231–33
  women's writing, xxi–xxii, 230, 234
  See also Czechoslavakia/the Czech
    Republic/Slovakia; Poland; Serbia;
    Yugoslavia
Eastern and Central Europe, translation
    and publishing (pre-1989)
  about, xx–xxi, 229–33, 249–50
  award winners, 231, 251n5, 266
  censorship, 214–15, 218, 230, 235–36,
    243–45
  copyright, 232, 238
  cultural agents, 231, 233, 239–41
  cultural diplomacy, 230–31, 256–57
  currency issues, 233, 238, 240, 242,
    243–47, 253n21
  economic presures on publishers,
    231–32
  fall of communism, 246, 249, 257–58
  funding, 232, 234
  history of, 234–35
  ideological interventions, 222–25,
    230–34
  literary criticism, 224–26
  material conditions, 229–32
  paratexts added to, 215–16, 224–26,
    227, 227n4, 233–34, 236, 246
  publishing industries and markets,
    230–32, 234–38, 246–47, 249–50
  readers, 233, 234–37, 242–43, 247–48
  state control, 251n4
  translations delayed or abandoned,
    230, 246
  university courses, 224
  women's writings, 230, 234
  See also Atwood, Margaret,
    translations; CEAC (Central
    European Association
    for Canadian Studies);
    Czechoslavakia, CanLit studies
    (pre-1989); Laurence, Margaret,
    translations; Munro, Alice,
    translations; Slovak translations
Eastern and Central Europe, translation
    and publishing (post-1989)
  about, xx–xxi, 234–35
  award winners, 248, 251n5
  Canadian government role, 234
  cultural diplomacy, 268
  currency issues, 235

Index 319

fall of communism, 246, 249, 257–58
funding, 234
paratexts added to, 246, 269–70
publishing industries and markets,
    234–35, 238, 249–50
translations delayed or abandoned,
    246, 248
women's writings, 234
See also Atwood, Margaret; CEAC
    (Central European Association
    for Canadian Studies); Czech
    Republic/Slovakia, CanLit studies
    (post-1989); Laurence, Margaret,
    translations; Montgomery, Lucy
    Maud, translations; Munro,
    Alice, translations; Seton, Ernest
    Thompson, translations
East Germany. See Germany, East (GDR)
    (pre-1989)
Eber, Dorothy Harley, 45
The Edible Woman (Atwood), xxi, 235–36,
    245, 252n13
Edugyan, Esi
    debates on "absence" of Canada in
        works by, 97n5
    Dreaming of Elsewhere, 112–13
    life of, 102, 105
    See also The Second Life of Samuel
        Tyne (Edugyan)
Edwards, Brent Hayes, 52, 100
Edwards, Whitney, 55
Edwardson, Ryan, 15
El-Hassan, Karla, 240–41
empathy and sympathy, 199–202
Engel, Howard, 57–58, 67, 68, 72
Engel, Marian, 30
England. See United Kingdom
The English Patient (Ondaatje), 266
environment
    anxieties in landscape photography,
        142–43
    degradation in speculative fiction,
        153–54
    UC priority theme, 25, 39–40
    See also Burtynsky, Edward; landscape
        photography
"Epistemologies of Respect" (Lai), 191
Erikson, Steven, 263

Ermine, Willie, 180–81, 189, 191
Ertler, Klaus-Dieter, 32–33
Essays in Red and White (Polish
    Association for Canadian Studies),
    26
Europe
    African Americans in interwar years,
        100
    Canada's literary position, 3–10
    Commonwealth studies in, 5–9, 224
    Eurocentrism and literary studies, 6
    European Network for Canadian
        Studies (ENCS), 261
    fall of communism, 246, 249, 257–58
    May's novels on the American West,
        220–21
    See also Czechoslavakia/the Czech
        Republic/Slovakia; Eastern and
        Central Europe; German-speaking
        countries; Poland; Serbia;
        Yugoslavia
European Network for Canadian Studies
    (ENCS), 261
Evans, Allen Roy, 222–23
Exalted Subjects (Thobani), 177–78

The Facts behind the Helsinki Roccamatios
    (Martel), 266
Fagan, Kristina, 189
Falls of the Kaaterskill (Cole), 144
fantasy and speculative fiction, 153–54
    See also speculative fiction
Faulkner, Peter, 118
Fee, Margery, 186
FEP (Faculty Enrichment Program),
    26–28, 36n3, 259, 260
Fielding, Joy, 262
film
    Atanarjuat, 41–43, 44
    Czech film criticism, 259
    I, Nuligak, 45–46
    translations and subtitles, 43
Findley, Timothy, 263, 269
First Nations. See Indigenous peoples
First Person Plural (McCall), 43, 45
Fleming, May Agnes, 256
folklore. See stories and storytelling

Fraile-Marcos, Ana María
    chapter on Helm's *Cities of Refuge*, xix, xxii, xxiii, 193–207
    on her study of CanLit, 303–4
francophones
    Czech author visits and translations, 259, 265, 268, 272n5
    Czech research on, 259
    Polish literary criticism, 30
Fraser, Brad, 263
FRG (Federal Republic of Germany). *See* Germany, West (FRG) (pre-1989)
"From Canadian Trance" (Coleman), 93, 95
FRP (Faculty Research Program), 26–28, 36n3, 259, 260
Frye, Northrop
    Canada's immature literary culture, 226
    Czech translations, 264
    definition of literary, 255
    fort as community, 85
    margins and centres, xviii, 125, 127–29
    support for Commonwealth literatures, 7
The Fur Trade in Canada (Innis), 125
The Future Is Queer (Labante and Schimel, eds.), 167

Gaining Ground (Kroetsch and Nischik, eds.), xxvi, 20n7, 232
Galea, Ileana, 247–48
Gandhi, Leela, 60, 62, 63
Gardening in the Tropics (Senior), 83, 86, 89–92, 96, 97n1
"Gastropoda" (Senior), 79–80
GDR (German Democratic Republic). *See* Germany, East (GDR) (pre-1989)
Gedge, Pauline, 263
gender
    gendered and sexual violence, 193–94, 196
    hybrid characters in speculative fiction, 158
    modernisms, 122–23

    posthuman singularities in "the multitude," xviii–xix, 165–68, 169n2
    transing, as term, xxiv
    See also women; women's writing
genres. *See* poetry; queer speculative fiction; speculative fiction
German-speaking countries
    Association for Canadian Studies, 261
    cultural diplomacy, 261
    currency issues, 253n21
    history of CanLit studies, 20n3
    Laurence's translations, 241–42
    publishing industries and markets, 232–38, 240–41, 246–47, 249–50, 251n7
Germany, East (GDR) (pre-1989)
    Atwood's translations, 236–37
    censorship, 235–36, 251n6
    currency issues, 253n21
    fall of communism, 246, 249
    Laurence's translations, 241–42
    May's novels on the American West, 220–21
    publishing industries and markets, 232–33, 238
    reception of Anglo-Canadian lit, 224
Germany, West (FRG) (pre-1989)
    Atwood's translations, 236–37
    Canada's position as a national literature, 3–10
    Commonwealth studies, 5–9
    cultural agreement with Canada, 5, 9
    currency issues, 253n21
    history of CanLit studies, 3–6, 20n3
    Laurence's translations, 241–42
    publishing industries and markets, 232–33, 238
Gibson, Graeme, 264
Gibson, William, 263
Gikandi, Simon, 100
Gilroy, Paul. See *The Black Atlantic* (Gilroy)
Gladwell, Malcolm, 264
Global Affairs Canada, name changes, ix
    See also DFAIT (Department of Foreign Affairs and International Trade)
Glover, Douglas, 30

Index **321**

Godard, Barbara, 75n11, 104, 114n9
Goetsch, Paul, 20n7
Good Bones (Atwood), 251n10
Goto, Hiromi
    about, xviii, 168
    affect modes, 160–62, 168
    genres, 169n6, 170n8
    her cultural background, 152, 168n1, 170n9
    hybrid characters, 152, 158, 160
    Japanese folklore, 160
    posthuman singularities in "the multitude," 153
    queer speculative fiction as genre, 153–56, 168
Goto, Hiromi, works
    Hopeful Monsters, 152, 169n6
    The Kappa Child, 152, 155, 160, 161–62
    The Water of Possibility, 152
Götz and Meyer (Albahari), 176
government of Canada, cultural policy. *See* Canada, cultural policy; Harper, Stephen, government; multiculturalism; Understanding Canada (UC) program
Goya, Francisco, 203–4
Graham, John, 12–13, 16, 34
graphic novels, 44–45
Grossman, Edith, 43–44
Group of Seven artists, 121–24, 134, 141–42
Growing Pains (Carr), 119–20, 121, 124
Gruesser, John Cullen, 100–101
Guattari, Félix, 198–99

Habermas, Jürgen, 195, 199
Hailey, Arthur, 262
Halberstam, Judith, 166
Haliburton, Thomas Chandler, 269
The Handmaid's Tale (Atwood), 235, 246
Haraway, Donna, 151–52, 156, 159–62
Hardt, Michael, xviii–xix, 151–53, 157–58, 165–68, 169n2
Harper, Stephen, government
    funding cuts, xii, 16–17
    isolationist approach, xx, 272
    neoliberalism and otherness, 13
    public protests against termination of UC, xii, 24, 33–36
    termination of UC, xii–xiii, 16, 19, 21n12, 24
Harris, Lawren, 121, 122, 141–42
Hay, Elizabeth, 24, 33–34
Haynes, Jeremy
    on his study of CanLit, 304
    introduction by, xi–xxvii
Head, Harold, 57–58, 60, 62, 64
Hébert, Anne, 30
Helm, Michael
    interview with, 202
    In the Place of Last Things, 202
    See also *Cities of Refuge* (Helm)
Henighan, Stephen, 205–6
Henitiuk, Valerie, 44–45, 46, 48n1
Highway, Tomson, 263, 265
The Highway of the Atom (van Wyck), 44
A History of Blacks in Canada (Walker), 102
history of Europe, Cold War era. *See* censorship in Eastern Europe (pre-1989); Czechoslavakia, CanLit studies (pre-1989); Eastern and Central Europe, translation and publishing (pre-1989); Germany, East (GDR) (pre-1989); Germany, West (FRG) (pre-1989)
history of Europe, post–Cold War era. *See* Czech Republic/Slovakia, CanLit studies (post-1989); Eastern and Central Europe, translation and publishing (post-1989); Europe
A History of French-Canadian and Québec Literature (Kyloušek), 259
Hodgetts, A.B., 11
Hodgins, Jack, 33–34
Hopeful Monsters (Goto), 152, 169n6
Hopkinson, Nalo
    about, xviii, 160–62, 168
    affect modes, 161–62, 168
    Caribbean folklore, 160–61
    genres, 169n6
    her cultural background, 152, 168n1, 169n3, 170n9
    hybrid characters, 152, 158, 160–61

posthuman singularities in "the multitude," 153
queer speculative fiction as genre, 153–56, 168
shapeshifters, 160, 170n9, 170nn12–13
slavery and plantations, 160–61, 170n13
social justice issues, 169n4, 170n13
Hopkinson, Nalo, works
    Falling in Love with Hominids, 155
    Midnight Robber, 152, 155, 160–62, 169n3
    The New Moon's Arms, 155, 160, 170n13
    The Salt Roads, 155, 170n13
    Sister Mine, 155
    Skin Folk, 152, 169n6
Houston, James, 222–23
Huggan, Graham, 169n5
humanism and posthumanism, 156–57, 160–61, 165–68
Hundreds and Thousands (Carr), 121, 122, 124
Hungary
    re-mapping of margins and centres, 128–29
    UC grants for literature, 29
"Hurricane Story" (Senior), 97n1
Hutchinson, Bruce, 135
Huttová, Mária, 224–25, 228n12
Huyssen, Andreas, xviii, 118

I, Nuligak (film), 45–46
ICCS (International Council for Canadian Studies), xii, 23, 25–26, 32
Ideas (CBC), 69
identity
    identity politics, 156–58, 162–63
    Indigenous peoples, 185–87
    landscape and, 146–47
    national identity, xxv–xxvi, 14–15, 224–25
    posthuman singularities in "the multitude," xviii–xix, 165–68, 169n2
    O. Senior's identity as choice, 84, 87, 92–93
    speculative fiction, 156–58, 162–63, 165–68
    storytelling and, xxii; 185–87
    transnationalism and, xxv–xxvi
    whiteness as hegemonic Canadian identity, 181–82
If This Is Your Land, Where Are Your Stories? (Chamberlin), 185–86
Igloolik Isuma Productions, 41, 45
Imbert, Patrick, 32–33
immigrants
    Canadian statistics, 189
    nostalgia for former nations, 179–80
    as outsiders in national vision, 177–78
    relations with Indigenous peoples, xxii, 175–78, 180–81, 188–89
    universalizing of experiences, 180–81
India, UC program, 29, 34
"An Indian at Olympic Plaza" (Albahari), 175–76, 178–81, 185–91
Indians, as term, 176–77
    See also Indigenous peoples
Indians, West. *See* Caribbean Canadian writing; West Indies writing
Indigenous peoples
    colonization, 180–83
    European images of, xxiii, 176, 220–21, 270
    influences on E. Carr, 120–22
    missing and murdered Indigenous women, 194, 207n1
    museum culture, 182–83
    as outsiders in national vision, 177–78
    preservation of culture and identity, 185–87
    relations with immigrants, 175–78, 180–81, 188–89
    residential schools, 192nn3–4, 200
    terminology, 176–77
    universalizing of experiences, 180–81
    See also Innu people; Inuit; Siksika people
Indigenous writing
    about, xxiii, 41–46
    colonization and names, 181–83
    disappearing figures, 185–88
    funding applications to cultural agencies, 41–43
    Inuit film makers, 41–46
    life writing, 45–46

new networks and research styles, 43–47
official languages, xvi, 41–42
storytelling, xxiii, 44, 183–90
translations, xxiii, 41–44, 263, 264–65, 270
trickster figures, 187–90
"Indigenous Place" (Coleman), 184, 185, 190
indigenous vs diasporic black Canadians, 104
In Other Worlds (Atwood), 153, 155
Innis, Harold, xviii, 125–27
Innu-aimun language, 37, 41–42
Innu people, 37, 41–42, 45, 46
  See also Indigenous peoples
interdisciplinarity vs transdisciplinarity, xxvi–xxvii
  See also transnational studies
inter-iconicity and photography, 131, 141–42, 144, 146–47, 147n1
International Council for Canadian Studies (ICCS), xii, 23, 25–26, 32
In the Place of Last Things (Helm), 202
Inuit
  Atanarjuat, 41–43, 44
  funding and grants, 41–43
  I, Nuligak, 45–46
  Inuktitut language, 41–42, 43, 45
  life writing, 45–46
  translation of works about, 222–23
  See also Indigenous peoples
Irvine, Dean, 118–19, 129–30
Isolation Peak (Harris), 142
Isuma Igloolik Productions, 41, 45
Ivanovici, Cristina
  chapter on translation in Eastern Europe, xix–xxi, 229–53
  on her study of CanLit, 304–5

The Jack Pine (Thomson), 140
Jamaica
  historical background, 81–83, 89, 94, 101
  See also Caribbean Canadian writing; Hopkinson, Nalo; Salkey, Andrew; Senior, Olive; West Indies writing
James, Patrick, 24, 34, 35

Jameson, Frederic, 118
Jan Evangelista Purkyně University, 257
  See also Masaryk University, Czech Republic
Japan
  Canadian Publishing Awards for Japan, 28, 36n3
  folklore in speculative fiction, 160
  translations and popular culture, 44–47, 48n1
Jaumain, Serge, 11, 35
A Jest of God (Laurence), 241–42
Jewish people, 54–55, 176
Jindra, Miroslav, 269
Johns Hopkins University, 7
Joly, Mélanie, xiii
Juráňová, Jana, 219
Justice, Daniel Heath, 184

Kaličanin, Milena
  chapter on dialogues of immigrants and Indigenous peoples, xix, xxii, xxiii, 175–92
  on her study of CanLit, 305
Kalliney, Peter J., 68
Kamboureli, Smaro
  call for new networks and research styles, 41, 43–44, 46–47
  chapter on cultural policy, xvi, 3–22
  on her study of CanLit, 305
  interview with Helm, 202
  Polish literary criticism on, 30
Kaplan, Karel, 214
The Kappa Child (Goto), 152, 155, 160, 161–62
Kay, Guy Gavriel, 263
Keats, John, 199, 201–2
Keefer, Janice Kulyk, 30
Keeshig-Tobias, Lenore, 187
Kelly, Robin D.G., 67–68
Khan, Ismith, 67, 71
Kincaid, Jamaica, 91
King, Thomas, xxiii, 24, 33–34, 263, 270
Klinck, Carl F., 4, 7
Kogawa, Joy, 30
Kokis, Sergio, 30
Komenský University, Bratislava, 258
Korte, Barbara, 224, 251n2

324 Index

Kostash, Myrna, 30, 264
Kroetsch, Robert, 129, 140, 141
Kroller, Eva-Maria, 33–34
Kunuk, Zacharias, 43
Kürtösi, Katalin
　Canada in Eight Tongues, 230, 234
　chapter on modernisms and E. Carr, xviii, 117–30
　on her study of CanLit, 305–6
Kúsa, Mária, 212
Kyloušek, Petr, 259

Labanté, Richard, 167
Lady Oracle (Atwood), 245
Lai, Larissa
　about, xviii, 158–62, 168
　affect modes, 160–62, 168
　definition of family, 159–60
　her cultural background, 152, 168n1, 170n9
　hybrid characters and languages, 152, 158–59
　poetry, 169n6
　political action, 159–60, 169n4, 184
　posthuman singularities in "the multitude," 153
　queer speculative fiction as genre, 153–56, 168
　shapeshifters, 169n4
Lai, Larissa, works
　"Epistemologies of Respect," 191
　Salt Fish Girl, 152, 155, 158–62, 166, 169n4
　When Fox Is a Thousand, 152, 155, 159, 167, 169n4
Lalonde, Robert, 30
Lamb, Harold Mortimer, 124
Lamming, George, 59–60, 64, 67
landscape photography
　about, xviii, 131–34
　cultural history in, 131–34, 136–37, 140–41
　exhaustion of landscape, 146–47
　genealogical approach, 132, 140–41
　imprints, 143–44
　inter-iconicity, 131, 141–42, 144, 146–47, 147n1

　nature and culture, xviii, 142–43, 146–47
　as object or process, xviii, 133
　technologies, 133, 136, 137
　timelessness vs change, xviii
　See also Burtynsky, Edward; Coupland, Douglas; Notman, William McFarlane
languages
　Canada's official languages, 40–41
　Czech and Slovak languages, 221, 227n1
　hybrid languages in speculative fiction, 158, 161
　Indigenous languages, 37, 41–47
　power relations, 42–44
　See also translations
Laurence, Margaret, translations
　about, 238–41, 249–50
　archives, 230, 238–40, 249–50, 252n15
　censorship, 241
　copyright, 238
　cultural agents, 239–42, 251n2
　currency issues, 240, 242
　Czech translations, 263
　funding, 234
　history of, 234–35, 237–41, 249–50
　paratexts added to, 227n4, 233–34
　readers, 234, 237–38
　statistics, 234
　translations delayed or abandoned, 230, 240–42, 251n2
　Western European publishers, 237–38
Laurence, Margaret, works
　The Diviners, 252n19
　A Jest of God, 241–42
　"The Loons," 252n19
　The Stone Angel, 240–41, 251n2, 251n8, 252n19
　This Side Jordan, 239–40, 241, 252n17
　The Tomorrow-Tamer, 240
Layton, Irving, 264
Leacock, Stephen, 228n13, 263
"Learning Cyrillic" (Albahari), 175, 182–84, 186, 190–91
The Life of Pi (Martel), 266
life writing, 45–46
Literary History of Canada (Klinck), 4, 255

Live Bait (Wood), 226
Livingston, Ira, 166
The Location of Culture (Bhabha), 92
London, Jack, 220–21, 228n7
"The Loons" (Laurence), 252n19
Lopičić, Vesna
    chapter on dialogues of immigrants and Indigenous peoples, xix, xxii, 175–92
    on her study of CanLit, 306
Lowe, Lisa, 60, 62, 67–68, 71
Lowry, Malcolm, 263
The Luck of Ginger Coffey (Moore), 223–24
Ludden, David, 19

MacDonald, Ann-Marie, 30, 263
MacIvor, Daniel, 263
MacLennan, Hugh, 20n7, 224–25
MacLeod, Alistair, 24, 33–34, 35
MacMillan, Margaret, 264
MaddAddam (Atwood), 155
"Making West Indian Literature" (Morris), 73–74
manga comic books, 44–45
Manske, Eva, 236
Manufactured Landscapes (Burtynsky), 148n10
Maracle, Lee, xxiii, 265, 270
margins and centres
    about, xviii, 117, 125–29
    arts and decentralization, 128–29
    Canada's history of, 125–26
    Canada's position in modernisms, 129–30
    hierarchies in, 127
    interpenetration principle, 128
    modernists, xviii, 118–23, 125–29
    multiculturalism, 181
    re-mapping of, 128–29
Markotić, Nicole, 163–64
maroon intimacy, 53–54, 59–60, 64–65, 70–72, 75n8
    See also Caribbean Canadian writing
Marryat, Frederick, 256
Martel, Yann, 30, 263, 264, 266
Martin, Paul, 35
Martín-Lucas, Belén
    chapter on queer speculative fictions, xviii, 151–71
    on her study of CanLit, 306–7
    on multitude as concept, xviii–xix, 165–67, 169n2
Masaryk University, Czech Republic, xxiii, 257–59, 267–68, 270
Massey Report, 10–11, 14, 76n23
    See also Canada, cultural policy
Matthews, Steven, 118
May, Karl, 220–21
Mayr, Suzette
    about, xviii, 162–65, 168
    affect modes, 168
    cannibalism, 163, 165, 171n14
    critique of multiculturalism, 162–65
    genres, 169n6
    her cultural background, 152, 168n1, 170n9
    hybrid characters, 152, 158, 162–65, 171n14
    Moon Honey, 153, 155, 162–63
    posthuman singularities in "the multitude," 153
    queer speculative fiction as genre, 153–56, 168
    vegetarian vampires, 153, 163–65
    Venous Hum, 153, 155, 163–65, 167, 171n14
McCall, Sophie, 43, 45
McCord Museum, Notman photography, 135, 148n4
McGill group of poets, 118–19
McLuhan, Marshall, xviii, 125–27, 264
media, broadcast. *See* BBC (British Broadcasting Corporation); CBC (Canadian Broadcasting Corporation)
"Meditation on Yellow" (Senior), 89–92
The Meeting Point (A. Clarke), 54–55
Meisel, John, 12–13, 34
Memorial University of Newfoundland, 39–40
Metayer, Maurice, 45–46
Miller, Kei, 64
Mirsepassi, Ali, 18
Mistry, Rohinton, 24, 33–34, 97n5, 263

Mitchell, W.T.J., 131, 138, 140
Mittleholzer, Edgar, 62–63
Miura, Reiichi, 165–66
modernisms
  about, 118–19
  Canada's history of, 125–26, 129–30
  E. Carr as marginal modernist, xviii, 119–24
  European modernism, 128–30
  gender issues, 122–23
  Group of Seven artists, 121–24
  interpenetration principle, 128
  margins and centres, xviii, 118–23, 125–29
  McGill group of poets, 118–19
Modest_Witness@Second_Millennium (Haraway), 159
Monarch, the Big Bear of Tallac (Seton), 222
Montgomery, Lucy Maud, translations
  Czech translations, 263
  Slovak translations, 214–15, 218–20, 226, 228n6
Month of Authors' Reading, Czech Republic, 265, 266, 267–68, 270
Moodie, Susanna, 269
Moon Honey (Mayr), 153, 155, 162–63
Moore, Brian, 223–24, 263
Moore, Lisa Jean, xxiv–xxv
More (A. Clarke), 60, 71–72
Morra, Linda M., 187
Morrell, David, 262
Morris, Mervyn, 73–74
Moses, Daniel David, 263, 265
movies. *See* film
Mowat, Farley, 222, 263, 269
Müller, Marianne, 241
multiculturalism
  acceptable cultural forms, 181–82
  bonding by storytelling, 183
  as colonialism, 181–82
  critique in speculative fiction, 153, 156, 162–65, 171n14
  dialogical space between marginalized peoples, 175–77, 181–84, 191–92
  government policies, 163
  multilingualism, xvi, 42
  nationalism and ethnicity, 54
  politics of recognition, 54
  respect for diversity, 180–82
  See also Canada, cultural policy; Canadian literature
Multitude (Hardt and Negri), 153, 169n2
multitude, as concept, xviii–xix, 165–67, 169n2
Munro, Alice, translations
  about, 246–50
  archives, 230, 238, 247–48, 249–50
  awards, 248
  copyright, 238
  cultural agents, 247, 248
  currency issues, 238, 247
  Czech translations, 263
  funding, 234, 238
  history of, 234–35, 238, 253n28
  paratexts added to, 227n4, 233–34
  post-1990 translations, 238, 253n28
  readers, 234, 247–48
  statistics, 234
  Too Much Happiness, 248, 253n29
  translations delayed or abandoned, 230, 248
  Western European publishers, 238
  Who Do You Think You Are?, 248
"Must All Blackness Be American?" (G.E. Clarke), 103
"My Father's Blue Plantation" (Senior), 86
myths and folklore. *See* stories and storytelling

Naipaul, V.S., 70
nationalism
  black networks as replacement for, 61, 76n18
  black writing and area studies, 54
  landscape and identity, 133–34, 146–47
  outsiders and corruption of idealized vision, 177–78
  public policy on culture, 14–15
  storytelling and preservation of culture, 185
Native people. *See* Indigenous peoples
Negri, Antonio, xviii–xix, 151–53, 157–58, 165–68, 169n2

Index   327

networks, black Atlantic. *See* black
    Atlantic
Never Cry Wolf (Mowat), 222
New, W.H., 33–34
Nickel Tailings series (Burtynsky), 144–45
Nischik, Reingard M., xxvi, 5, 11, 232
Nolette, Nicole, 42
Nordic Association for Canadian Studies, 272n3
Northwest Territories, languages, 41
Notman, William McFarlane
    about, xviii, 131, 134–37, 146–47
    archives, 148n4
    assumption of progress, 142
    documentary style, 136, 146–47
    exhaustion of landscape, 146–47
    genealogical approach to his works, 132, 140
    life of, 134–36, 148n5
    online exhibition, 135, 148n4
    photography technologies, 136, 137
    Romantic landscapes, 137
    shadow and light, 140
    tension between medium and message, 132, 137–40
    transportation history, 136–37, 143
Notman, William McFarlane, works
    Douglas Pine Trees, 138–40, *139*
    Scuzzie Falls, 137
    Young Canada, 135
Nouwen, Henri, 264
Nuligak, 45

Oeding, Brita, 4, 5, 237
"Of Aliens, Monsters, and Vampires" (Martín-Lucas), 156
Ollivier, Émile, 30
Omhovère, Claire
    chapter on landscape photography, xviii, 131–49
    on her study of CanLit, 307–8
Ondaatje, Michael, 30, 35, 97n5, 205–6, 263, 266
On Photography (Sontag), 132
Oryx and Crake (Atwood), 155
Ostenso, Martha, xxi, 228n8
O'Sullivan, Simon, 198, 205

Otrísalová, Lucia
    chapter on Slovak translations, xix, xx–xxi, 211–28
    on her study of CanLit, 307–8

Pache, Walter, 3–10, 20n4, 20n7
Padolsky, Enoch, 104
painting and drawing. *See* arts, visual
Palacký, František, 271
paratexts added to translations, 215–16, 224–26, 227, 227n4, 233–34, 236, 246, 269–70
    See also translations
Pearson, Wendy, 168, 170n8
Penashue, Elizabeth, 37, 41–42, 46
People from Our Side (Pitseolak and Eber), 45, 46
Petruț, Margareta, 245–46
Philip Sherlock Lecture (Senior), 94
photography
    cultural history in photos, 135–37
    genealogical approach, 132
    Peirce's semiotic system, 148n9
    still life photos, 132, 145–46, 148n11
    See also Burtynsky, Edward; Coupland, Douglas; landscape photography; Notman, William McFarlane
Pierce, C.S., 148n9
The Pillow Book (Henitiuk, trans.), 44–45, 46
Pitseolak, Peter, 45
"The Poem as Gardening" (Senior), 94
poetry
    dub poetry, 73–74, 75n5
    McGill group, 118–19
    poet as "tribal drummer," 88
    speculative fiction, 169n6
    translations in Eastern Europe, 235
    See also Senior, Olive
Poland
    Atwood's translations, 243–45, 253n24
    Munro's translations, 248–49, 253n28
    Polish journals and associations, 26, 29–30
Polyfoam Resurrections (Burtynsky), 146
Pospíšil, Tomáš, 220–21
"Postcolonial Diasporas" (Chariandy), 61, 75n12, 76n18

Postcolonial Intimacies (Antwi), 61–62
postcolonialism
    postcolonial intimacy, 61–64, 70–71
    resistance, 62–65
The Posthuman (Braidotti), 156–57, 159
posthumanism
    affirmative politics, 154
    definition of posthuman, 166
    humanism and posthumanism, 156–57
    speculative fiction, 156–62, 165–68
    theorists, 151–52
power relations
    black politics of recognition/erasure, 55–56
    government cultural policy, 18
    mobility and asymmetrical exchanges, 19
    personal responsibility and ethics, 191
    translations, 42–43
Prague Writers' Festival, 264, 266, 267
Procter, James, 65
Puar, Jasbir, 156
public policy. *See* Canada, cultural policy
publishing translations in Europe. *See* Czechoslavakia/the Czech Republic/Slovakia; Eastern and Central Europe; German-speaking countries

Quebec francophones
    Czech research on, 259
    translations, 259, 272n5
queer culture
    black postcolonial intimacy, 63–64
    Canadian aspects of, 170n8
    queer as category, 155–56, 166–67
    terminology, xxiv, 64
queer speculative fiction
    about, xviii, xxi, 152–56, 168
    affect modes, 155–56, 160–62, 168
    autoethnographic mode, xviii, 169n5
    cannibalism, 165, 171n14
    critique of multiculturalism, 153, 156, 162–65, 171n14
    folklore, 152, 160–61
    genres, 169n6
    humanism, 156–57, 160–61
    hybrid characters and languages, 158–61
    identity politics, 156–58, 165–68
    mutant monsters, 152–53, 157, 166–67
    new forms of subjectivity, 157–58
    posthumanism and posthumans, 152, 156–65, 165–68
    posthuman singularities in "the multitude," xviii–xix, 165–68, 169n2
    queer as category, 155–56, 166–67
    science fiction vs speculative fiction, 153–54
    shapeshifters and morphing bodies, 152, 156, 166, 169n4, 170nn12–13
    social justice issues, 153–56, 167, 169n4, 169n6
    transhuman, defined, 170n10

race and ethnicity
    black racism, xxii, 69–71, 109–10, 112
    cross-racial alliances in media, 68, 73
    identity choices, 87
    monsters as mixed-race characters, 163–64
    multiculturalism and racialization, 181–82
    posthuman singularities in "the multitude," xviii–xix, 165–68, 169n2
    speculative fiction, 155, 158, 162–64, 171n14
    whiteness as hegemonic identity, 181–82
    See also multiculturalism
radio networks. *See* BBC (British Broadcasting Corporation); CBC (Canadian Broadcasting Corporation)
Railcuts (Burtynsky), 143
Reder, Deanna, 187
Re-Exploring Canadian Space / Redécouvrir l'espace canadien (den Toonder and van Hoven, eds.), 27, 30–31
Reid, Victor, 67
Reimer, Sharlee, 159
Reindeer Trek (Evans), 222–23

Remi, Cornelius, 30–31, 40
research, transnational. *See* Canada, cultural policy; transnational studies; Understanding Canada (UC) program
Resnick, Philip, 14–15
Revue svetovej literatúry (journal), 224
Richler, Mordecai, 263
Robinson, Eden, xxiii, 265, 270
Rolf in the Woods (Seton), 222, 228n6
Romania
    Atwood's translations, 245–46, 252n12
    Munro's translations, 247–48
    UC grants for literature, 29
Ross, Ian, 265
Rothberg, Michael, 113
Rowell, Charles, 93–94

SACS (Special Awards for Canadian Studies), 28, 36n5
Said, Edward, 43
Salkey, Andrew, 54, 62, 70–72, 77n28
Salt Fish Girl (Lai), 152, 155, 158–62, 166, 169n4
Samcová, Jarmila, 224
same-sex relations. *See* queer speculative fiction; sexuality
Schimel, Lawrence, 167
Schwarz, Bill, 60
science fiction and speculative fiction, 153–54
    See also speculative fiction
Scott, F.R., xvii, 119
Scuzzie Falls (Notman), 137
The Second Life of Samuel Tyne (Edugyan)
    about, xvii–xviii, 101, 105–12
    black relations with blacks, 101, 107–13
    generational differences, 109
    heterogeneity of black populations, 106–9, 112–13
    historical background, 102
    memory and forgetting, 113, 114n13
    new vs old diaspora, 106–8, 112–13
    politics of belonging, 108, 112
    reparation and reconciliation, 105, 109–13
    systemic racism, 109–10, 112
    text variations in editions, 111–12
    twins as doubles, 109–12
Sedgwick, Eve, 158
Selvon, Samuel, 54, 59, 64–67, 70–71
Senior, Olive
    art as a quiet hurricane, 79, 97n1
    Canadian relationship to Caribbean, xxvii
    Caribbean stories as subversion, 92–93
    "civility" of, 85, 92–93
    debates on "absence" of Canada in works by, xvii, 79–81, 84–89, 93–96, 97n5
    historical connections, 96–97
    identity as Jamaican, 81, 84, 87, 92–93
    interviews with, 87, 93–94
    life of, 81, 84–89
    nostalgia and loss, 88–89
    slavery and sugar plantations, 81–83, 89, 94
    visible minority, 81, 87
Senior, Olive, works
    "At the Slave Museum," 80
    "Bamboo," 86
    "Canefield Surprised by Emptiness," 81
    "Colonial Girls School," 98n7
    "Crossing Borders and Negotiating Boundaries," 80–81, 96–97
    Gardening in the Tropics, 83, 86, 89–92, 96, 97n1
    "Gastropoda," 79–80
    "Hurricane Story," 97n1
    "Meditation on Yellow," 89–92
    "My Father's Blue Plantation," 86
    Philip Sherlock Lecture, 94
    "The Poem as Gardening," 94
    Shell, 79–82, 94–95
    "Shell Blow," 95
    Talking of Trees, 82–83
    "Talking of Trees," 83
    "Whirlwinds Coiled at My Heart," 92–93
    "Yemoja: Mother of Waters," 96
Serbia, 175–76, 178–79, 187, 190–91
    See also Albahari, David; Yugoslavia

Seton, Ernest Thompson, translations
  Czech translations, 263
  Slovak translations, 215, 218, 220–22, 224, 226, 228n6, 228n9
  visit to Czechoslovakia, 222, 228n11
The Settlers of Canada (Marryat), 256
sexuality
  hybrid characters in speculative fiction, 162–63
  posthuman singularities in "the multitude," xviii–xix, 165–68, 169n2
  queer as category, 155–56, 166–67
  social justice issues in speculative fiction, 155–56, 162–65, 168
  technological advances, 167
Shadbolt, Doris, 123
Shanghai Jia Tong University, 38, 39–40
Shell (Senior), 79–82, 94–95
"Shell Blow" (Senior), 95
Sherman, Jason, 265
Shields, Carol, 30, 263
Shimmering Water (Harris), 141
Show Room and Office (Burtynsky), 149n12
Siamon, Sharon, 263
Siksika people, 182–84, 190
  See also Indigenous peoples
Šimečková, Darina, 223–24
Simpson, Jeffrey, 34
Sinclair, James, 183–84
Skilling, Gordon, 264
Slipperjack, Ruby, xxiii, 270
Slovakia. *See* Czechoslavakia/the Czech Republic/Slovakia
Slovak translations
  about, 212–16, 226–27, 228n6
  bourgeois realism, 215, 223–24
  Carter's pro-Soviet novel, 215–18, 227n5
  censorship, 214–15, 218
  gender issues, 219–20
  ideological interventions, 213–15, 218–19, 222–25
  images of Canada, xxi, 211–12, 214–15, 219–20, 222, 226–27
  Indigenous peoples of Canada, 222–23

  literary criticism, 224–26, 228n12
  morality and freedom in nature, 222–23, 226–27
  national identity of Canada, 225
  paratexts added to, 215–17, 224–26, 227, 227n4, 233–34, 236, 246
  publishing industries and markets, 226, 228n6
  religious content, 218–19
  university courses, 224
  wilderness culture, 211–12, 220–23, 226–27
  See also Czechoslavakia, CanLit studies (pre-1989); Montgomery, Lucy Maud, translations; Seton, Ernest Thompson, translations
Snow, Michael, 7–8
Snow Man (Albahari), 175, 177, 179–80, 182, 186, 191
Snyder, Joel, 136
social class in speculative fiction, 158, 162–63
Social Formation and Symbolic Landscape (Cosgrove), 133
social justice
  humanism and posthumanism, 156–57
  issues in queer speculative fiction, 153–56, 167, 169n4, 169n6
  stories for confronting injustices, xxiii
Somerville, Janet, 67, 69
Sontag, Susan, xxii, 132, 195–98, 203–5
Souvenir of Canada 1 & 2 (Coupland), 135, 145–46, 149n12
Soviet Union
  fall of communism, 246, 249, 257–58
  See also Cold War era in Europe (pre-1989)
Spain
  Canadian Studies and UC programs, 37–39
  funding for research on CanLit, 31–32
Sparling, Don
  chapter on Canadian writing in Czech Republic, xx–xxi, 255–73
  on choice of texts for translation, 212–13
  on his study of CanLit, 308

Index 331

on May's novels on the American
    West, 220–21
Special Awards for Canadian Studies
    (SACS), 28
speculative fiction
    literary genre, 153–56, 168
    posthumanism and new forms of
        subjectivity, 156–58
    See also queer speculative fiction
Spivak, Gayatri, 95
Squire, Shelagh, 220
SSHRC (Social Sciences and Humanities
    Research Council of Canada),
    funding applications, 41–42
Staines, David, 33–34, 126
Stephens, Michelle Ann, 52
The Stone Angel (Laurence), 240–41,
    251n2, 251n8, 252n19
stories and storytelling
    bonding of marginalized peoples,
        183–84, 188–90
    Caribbean stories, 92–94, 160–61
    Corn Woman story, 185–90
    dialogical space between
        marginalized peoples, 175–77,
        181–85, 191–92
    dismantling of stereotypes, 184
    ethical value, xxii
    folklore in speculative fiction, 152,
        160–61
    geography and access to, 44
    hybrid characters in speculative
        fiction, 160, 162–64
    identity, xxii, 185–86
    Indigenous stories, xxiii, 183–90
    monsters as mixed-race characters,
        163–64
    new networks and research styles,
        45–46
    preservation of culture, 184–87
    trickster figures, 187–90
Stouck, Jordan, 86
Stryker, Susan, xxiv–xxv
Süddeutsche Zeitung (newspaper), 3–4, 9
Surfacing (Atwood), 235–36, 243–45,
    251n8, 252n14
Survival (Atwood), 245
Swanzy, Henry, 67, 76n24

Symons Report, 11–12, 14
    See also Canada, cultural policy
sympathy and empathy, 199–202

The Tale of Genji (Henitiuk, trans.),
    44–45, 46
Talking of Trees (Senior), 82–83
"Talking of Trees" (Senior), 83
Tamarack Review (journal)
    Caribbean writing, 66–68, 72–73
Tanti, Melissa
    on her study of CanLit, 308
    introduction by, xi–xxvii
Taylor, Charles, 118, 121, 264
Taylor, Drew Hayden, 263, 265
Taylor, Timothy, 33–34
Thaler, Ingrid, 154, 166, 169n3
Theories of Bilingual Education
    (Yu and Yeoman), 38
Thien, Madeleine, 265
Thiong'o, Ngũgĩ wa, 81–82
"This Dance" (Miller), 64
This Side Jordan (Laurence), 239–40, 241,
    252n17
Thobani, Sunera, 177–78, 189
Thomson, Tom, 140
Thomson-Wohlgemuth, Gaby, 251n6
Times Literary Supplement (*TLS*)
    CanLit issue, 7–9, 20n9
Tinsley, Omise'eke Natasha, 61–62,
    63–64, 76nn19–20
Tomorrow Is with Us (Carter), 215–18,
    227n5
The Tomorrow-Tamer (Laurence), 240
Too Much Happiness (Munro), 248,
    253n29
Traill, Catharine Parr, 269
TransCanadiana (Polish Association for
    Canadian Studies), 26, 29–30
transdisciplinarity, xxvi–xxvii
transhuman and posthumanism, 170n10
transing, as term, xxiv–xxvi
    See also transnational studies
Translating Canada (von Flotow and
    Nischik, eds.), 230, 232
translations
    about, 41–44, 212–13
    adaptations to new forms, 44–46

antipathy to translated works, 43
collaborations, 43, 45
as cultural diplomacy, 230–31, 272n7
for export of culture, 3
for funding applications to cultural
    agencies, 41–43
history of government support, xi–xii
ideological interventions, 213
of Indigenous languages, 37, 41–47
paratexts added to translations,
    215–16, 224–26, 227, 227n4,
    233–34, 236, 246
power relations, 42–43
source and target cultures, 212–13
translator's personal initiative, 212
translation in Eastern and Central
    Europe. *See* Eastern and Central
    Europe, translation and publishing
    (pre-1989); Eastern and Central
    Europe, translation and publishing
    (post-1989)
Transnational Canadas (Dobson), xxvi
transnational studies
  about, xxiv–xxvii
  area studies, 13–14, 18–19, 46–47, 54
  associations for Canadian studies, xiv,
    11, 25–26
  conference on, xiv–xvi
  critical hierarchy, xxv
  funding, 47
  mobility as factor in research, 19
  new networks and research styles,
    17–20, 43–44, 47
  terminology, xxiv–xxvi
  transdisciplinarity vs
    interdisciplinarity, xxvi–xxvii
  universal and contextual knowledge,
    19
  See also Canada, cultural policy;
    Canadian literature; translations;
    Understanding Canada (UC)
    program
"Treason in the Fort" (Almonte), 85
Trehearne, Brian, 33–34
Tremblay, Tony, 126
Trudeau, Justin, government, xiii, 272
Trudeau, Pierre Elliott, multiculturalism,
  163

Truth and Reconciliation Commission,
    192nn3–4, 200
Two Little Savages (Seton), 222, 228n6
Two Solitudes (MacLennan), 224–25
Ty, Eleanor, 158, 169n4
Tymoczko, Maria, 43, 213

UC. *See* Understanding Canada (UC)
    program
Udall, Sharyn, 120
Ulrikabe, Abraham, 45, 46
Understanding Canada (UC) program
  about, 12–13, 25–30
  administration of (DFAIT, ICCS), xiv,
    23, 25–26
  benefits of, 271–72
  conference focused on, xiv–xvi, xxiv
  conference travel assistance (CONF),
    27–28
  cost of, xii, 24, 34, 36n1, 39
  critical questions on, 15, 17
  cultural diplomacy, 12–13, 21n11,
    271–72, 272n7
  doctoral student research (DSRA),
    26–28, 36n3
  economic benefits of, 15, 16–17, 24,
    36n1, 39
  faculty enrichment (FEP), 26–28,
    36n3, 259, 260
  faculty research (FRP), 26–28, 36n3,
    259, 260
  funding, xiv–xv, 23, 25
  mandate and goals, 17, 33–34
  national vs international studies,
    25–26
  power relations, 18
  priority countries, xiv–xv, xxvi–xxvii
  statistics, 15, 16–17, 24, 36n1
  visiting scholars' obligations, 33
  See also Canada, cultural policy;
    transnational studies
Understanding Canada (UC) program,
    termination
  about, xii–xiii, 16, 21n12, 24
  new networks and research styles
    after, xiii–xiv, 17–20, 43–44, 47
  protests about, xii, 24, 33–36, 35

Understanding Canada (UC) program, themes
　about, 23–25, 27t
　economic development, 25
　environment/energy, 25, 39–40
　grants for, 27–29, 27t
　influence on research, 47
　literary studies excluded, 23–25, 29
　literary studies under other themes, 27–33, 39
　managing diversity, 25, 28–29, 39–40
　peace in Afghanistan, 25
　thematic constraints, 23–24, 31–32, 47
Understanding Media (McLuhan), 127
United Kingdom
　"becoming West Indian," 59–60, 75n14
　black Britain, defined, 101
　British Association for Canadian Studies, 7
　Caribbean writers, 65–66, 67, 70, 75n13
　Commonwealth studies, 6–7
　cultural diplomacy, 256
United States
　area studies model, 13–14, 18–19
　Association for Canadian Studies in the US (ACSUS), 7, 273n9
　black migrants to Canada, 101–2, 106–7
　cultural diplomacy, 256
　protests on termination of UC, 35
　representations in German novels, 220–21
Université de Bordeaux, 7
universities and transnational studies. *See* transnational studies
University of Bayreuth, 5
University of Salamanca, 38–40
University of Toronto, 5
University of Vermont, 35
Unruly Penelopes and the Ghosts (Darias-Beautell, ed.), 27, 31–32
Updike, John, 206
Urquhart, Jane, 33–34
Urry, John, 196
Us—Them—Me (Kyloušek), 259

utopian fiction and speculative fiction, 154
　See also speculative fiction

Van Herk, Aritha, 33–34, 264, 265
Vanier, Jean, 264
Van Vogt, A.E., 262
Van Wyck, Peter, 44
Venous Hum (Mayr), 153, 155, 163–65, 167, 171n14
Venuti, Lawrence, 212–13
Verduyn, Christl
　chapter on Understanding Canada program, xvi, 23–36
　on her study of CanLit, 308–9
　on transdisciplinarity, xxvi–xxvii
Vermont Marble Company series (Burtynsky), 141
Vernon, Karina, 108
Vinnetou Doesn't Live Here, xxiii, 270
visual arts. *See* arts, visual
von Flotow, Luise, 3–5, 10, 237

Wachowich, Nancy, 41
Waiting for Coyote, 264–65, 268
Walcott, Derek, 53, 67
Walcott, Rinaldo
　Black Like Who?, 52–53, 55, 75n15, 102–5, 114n7
　detour routes, 55, 60, 75n15, 103–4
　hypervisibility of Caribbean writing, 53, 56, 103–4
　politics of recognition/erasure, 53, 55–56
　power relations, 56
　rudeness to power, 57–58, 93
　terminology for black Canadians, 104
Walker, James W. St. G., 102
Walker, Stephanie, 120, 123–24
Walking Woman (Snow), 7–8
The Water of Possibility (Goto), 152
Weaver, Frederick, 18
Weaver, Robert, 62–63, 67–69, 76n23, 76nn25–26
West Germany. *See* Germany, West (FRG) (pre-1989)
West Indies writing
　"becoming West Indian," 59–60, 75n14

dub poetry, 73–74, 75n5
literary history, 73–74
Salkey's writing, 54, 62, 70–72, 77n28
See also Brathwaite, Edward Kamau; Caribbean Canadian writing; Clarke, Austin; Hopkinson, Nalo; Senior, Olive
What We All Long For (Brand), 114n14
When Fox Is a Thousand (Lai), 152, 155, 159, 167, 169n4
"Whirlwinds Coiled at My Heart" (Senior), 92–93
White Dawn (Houston), 223
Who Do You Think You Are? (Munro), 248
Wiebe, Rudy, 24, 33–34
Wieniewska, Celina, 239, 252n16
Wilfrid Laurier University Press, 31
Williams, David, 127
Williams, Raymond, 43, 199
Wilson, Richard Ashby, 199
Wing, Willis K., 240
Winks, Robin, 102
women
　missing and murdered Indigenous women, 194, 207n1
　social justice issues in speculative fiction, 155–56
　violence against women, 193–96, 198, 207n1
women's writing
　Ostenso's early translation, xxi, 228n8
　translations, xxi–xxii, 230, 234–37, 249–50
　See also Atwood, Margaret; Edugyan, Esi; Hopkinson, Nalo; Laurence, Margaret, translations; Montgomery, Lucy Maud, translations; Munro, Alice, translations; Senior, Olive

women's writing, queer speculative fiction. *See* Goto, Hiromi; Hopkinson, Nalo; Lai, Larissa; Mayr, Suzette; queer speculative fiction
Wong, Orlando, 73–74
Wood, Ted, 226
Workbench (Burtynsky), 149n12
Wright, Eric, 262

The Year of the Flood (Atwood), 155
Yelistratova, Anna, 215–17
"Yemoja: Mother of Waters" (Senior), 96
Yeoman, Elizabeth
　chapter on Indigenous writing, xvi, 37–50
　on her study of CanLit, 309
York, Lorraine
　on her study of CanLit, 309–10
　introduction by, xi–xxvii
Young Canada (Notman), 135
The Young May Moon (Ostenso), xxi, 228n8
Yu, Liming, 38, 39
Yugoslavia
　dialogical space between immigrants and Indigenous peoples, 182–84, 191–92
　historical background, 176, 178–80
　nostalgia for, 179–80
　See also Albahari, David

Zajtrajšok je náš (Carter), 215–18, 227n5

Other Titles from The University of Alberta Press

Retooling the Humanities
The Culture of Research in Canadian Universities
Daniel Coleman & Smaro Kamboureli, Editors

Twelve essays examine challenges that an intensified culture of research capitalism imposes on the humanities.

Cultural Mapping and the Digital Sphere
Place and Space
Ruth Panofsky & Kathleen Kellett, Editors

Fourteen essays map Canadian literary and cultural products via advances in digital humanities research methodologies.

Narratives of Citizenship
Indigenous and Diasporic Peoples Unsettle the Nation-State
Aloys N.M. Fleischmann, Nancy Van Styvendale & Cody McCarroll, Editors

Thirteen essays examine music, travel guides, ideographic treaties, film, and especially the literary arts to conceptualize citizenship as a narrative construct.

More information at www.uap.ualberta.ca